EVALUATION

EVALUATION
A SYSTEMATIC APPROACH

Third Edition

Peter H. Rossi
Howard E. Freeman

SAGE PUBLICATIONS
Beverly Hills   London   New Delhi

For information address:

SAGE Publications, Inc.
275 South Beverly Drive
Beverly Hills, California 90212

SAGE Publications India Pvt. Ltd.
M-32 Market
Greater Kailash I
New Delhi 110 048 India

SAGE Publications Ltd
28 Banner Street
London EC1Y 8QE
England

Printed in the United States of America

Library of Congress Cataloging-in-Publication Data

Rossi, Peter Henry, 1921-
    Evaluation: A systematic approach

    Includes index.
    1. Evaluation research (Social action programs)
I. Freeman, Howard E.   II. Title.
H62.R666   1985   361.6′1′072   85-18413
ISBN 0-8039-2488-7

Third Printing, 1987

To

Bert Brim, Pat Moynihan,
and Howard Rosen

*Architects and Builders
of the Evaluation Enterprise*

*I*n both previous editions of this book, we pointed out its cosmopolitan origins: At a UNESCO meeting on evaluation research in the mid-1970s, we each presented separate papers on evaluation approaches and procedures. The papers had a surprising amount of overlap in content and emphases. Indeed, at the time, we jokingly accused each other of plagiarism, much to the discomfort of the largely non-American audience, who were unused to frivolity about what they regarded as serious professional misconduct.

Happily, the Staff of the Organization for Economic Cooperation and Development (OECD) who attended the conference understood that we were simply emphasizing our surprise discovery of consensus. They asked us to integrate the papers, add to them, and develop a primer on evaluation useful for persons working in lesser developed countries. We prepared a draft, revised it after two working meetings in Paris, at which we benefited from the advice of groups of international experts, and OECD published it in English and French (Freeman, Rossi, and Wright, 1979). Its derivative, the first edition of this book, was published in the same year.

In 1982, we undertook a substantial revision of *Evaluation: A Systematic Approach* (Rossi and Freeman, 1982). Sonia Rosenbaum (formerly Sonia R. Wright), who co-authored the UNESCO paper with Rossi, was the third author of the first edition. She shifted career interests after it was published, and did not participate in writing either the second or this third edition. We did acknowledge her contributions to the enterprise, however, by listing her as a collaborator in the second edition.

This third edition is still further removed from the original one, and only the two of us are responsible for whatever virtues and defects it may have.

Although this edition covers many of the same topics treated in earlier editions, there are many changes in specific content. In large part, the changes reflect the fact that we are not only older but, we hope, wiser. Close to a decade has passed since we began work on the first edition: During this period each of us has undertaken a number of evaluations and consulted on many more. Indeed, we have found ourselves on at least one occasion on opposite sides of the table, with one of us a consultant to and to some extent an advocate for a project, and the other a critic and adviser to the funding agency that was considering supporting it. Our arguments and counterarguments about the projects must have been puzzling to the others present, who must have wondered how we could ever agree on a manuscript.

Certainly our personal experiences in doing evaluations and advising about them have changed our views and expanded our ideas about evaluation research. In addition, the field of evaluation has changed considerably during the last decade and shows every promise of continuing to evolve. Some of the changes are technical and technological. For example, a decade ago, econometric modeling was not part of the repertoire of many persons in the field, but that is no longer the case. The widespread adoption of microcomputers has been an enormous technological change, not only in terms of statistical analysis but, for example, in implementing monitoring procedures in small and medium-sized programs. We have attempted to reflect those changes in the field in this new edition.

In the middle of the last decade, the political climate changed dramatically. When we were writing the first edition, there was much more political and public support for social programs, and for innovative initiatives. Even while the second edition was in our typewriters, we could count on support for both programs and evaluations, although at a slightly reduced level. But now the climate is much different, with less support available for programs and for evaluations. This change has affected the distribution of effort in the field, the motivations of sponsors for supporting evaluations, and the allegiances of evaluators themselves. Indeed, the political use of evaluation has changed. During the 1970s, it was rare that evaluations were undertaken of large-scale, well-established, national programs for the purpose of promoting their dismantlement and demise. The exciting experimental work of the 1970s is not likely to be matched in this period. Indeed, it is now rare to find support for multimillion-dollar social experiments whose documented success might lead to major additional commitments of public funds. There is no doubt that the changed times are reflected at least in the emphasis given to certain topics in this edition compared with the earlier ones.

But in revising this book, we have been most influenced by the responses of our colleagues in the field and by the reactions of teachers and students to the contents of earlier editions. Both of us have used the text a number of times in our own courses. In addition, the book has been the text in literally hundreds of graduate classes in just about all of the social science disciplines, and in courses in a large number of professional schools as well. Moreover, we are most grateful that so many teachers (and actually a few students) have taken the trouble to provide us with feedback about the material included in earlier editions. If this edition is better, clearer, and more comprehensive, we owe it to them.

We are proud of this book. Collaborating on it turned an acquaintance-ship into a friendship, and since the first edition we have collaborated on other efforts. This book has also, we like to think, helped to build closer relationships between persons in different disciplines and with different professional backgrounds; we hope that it has reduced the gap between persons in positions in policy development and social program implementation and those in evaluation research. At least these were our reasons for first writing it, and for revising it this time as well.

June 1985   *P.H.R.* and *H.E.F.*

1

Programs, Policies, and Evaluations

Systematic evaluations of the extensive range of existing and innovative social programs are now commonplace. Evaluation research is a robust area of activity devoted to collecting, analyzing, and interpreting information on the need for, implementation of, and effectiveness and efficiency of intervention efforts to better the lot of humankind by improving social conditions and community life. Evaluations are undertaken for a variety of reasons: to judge the worth of ongoing programs and to estimate the usefulness of attempts to improve them; to assess the utility of innovative programs and initiatives; to increase the effectiveness of program management and administration; and to meet various accountability requirements. Evaluations may also contribute to substantive and methodological social science knowledge.

In planning social intervention programs, the focus of evaluations is on the extent and severity of problems requiring social intervention, and on the design of programs to ameliorate them. In the conduct of ongoing and innovative programs, the concern is that programs are reaching their intended target populations and are providing the resources, services, and benefits envisioned. As interventions are implemented and continued, there is interest in whether they are effective and, if so, what the magnitudes of their impacts are. For accountability purposes, and for decision-making on the continuance, expansion, or curtailment of programs, it is important to consider costs in relation to benefits, and to compare an intervention's cost-efficiency to that of alternative resource allocation strategies.

Some evaluations are comprehensive and consider all of these questions; others are directed at only some of them. In all cases, the aim is to provide the most valid and reliable findings possible within political and ethical constraints and the limitations imposed by time, money, and human resources.

KEY CONCEPTS

---

*Comprehensive
Evaluation:*

Analysis covering the conceptualization and design of interventions, the monitoring of program implementation, and the assessment of program utility.

*Conceptualization
and Design Analyses:*

Studies of (1) the extent and location of problems for intervention, (2) ways targets can be defined in operational terms, and (3) whether the proposed intervention is suitable.

*Cost-Benefit
Analyses:*

Studies of the relationship between project costs and outcomes, usually expressed in monetary terms.

*Cost-Effectiveness
Analyses:*

Studies of the relationship between project costs and outcomes, usually expressed as costs per unit of outcome achieved.

Delivery System:

Organizational arrangements, including staff, procedures and activities, physical plants, and materials, needed to provide program services.

Formative Research:

Design and development testing to maximize the success of intervention.

*Impact
Assessment:*

Evaluation of the extent to which a program causes changes in the desired direction in a target population.

Intervention:

Any program or other planned effort designed to produce intended changes in a target population.

Monitoring:

Assessment of whether or not an intervention is (1) operating in conformity to its design, and (2) reaching its specified target population.

Program Utility Assessment:	Study of the effectiveness (impact) and efficiency (costs-to-benefits ratios or cost-effectiveness analyses) of programs.
Target Populations:	Persons, households, organizations, communities, or other units at which interventions are directed.
Target Problems:	Conditions, deficiencies, or defects at which interventions are directed.

• With support from the U.S. Department of Justice, a number of communities have developed programs to increase the visibility of the police, on the assumption that both personal and property crimes will be reduced by community perceptions of increased police presence. One program provides police officers with marked cars to use as personal automobiles as well as when they are on duty; another increases the number of hours of police "beat-walking." These efforts have had a modest influence on crime rates.

• In four major cities in the United States, a large private foundation provided the initial operating costs for community health centers in low-income areas. These centers are trying to reduce costly ambulatory-patient care now provided by hospital outpatient clinics and emergency rooms, and to offer an alternative to lengthy and expensive in-hospital care. A variety of other efforts to provide economical medical care to the poor and to contain the costs of health care are being undertaken throughout the United States. Evaluations suggest that community health centers are cost-beneficial in comparison with hospital clinics.

• In a large Latin American country, educational television is used in efforts to raise the low literacy levels of the population. An educational television program, *Plaza Sésamo,* was created by modifying a U.S. television program, *Sesame Street,* and showing it at times when school-children would have opportunities to view it. Similar educational television programs have been attempted in many other countries. The utility and efficiency of these efforts in terms of costs to benefits is open to question.

• A community mental health center in a medium-sized New England city has developed an extensive program using local community members to counsel teenagers and adults about their emotional, sexual, and educational problems. Compared with persons treated by psychiatrists and social workers, the clients of the indigenous workers seem to do as well in terms of need for hospitalization, maintaining treatment, and self-reports of satisfaction with the center. This finding holds even when the clients' psychological and social characteristics are taken into account.

• The federal government has had many employment training programs designed to help unemployed persons develop the skills that would facilitate their gainful employment. A large program that was abolished a few years ago was CETA (the Comprehensive Employment and Training Act). Under this program, federal funds were allocated to local governments to provide jobs in public service projects for chronically unemployed persons. Many of the jobs and work settings were "unusual" compared with the ordinary opportunities available to people who had been unemployed for long periods. However, periods of employment for CETA workers were usually short, lasting less than one year. Whether or not CETA jobs led to careers of gainful employment was a key evaluation question for the U.S. Department of Labor for many years. Currently, a new program, the Job Training Partnership Program, with which CETA was replaced by the Reagan administration, emphasizes training for jobs for the unemployed in the private sector. It is faced with the same evaluation question, namely, does participation in the program lead to careers of gainful employment in the private sector?

• Fully two-thirds of the world's rural children suffer mild to severe malnutrition resulting in documented negative consequences for their physical growth, health status, and mental development. A major demonstration of the potential for improving the health status and mental development of children through diet supplementation was undertaken in Central America. Pregnant women, lactating mothers, and children from birth through age 12 were provided daily with a high-protein, high-calorie food supplement. Results show major gains in physical growth and modest increases in cognitive function.

• A large manufacturing company, in an effort to increase worker productivity and product quality, has reorganized its employees into independent work teams. Within the teams, workers designate and assign tasks, recommend productivity quotas to management, and vote on the distribution of bonuses for productivity and quality improvements. Information obtained in monitoring the program suggests it reduces days absent from the job, turnover, and similar measures of employee inefficiency.

These are but a few illustrations of the diversity of human resource programs that are undertaken and evaluated with the support of local, state, and federal government agencies, international organizations, private foundations and philanthropies, and both nonprofit and for-profit associations and corporations. Evaluation research, by any standard, is a large enterprise. During the 1970s, it was estimated that annual federal expenditures ranged between $.5 billion and $1 billion. Given the cutbacks in governmentally supported social programs that have occurred during the 1980s, it is probable that total expenditures for evaluation activities may be somewhat lower. At the same time, the use of evaluation procedures has been diffused during the past few years, and such procedures are now commonplace at all levels of government, among private foundations, and among commercial and industrial organizations. While there is no way of providing a firm estimate, the total volume of work being done probably is not much lower than that done in the 1970s, despite the federal cutbacks. However, the proportion of the enterprise supported directly by the federal government clearly has declined.

In addition, there continue to be extensive commitments to evaluation activities internationally, particularly for assessing programs in the Third World. There is no way to estimate international expenditures. Even in the 1970s, however, in the family planning area alone, the World Bank had identified more than 100 social action programs of varying size, and in which citizens of more than 25 different nations have participated. Evaluation activities, internationally, continue to constitute an important segment of the total volume of work being done.

There is no need to belabor the obvious—many human beings suffer serious deficiencies in the quality of their lives, defects that exist both in industrialized countries and in lesser developed nations. The challenge to improve existing purposive, organized-action efforts to remedy human and social conditions, and to implement creative new initiatives, continues. True, there are increased resource restraints in the United States and internationally as well. Moreover, the experiences of the past several decades have brought about a more realistic perspective about the barriers to successful implementation of social programs, and about the magnitude of outcome that can be expected from them (Weick, 1984). Reduced resources and increased realism, however, increase the need for evaluation efforts and present the challenge of undertaking evaluations in ways that maximize efforts to deal with the myriad human and social problems that persist.

In order to distinguish useful current programs from ineffective and inefficient ones, and to plan, design, and implement innovative efforts that have effective and efficient impact on community members and their environments, it is critical that policymakers, funding organizations, planners, and program staffs obtain answers to a range of questions, including:

- What is the nature and scope of the problem requiring actions?
- What interventions may be undertaken to ameliorate the problem significantly?
- What is the appropriate target population for the intervention?
- Is the intervention reaching that target population?
- Is the intervention being implemented in the ways envisioned?
- Is it effective?
- How much does it cost?
- What are its costs relative to its effectiveness and benefits?

Answers to such questions are necessary not only for broad, complex programs—such as nationwide family planning or income maintenance efforts—but also for local, specialized projects, such as those offering occupational training in a rural village or increasing public safety in a large city. Providing those answers is the heart of evaluation research.

WHAT IS EVALUATION RESEARCH?

We begin this volume with a simple definition of evaluation, or evaluation research (and we will use the terms interchangeably): *Evaluation research is the systematic application of social research procedures in assessing the conceptualization and design, implementation, and utility of social intervention programs.* In other words, evaluation research involves the use of social research methodologies to judge and to improve the planning, monitoring, effectiveness, and efficiency of health, education, welfare, and other human service programs.

Note that this definition does not imply that evaluation studies follow one or another or some particular combination of the different social research styles currently in use. Evaluation research is a social science activity, and its methods cover the gamut of social research paradigms.

Evaluations are systematic to the extent that they employ social science approaches to gathering valid, reliable evidence. It is the commitment to the "rules" of social research that is at the core of our perspective on evaluation.

In describing evaluation activities, Cronbach et al. (1980) make the following points:

1. The intention of an evaluation is to influence social thought and action during the investigation or in the years immediately following. (It is reasonable to hope for long-term influences as well.)

2. Evidence is collected on experience with an already existing program or one installed for research purposes. After the analysis, the investigators set forth just how they reached their conclusions, documenting their observations and reasoning so that readers can judge the plausibility of each conclusion.

3. Evaluators aim to give a comprehensive and disciplined interpretation. The account is intended to impress fair-minded persons, including those whose preconceptions or preferences run counter to the findings. Furthermore, the information collected is made available for others to scrutinize and interpret independently.

Although this text emphasizes the application of social research procedures to the evaluation of social and human service programs, the approaches considered have utility in other spheres of activity as well. For example, the mass communication and advertising industries use fundamentally the same approaches in assessing media programs and marketing products; commercial and industrial corporations evaluate the procedures they use for selection and promotion of employees and organization of their work forces; political candidates develop their campaigns by evaluating the voter appeal of different strategies; consumer products are subjected to market testing; and administrators in both public and private sectors are continually assessing the clerical, fiscal, and interpersonal practices within their organizations. The distinction lies primarily in the intent of the effort to be evaluated. Our emphasis in this text is on programs that are designed to benefit the human condition; others use evaluation procedures to increase profit, to amass influence and power, or to achieve other goals important to them. Our focus on social programs stems not from a sense of righteousness about the evaluation of social programs compared with the application of social research methods in evaluating other activities, but rather from a heuristic need to limit the scope of the book.

A BRIEF HISTORY

Systematic, data-based evaluations are a relatively modern development, coinciding with the growth and refinement of social research methods, as well as with ideological, political, and demographic changes that have occurred during this century. Actually, evaluation research can be traced back to the rise of the scientific enterprise during the 1600s. As Cronbach et al. (1980) describe, Thomas Hobbs and his contemporaries were concerned with numerical measures to be used in assessing social conditions and in identifying the causes of mortality, morbidity, and social disorganization.

"Social experiments" certainly preceded the establishment of the organized set of activities that are undertaken under the rubric of evaluation research. In the 1700s, for example, having observed the lack of scurvy among sailors serving on the ships of Mediterranean countries and the inclusion of citrus fruit in their rations, a British ship's captain made one-half of his crew consume limes while the other half continued with their regular diet. Despite much grumbling among the crew in the "treatment" half, the experiment was carried out and showed that consuming limes could avert scurvy.

The good captain probably did not have an explicit "impact model" (a term we will discuss later in detail), that is, that scurvy is a consequence of a vitamin C deficiency and that limes are rich in vitamin C. Nevertheless, based on the results, British seamen eventually were forced to consume citrus fruit—this is the derivation of the label "limeys," which is still sometimes applied to the English. Parenthetically, it should be noted that it took about fifty years before the captain's "social program" was widely adopted. Then, as now, diffusion and acceptance of evaluation findings often are problematic, and implementation difficult.

The Rise of Evaluation Research

In the modern era, commitment to the systematic evaluation of programs in such fields as education and public health can be traced to efforts at the turn of the century to provide literacy and occupational training by the most effective and economical means, and to reduce mortality and morbidity from infectious diseases. As far back as the 1930s, there were social scientists who advocated the application of rigorous social research methods to the assessment of programs (Freeman, 1977): Dodd's attempt to introduce water boiling as a public health practice in Middle Eastern villages was one of the landmark studies in the pre-World War II empirical sociological literature; Lewin's field studies and Lippitt and White's work on democratic and authoritarian leadership have been well known to psychologists for decades; and the famous Western Electric study that contributed the term "Hawthorne Effect" to the social sciences was undertaken half a century ago. (See Bernstein and Freeman, 1975, for a more extended discussion. Also see Cronbach et al., 1980, and Bulmer, 1982, for somewhat different historical perspectives.)

Indeed, it was more than forty years ago when an Arkansas sociology professor pleaded for evaluations of President Roosevelt's New Deal social programs (see Exhibit 1-A). From such beginnings in the 1930s and earlier, applied social research received considerable impetus. Its employment increased during World War II; Stouffer and his associates worked with the U.S. Army (Stouffer et al., 1949) to develop continual monitoring of soldier morale as well as to evaluate personnel and propaganda policies. The Office of War Information used sample surveys to measure civilian morale continually. At the same time, a host of smaller studies assessed the efficacy of price controls and campaigns to modify American eating habits. Similar social science efforts were mounted in Britain and elsewhere (see Exhibit 1-B).

The Boom Period in Evaluation Research

The period immediately following World War II saw the beginning of large-scale programs designed to meet needs for urban development and housing, technological and cultural education, occupational training, and preventive health activities. It was also during this time that major com-

(text continues on page 25)

Exhibit 1-A: The New Deal and Social Research

No one can deny the progress in the social sciences. But with all the exacting methods developed, the economists, sociologists, and political scientists have suffered from a lack of large-scale experimental set-ups to match the everyday resources of the scientists in the laboratory.

The current enthusiasm over planning schemes now being devised by the alphabetical corporations of the federal government furnishes some hope that this deficiency may be partially remedied. The blueprints of these agencies and the carrying out of their plans may well be looked upon as the creation of experimental laboratories for the social scientists, and for the social workers, educators, and administrators who may profit from their research.

These laboratories, set up by the planning agencies of the New Deal, permit a more effective use of the experimental method in the research projects of the social scientists. This research, in turn, would not only be an addition to science but would also be a form of social auditing for the planning authorities in noting and accounting the changes wrought by the programs.

Do slums make slum people or do slum people make the slums? Will changing the living conditions significantly change the social behavior of the people affected? The public housing projects may furnish the made-to-order test tubes to help in answering these fascinating and bewildering questions.

The accumulating studies of the sociologists reveal the slums as the sore spots of our modern industrial civilization. In the slum areas of our urban centers are found high rates of delinquency, adult crime, dependency, tax delinquency, insanity, and similar conditions, together with such characteristic groups as delinquent gangs and institutions of vice. These institutions and conditions epitomize the so-called viciousness of the slum. The implication is that if these people lived under more wholesome conditions there would not be as much delinquency, dependency, sickness among them. No doubt—but how much less delinquency, dependency, sickness? Compare a slum group with the people living in a suburb. Less delinquency, dependency, and sickness? To be sure. But the people living in the suburbs are not similar to the people living in the slums in terms of certain significant factors. They are usually wealthier, better educated, healthier than the slum dwellers. The layman would call this an unfair comparison. The best way we can answer this problem, perhaps, is to compare the social indices (rates of delinquency, dependency, adult crime, sickness, and similar factors) characteristic of a given population while living in the slum with the social indices of the same or a similar population after living in the changed environment of a model community. This would mean a "before and after" study. In other words, we would have to employ the exacting techniques of an experimental approach. This would permit controlled observation and enable us to know with more precision the difference that may occur in social behavior accompanying a change in social environment brought about by the altering of living conditions. Graphically, it would be like transferring a population mass from Test Tube 1 of Liquid A to Test Tube 2 of Liquid B and finding out what happens.

Certain of the social indices may be reduced to monetary items of costs to the government (costs of delinquency, adult crime, dependency, police protection, sickness, and similar factors) and a comparison made of the costs to the government preceding and following slum clearance of the transference of a slum population to a model community on more open land. Specifically, such a program may reduce delinquency and adult crime. The cost per delinquent and the cost per adult criminal may be computed and the differential in lower costs to the state that may result from the housing program calculated. A computation may be made of the social cost differential in favor of the new communities, which may be logically considered a governmental and social saving. Such a body of data may even serve as a basis for recruiting financial support to future housing programs.

SOURCE: Adapted, with permission, from *Social Forces*, 13 (May 1935): 515-518. "Prospects and Possibilities: The New Deal and the New Social Research" by A. S. Stephan. Copyright © The University of North Carolina Press.

Exhibit 1-B: Early Experiments in Mass Communications

In designing Army orientation programs, an issue that was frequently debated was this: When the weight of evidence supports the main thesis being presented, is it more effective to present only the materials supporting the point being made, or is it better to introduce the arguments of those opposed to the point being made?

1. The Two Programs Used

At the time the experiment was being planned (early 1945), the war in Europe was drawing to a close and it was reported that Army morale was being adversely affected by overoptimism about an early end to the war in the Pacific. A directive was issued by the Army to impress upon troops a conception of the magnitude of the job remaining to be done in defeating Japan. This furnished a controversial topic on which arguments were available on both sides, but where the majority of experts in military affairs believed the preponderance of evidence supported one side. It was therefore chosen as a suitable subject for experimentation.

2. The Study Groups

The preliminary survey was administered during the first week of April 1945 to eight quartermaster training companies. One week later eight platoons, one chosen at random from each of the eight companies, heard Program I (which presented only one side) during their individual orientation meetings. Another group of eight platoons, similarly chosen, heard Program II (which presented both arguments). Immediately after the program the men filled out the second questionnaire, ostensibly for the purpose of letting the people who made the program know what the men thought of it. Included in this second questionnaire, with appropriate transitional questions, were some of the same questions that had been included in the earlier survey, asking the men how they personally sized up the Pacific War. A third group of eight platoons served as the control, with no program. They filled out a similar questionnaire during their orientation meeting, which, in addition to asking the same questions on the Pacific War, asked preliminary questions about what they thought of their orientation meetings and what they would like in future orientation meetings. For the control group, the latter questions—in lieu of the questions about the transcriptions—were represented to the men as the main purpose of the questionnaire.

3. Summary of Results

• Presenting the arguments on both sides of an issue was found to be more effective than giving only the arguments supporting the point being made, in the case of individuals who were initially opposed to the point being presented.

• For men who were already convinced of the point being presented, however, the inclusion of arguments on both sides was less effective, for the group as a whole, than presenting only the arguments favoring the general position being advocated.

• Better-educated men were more favorably affected by presentation of both sides; less well-educated men were more affected by the communication that used only supporting arguments.

SOURCE: Adapted from Carl I. Hovland, Arthur A. Lumsdane, and Fred D. Sheffield, *Experiments in Mass Communication*, Vol. III, *Studies in Social Psychology in World War II*. Copyright 1949, © renewed 1977 by Princeton University Press. Excerpt reprinted with permission of Princeton University Press.

mitments were made to international programs for family planning, health and nutrition, and rural community development. Expenditures were huge, and consequently were accompanied by demands for "knowledge of results."

By the end of the 1950s, large-scale evaluation programs were commonplace. Social scientists were engaged in evaluations of delinquency-prevention programs, felon-rehabilitation projects, psychotherapeutic and psychopharmacological treatments, public housing programs, and community organization activities. Not only were such studies undertaken in the United States, Europe, and other industrialized countries, but in lesser developed nations as well: Increasingly, programs for family planning in Asia, nutrition and health care in Latin America, and agricultural and community developmemt in Africa included evaluation components (Levine et al., 1981; Freeman et al., 1980). Knowledge of the methods of social research, including sample surveys and complex statistical procedures, became widespread. Computer technology made it possible to conduct large-scale studies and sophisticated statistical analyses.

During the 1960s, the numbers of papers and books on the practice of evaluation research also grew dramatically. Suchman's (1967) review of evaluation research methods, Hayes's (1959) monograph on evaluation research in lesser developed countries, and Campbell's (1969) call for social experimentation are but illustrations. By the late 1960s—in the United States and internationally—evaluation research, in the words of Wall Street, had become a "growth industry."

In the early 1970s, a variety of books on evaluation appeared, including a text (Weiss, 1972), collections of readings (Caro, 1971; Rossi and Williams, 1972), critiques of the methodological quality of various studies (Bernstein and Freeman, 1975), and discussions of the organizational and structural constraints on the successful conduct of evaluation research (Riecken and Boruch, 1974; Wholey et al., 1970). Guttentag and Struening's two-volume *Handbook of Evaluation Research* was published in 1975. *Evaluation Review,* a journal started in 1976, is widely read by evaluation researchers, and now there are other journals as well, such as *Evaluation News, Evaluation and the Health Professions,* the *Journal of Evaluation and Program Planning,* and *New Directions for Program Evaluation.* The proliferation of publications and conferences, the formation of professional associations, and special sessions on evaluation studies at the meetings of academic and practitioner groups are testimony to the rapid development of the field. These efforts to improve, refine, and promote evaluation activities continue today. As Cronbach and his associates (1980: 12-13) put it, "Evaluation has become the liveliest frontier of American social science."

Evaluation research prospered to a large extent because of the post-World War II developments in research methods and statistics applicable to the study of social problems, social processes, and interpersonal relations. At the same time, the need for sophisticated methods for use in evaluating social programs stimulated methodological work. In particular, systematic data collection by the refinement of survey research procedures and the ability to examine large numbers of variables analytically by multivariate statistics were essential inputs into the development of the field. Needless to say, the "computer revolution" was an important stimulus to the growth of evaluation research. The symbiotic relationship between technological and methodological developments in social research continues to this day.

But history can obscure as well as illuminate: While there is continuity in the development of the evaluation field, a qualitative change has occurred. Even as late as 1967, Suchman's definition of evaluation research as the application of social research techniques to the study of large-scale human service programs was a useful and sufficient delineation of the field.

Indeed, we offered a somewhat extended version of this definition at the outset of this chapter. It fails to take into account, however, the extensive influence on the evaluation enterprise of its consumers—policymakers, program planners, and administrators.

Evaluation research is more than the application of methods. It is also a political and managerial activity, an input into the complex mosaic from which policy decisions and allocations emerge for the planning, design, implementation, and continuation of programs to better the human condition. In this sense, evaluation research also needs to be seen as an integral part of the social policy and public administration movements.

Social Policy and
Public Administration Movements

A full treatment of the development of the overlapping social policy and public administration movements would require not only tracing the remarkable growth of population and industrialization in the United States during the first part of this century, but also detailing the changing social values related to the shift of responsibility for community members' welfare from volunteers and family members to public groups. At least a few highlights are important here.

Emergence of the Government Role

First, as Bremner (1956) has noted, before World War I obtaining human services was seen primarily as a personal responsibility. Poor people, physically and mentally handicapped persons, and troubled families were the clients of local charities staffed mainly by volunteers drawn from the ranks of the more fortunate. The image of these volunteers as wealthy matrons toting baskets of food and hand-me-down clothing to give to the poor and unfortunate is only somewhat exaggerated. Along with civic associations and locally supported "charity hospitals," county and state asylums, locally supported public schools, state normal schools, and sectarian old-age homes, volunteers were the bulwark of our human service "system."

Second, government—particularly the federal government—was comparatively small before the 1930s. There were few national health, education, and welfare programs and therefore no need for an army of federal employees. The idea of annual federal expenditures of billions of dollars for health research would have completely bewildered the government official of the 1920s. The idea of even more billions going to purchase medical care for poor persons would be even more mind boggling to the civil servant of the early part of the twentieth century. Federal support of public education was infinitesimal; for public education alone, more dollars now flow from

Washington in six months, even under the Reagan administration, than were spent in the entire first decade of this century.

The scope and utilization of social and economic information mirrored the sparseness of government program operations. Lynn (1980) records that even in the late 1930s, federal expenditures for social science research and statistics were between $40 and $50 million; forty to fifty times that amount is spent today.

Finally, the human services field and government operate currently with different norms than previously. Key government officials and even ordinary staff members once were selected without consistent regard to objective competence criteria; indeed, there were few ways of determining competence objectively. The professional civil service was a fraction of its current size, most jobs did not require technical know-how, and formal training programs were rarely available. Moreover, as its activities and influence were comparatively small, there was relatively little interest in what went on in government—at least in terms of human service programs. Government bureaucracies operated in such ways that it was difficult to find out anyway. For example, the Federal Freedom of Information Act, which allows public access to government documents, is comparatively recent.

Growth of Social Programs

Human services programs grew at a rapid pace with the advent of the Great Depression, and of course so did government in general during the period surrounding World War II. In part because of the unwieldiness that accompanied this accelerated growth, there was strong pressure to apply the concepts and techniques of so-called scientific management, which were well thought of in industry. These ideas first took hold in the area of defense and then filtered to other government organizations, including human services agencies. Concepts and procedures for planning, budgeting, quality control, and accountability, as well as, later, more sophisticated notions of cost-benefit analysis and systems modeling, became the order of the day in the human resources area.

At the same time, persons with social science training, particularly in political science, began to apply themselves to understanding the political, organizational, and administrative decision-making that took place in executive departments and other government agencies. Economists were simultaneously perfecting models for planning and decision-making and refining macroeconomic theories (Stokey and Zeckhauser, 1978). In part, the interests of social scientists in government were purely "academic": They wanted to know how government worked. Some, however, recognized that their concepts and methods could facilitate and improve the governmental operations and actions they were documenting.

Likewise, persons in leadership positions in government agencies, groping for ways to deal with their large staffs and full coffers, recognized the critical need for orderly, explicit ways to deal with their policy, administrative, program, and planning responsibilities. They became convinced that concepts, techniques, and principles from economics, political science, and sociology could be useful. The study of the public sector grew into a specialty that most commonly is termed "policy sciences" or "policy analysis."

Moreover, as the federal government was becoming increasingly complex and technical, it could no longer be managed and conducted by persons hired either as intelligent generalists or because of their connections with political patrons, relatives, or friends. Most midlevel management jobs and many senior executive positions required specific substantive and technical skills, and those who filled such positions needed either training or extensive experience to do their work completely (see Exhibit 1-C). State and local counterparts of federal agencies expanded at a similar rate, in part stimulated by federal initiatives and funding, and they too required skilled staffs.

As we have noted, university social science departments provided some of the needed human resources for government positions. Now, in response to the demand for government "technocrats," graduate schools of management, public health, and social work began programs to meet the need for executives and technicians, and special schools, generally with "public administration" in their titles, were organized or expanded.

In short, a new army of professionals emerged. The institutionalization of policy analysis and public administration programs in universities has maintained the momentum of the intertwined policy science and public administration movements. Concepts and methods from the social sciences have become the core of the educational programs from which many of our public officials and program managers are drawn, and these programs stress training in evaluation research. The importance of evaluation is now acknowledged by those in political as well as executive roles. For example, the General Accounting Office, Congress's "watchdog," established a special evaluation division in 1980 in response to congressional interest in the conduct of program assessment. Evaluation research has become more than an isolated academic concern; it thrives in the context of the social policy and public administration movements.

POLITICAL IDEOLOGY AND THE EVALUATION ENTERPRISE

Evaluation activities had their most rapid growth during the Kennedy and Johnson eras, when domestic social programs undertaken under the

Exhibit 1-C: The Rise of Policy Analysis

The steady growth in the number, variety, complexity, and social importance of policy issues confronting government is making increasing intellectual demands on public officials and their staffs. What should be done about nuclear safety, teenage pregnancies, urban decline, rising hospital costs, unemployment among black youth, violence toward spouses and children, and the disposal of toxic wastes? Many of these subjects were not on the public agenda twenty years ago. They are priority issues now, and new ones of a similar character emerge virtually every year. For most elected and appointed officials and their staffs, such complicated and controversial questions are outside the scope of their judgment and previous experience. Yet, the questions cannot be sidestepped; government executives are expected to deal with them responsibly and effectively.

To aid them in thinking about and deciding on such matters, public officials have been depending to an increasing extent on knowledge derived from research, policy analysis, program evaluations, and statistics to inform or buttress their views. More often than in the past, elected and appointed officials in the various branches and levels of government, from federal judges to town selectmen, are citing studies, official data, and expert opinion in at least partial justification for their actions. Their staffs, which have been increasing in size and responsibility in recent decades, include growing numbers of people trained in or familiar with analytic techniques to gather and evaluate information. Increasing amounts of research, analysis, and data-gathering are being done.

Because the power to influence policy is widely shared in our system of government, public officials seeking to influence policy—to play the policy game well—must be persuasive. Because of the changing character of policy issues, it is probably harder to be persuasive than it used to be. Seniority, affability, and clever "wheeling and dealing" may be relatively less influential than being generally knowledgeable and tough-minded, having the ability to offer ideas and solutions that can attract a wide following, or having a reputation as a well-informed critic. Increasingly, officials from the president on down lose influence in policy debates when they cannot get their numbers right or when their ideas and arguments are successfully challenged by opposing experts. Indeed, thorough and detailed command of an issue or problem is often mandatory. Legislatures are requiring executives to be experts in the programs and issues under their jurisdiction. Judges are requiring detailed proof that administrative decisions are not arbitrary and capricious. Budget officials demand positive program evaluations. The public demands accountability. Thus the dynamic processes whereby our political system confronts social problems are perceptibly, if not dramatically, raising the standards of substantive and managerial competence in the performance of public responsibilities.

SOURCE: Adapted, with permission, from Laurence E. Lynn, Jr., *Designing Public Policy.* Copyright © 1980 by Scott, Foresman and Company.

rubrics of the War on Poverty and the Great Society provided extensive resources to deal with unemployment, crime, urban deterioration, access to medical care, and mental health treatment. It was a period in which the emphasis was on innovation, and the testing of local and national "demonstrations" literally produced more opportunities to conduct evaluations than there were persons equipped to undertake them. During this period, the primary emphasis was on documenting the gains in improved social and human conditions from social programs. At least a portion of these programs, often hurriedly put into place, were poorly conceived, improperly implemented, and ineffectively administered.

As a consequence, the decade of the 1970s increasingly saw serious questioning of the continued expansion of government programs (Freeman and Solomon, 1979). The reaction is most clear in such referenda as California's Proposition 13, which limited local tax revenue, and "sunset" laws, which require the automatic shutdown of ineffective programs (Adams and Sherman, 1978). As a consequence, governmental—and to some extent private foundation—resources for innovative social programs declined. The result has been a change in emphasis in the evaluation field. In particular, there is increased concern with documenting the worth of social program expenditures in comparison to their costs and increased attention to fiscal accountability and the management effectiveness of programs. Paradoxically, fiscal and political conservatives, often skeptical about social science methods, have joined the advocates of expanded social action programs in pressing for the types of information that evaluations provide.

The evaluation enterprise must acknowledge the impact on its activities of the changing mood of the times, and, in particular, the mentality of the

Reagan administration. The federal government apparently will continue to try to control inflation and reduce the federal deficit by advocating the curtailment of domestic federal expenditures, including, of course, those for social programs. A similar posture is manifest in many states and cities; some of the local and state reactions to the current economic situation have been particularly severe. This is not simply a consequence of the distrust, hostility, and political actions of community members dismayed by the burdensome and growing bite of income and property taxes. It also results from disenchantment with the outcomes and implementation of a large share of the programs advocated by public officials, planners, and politicians in the past several decades.

It is clear that Reagan's 1980 election and overwhelming reelection vote in 1984 is interpreted by many as a continued mandate for reduced or at least rearranged human and social program efforts. Elections in a number of Western European countries during the first half of the 1980s suggest this is a widespread phenomenon.

On the intellectual front, several conservative criticisms of Great Society programs have appeared (see especially Murray, 1984). These criticisms are based more on ideological grounds than on grounds of ineffectiveness, but some nevertheless draw heavily on evaluation research results for condemnations of social programs as providing perverse incentives that increase the social problems they were intended to ameliorate.

Whether this is a sustained reaction to the Great Society outlook of the 1960s and early 1970s that will persist for the rest of this decade or longer or simply a shorter-term "pendulum swing" is a matter of conjecture, although the latter view is supported by some experienced analysts of the social program arena (Chelimsky, 1983). Nevertheless, the role of evaluation remains substantial, and, in some types of evaluation, activities may actually increase (Chelimsky, 1983; Rossi, 1983).

Fundamentally, a "conservative" outlook does not change the role of evaluation research in the social program arena (Freeman, 1983). Rather, it results in the raising of a partially different set of evaluation questions, or in shifts in emphases of the concerns of the stakeholders. Given the tenor of the times, we can expect that there will continue to be intensive scrutiny of existing programs, because of the pressure to curtail or dismantle those for which there is limited evidence of program efficacy and efficient delivery of services. Evaluations of the wide range of established programs are likely to increase if the present political outlook continues. At the same time, however, evaluations will be needed to assess less costly alternatives to programs that are curtailed and forsaken, as well as assessments of revised ways of delivering services.

EVALUATION RESEARCH IN PRACTICE

Perhaps the most challenging aspect of applying social research procedures to the study of social programs, and the most distinctive feature of
evaluation research, is the inherent requirement that evaluators conduct
their work in a continually changing milieu. A number of features of social
interventions are associated with the highly volatile character of social
programs. First, the relative influence, resources, and priorities of the
sponsors of social programs change frequently. Some of these changes
are associated with political shifts. For example, with the change of
national administrations, governmental endorsement of family planning,
especially in the form of abortions, has been sharply curtailed both domes-
tically and internationally. Clearly this must have an impact on any ongoing
evaluations of family planning programs.

Second, the interests and influence of the various stakeholders may
change. Programs that require the cooperation of particular organizations
or individuals may be benefited or hurt by these changes. For instance, a
police chief who agreed to provide certain information to a program and its
evaluators may change his outlook in the face of mass media attention to
police invasions of privacy.

Third, there may be marked modifications in the priorities and responsibilities of the organizations and agencies implementing programs. For
example, a school system released by the courts from forced school
busing may no longer be as interested in its programs to increase acceptance by white students of attendance in predominantly minority schools
as it was while court-required busing was in effect.

Fourth, unanticipated problems with delivering the intervention or with
the intervention itself may require modifying the program and consequently the evaluation plan as well. For example, a program to reduce the
absenteeism of low-income high school students by providing comprehensive medical care was thwarted because more than two-thirds of the
students with high rates of absence refused the medical care offered.

Fifth, partial findings from an evaluation may result in reasonably secure
knowledge of the lack of intended outcomes from the intervention. For
example, a study of the impact of an alcohol treatment program included
six-month and one-year follow-ups of the clients. The six-month follow-up
revealed very high rates of drunkenness among the treatment group, with
the result that the program staff modified the intervention markedly.

Sixth, unanticipated problems may occur in implementing the evaluation design. For example, a foundation sponsored a program to improve
the delivery of emergency care that, since it was not costly to implement,
was also undertaken in many locales that were not provided with founda-

tion funding for the intervention. As a consequence, the planned comparisons between funded and unfunded groups was not possible, and the evaluation strategy had to be revised sharply.

Some social programs and their accompanying evaluations, of course, suffer minimally from these and related problems. For example, a study to evaluate the impact of different dental prevention programs was undertaken nationally without significant modifications in the intervention plan, with high rates of provider and student cooperation, and with virtually complete adherence to the original evaluation design (Bell et al., 1984). Others, however, depart markedly from "ideal" studies in their design and data collection procedures and, in the case of impact evaluations, in the degree of control the investigator has over the implementation of the treatments. Thus, within the evaluation field there is considerable controversy over whether or not evaluation research is qualitatively different from "scientific" research.

Scientific versus Pragmatic Evaluation Postures

Perhaps the single most influential article in the evaluation field is the 1969 paper by Donald Campbell. This paper provided a review of experimental approaches for the study of the impact of social programs. But it was much more than that; it outlined an ideological position that Campbell has advanced for more than twenty years. His perspective is that policy and program decisions should emerge from the continual testing of ways to improve the social condition, and that the social change efforts of the society should be rooted in social experimentation. In a real sense he argues that the community and the nation, if not the world, should be seen as a laboratory for social experimentation. Further, not only does he hold this position in the abstract, but he contends that the technology of social research permits the feasible implementation of such an outlook. He and his colleagues have thus consistently sought to promote this position and at the same time to refine and improve the methodology of social research in order to undertake efforts to convert us into an "experimenting society" (for example, see Cook and Campbell, 1979). Campbell, then, has sought to impose the experimental model on evaluation research, as he originally practiced it in social psychology. While in some of his writing he tempers his position, it is fair to characterize him as seeing evaluation research fitting into the scientific social research paradigm.

In contrast is the viewpoint of another giant in the evaluation field, Lee Cronbach. Cronbach, a superb statistician and highly respected researcher, argues that evaluation research is an art, and different from scientific research (Cronbach, 1982). According to Cronbach, every evaluation represents, or should represent, an idiosyncratic effort directed at providing maximally useful information to program sponsors and stakeholders. This is in contrast to "scientific investigations," the design and implementation of which strive to meet the standards of the investigators' peers. According to Cronbach, it is the contrast in purpose and intent that differentiates evaluations from scientific investigations. Both may use the same logic of inquiry and research procedures, but scientific studies strive to meet a set of research standards, while evaluations need to be developed in ways that recognize both the policy and program interests of the sponsors and stakeholders, and to be formulated and conducted so they are maximally useful to the decision-makers, given the resources, political circumstances, and program constraints that surround them.

In some cases, for example, evaluations may be undertaken that are "good enough" for answering the policy and program questions, although from a scientific standpoint they are not the "best" designs. If it is known in advance, as an illustration, that one program will be substituted for another only if its impact is twice as large as that of the one in place, decisions on the size and composition of the study group will be different than they would be in an investigation to test a hypothesis derived from some social science theory. In contrast, an evaluation might be tested on a sample of a target group many times larger than that needed to demonstrate the impact of an intervention because the evaluators are aware that political decision-makers will act only if several thousand, in contrast to several hundred, subjects constitute the target sample. Then, too, some evaluations necessarily begin with an awareness that, from the standpoint of the scientific community, the study will be viewed as "sloppy" because either the program conditions or the resources available limit its rigor.

Actually, we have described Campbell's and Cronbach's positions in polar terms for didactic purposes. In fact, as Cronbach acknowledges, there is not so extreme a difference between his views and Campbell's. On the one hand, there are a significant number of evaluations that do approximate "perfect" designs by scientific standards, either because such designs are required to be maximally useful to sponsors and stakeholders or because the evaluators are committed to meeting the requirements of their scientific peers as well as those of the sponsors and stakeholders of the evaluation. Boruch and his associates (1978), for example, have collected a large number of "true" experiments conducted as evaluations that are as close to "perfect" in terms of scientific standards as those undertaken as "basic research" studies.

On the other hand, persons whose primary purpose in doing a study is "science" often face the same constraints of resources and research milieus as evaluators and are aware from the outset that their investiga-

Exhibit 1-D: Issues in Planning Evaluations

Designing an evaluative investigation is an art. The design must be chosen afresh in each new undertaking, and the choices to be made are almost innumerable. Each feature of a design offers particular advantages and entails particular sacrifices. Further merits and limitations come from the way various features combine. A broad theory of validity and utility is thus required to provide a base both for judging research plans and for generating more satisfactory ones.

A design is a plan for allocating investigative resources. In evaluation—as in basic science—the designer's task is to produce maximally useful evidence within a specified budget of dollars, a specified number of person-years from the evaluation staff and of person-hours from informants, and other such constraints. "Maximally useful" is a key phrase. Most writings on design suggest that an investigation is to be judged by its form, and certain forms are held up as universal ideals. In contrast, I would argue that the investigations have functions and that a form highly suitable for one investigation would not be appropriate for the next. This is to be, then, a functional theory of design.

The central purpose of evaluation differs from that of basic social research, and evaluations fit into a different institutional and political context. The strategy of evaluative research therefore requires special consideration. Logic is necessarily the same in all disciplined inquiry, but the translation of logic into procedure should depend upon context, purpose, and expected payoff. Many recommendations appropriate for long-term programs of scientific research are ill suited to evaluation. Hence, general writings on design and scientific method are inadequate to guide the evaluator. General recommendations on evaluation can also mislead; evaluations should not be cast into a single mold. For any evaluation many good designs can be proposed, but no perfect ones.

SOURCE: Lee J. Cronbach, *Designing Evaluations of Educational and Social Programs.* San Francisco: Jossey-Bass, 1982 (pp. 1-2). Reprinted by permission.

tions will be less than "perfect." At a more philosophical level, the difference in positions can be seen as a carry-over from a long-standing debate about the "objective" qualities of social research and the extent to which investigators' values impinge on the design, scope, and conduct of studies (Krasner and Houts, 1984).

Nevertheless, the distinction is a real one. Our outlook in many respects is fairly close to Cronbach's, although we do hold that in many instances evaluations can be maximally useful to decision-makers and yet meet the requirements of scientific investigation. In a sense we are like religious reformists who are deeply respectful of the orthodox roots of their enterprise but recognize the realities of the real world in which they are operating. In other words, evaluations need to be formulated and executed with an awareness that evaluators must be pragmatic in their outlooks.

From extensive experience in doing evaluations, we are aware that there is an art as well as a science to evaluation research. At the same time, certainly via the written word, there are limits to how much of an art form can be taught. By analogy, it is like the training of physicians to be diagnosticians. Any intelligent person can be taught to understand the values obtained from laboratory tests and to use them in reaching a diagnosis; at the same time, practice, experience, and understanding of the individual case clearly are essential in order for a doctor to become an astute diagnostician and maximally benefit his or her patients. In this sense, learning from a text provides only part of the knowledge base one needs to undertake maximally useful evaluations.

Finally, it should be acknowledged that some persons in the field, individuals with strong commitments as evaluators, minimize the importance of the social research outlook, whether it be the scientific perspective of Campbell or the art-form view of Cronbach, or our somewhat more middle-ground pragmatic outlook. True, they may use social research procedures to obtain some or all of the information they think is required. But at the heart of their activities as evaluators is a belief that their experience in studying a particular social problem area, their intuition and wisdom, and their feel for the needs of sponsors and stakeholders are (and should be) the major inputs into their work. For them, each assignment is truly a unique case.

In our view, persons with this perspective are not engaged in evaluation research—indeed, although we use the terms "evaluation" and "evaluation research" as synonyms, some in the field reserve the former for description of such persons and their activities and retain the latter term for work rooted primarily in the scientific tradition. From our standpoint, it is not possible to "teach," at least via a text, this approach to social program evaluation. (For an elegant presentation of this side of evaluation, see Guba and Lincoln, 1981.)

AN OVERVIEW OF EVALUATIONS

Evaluations may be undertaken for a variety of reasons (Chelimsky, 1978): for management and administrative purposes, to assess the appropriateness of program changes, to identify ways to improve the delivery of interventions, or to meet the accountability requirements of funding groups. They may be undertaken for planning and policy purposes, to test innovative ideas on how to deal with human and community problems, to decide whether to expand or curtail programs, or to support advocacy of one program as opposed to another. Finally, they may be undertaken to test a particular social science hypothesis or a professional practice principle (the particular program studied in this case may be mainly a matter of convenience). For all these purposes, the key goal is to design and implement an evaluation that provides a firm assessment, one that would be unchanged if the evaluation were replicated by the same evaluators or conducted by another group.

Foci of Evaluations

The scope of each evaluation, of course, depends on the specific purposes for which it is being conducted. Furthermore, the ways the evaluation questions are asked and the research procedures undertaken depend on whether the program under evaluation is an innovative intervention, a modification or expansion of an existing effort, or a well-established, stable human service activity.

"Evaluation," in our sense, encompasses several related sets of activities. It is useful to distinguish among three major classes of evaluation research: analysis related to the conceptualization and design of interventions, monitoring of program implementation, and assessment of program utility. Although it is not always possible to do so fully, the evaluation of social programs may need to include all three classes of activities. Evaluations that do so are termed "comprehensive evaluations." An expanded discussion of the variations in evaluation strategies in relation to types of programs is the central topic of Chapter 2. Here we discuss the three foci of evaluations in general terms, listing the major questions adhering to each.

Program Conceptualization and Design

Interventions, particularly during their planning but also throughout their existence, can be seen as responses to either perceived or incipient communal problems. The origin of a social program is the recognition of a "social problem"—by which we mean defects in the human and social condition—and a resolve to take purposive, organized action to remedy the problem. The impetus for a program to raise educational skills, for example, is usually the recognition that a significant number of persons in a given population are deficient in reading and mathematics skills. An ongoing program may be justified by the persistence of a social problem: Driver education in high schools receives public support and is subject to evaluations because of the continuing high rates of automobile accidents, particularly among adolescent drivers. Chapter 2 discusses the relationships among problem identification, program design and planning, and evaluation activities. In Chapter 3, we examine "diagnostic" evaluation activities, that is, concepts and procedures to allow the specification of a social problem in ways that enhance both the design of appropriate interventions and their evaluations.

Program Conceptualization and Design Questions

- What is the extent and distribution of the target problem and/or population?

- Is the program designed in conformity with intended goals; is there a coherent rationale underlying it; and have chances of successful delivery been maximized?

- What are projected or existing costs and what is their relation to benefits and effectiveness?

**Monitoring and Accountability
of Program Implementation**

There are many reasons for monitoring programs. First, proper management and administration of human resource programs require that program managers, on a day-to-day basis, conduct their activities as efficiently as possible. Program managers and supervisors who have reputations for wasting funds, inappropriately using staff resources, and in other ways being ineffective often not only endanger their own positions but jeopardize the futures of their programs.

Second, program sponsors and stakeholders require evidence that what presumably was paid for and deemed desirable was actually undertaken. Increasingly, there is concern with the lack of accountability of programs, particularly public programs. In many programs, the regular feedback of evaluation information is one of the most powerful tools the program manager has for documenting the operational effectiveness of his or her organization, for justifying the ways staff are employed, for requesting further program support, and for defending the performance of his or her program compared with those undertaken by other organizations in the same social program sector.

Third, there is no point in being concerned with the impact or outcome of a particular project unless it did, indeed, take place and did serve the appropriate participants in the way intended. Many programs are not implemented and executed according to their original design. Sometimes personnel simply are not available or equipment is in disrepair; sometimes project staffs may be prevented by political or other reasons from undertaking what they intended. Some project staff members may not have the motivation or know-how to carry out their tasks as outlined. In still other instances, either poor budget estimates or inflation leads program staffs to modify their efforts.

There are also instances in which the intended project participants do not exist in the numbers required, cannot be identified precisely, or are not cooperative. For example, in certain communities, funds have been provided for projects in which the participants are identified as children with congenital heart conditions. For some of these projects, locating potential participants has been so costly that funds are short for supporting the treatments intended.

Monitoring can alert project personnel to such problems by providing a systematic assessment of whether or not a program is operating in conformity to its design and reaching its specified target population. As a result of such an evaluation, staff of the New York City School Lunch Program discovered some serious deficiencies in their services (see Exhibit 1-E). Monitoring and accountability are discussed in detail in Chapter 4.

Program Monitoring Questions

- Is the program reaching the specified target population or target area?
- Are the intervention efforts being conducted as specified in the program design?

Assessment of Program Utility

It obviously is critical to know both the degree to which a program has an impact and its benefits in relation to costs. The former is referred to as the program's "effectiveness" or "impact" and the latter as its "efficiency" (its cost-effectiveness and cost-efficiency, to be discussed in more detail in Chapter 8).

Unless programs have a demonstrable impact, it is hard to defend their implementation and continuation; hence the need for impact assessments.

Exhibit 1-E: A Monitor's Report on a Free Meal Program

A monitoring committee consisting of volunteers with expertise in education, nutrition, research, and children's services conducted visits to New York City schools to describe the free lunch program. Twenty-four schools in nine districts were selected, and school staffs were interviewed informally. Monitors also observed lunchroom and cooking facilities. In addition, 1,322 mailed questionnaires from lunchroom workers were analyzed.

In March 1975 in New York City, there were 1,292 schools and institutions serving an average of 537,359 meals daily. Of these, 90 percent of the meals were free, the remainder full price. Until the end of 1975, New York City had no reduced-price school meal program. It is currently being introduced in response to federal legislation that mandates it. About 57 percent of the children registered in elementary and junior high schools are eligible for free meals. Of these, 87 percent participate in the School Lunch Program. If reduced-price meals were available, the monitors estimated that based on 1970 Census data, at least 250,000 additional children would be eligible for them.

As of June 1975, twenty-two of the thirty-two community school districts served an average of 63,838 daily breakfasts in 365 schools. Only 13 percent of the eligible children in New York City received free breakfasts. At least 400,000 others who now eat a free lunch are eligible for a free breakfast, but are not being served.

Program Administration

The monitors found that centralized food distribution is not necessarily the cheapest or most efficient way of getting food to children in school. Monitors observed during visits to schools that food purchased in bulk through the Bureau of School Lunches frequently was more expensive than it would have been at a local market. For instance, chicken bought through the Bureau was $.67 a pound, while the price at the local market was $.47. In addition, school officials complained that the Bureau often paid for larger produce deliveries than were ordered or could be used.

Quality of Meals

In general, the monitors were dissatisfied with both the appearance and the taste of the food served in these programs. They rated the food in only three of the fourteen breakfast programs and twelve of the thirty lunch programs visited, as "appetizing in appearance"; the food in four breakfast and ten lunch programs tasted good. They observed greenish hot dogs and tasted cloyingly sweet baked beans, unidentified mixtures of rice and meat, stale rolls, soggy vegetables, and other unappetizing dishes. Most of the lunch programs and nearly all the breakfast programs offered no choice of food. Some monitors reported overly small portions for older children, although when the meal is disliked, even small portions remain uneaten.

Menu Planning and Distribution

Schools do not distribute menus regularly or widely. Neither parents nor children know the menus in advance, nor are they consulted in menu planning, even though the parents have requested it in some schools. The monitors noted that in one school on the Lower East Side, parents are involved in menu planning with the result that the school is serving appetizing and nutritious meals. No provisions are made for special dietary needs or problems. Although lunchroom workers said they frequently knew children's preferences—such as extra peanut butter with a meal-pack or frozen meal; beans instead of sauerkraut which the children will not eat; one extra slice of bread so children can make sandwiches—they were unable to influence menu planning to reflect them.

Lunchroom Atmosphere

Many schools are ill equipped to feed large numbers of children. Lunchrooms are small and lunch sometimes is served in shifts from 10 a.m. to 2 p.m. The monitors found many lunchrooms very crowded and, in more than half of the schools visited, children eat with their coats on and books in their laps. Times for meals and times for recreation are not separated in most schools, with the result that in some lunchrooms, children rush through their food or skip it entirely so that they will have an extra few minutes to play and talk, making the atmosphere extremely noisy and unsettled for those still eating.

There is a significant amount of waste, and several schools were described as having an insufficient number of garbage cans. Tables and floors, and the areas around the garbage cans, were often strewn with leftover food.

Separation of Free-Lunch Recipients from Other Students

There was evidence that children who receive free lunches and those who pay for lunch or bring their own were separated. Of the schools visited that served both free and paid lunches, half separated nonpaying children by maintaining different waiting lines or separate tables, and/or by the use of tickets instead of money.

SOURCE: Adapted, with permission, from Trude W. Lash and Heidi Sigal, *State of the Child: New York City.* New York: Foundation for Child Development, 1976.

But knowledge of effectiveness simply is insufficient in most cases; outcome or impact must be judged against input costs. Some programs may not be supportable because of their high costs in comparison to their impacts. For example, some universities, in the face of budget problems, have terminated their student counseling programs because costs are high and benefits slight. Other programs may be expanded, retained, or terminated on the basis of their comparative costs. For instance, findings about the impact of institutional versus community care for adolescent offenders suggest that community programs are preferable because of their markedly lower costs. The need to determine the relation of such costs to effectiveness necessitates efficiency assessments.

Impact Assessments

An impact assessment gauges the extent to which a program causes change in the desired direction. It implies that there is a set of specified, operationally defined goals and criteria of success. A program that has impact is one that achieves some movement or change toward the desired objectives. These objectives may be social-behavioral ones, such as lowering functional illiteracy or reducing nutritional deficiencies among children; they may be community related, such as reducing the frequency of certain crimes; or they may be physical, such as decreasing water pollution or increasing the number of bus trips that conform to a time schedule.

Exhibit 1-F: Infant Day Care

The question that provoked the work can be put in deceptively simple form. Do infants attending a well-run, nurturant, responsible group-care center five days a week for a little over 100 weeks display different patterns of psychological development during or at the end of that period when compared with children of the same sex and family background who are being reared in a typical nuclear family context in the northeastern United States?

A longitudinal investigation was designed to assess the psychological effects of an experimentally conducted day-care program on children ages 3.5 to 29 months. The subjects were Chinese and Caucasian children from working- and middle-class families who were cared for at a special group-care center five days a week; the major control group consisted of children reared totally at home and matched with the experimental children in terms of ethnicity, social class, and sex.

The central question that provoked the investigation can be answered with some assurance: Attendance at a day-care center staffed by conscientious and nurturant adults during the first 2.5 years does not seem to sculpt a psychological profile very much different from the one created by total family rearing. This conclusion is based not only on formal assessments but also on informal observations of the children over the 2.5-year period. These data did not confirm several popular notions about early group care. Although it is reasonable to assume that daily encounter with other children during the first two years might speed up the maturation of the social interaction sequences usually seen in 3- and 4-year-olds, the data did not provide dramatic support for that prediction. The 20- and 29-month-olds were simply not very social and did not often initiate play with other children. Both cooperative and aggressive play occurred infrequently among both groups. There were as many shy children among the day-care groups as there were among the home controls. The day-care children were neither more cooperative nor more aggressive than home controls. In brief, the evaluation revealed a remarkably similar growth function for both day-care and home controls.

SOURCE: Adapted from J. Kagan, R. B. Kearsley, and P. R. Zelazo, "The Effects of Infant Care on Psychological Development," Evaluation Quarterly 1 (February 1977): 109-142.

To conduct an impact evaluation, the evaluator needs a plan for data collection in order to demonstrate in a persuasive way that the changes are a function of the intervention and cannot be accounted for in other ways. Specific impact assessment plans may vary considerably: Sometimes it is possible to use classic experimental designs in which there are control and experimental groups that receive different treatments and are constructed through randomization. (Basic strategies for impact analysis are found in Chapter 5; randomized experiments are discussed in Chapter 6.)

For practical reasons it is often necessary, however, to employ non-experimental approaches rather than true experiments. Nonrandomized experiments and nonexperimental methods are commonly employed in impact assessments. With proper safeguards and appropriate qualifications, such nonexperimental designs can provide reasonably firm estimates of effects. (These designs are found in Chapter 7.)

Impact evaluations are essential when there is an interest in either comparing different programs or testing the utility of new efforts to ameliorate a particular community problem. An illustration is the evaluation of a program to maximize psychosocial development in children (see Exhibit 1-F).

Efficiency Assessments

Because resources present a constant and increasing problem, programs demand efficiency assessments. Interventions compete with each other for funds from foundations, international organizations, and the various levels of government. Similarly, specific interventions within programs often compete for funds and resources. Choices must be made continually between funding or not funding, continuing or discontinuing, and expanding or contracting one program as opposed to another.

At least some of the considerations that go into such choices concern economics: Is a program producing sufficient benefits for the costs incurred? Is it intended to produce a particular benefit at a lower cost per unit of outcome than other interventions or delivery systems designed to achieve the same goal? The techniques for undertaking evaluations to answer these types of questions are found in two closely related approaches: cost-benefit and cost-effectiveness analyses. (See Exhibit 1-G for an illustration of cost-benefit analysis.) The ideas underlying the two approaches and further illustrations of them are presented in Chapter 8.

Program Utility Questions

- Is the program effective in achieving its intended goals?
- Can the results of the program be explained by some alternative process that does not include the program?

- What are the costs to deliver services and benefits to program participants?
- Is the program an efficient use of resources, compared with alternative uses of the resources?

PROGRAM STAGES

As we have just discussed, evaluations are conducted to answer a variety of questions related to what we have listed as the three foci of evaluation research: program conceptualization and design, program implementation (monitoring and accountability), and program utility (impact and efficiency assessments). Beyond dealing with these questions, an evaluation must be tailored to the stage of development of the intervention being addressed. This may be found by locating the program on a continuum with poles at "innovative" programs and "established" programs, with those in need of "refinement," "modification," or "fine-tuning" lying somewhere between. While many of the same procedures characterize all evaluations, the state of the program's development—what we shall refer to as the "program stage"—determines the level of effort and technical procedures undertaken during the evaluation.

Evaluation of Innovative Programs

Completely new interventions are relatively rare. Most programs introduced as "new and innovative" are ordinarily modifications of existing practices. What makes an intervention "innovative" in our sense is that the "treatment" has never been applied to the population specified. It may have been tried as a small-scale, impressionistically judged demonstration, but never with the realistic intent of having it implemented on a broad scale.

In our terms, a program is innovative if it has not been subject to implementation and assessment in the following ways:

1. The intervention itself is still in an emerging or research and development ("R&D") phase. That is, there is no evidence, or very limited evidence, that it has an impact as an installed program. For example, hospices, which are nonmedically oriented settings for terminally ill patients, are now being evaluated as an innovative alternative to long-term hospitalization. While hospices have been operating for some years, only recently have they been seen as a widespread initiative possibly meriting governmental and national foundation support.

2. The delivery system or parts of it have not been tested adequately. Such a program would be one that includes the untested idea of having high school students provide nutritional education and information to the elderly.

Exhibit 1-G: Ambulatory Surgery in an HMO

In recent years the subject of ambulatory surgery has become one of great interest in the health-care field. Interest in it has been stimulated by the opening of free-standing surgical care centers throughout the country and by the increasing efforts of health regulatory agencies to contain the rapidly rising costs of health care.

This study is a retrospective examination of data taken from a self-contained medical care system that introduced a change in surgical services in its hospital. The ambulatory surgery services it provides are similar to those offered in free-standing surgical care centers. Surgeons of the Kaiser-Permanente Medical Care Program (KMCP) in Portland, Oregon, have been performing ambulatory surgery for more than 20 years. As early as 1961, 10 percent of their patients having surgery performed in the hospital operating rooms were not admitted either before or after the surgery. As of 1977, about 41 percent of operating-room surgical patients in the Kaiser-Permanente Medical Care Program were not admitted to the hospital.

Analysis of Cost Savings

The study investigated the process differences between the inpatient and ambulatory modes and found that the only significant differences were that ambulatory patients were not admitted (thus saving inpatient costs) but required longer recovery-room time than inpatients. These differences were then priced out as follows, to find the cost savings. The savings made from shifting certain procedures from inpatient to ambulatory mode were calculated based on the assumption that (except in a few cases noted in the cost analysis of selected procedures), had the ambulatory mode not been available, the patient would have been admitted. Therefore, when the procedure is performed as an ambulatory case, inpatient costs are saved. Inpatient costs include routine service per-diem costs and costs of physician inpatient visits. They are partially offset by the extra costs for ambulatory patients' recovery-room time, which is longer than for inpatients.

**Cost Savings per Ambulatory Case for Selected Procedures
(based on 1974 ambulatory procedures applied to 1977 dollars)**

Procedure	Total Routine Inpatient Costs ($)	Subtracted Recovery- Room Costs ($)	Total Cost Saved per Ambulatory Case ($)
Dilation and curettage of uterus	210.45	28.91	181.74
Excision and destruction of lesion of skin and subcutaneous tissue	274.00	7.45	271.16
Bilateral ligation and division of fallopian tubes and bilateral salpingectomy	147.02	24.97	122.05
Myringotomy	147.02	12.70	134.32
Biopsy of breast and partial mastectomy	210.45	25.84	184.61
Excision of lesion of muscle tendon and fascia	274.00	17.96	258.74
Exploration and neurolysis of peripheral nerve	274.00	18.83	255.17
Circumcision	147.02	37.67	109.35
Partial excision of bone	274.00	7.45	271.02
Trachelectomy (conization)	147.02	25.40	121.62
All selected procedures (weighted average of all cases for 1974)			192.19

Conclusions

This study found that ambulatory surgery can save a great deal of money for health-care consumers. If implemented nationally at a rate similar to the rate of ambulatory surgery in the Oregon Region of the Kaiser-Permanente Medical Care Program, approximately three-quarters of a billion dollars would be saved annually (based on 1977 figures). The study also found that both patients and providers of care were very satisfied with ambulatory surgery and that the quality of care was very high.

The results of the study clearly indicate that a widespread program of ambulatory surgery would be beneficial to the entire health-care system. The study also gives indications that such a program could be implemented easily.

SOURCE: Adapted, with permission, from Sylvia D. Marks et al., "Ambulatory Surgery in an HMO." *Medical Care,* xviii (February 1980): 127-146.

3. The targets of the program are markedly new or expanded. An intervention of this type might offer cassette-recorded language training to immigrant schoolchildren who are not present in large enough numbers in an individual school to justify bilingual educational classes.

4. A program originally undertaken in response to one goal is continued or expanded because of its impact on another objective. For instance, a program providing marked automobiles to police for their personal use may have been initiated to cut the crime rate, but is continued to curtail job instability and keep police close to their precincts.

Evaluations for Fine-Tuning

Once programs are under way, it is often important to test variations in the ways they operate. The major reason to do so is to improve either their efficacy or their efficiency—that is, to increase the magnitude of their impact or to decrease their costs per unit of impact. An example of the former would be a weekly tutoring program for economically disadvantaged children that is improving educational skills to a fair extent, but that program staff feel could be more effective if the children were provided learning opportunities beyond once-a-week tutoring sessions. Accordingly, a supplemental "homework" program is introduced and evaluated. An example of the latter is a program that involves three months of daily counseling for previously hospitalized alcoholics. Because the costs of the program are high, reducing the program's duration from three to two months may become the subject of an evaluation.

There are other reasons to undertake fine-tuning of evaluations. One is to provide equitable service delivery—that is, to see that a program's services are delivered to its target population just as these services are delivered to persons in the general population. In a health-care clinic, this may involve putting in an appointment system, thereby cutting down on client waiting time. Here the issue would be whether or not patient satisfaction with the delivery system is increased without loss of efficiency. Another basis for fine-tuning a program is to reduce dropouts from the target population. In our hypothetical clinic, this might be a second rationale for putting in the appointment system.

It should be emphasized that there is no clear-cut line between innovative and fine-tuning or modification efforts. Sometimes the changes being tested are minor and clearly modificatory. Other times, however, they are costly and may have broad ramifications for human service networks. For example, fine-tuning that integrates formerly free-standing community health centers with teaching hospitals does not change the basic concept underlying delivery of medical care to low-income persons. However, it may have major consequences for the costs of such care on a national basis and may alter the quality of services received markedly.

Evaluations of Established Programs

Programs mandated by legislation and even those in existence for decades may also be subjected to evaluation for a series of different reasons. First, a program may have been instituted for a complex set of political and other external reasons, and it is important to have hard data on its impact and the ratio of benefits to costs in order to justify its continuation, expansion, or termination. Changes in resources available, political outlooks, community members' priorities, and real or asserted declines in the extensiveness or severity of the target problem may provoke evaluation activities. Perhaps most important in stimulating evaluation of an established program is evidence of or suspicion that programs are either ineffective or inefficient. Moreover, as mentioned, many state and local programs, and a growing number of federal programs, must meet the requirements of "sunset" legislation, which provides for regular program reviews and "automatic" termination of programs failing to demonstrate utility.

Evaluations of established programs may focus on impact and costs-to-benefits ratios. Often, however, the assessments are limited to examinations of service delivery. In such cases, the evaluation centers on monitoring questions: whether or not appropriate target groups are served, and the extent to which program staff and management are meeting commitments with respect to the quality and quantity of services delivered. The human service area is highly vulnerable to serious, responsible questioning of the ways programs are conducted, as well as to political or publicity-related attacks. Evaluation results, both from monitoring program implementation and from assessing impact and efficiency, can influence decisions on the expansion, continuation, or termination of programs and the organizations responsible for them.

HOW EVALUATIONS ARE USED

Not only do evaluations differ according to states of program development, but the uses to which they are put also vary. The scope and design of evaluations must take into account these varying uses. Again, no clear-cut distinctions are possible, but the range of uses nevertheless can be described with some degree of specificity by considering evaluation uses in terms of decision-making modes. Use can also be examined in terms of the consequences or ramifications of the evaluation effort. Both perspectives are relevant to how evaluators go about their work.

Modes of Decision-Making

As is the case in all applied research, evaluations are undertaken to influence the actions and activities of individuals and groups who have or are presumed to have an opportunity to tailor their actions on the basis of the results of the evaluation effort. In the simplest case, the results are directed at an individual executive, such as a key public official who has the authority and responsibility to allocate resources and shape a human service program. For example, within limits, police chiefs can decide on how to assign their officers, how to structure communication between various divisions, and how to deal with emergencies and other unforeseen occurrences.

In other cases, of course, the situation is more complex; a variety of parties influence the ways human resource programs are designed and implemented. For example, a national health insurance initiative would require agreement on program outlines by both the congressional and the executive branches of the federal government, and would involve attention to the views and interests of a variety of stakeholders, including health professionals and their organizations, labor and management groups, insurers, and consumer aggregates. The various permutations and combinations of stakeholders and the range of influences and decision-making processes encountered across human resource activities are subject to both speculative and systematic inquiries. There are three modal alternatives; we discuss them below.

Go/No-Go Decisions

At various points in programming human services, decisive actions are required. For example, the secretary of Health and Human Services must recommend to either Congress or the White House whether or not to provide training for different categories of health practitioners, what types of patients to admit into federally supported hospitals, eligibility requirements for welfare programs, and so on. At a local level, a school superintendent and board may have to decide whether or not to impose standards of classroom size, to establish a work-study program for high school students, or to terminate kindergarten instruction.

There are probably relatively few instances wherein decisions are made solely on evaluation findings, although if they are strong enough and the studies are defensible from the standpoint of rigor, the findings may dominate decision-making.

Developing a Rationale for Action

More often, evaluations influence the determinants of decisions; political, practical, and resource considerations; and the wisdom and personal experience of those with influence. Sometimes evaluations directly affect the underlying rationale of a program and consequent professional, political, and legal decisions about it. For example, the pressure to deinstitutionalize the treatment of mentally ill and retarded persons is accompanied by a large number of political, legal, and practical issues. The first court-ordered deinstitutionalization of a state facility for mentally retarded persons was accompanied by a federally supported evaluation to determine the consequences of deinstitutionalization on the severely retarded, their families, and community members living close to where they would reside. The results may have important consequences for future legislative and legal decisions in various states and at a national level.

Other times, evaluations have an indirect or delayed effect. Those conducted either to develop knowledge or for a particular program purpose may have subsequent impact. This type of evaluation impact is sometimes referred to as the "conceptual use" of evaluation results. For example, some years ago a carefully controlled study examined the impact of psychotherapy in prisons. Findings suggesting that psychotherapy had limited, if any, utility, at least when delivered by prison staff, were available for a number of years prior to the surge of concern about the efficacy and efficiency of prison rehabilitation programs (Kassebaum et al., 1971). Efforts to expand psychotherapy in prisons were thwarted by the evidence of inefficacy provided by the evaluation. In this sense, although difficult to gauge, evaluations may make important contributions to the human service area. Likewise, evaluations serve to "discipline" program decision-making. As we will discuss later, the emphasis of evaluations on explicit goals, criteria, and specification of intervention activities may influence how much weight other decision determinants are given.

Legitimation and Accountability

Evaluation also may serve either program advocates or opponents as inputs into the oversight of programs. Information on how well interventions are implemented, the extent to which they reach targets, their impacts, and their costs may help advocates or opponents of a particular program to ward off their adversaries. Legitimation may be required at different levels. For example, the board of a foundation supporting a school health program may be concerned with whether or not the activity is providing treatment to a sufficient number of children, and with the per-child costs of care. The state administration of such a program may use regular reports on such information to judge the production and performance of the school health teams that are located in local school systems throughout the state.

Evaluations for legitimation purposes need not be used, of course, to justify the status quo with respect to programs. Rather, they alert program sponsors and managers to "soft spots," serving as the basis for the modification, expansion, or reduction of interventions. For example, different rates, by districts, of disabled persons returning to the labor force may suggest to a state agency director the need either to reallocate staff resources or to redraw the boundaries of districts to shift the attention to population groups with the greatest needs.

As the field of evaluation has matured, considerable attention has been paid to the uses of evaluations, and the barriers to their utilization in program and policy decision-making. This topic is discussed in detail in the last chapter of the book. Here it is important to note that, while evaluation findings constitute only one input into the complex process by which policymakers, program managers, and stakeholders decide on the allocation of resources and the ways programs are staffed and implemented, evaluation results are a discernible and important input into the policy and administrative processes. For example, Leviton and Boruch (1983) review a major set of national educational evaluations and are able to document their use as an input into a range of specific decisions and into the overall program thrusts of the educational establishment (see Exhibit 1-H).

Policy and Administrative Studies

The literature on evaluation research—indeed, much of the commentary on all of applied research—refers to the "policy-relevance" of work in the field. Policy evaluations may be described generally as those that have potential impact on large segments of the population, result in major organizational changes in the structure and activities of groups delivering interventions, or are critical to the allocation of monetary, staff, and other resources. At the margins it is easy to separate policy from administrative evaluations. In practice, however, the distinction rests with the ways the stakeholders perceive the consequences of the assessment.

For example, it is clear that the evaluation of a program such as *Sesame Street* can be considered a policy study. Results have implications for public funding, requirements of television stations regarding time allotments for public service broadcasting, and the types of other school-readiness programs that are implemented. In contrast, the decision of a government agency to evaluate "flexitime" for its professional staff (allowing personnel to work at times of their own choosing, so long as they put in the required number of hours) may be seen as an administrative evaluation, although it may affect the families of the workers themselves.

Exhibit 1-H: Contributions of Evaluation

This study of use of evaluations stems from a congressionally mandated appraisal of educational evaluations at the national, state, and local levels of government. A sample of fourteen evaluations out of three U.S. Office of Education studies completed in 1978 and 1979 was first drawn. In addition, seven highly visible educational evaluations sponsored by other agencies were examined.

Evaluations do contribute to policy and program decisions, and to actual changes. It was possible to trace numerous contributions to law, regulation, management, and budgets. The reported contributions of evaluations were classified into those (1) having impact on programs or policies, (2) having influenced decision-making although they had not, at least at the time of the study, had direct impact on programs and policies, and (3) those that were considered seriously by persons and agencies but for which there was not clear evidence they had contributed to either impact or decision-making. Some 156 verified distinct contributions of these 21 evaluations were located; when unconfirmed instances are included, the total rises to 180. The verification trail led to reports of impact 68 times (76 if the unverified are included), of influence on decisions 61 times (67 including unverified instances), and to "serious consideration" 27 times (37 with unverified instances).

This is not to say that evaluations alone caused either the decisions or the changes. It is to say that evaluations can be considered seriously, and they can influence the content of decisions. They can sometimes even motivate a decision. After a decision is made, findings can support arguments in its favor and thus contribute to impact. But many other considerations go into decisions, and many other forces determine program changes. In highlighting some of these contributions, the investigators tried to indicate the forces at work in each situation.

Because the findings contradict the truism that evaluations are not used, the investigators maintain it is necessary to reassess their methods and state why they should be believed. First, although their sample was purposive, they examined almost half of the eligible studies completed in two years by the Office of Education's evaluation unit. Even if the rest of the studies contributed nothing to decision-making (and they know some of them did), the extent to which OE's evaluations contributed would still be a striking disproof of current beliefs. The investigators do not maintain that their findings generalize beyond two years of OE studies. The study that samples evaluations across many policy sectors and many years remains to be done. Yet, it is now reasonable to believe that such evaluations might contribute something to decision-making.

Second, it is always possible the respondents embroidered on the truth, and decisions were not influenced by the evaluations. This may be a serious problem, given that the study was undertaken for Congress. However, they verified the claims of each respondent as extensively as possible, through independent statements and documentation. A conspiracy would have to stretch from congressional staffers themselves, to independent researchers, to bureaucrats who had varying perspectives and no particular love for evaluation. The investigators discovered only two instances in which respondents flat out disagreed with each other, and in both cases the likely explanation is a simple mistake. In summary, their methods, though flawed, are adequate to support the contention that these studies contributed to decisions and to impact on policies and programs.

SOURCE: Adapted from L. C. Leviton and R. F. Boruch, "Contributions of Evaluations to Educational Programs," *Evaluation Review* 7 (October 1983): 563-599.

Certainly, as evaluations become more generalizable and provide input into decisions that are costly and difficult to reverse (i.e., when the changes they effect have impact directly and indirectly on large numbers of persons), they are more likely to be candidates for the "policy evaluation" label. It is important, however, that the extensiveness of policy evaluations not be overemphasized, and that the worth of administrative assessments not be downgraded. In many programs, small and large, evaluations of the implementation of technology, of changes in bureaucratic procedures, and of minor modifications in delivery systems may have important consequences for the effectiveness and efficiency of programs.

We should also stress that the distinction between policy and technical-administrative studies is arbitrary. In part, it depends on the perspective of the person determining the level of the evaluation. For example, many would view a study of the impact on crime rates of police using marked cars as personal autos as a technical or administrative study. For police administrators, however, matters of cost, insurance liability, police morale, and public acceptance raise major policy issues.

The way a study is viewed also depends on how a program can be and is formulated. There are two national child health programs currently being supported and evaluated. One, conducted at UCLA, consists of developing primary-care ambulatory centers in public schools, staffed by nurse-practitioners (with physicians as backups) who provide services to children of low-income families. If effective and efficient, it could be a model for a federally supported, nationwide program. The nature of the intervention minimizes opportunities for studying individual program components; only the broad intervention question is amenable to full assessment.

The second program, evaluated by the Rand Corporation, is designed to improve the dental health of schoolchildren. It is an experiment in which a large number of schools and classrooms across the country are assigned to different treatment programs. The most comprehensive consists of dental health education, brushing and flossing of the teeth, fluoridation of teeth, and annual applications of a sealant to suppress cavities. The design of the experiment includes an opportunity to study the impact and cost-benefits ratio of the program components separately and in all of their combinations. It would be possible, depending on the findings, to implement any individual program element. In many ways this could be considered a massive technical study, but it is seen by staff of the funding foundation and by health planners as a policy-level study because of the impact of its findings on the costs of dental care, including the earnings of private dentists (Robert Wood Johnson Foundation, 1980).

The level of the evaluation, of course, has consequences for its design and implementation in terms of funding support, time for completion, and staffing requirements. To repeat our view that evaluations must be pragmatic, we hold that successful evaluators are those who have made clear to themselves, and to their sponsors and program staffs, how the evaluation is to be used and its level of application. This is necessary whether the evaluation is of an innovative program, a program in need of fine-tuning, or an established program.

WHO CAN DO EVALUATIONS?

Systematic evaluation studies are grounded in social science research techniques that have application in evaluation studies. Hence, most evaluation specialists have had social science training. At first glance, someone unacquainted with evaluation research would undoubtedly find professional discussions of evaluation difficult to comprehend. As in any other professional field, evaluators have developed their own vocabulary, short-hand expressions, and rules for doing the work. One of the main purposes of this book is to introduce readers to the special language employed by evaluators. In order to facilitate learning this vocabulary, we provide a glossary of special terms, or key concepts, at the beginning of each chapter.

Some of the complexity of evaluation stems from the inherent tendencies of those in a professional field to develop their own language, but at least part of the need for special terminology derives from the unique concepts and insights developed in each field. At the most complex level, evaluation activities can be so technically complicated, sophisticated in conception, costly, and of such long duration that they require the dedicated participation of highly trained specialists at ease with the latest in social science theory, research methods, and statistical techniques. Such highly complex evaluations usually are conducted by specialized evaluation staffs. At the other extreme, there are many evaluation tasks that can easily be understood and carried out by persons of modest expertise and experience.

It is the purpose of this book to provide an introduction to the field for those whose current positions, academic interests, or natural curiosity inspires them to want to learn how evaluations are conducted. It is but a start along the pathway to becoming a technical expert in evaluation. An equally important aim is to provide persons faced with the administration and management of human resource programs with sufficient understanding of evaluation tasks and activities to be able to judge for themselves what kinds of evaluations are appropriate to their programs and projects, and to comprehend the results of completed studies relevant to their organizations. We have tried to provide a work that is helpful to those who conduct (or plan to conduct) evaluations, who contract for them, who oversee evaluation staffs, and who are consumers of evaluation research done by others.

2

Tailoring Evaluations

Every evaluator cannot be a planner and program implementor.
But the inevitable links between program and evaluation do
require mutual understanding of the tasks and processes
involved on both sides—thus the need to introduce
considerations of program planning, design, and implementation.
Every evaluation must be tailored to its program. The tasks
undertaken by evaluators differ depending on the stage of
activity at which they are brought in, and the needs and interests
of such stakeholders as policymakers, program managers, and
funding groups.

KEY CONCEPTS

Evaluability Assessment:	A set of procedures for planning evaluations so that stakeholders' interests are taken into account in order to maximize the utility of the evaluation.
Goals:	Statements, usually general and abstract, of desired states in human conditions and social environments.
Impact Model:	The set of guiding hypotheses underlying the planning and implementation of a program.
Objectives:	Specific and operational statements regarding the desired accomplishments of the social intervention programs.
Planning:	The process of converting goals into objectives, formulating specific interventions, and defining relevant target populations.
Management Information System (MIS):	An ongoing data collection and analysis system, usually computerized, that allows timely access to service delivery and outcome information.

*E*valuation research is an integral part of broader sets of activities usually described as rational policymaking, scientific decision-making, or program planning and implementation. It must be recognized, however, that no program is designed and implemented according to a set of "rules" or prescribed procedures. Rather, the design and implementation of programs almost always emerge from a complex mixture of political considerations, the personal influence of key stakeholders, economic constraints, and the availability of necessary program staff and technology (see Exhibit 2-A). Evaluation research is just one of the many considerations that go into the instigation and conduct of programs.

In order to maximize their influence, evaluators, on the one hand, must understand the formal and informal organizational arrangements of the environments in which they work. Policymakers and program managers, on the other hand, must see that decision-making, planning, and implementation are conducted in clear-cut, explicit ways if interventions are to benefit from the efforts of evaluators.

Two cautions should be noted. First, the discussion that follows provides an ideal view of the relations between evaluation activities and program planning, development, and implementation. It presumes there is general agreement between involved parties on the steps of implementation and the order in which they are to be taken. The reader should recognize that actual task allocation and sequences vary markedly within and between human service areas.

Second, there is wide variation in organizational arrangements. At one extreme, evaluators may do their work almost independently of either planning or program staff. At the other extreme, the same group or person is responsible for program planning, design, implementation, and evaluation. It is rare that programs are so well planned, designed, and implemented before the evaluator gets on board that he or she can concentrate solely on what may narrowly be conceived as technical evaluation tasks.

The evaluator's work often includes participating, at least to some degree, in activities that ideally should precede the design and conduct of the evaluation, or at least should be the responsibility of others. Indeed, some evaluators argue that participation in the broader processes of program design and implementation is a major contribution of the evaluation effort (Wholey, 1979). In the past few years, there has been increasing attention within the field of evaluation to the study of the design and development of programs, and "implementation research" is a growing activity. Persons who have engaged in program implementation activities are insistent that converting policies into viable interventions that correspond to the original intentions of the sponsors is the most

(text continues on page 64)

Exhibit 2-A: The History of the New Jersey-Pennsylvania Negative Income Tax Experiment

Negative income tax programs as substitutions for welfare have been advocated by such diverse persons as Milton Friedman, a well-known conservative economist, and many much more liberal economists and welfare planners. Traditional public welfare programs, in theory if not in practice, are predicated on the idea that the purpose of the program is to "rehabilitate the client," and financial support is seen as an input into the client's and his or her family's "treatment," leading to rehabilitation, defined as moving to self-reliance.

Income security or negative income-tax programs are based on a simpler assumption: It is their goal to establish an income "floor" for all families, with a payment plan that starts payments to families when their incomes fall below that income floor. Families earning income would have reduced payments, proportionally, until they reach a point when no payments are given. The floor is defined as that level of income under which it is not possible for persons and families to live at a decent, subsistence level. Taking into account family size, such programs provide sufficient payments that the total household income is at this floor. Income maintenance, or negative income tax, plans such as that discussed here are modeled to a large extent after those in place in Western European countries.

In 1965, an attempt was made by OEO staff to convince the president's office of the attractiveness of some such program, but without success. One of the major objections was that the plans offered strong incentives to poor families to stop working and to rely on payments exclusively. Failing to get political approval, the staff sought ways to produce hard evidence on its feasibility and especially on how much of a work disincentive negative income tax plans would constitute.

In 1966 and 1967, a number of plans were submitted to OEO to launch some field tests of various negative income tax plans. The most attractive plan was submitted by Mathematica, a firm in Princeton, New Jersey. While the OEO staff was disposed to accept and fund this proposal, OEO Director Sargent Shriver was unwilling to make so large a grant to a profit-making firm, insisting that the project be carried out with principal responsibilities going to the

Institute for Research on Poverty at the University of Wisconsin as the prime contractor and Mathematica as the subcontractor.

In the middle of 1967, contracts were signed. Fourteen months were spent in designing the study. It was designed as a randomized controlled experiment in which negative income tax payments were systematically varied on two dimensions, minimum income guarantees and applicable tax rates. From the fall of 1968 through the fall of 1972, payments were given to families in experimental groups and both experimentals and controls were meticulously followed through personal interviews.

Throughout the course of the experiment, several events occurred that illustrate the interaction between political events and the conduct of evaluative activity. The first event was a shift in the welfare policy of the State of New Jersey, shortly after the experiment got under way. New Jersey was picked as a site partially because the then current welfare policy covered only female-headed households under AFDC (Aid to Families with Dependent Children). The change made families with unemployed fathers eligible, a shift that made welfare policies in New Jersey competitive with some of the less generous plans.

The same New Jersey policy shift caused other problems. Local welfare officials became concerned with experimental families who were accepting both welfare payments and experimental payments. The director of the project was subpoenaed in the New Jersey courts and ordered to produce experimental records. Although the subpoena was not enforced, Mathematica was required to compensate local welfare departments for overpayments to experimental families.

Later in 1969, as Congress considered welfare reform, pressure was exerted on the research staff to produce results from the experiment that would be relevant to the legislation being considered. Preliminary data were hastily compiled and presented in testimony before the House Ways and Means Committee. Opponents of the legislation, however, saw the experimenters as advocates of the proposed welfare reform and asked the General Accounting Office to conduct a critical analysis of the experiment, including a search of original data and reinterviews with experimental subjects.

SOURCE: Adapted, with permission, from D. Kershaw and J. Fair, *The New Jersey Income-Maintenance Experiment,* Vol. 1. New York: Academic Press, 1976, pp. 4-5.

difficult activity in the social program arena (Schneider, 1982). Faulty program implementation accounts for many evaluation findings of no impact (see Exhibit 2-A). A shared commitment to develop and undertake programs in ways that maximize the likelihood of rigorous evaluations is essential. Outlining these activities is the thrust of this chapter.

PLANNING EVALUATIONS OF INNOVATIVE PROGRAMS

The planning process includes the following:

identification of the goals of the organization sponsoring and implementing the intervention, and of the other stakeholders involved;

assessment of the extent to which the actual conditions under which the program will operate limit the realization of these goals;

the development of a general framework or strategy for achieving the desired goals by modifying conditions or behavior; and

specification of necessary human and financial resources, designation of individuals responsible for carrying out intervention activities, and creation of a schedule for meeting objectives.

Planning and implementation of social program initiatives usually are predicated on a need to reduce the gap between the desired state of affairs and what actually exists; in other words, the disparity between a "goal" and "reality." For example, the goal of a program may be to prevent persons who have consumed alcohol from driving an automobile; the existing situation may be one in which 15 percent of persons driving between five and seven in the evening have consumed three or more ounces of alcohol. The intervention in this case is to deal with the 15 percent of drivers whose alcohol use increases their risk of accidents.

In some instances, however, the goal may be to maintain the status quo in the face of an anticipated decline or deterioration in the existing situation. For example, the goal may be to avoid further increases in the costs of hospital care for poor persons whose health services are paid for under such government programs as Medicaid. In the face of the rising costs of such care over the past decade, maintaining the status quo would be regarded as the appropriate goal.

The designs of all evaluations have many generic qualities. Although the ensuing discussion examines these characteristics in relation to innovative programs, many of them are applicable, as we will discuss, to evaluations of established programs and fine-tuning of existing interventions.

Setting Goals and Identifying Objectives

Social intervention programs can be developed only in relation to one or more goals. Goals are generally abstract, idealized statements of desired social program outcomes. For evaluation purposes, goal-setting must lead to the operationalization of the desired outcome; that is, it is essential that there be detailed specification of the condition to be addressed and identification of one or more measurable criteria of success. Evaluation researchers often refer to these operationalized statements as *objectives*.

Defining Objectives

The distinction between goals and operationalized objectives is vital: Many programs, especially those with large target populations or far-reaching effects, state their goals initially in broad and rather vague terms. For a worthwhile evaluation to be undertaken, such goal statements must be refined and stated in operationalized terms. For example, each year the components of federal executive departments, such as the Department of Health and Human Services, submit "forward plans" or strategy papers to their secretaries with goals reflecting their departments' aspirations. Such a document may state that an important priority is to reduce the number of homeless persons in large urban centers, or to increase the number of pregnant women who receive prenatal care, or to improve the standard of living for persons on public welfare.

Unless these goals are operationalized into specific objectives, however, it is unlikely that a plan can be implemented that is consistent with these goals. For example, in connection with the homeless, the objective may be to increase by 200 percent the availability of permanent living quarters for currently homeless persons; in terms of prenatal care, it may be to increase to 90 percent the proportion of pregnant women who visit a doctor during the first three months of their pregnancies; for persons on welfare, it may be to provide funds that allow the same quality and quantity of food as such persons now receive and dwellings that meet current standards of adequate housing (see Exhibit 2-B).

Objectives may be defined in either *absolute* or *relative* terms. Achieving an absolute objective requires either that an undesirable condition be totally eliminated or that a desirable one be attained for everyone. An absolute objective in the health area might be the immunization of all persons against such illnesses as measles or whooping cough. Educators might advocate another absolute objective, the total elimination of illiteracy. Relative objectives establish standards of achievement in terms of some proportionate improvement of the conditions that exist. The reduction of gonorrhea by 50 percent would be a relative objective. The relative

Exhibit 2-B: If You Don't Care Where You Get To, Then It Doesn't Matter Which Way You Go

In order to allow a program to be managed to achieve objectives, the program must satisfy three criteria:

a. Measurable objectives have been specified (i.e., those in charge of the program, such as policymakers and program managers, have agreed to measurable objectives for the program, including any necessary measures of program costs, program activities, intended program outcomes, and intended impact on the problem addressed by the program).

b. There exist plausible, testable assumptions linking application of resources to the program activities, linking program activities to intended program outcomes, and linking program outcomes to program objectives.

c. Those in charge of the program have the motivation, ability, and authority to manage.

It is recognized that programs may be more or less manageable, according to the extent to which these three criteria are or are not satisfied. The researchers found that the typical federal social program is unmanageable because it fails to meet one or more of these criteria.

Although every federal program has a number of objectives, the objectives are generally not defined by those in charge (policymakers and program managers) in such a way that progress toward objectives can be measured or important underlying program assumptions tested. The programs are sufficiently well defined to be funded, but are not sufficiently well defined to be managed to achieve specific objectives related to the goals implied in the authorizing legislation. In such programs, whatever activities are carried out tend to become synonymous with objectives; i.e., from a "management" perspective, the intended effect is achieved when the program activities are carried out, regardless of program outcome or subsequent impact on the problem addressed by the program.

SOURCE: Adapted from J. N. Nay et al., "If You Don't Care Where You Get To, Then It Doesn't Matter Which Way You Go," in C. C. Abt (ed.) *The Evaluation of Social Programs.* Beverly Hills, CA: Sage Publications, 1976, pp. 97-98.

counterpart of our education example might be reducing the number of persons with less than sixth-grade educational skills by 75 percent.

Clearly, setting goals and specifying objectives require either assumptions or knowledge about two fundamental aspects of the social situation: values and existing conditions. The immunization goal reflects certain basic values favoring good health and low death rates. The goal to eliminate illiteracy assumes the importance of educational skills to productive participation in our economic system. Like all goals, they are based on an assumption that there is room for improvement—that is, that there is some significant discrepancy between the actual conditions and the desired outcome of implementing a program.

Although a deficiency in existing conditions may be easy to recognize, a precise assessment of the empirical situation is usually required before one can formulate realistic goals and objectives and plan programs to achieve them. Procedures for diagnosing social problems are discussed in Chapter 3. After refined estimates of existing conditions have been obtained, goals and objectives may have to be modified. Modifications may be necessary because of external conditions that limit the methods and intensity of the intervention, the resources available to support the program, the difficulties of identifying the target population and securing their cooperation, and the availability of intervention approaches to deal with the problem. For example, the planners of an antismoking program may start out with the absolute objective of eliminating all cigarette smoking. But the planners may soon find that the stubborn persistence of smoking habits necessitates reducing their aspirations to the relative objective of reducing the number of smokers by some specified percentage.

Modification of goals and objectives may also result from conditions within the intervention effort. For instance, it is essential that evaluators, planners, program staff, and sponsors achieve consensus on the criteria to be used in assessing achievement of objectives. If a housing program is evaluated partly on the basis of morbidity, specific measures of morbidity (such as the number of days absent from work or school due to illness) must be agreed upon as indicators of outcome. Failing such agreement, the evaluation may be confronted with rancorous conflict between evaluators and project planners, staff, and policymakers when evaluation results are presented.

As we will discuss subsequently in detail, if adequate resources are available, sometimes the solution is to include multiple criteria that reflect the interests of the various parties involved. Another solution is to include objectives in addition to those originated by the stakeholders, based on current viewpoints and theories in the relevant substantive field (Chen and Rossi, 1980). For example, sponsors of a job-training program may be interested solely in the frequency and duration of postprogram employ-ment. But the evaluator may try to have measures of stability of living arrangements, competence in handling finances, and efforts to obtain additional education included as outcome measures because these life-style features also may change with both increased employment and improved self-image as a result of being able to cope with the social milieu.

Consequently, an early task for the evaluator often is to collaborate with planners, project managers, and sponsors to transform ambiguous or contradictory objectives into clear, consistent, operational statements. The closer the objectives are to outcomes that can be measured directly and reliably, the more likely it is that a competent evaluation will result. Exhibit 2-C presents helpful rules for specifying objectives.

Formal Procedures

There are a number of formal ways to establish objectives, the technical details of which are beyond the scope of this book. A well-known proce-dure in the evaluation field is the decision theoretic approach (Edwards et al., 1975). This approach permits the formal explication and ranking of the objectives of diverse groups. Each group first defines and ranks its objec-tives, providing information on those it considers most important. Then, by a set of procedures known as Bayesian statistics, the choices are analyzed and reported back to the groups. On this basis, priorities are reordered. The process of providing information, linking objectives to inferences, and reordering objectives is continued until the groups arrive at a solution that takes into account their diverse views.

Formal approaches such as the one just described are especially useful when the different stakeholders hold sharply conflicting views and the pool of potential objectives is beyond informal reconciliation. They are part of a family of consensus methods used to elicit, refine, and operationalize views of various parties to a particular activity, event, or value domain (Fink et al., 1984). Another formal approach, evaluability assessment, seeks to produce evaluations with maximal potential utility. Although evaluability assessment is applicable to all evaluations, including those of innovative programs, it is most often undertaken in connection with established programs and will therefore be discussed in this chapter.

Goal-Attainment Scaling

Although most evaluations rely on statements of objectives that involve measuring change in the target group as a whole, goal-attainment scaling makes it possible to tailor goals to individual units within the target population. The results can be summarized to provide a composite esti-mate of program impact (Kiresuk, 1973). The approach uses relative

Exhibit 2-C: Some Rules for Specifying Objectives

Four techniques are particularly helpful for writing useful objectives:
(1) using strong verbs, (2) stating only one purpose or aim, (3) specifying a single end-product or result, and (4) specifying the expected time for achievement [Kirschner Associates, 1975].

A "strong" verb is an action-oriented verb that describes an observable or measurable behavior that will occur. For example, "to increase the use of health education materials" is an action-oriented statement involving behavior that can be observed. In contrast, "to promote greater use of health education materials" is a weaker and less specific statement. The term "promote" is subject to many interpretations. Examples of action-oriented, strong verbs include: "to write," "to meet," "to find," "to increase," and "to sign." Examples of weaker, nonspecific verbs include: "to understand," "to encourage," "to enhance," and "to promote."

A second useful suggestion for writing a clear objective is to state only a single aim or purpose. Most programs will, of course, have multiple objectives, but within each objective only a single purpose should be delineated. An objective that states two or more purposes or desired outcomes may well require different implementation and assessment strategies, making achievement of the objective difficult to determine. For example, the statement "to begin three prenatal classes for pregnant women and provide outreach transportation services to accommodate twenty-five women per class" creates difficulties. This objective contains two aims—to provide prenatal classes and to provide outreach services. If one aim is accomplished but not the other, to what extent has the objective been met? It is better to state a single aim for each objective, such as "*start three prenatal classes* for pregnant women," "*provide outreach services* to twenty-five pregnant women per class."

Specifying a single end-product or result is a third technique contributing to a useful objective. For example, the statement "to begin three prenatal classes for pregnant women by subcontracting with City Memorial Hospital" contains two results, namely, the three classes and the subcontract. It is better to state these objectives separately, particularly since one is a higher-order objective (to begin three prenatal classes) that depends partly on fulfillment of a lower-order objective (to establish a subcontract).

A clearly written objective must have both a single aim and a single end-product or result. For example, the statement "to establish communication with the Health Systems Agency" indicates the aim but not the desired end-product or result. What contributes evidence of communication—telephone calls, meetings, reports? Failure to specify a clear end-product makes it extremely difficult for assessment to take place.

The reverse is equally true. That is, statements can exist that specify an end-product but no aim or purpose. "To provide all monthly discharge abstracts to the Commission of Professional and Hospital Activities" is an example of a statement with an end-product but no aim or purpose. The implicit aim may be to improve medical staff accountability and management or to improve the quality of medical care, but it is not clear that submitting case abstracts will meet this objective, nor can the objective be assessed in a meaningful way without such a statement of purpose. Those involved in writing and evaluating objectives need to keep two questions in mind. First, would anyone reading the objective, with or without knowledge of the program, find the same purpose as the one intended? Second, what visible, measurable, or tangible results are present as evidence that the objective has been met? Purpose or aim describes what will be done; end-product or result describes evidence that will exist when it has been done. This is assurance that you "know one when you see one."

Finally, it is useful to specify the time of expected achievement of the objective. The statement "to establish a walk-in clinic as soon as possible" is not a useful objective because of the vagueness of "as soon as possible." It is far more useful to specify a target date, or, in cases where considerable doubt exists, a range of target dates—for example, "sometime between March 1 and March 30."

SOURCE: From Stephen M. Shortell and William C. Richardson, *Health Program Evaluation.* St. Louis, MO, 1978: The C. V. Mosby Co., pp. 26-27. Reprinted by permission.

rather than absolute measures, an idea we have already discussed. For example, an alcohol treatment program may have as its objective the reduction in the number of days workers are absent from work because of excessive drinking. In the case of worker A, who is primarily a "weekend drinker," the goal may be to reduce the number of Sundays of drunkenness over a three-month period so that the worker gets to work on Mondays. For worker B, who is a "binge drinker," the goal may be to reduce the duration of drinking bouts so that the "drying out" period is reduced and the number of days he or she misses work is also reduced.

Objectives for the delivery system can also be developed in this way. For example, the frequency with which therapy appointments are missed can be computed for each individual as in the above example. The evaluator can then calculate difference scores, pooling individual estimates to arrive at a composite result. Goal-attainment expectations can be based on the views of practitioners, those of the targets, those of outside judges, or some combination of the three.

While goal-attainment scaling has utility for evaluations in many areas, such as psychotherapy and special education, it has its limitations as well. First, it is time-consuming and expensive for large-scale studies involving many targets. Second, it runs counter to the intervention approaches of the many programs that are concerned with consistent outcome results for all in the target population. Third, goal-attainment scaling may result in depressed objectives. For example, a weight-reduction clinic might designate a loss of five pounds as the objective for a patient who is thirty pounds overweight, thereby equating "success" with minimal impact. Despite those cautions, however, the method remains attractive for some evaluations.

Program Design and Development

In some instances, evaluators take the lead in designing and developing the programs they evaluate. Most commonly, however, this task is primarily the responsibility of program planners and designers or is mandated by program sponsors, such as foundation executives and legislators. Regardless of who does the work, in order to undertake a successful evaluation, both explicit, agreed-upon objectives and a detailed description of how they are to be achieved are required.

The absence of a well-specified impact model severely limits opportunities to control a program's quality and effectiveness (Freeman and Sherwood, 1970). By analogy, a computer software package is useless if it has not been documented adequately. Even if a program is successful in delivering services and achieving the objectives set for it, without an explicit impact model there is no basis for understanding how and why it worked or for reproducing its effects on a broader scale in other sites and with other targets. If, when an evaluation is undertaken, there is no impact model (or only an incomplete one), the evaluators must either inspire program staff and sponsors to create one or do so themselves.

Elements of the Impact Model

An *intervention* or *impact* model is an attempt to translate notions regarding the regulation, modification, and control of social behavior or community conditions into hypotheses on which action can be based. Fully explicated models are rare. Too often, the intervention "model" consists of nothing more than the assumptions underlying a program's operation. These assumptions may have been drawn from previous studies—often undertaken on small samples or in other locales—or may have little or no empirical basis, being drawn instead from the untested ways in which practitioners have performed in the past.

An impact model takes the form of a statement about the expected relationships between a program and its goal; it sets forth the strategy for closing the gap between the goal set during the planning process and the existing behavior or condition. It must contain a causal hypothesis, an intervention hypothesis, and an action hypothesis.

The Causal Hypothesis

At the heart of any impact model is a hypothesis about the influence of one or more processes or determinants on the behavior or condition that the program seeks to modify. Although there are a number of different ways of thinking about causes, a simple idea of cause suffices in the example that follows.

Many social scientists believe, for example, that lack of employment among released felony offenders results in a return to crime (recidivism). A number of investigators (for example, see Irwin, 1970) maintain that if released prisoners are unable to find legitimate employment, they will be likely to seek out illegal modes of obtaining income. The causal hypothesis in this case, then, would be that recidivism results from unemployment. But in order to be useful, all hypotheses, including causal ones, must be stated in a way that permits testing, or measurement. This is the process of *operationalization*. To operationalize the hypothesis, the evaluator might state that rearrests for crimes are most likely among released prisoners who either have minimal vocational qualifications or encounter poor employment markets.

It should be noted that this formulation is not the only one consistent with the causal hypothesis. Recidivism could be measured by whether or not a person is convicted of a felony; vocational qualifications can mean previous employment history, vocational training while in prison, or scores on various aptitude tests; community employment markets could be measured by vacancies listed with employment agencies, the measured level of unemployment in the community; and so on.

The important point is that recidivism, employment qualifications, and employment opportunities have to be measured in the evaluation of any program that is designed to lower recidivism among ex-prisoners. Therefore, part of the task of developing an impact model is to specify the causal variables in operational—that is, measurable—terms.

The Intervention Hypothesis

An intervention hypothesis is a statement that specifies the relationship between a program, what is going to be done, and the process or determinant specified as associated in the causal hypothesis with the behavior or condition to be ameliorated or changed. The intervention hypothesis in the recidivism reduction program example might be that postrelease employment is related to completing a program of vocational training successfully. Thus, the impact model for reducing recidivism would state as the intervention hypothesis that providing vocational training for released prisoners leads to a reduction in recidivism.

Other intervention hypotheses are also consistent with the causal hypothesis. An intervention hypothesis that directly provided employment opportunities by somehow motivating employers to hire released prisoners (possibly through tax subsidies) would be an alternative to vocational training. So would an intervention hypothesis that emphasized job-search assistance for released prisoners. Indeed, an agency trying to develop an effective program for reducing recidivism might try all three approaches separately and in combination to develop the most effective and efficient intervention program.

The Action Hypothesis

A third kind of hypothesis is also required. An action hypothesis is necessary if one is to assess whether the intervention, even if it results in a desired change in the causal variable, is necessarily linked to the outcome, that is, to the behavior or condition one is seeking to modify. This third hypothesis is required because, although a natural change in existing conditions may cause a desirable chain of events, the introduction of that change by means of an intervention may not result in the behavioral and social processes that occur naturally. An action may be planned and carried out as an intervention, but conditions may necessarily differ from when such actions "ordinarily" occur. Thus, the competencies that result from vocational training may not be the same as those that result from learning that takes place during regular work experiences. Ex-felons who have gone through vocational training courses, for example, may not have—or may not be viewed as having—the range of qualifications required by employers.

The importance of the action hypothesis can be seen in an interesting piece of research conducted a number of years ago (Festinger, 1964) on lowering racial discrimination in employment. Causal links were presumed between (1) understanding and knowledge of blacks and (2) prejudice, on the one hand, and between prejudice and (3) discrimination, on the other. A program was developed for employment managers to increase their understanding and knowledge of blacks in order to decrease their prejudice. The unexpected result of the program was that those employment managers whose attitudes changed the most discriminated more than they had before. Festinger explained this result by arguing that the input of new information led to a polarization of behavior. In other words, in the face of the program, it was impossible for the employment managers to continue behaving as they had before. Therefore, while some of them became less discriminatory in their hiring practices, others became more so. Neither the findings of the study nor Festinger's explanation vitiates the causal links that exist in the normal course of socialization. The point is that even if changes occur in a natural state, we may not be able to induce them. The action hypothesis is, therefore, as important as the other hypotheses in evaluation, and needs to be studied empirically.

Sources of Hypotheses

Ideally, the hypotheses embodied in impact models should stem from experimental studies that permit causal inferences, well-developed theories, or both. In actuality, causal studies, based on true experiments, and fully developed theories of social behavior and social processes are scarce.

At the same time, modern analytical procedures now permit the identification, with reasonable degrees of plausibility, of causal processes, and these serve well as the departure points for the development of impact models. Knowledge development continues to be uneven, however, and in many social program areas impact models necessarily are derived either from clinical impressions or from unsophisticated statistical studies of associations between independent (presumably causal) variables and dependent (or outcome) measures that minimally rule out other reasonable causal explanation.

Another important source of hypotheses is the results of other social programs in the same sector. Indeed, one of the arguments for conducting evaluations is that their cumulative results form a valuable source of information for the development of impact models.

A useful approach for searching the existing literature on empirical knowledge about some phenomenon—meta-evaluations—is described in Chapter 5. It constitutes a formal approach to pooling the results of a set of evaluations in the same program area. Meta-evaluations represent a means of establishing impact models on the basis of knowledge of program findings.

Clearly, programs that are successful in both delivery and outcome are most likely when reasonably definitive knowledge—be it on the basis of research, informed clinical impressions, or previous program evaluations—is available for impact model development.

Manipulability and Feasibility

For impact models to be useful, they must deal with variables that are subject to manipulation through intervention. That is, the intervention must consist of some actions that can be taken in practice. First, the model must specify intervention variables that are action-relevant to the target population—that is, interventions that, within the time frame of the program, can affect targets directly or indirectly. If an undesirable condition exists because its targets became subject to the condition in a particular manner at a point in time prior to the stage at which the intervention operates, manipulability is precluded. This apparently is partly the case in the area of educational achievement. Much of the variance in students' performance in the high school, for example, is evidently not primarily a function of what happens to them in high school; instead, it is due mainly to the influence of their families and early environments (Sewell and Hauser, 1975). If poor performance in high school is so determined, any intervention would have to take place when students are younger, even if children of high school age would be "sacrificed." The focus of a program clearly needs to be on the variables that are manipulable, and must also take into account the time frame in which the intervention can be expected to result in the desired change.

Second, one must avoid selecting interventions with low feasibility. Low feasibility may be due to a lack of program acceptance by sponsors, targets, and other stakeholders, the contradictory ideological values and imperatives of community life, or the risk of undesired side effects. For example, in a program developed to reduce air pollution, certain conditions, such as the amount of fumes given off by automobiles, may be found to be manipulable. Other conditions, such as the amount of waste from industrial operations, may be found not to be manipulable, because of either a lack of technical knowledge about reducing industrial fumes or the unwillingness of industry to pay the costs. Ideological and political imperatives can be illustrated by another problem. Social class has been found to be correlated with mental illness, but a revolutionary change in our economic structure is hardly an intervention that would be endorsed by the typical policymaker. As another illustration, undesirable side effects may result from the use of telephone-tapping to identify certain criminals, such as bookmakers. Given that telephone-tapping would of necessity include listening in on the innocent as well as the guilty, its use would be an invasion of privacy and would be opposed intensely by civil libertarians.

Evaluators, along with program sponsors and program staff, need to be sensitive to the manipulability potential of the variables or program components of the impact models they formulate. Therefore, they must be concerned with obtaining a correct appreciation of the current "policy space"—the set of programs that are politically feasible; that is, the programs that are likely to be acceptable to current policymakers. Clearly the concept of policy space implies that it makes little sense to propose programs that are not likely to attain the support of the stakeholders involved. (A more detailed discussion of policy space can be found in Chapter 9.)

Selecting Target Populations

There is interplay, of course, between selecting the target population and developing the impact model of any intervention. In some ways the distinction between the two tasks is artificial. The impact model must include a set of hypotheses about the plausibility of one event leading to another. Such hypotheses rest on predictions about the characteristics of the target population in relation to the intervention.

In considering the selection of the target population, the researcher should be aware that it is often desirable to distinguish between the group that will be subjected to intervention immediately (the direct targets) and the total population that benefits from the program eventually (the indirect targets). Some impact models imply such distinctions. For example, suppose the problem is to increase the income of the unemployed. Were the government to provide increased welfare payments to the unemployed, the direct and indirect target populations would be the same—those out of work. However, the government might decide to make employers the direct targets, permitting special tax deductions for those who hire workers with a history of unemployment (who are now the indirect targets). To predict the effect of such intervention, the evaluator would have to assess, either from past studies or by collecting new data, the relationship between such tax incentives to employers and increased employment, a task surely as important as specifying the characteristics of the target population of unemployed workers. (See Chapter 3 for further discussion of direct and indirect targets.)

In addition, because of the relationship between the way programs are organized and their acceptance and utilization by target populations, impact models need to take into account the way a program is organized in terms of target acceptance. The health field provides a useful illustration: Studies suggest that lack of prenatal care, particularly during the last months of pregnancy, is related to subsequent health problems for both the mother and the baby—among them, a higher likelihood that the child will be mentally retarded. A major subgroup of the target population is unmarried mothers, particularly in low-income areas. The solution advocated is often simplistic: Increase the available medical facilities in low-income areas that have large populations of young women. It does not necessarily follow, however, that an increase in facilities will lead to increased use of the medical services by unmarried mothers. The latter may simply not use the facilities made available to them.

The choice of a target population is a strategic decision. The focus of a program must shift dramatically if it is found that the characteristics of its target population are not what they were originally thought to be. For that reason we shall devote Chapter 3 to a discussion of how targets are identified and estimated.

Delivery System Design

Interventions, no matter how well conceived, cannot be effective and efficient unless there are carefully developed delivery systems. Some delivery systems are comparatively simple, particularly when targets are "semicaptives": Providing health education in classroom settings is a comparatively simple proposition. Other delivery systems are highly complex: Special health care for prospective mothers experiencing "high-risk" pregnancies may require family physicians, obstetrical and pediatric specialists, general hospitals, and centers specializing in infant care.

Elements of the Delivery System

In order to document and assess a program, the components of the delivery system must be explicated and criteria of performance developed and measured. Among the elements usually monitored, as will be discussed further in Chapter 4, are the following:

- appropriateness of the target population served
- treatments and services provided
- qualifications and competencies of staff
- mechanisms for recruiting and obtaining the cooperation of the targets
- means of optimizing access to the intervention, including location and physical facilities at the service delivery sites

- referral and follow-up efforts

Every program, of course, has its own set of delivery system elements. An illustration may be useful. A rare but invariably fatal neurological infant disorder is Tay-Sachs disease. It is genetically transmitted and confined almost exclusively to Jews of Eastern European background. In one of four pregnancies where both prospective parents carry the recessive defective gene, the child will be affected. (Targets are identified.)

One of the interventions in place to prevent such pregnancies is to offer Tay-Sachs blood tests to persons of Eastern European background; carriers are counseled about the risks with prospective sexual partners who also have the recessive gene; carriers who are pregnant are advised to seek diagnostic evaluation of the *in utero* baby; and in the case of a Tay-Sachs fetus, the medical recommendation is to seek a therapeutic abortion. (Procedures and services provided.)

The program is under the supervision of a genetic counselor; there are nurses to take the blood tests; and a publicity specialist has developed a variety of mechanisms to reach and recruit targets. Since young people of marriageable age are concentrated on college campuses, the program concentrates on college campuses (among other places where young people are found in relatively large numbers). A campaign is conducted on college campuses each semester, in convenient places such as student unions. Positive cases are referred to the genetic counselor, who is located at the campus clinic. (Recruiting, access to sites.) Students who are found to be carriers and fail to seek counseling are contacted as frequently and as aggressively as possible. Once identified, they are contacted annually by mail to encourage testing of prospective or current partners. (Target retention.)

In addition to assessment of the various elements of the delivery system, provision has to be made for collecting data on costs if the evaluation plan includes an efficiency evaluation. Salaries, supplies, fees, and advertising costs would be relevant in the illustration given above. (See Chapter 4 on monitoring and Chapter 8 on efficiency studies.)

Formative Studies

In the design and development of many programs, it is useful and frequently necessary to undertake evaluative activities during the intervention's design. In many cases, it is wise to pilot test all or parts of the intervention program prior to implementing it routinely. It is obvious that programs can be operated most effectively and evaluations can be undertaken most rigorously if most of the "kinks" in the program can be eliminated during a trial period. Experience strongly suggests that putting programs in place without pilot testing often jeopardizes their futures. "Formative evaluations" refers to assessing the conduct of programs during their early stages.

Formative evaluation activities may be quite simple or as complex and comprehensive as any other evaluations. Sometimes they are directed at specific questions related to developing the delivery system, selecting targets, and structuring the intervention. Other times they are "mini-impact" evaluations conducted in order to gather estimates of the magnitude of impact to be expected with a particular intervention. The need for formative evaluation is a major reason for allowing adequate lead time for program planning and development. It bears emphasis that many programs fail either in the design phase or during early periods of operation because insufficient time and resources were invested in formative efforts.

Formative evaluations may include the testing and assessment of a program either at one or a few sites or with a small sample of targets prior to full-blown implementation. For example, as part of the planning and design of *Sesame Street*, program staff were concerned about which particular TV characters should be chosen to be the agents of the messages communicated. Relatively simple experiments were undertaken: The same learning messages were transmitted by different characters and in different sequences. Groups of children viewed the presentations on a television screen and variations in their attention to the screen were measured. It was on this basis that decisions were made regarding the format of the program (see Exhibit 2-D).

In another example of a formative study, a "typical" portion of the target population is selected to participate in a trial run of the intervention. Such a study was conducted to estimate the number of targets who would utilize a community mental health program requiring attendance at weekly meetings. Careful records were kept of the various means of recruiting targets, the proportion who attended for the full eight-week course, and those who dropped out. Dropouts were interviewed in order to discover their reasons for not completing the program and to find better means of retaining targets.

Formative studies vary, as noted, in the extent to which they are rigorous and in the sophistication of their data collection and data analysis. In many cases, however, even simple studies provide insight into the problems an intervention may face and ways to overcome them. Further, formative studies allow opportunities, in many cases, for "pretesting" evaluation procedures and instruments, as well as the intervention itself. Evaluators engaged in formative studies obviously must become involved in the actual design and programming effort, because the emphasis here is

Exhibit 2-D: Formative Research for *Sesame Street*

An important part of the formative research that went into the year-and-a-half planning for *Sesame Street* involved measuring the audience appeal of possible programs before they went on the air, since appeal was a vital ingredient if *Sesame Street* was to reach and keep its audience. Small groups of children of the appropriate age and apparent cognitive skills were recruited to come to the Children's Workshop studios to view proposed programs and segments of programs. The program was projected on a monitor set while, on an adjoining wall, slides were projected at an angle to the child. Observers rated the proportion of each 7.5-second schedule that the children viewed the program rather than the projected slide. Producers could then relate the content of the program (or segment of a program) at any one point to the degree of attention that the program or segment attained from the test audience of children. From these findings, in addition to accepting or rejecting versions of programs, generalizations were drawn about program features that did or did not attract the attention of economically disadvantaged children. The formative research played a crucial role, producers believed, in reducing the risk that *Sesame Street* would not hold its audience once it reached them.

SOURCE: Adapted, with permission, from B. F. Reeves, *The First Year of Sesame Street: The Formative Research*. New York: Children's Television Workshop, 1970.

on increasing the success of subsequent intervention efforts and their evaluations. Thus, the evaluator frequently becomes an advocate and a partisan participant in program activities.

Program Simulations

Often, time, costs, and other demands preclude the use of "on-site" formative studies in the design of innovative activities. In such cases, program staff and evaluators may turn to program simulations (see Exhibit 2-E). Simulations can also complement formative efforts. Some simulations are highly quantitative and formal, incorporating sophisticated computer-based modeling (including *ex ante* efficiency studies, discussed in Chapter 8). Others apply qualitative approaches, such as scenarios about the consequences of different ways to identify, delimit, and recruit

Exhibit 2-E: Involuntary Patient Flow

Following fairly solid experiences of success in aerospace, military, computer science, and business settings, the technique of computer simulation is appearing more and more in social welfare applications. Although in the latter cases the systems being modeled are often less well structured, and outcome variables are frequently less well defined, such simulations are undertaken for reasons typical for the technique: A system of variables exists that is so complexly interrelated that the relationship between input and output is not intuitively obvious and is difficult or impossible to approach analytically. If the system can be represented adequately in a model, then the outputs resulting from particular patterns of input can be estimated, and this information used in whatever decision process is at hand.

In the summer of 1975 data were collected for the period from September 1974 through April 1975 that would allow a description of the numbers of patients following each branch of the decision tree, and the distributions of length of stay for each segment of stay. Subjects were all patients who entered the ward over that period. The primary data source was a computerized data system for a related community mental health center, which at the time also covered all patients entering the psychiatric ward. Additional data were obtained from county records generated by the mental health professionals who performed the initial screening of potential involuntary patients. The data collected included referral source into and disposition out of the ward, dates of admission and discharge, and dates of each hearing and/or change of status while on the ward.

Each patient was then classified as to his or her status for each day on the ward, where the status categories were voluntary admission, converted voluntary (admitted involuntarily, but subsequently agreed to become voluntary), or patients on 72-hour hold, 14-day commitment, or 90-day commitment.

Given this set of patient classifications, computer programs were written that would summarize referral sources and disposition into and out of the ward, changes in patient status, frequencies and types of legal hearings, distributions of lengths of stay, distributions of numbers and types of admissions, and a day-by-day profile of how many ward beds were occupied by each class of patient.

These outputs were considered useful by the ward psychiatrist, particularly the day-to-day profiles and the information on admissions, hearings, and status changes. A fairly natural reaction to these materials, and in fact the one that occurred, was "What would happen if . . . ?" The two major versions of the question were (a) What would happen if the mix of voluntary/involuntary patients changed? and (b) What would happen if the judges began increasing or decreasing the rate at which they made commitments at the first hearing? These factors are of special interest due to their impact on the mix of voluntary/involuntary patients (since this affects the program), average length of stay, and bed utilization rates. Such issues were of particular salience at the time because the law, which represented a moderately radical change in procedure, was still relatively new, and procedures for responding to it were still settling down. A simulation study seemed an appropriate way to address the questions.

The second, broader purpose of the simulation study was to gain some experience with the technique of simulation in an effort to evaluate its utility for program evaluation and evaluation research functions.

SOURCE: Adapted from Gary B. Cox, "Involuntary Patient Flow: A Computer Simulation of a Psychiatric Ward," *Evaluation Review* 4 (October 1980): 571-584.

target populations. Likewise, levels of impact are estimated for programs of various intensities. Finally, evaluators often simulate results from studies of similar programs, so that sponsors, planners, and designers can be prepared for the type and magnitude of outcomes they may achieve.

Much of the simulation work evaluators do during the design phase of the program and throughout its evaluation is similar to what takes place in all research studies. A commonly requested attachment to evaluation designs, for example, is a set of "dummy tables," essentially mockups that show what the results of an evaluation may look like, and into which a range of utilization and impact estimates can be inserted. Dummy tables may alert staff, sponsors, and evaluators to whether or not appropriate evaluation questions are being asked, suggest reasonable estimates of impact, and thereby form expectations regarding adoption of the program on a broader basis or its continued support at any level.

A simulation is only as good as the assumptions used in its construction. Hence, simulations are a useful approach for formative evaluations in an area about which a great deal of empirically based knowledge exists.

Correspondingly, they are less useful in formative evaluations of areas about which little is known, and they may actually be misleading in such cases.

The Evaluation Plan

A key outcome of the planning of an innovative program should be the plan for conducting the evaluation. It may be a comprehensive evaluation that involves all of the evaluation tasks discussed in this book, or it may include only some of the activities discussed here, such as procedures for monitoring the program and for undertaking an impact evaluation. The planning of an initiative and the development of the evaluation plan go hand in hand. For example, the program staff may feel that a sample of 100 participants is large enough for the program. On the basis of an understanding of statistical inference, however, the evaluator may believe that this group size will not be sufficient to yield firm results of impact. Such a situation would require reconsideration of the size of the program. The reverse situation may also occur: The evaluator may believe that the number of participants planned for is too large and will not leave enough "unexposed" targets to permit the comparison of "experimental" and "control" groups.

Indeed, planning the evaluation together with the development of the program provides both evaluators and program staff with realistic expectations of the evaluation requirements and the resources that need to be allocated to the evaluation. In such cases there is less likelihood of conflict between the two groups.

Summary of Innovative Evaluation Activities

It should be stressed that the evaluator, in planning, designing, and testing new programs, must be capable of undertaking a wide range of activities. These will vary, depending on the type of program, the relationship of the evaluator to the program, the amount of time available before implementation, the program's political and resource demands, and the particular skills of program staff and evaluation groups. In most evaluations of innovative programs, the evaluator will participate in many if not all the tasks we have examined in this section:

1. identifying and describing the problem being addressed by the program

2. operationalizing objectives for the program

3. developing the intervention model

4. defining the target population

5. designing the delivery system

6. specifying procedures for monitoring the program

7. assessing impact and estimating efficiency

EVALUATING ESTABLISHED PROGRAMS

While the evaluation of innovative programs represents an important activity for the field, by far the greater proportion of program resources, and thus evaluation efforts, goes into the assessment of established, ongoing programs. The evaluation efforts related to established programs are less visible than those connected with program innovations. More are conducted "in house," either by staff connected with operating agencies or by such governmental groups as the General Accounting Office, than by university, for-profit, or nonprofit groups. While reports of these evaluations are available, they typically are less widely distributed than "outside" evaluations. Second, part of the evaluation of established programs is associated with the managerial concerns of maintaining and improving program effectiveness and efficiency, and there is often less broad interest in their findings.

At the same time, as noted in Chapter 1, the current conservative outlook regarding public support of social programs has increased pressures for scrutinizing established programs. Furthermore, since many established programs are costly, the results of evaluations that eventuate in their curtailment or modification may yield large program savings. For example, a General Accounting Office evaluation changed the way earned income was figured into decisions about the eligibility of families for aid to dependent children. As described in Exhibit 2-F, these modifications in the eligibility requirements (referred to as the "OBRA" changes, because they were contained in the 1981 Omnibus Budget Reconciliation Act) reduced annual costs of the program by about $1 billion. While persons with different social welfare outlooks may regard these modifications in program eligibility either positively or negatively, clearly the evaluation of this and other established federal programs, and those at state or city level, represent important inputs into the way human services resources are allocated and distributed.

Evaluating established programs requires an understanding of the social and political situations that existed when they were initiated, and the tracing of how they have been modified from their emergence until the time of the evaluation. Established programs are generally a historical response to social concerns. Most have sprung from traditional, long-standing ameliorative efforts, and often there is considerable opposition from some of the stakeholders to the questioning of their fundamental

Exhibit 2-F: The 1981 AFDC Changes

The Omnibus Budget Reconciliation Act of 1981 (OBRA) made major changes in the Aid to Families with Dependent Children (AFDC) program, particularly with regard to AFDC recipients' earnings. These changes resulted in the loss of AFDC benefits for many working recipients, and reduced benefits for many others.

From its survey of state public assistance agencies and an analysis of 10 years of Department of Health and Human Services program data, the General Accounting Office (GAO) estimates that when the declines in caseload and outlays stabilized, OBRA had decreased the national AFDC-Basic monthly caseload by 493,000 cases and monthly outlays by $93 million. However, because the caseload rose faster than predicted after this point, long-term effects are less certain.

GAO conducted in-depth evaluations of OBRA's effects on individual AFDC families in Boston, Dallas, Memphis, Milwaukee, and Syracuse, using case records and interviews. These evaluations indicate that by fall 1983, most working recipients who lost benefits because of OBRA had not quit their jobs and returned to AFDC.

In interviews with former working recipients more than a year after their termination from AFDC because of OBRA, GAO found that OBRA changes to the food stamp program appear to have resulted in a simultaneous loss of AFDC and food stamps for many families in Boston, Milwaukee, and Syracuse. Although earnings increased for many who remained in the labor force, the respondents as a whole (including those no longer working) experienced significant income losses in all five sites. Apparently they did not make up the loss of income from AFDC and food stamps by working. Additionally, in Dallas and Memphis, about half of these families remained without health insurance coverage after having lost medicaid.

SOURCE: From General Accounting Office, *Evaluation of the 1981 AFDC Changes: Initial Analysis*. Washington, DC: General Accounting Office, 1984.

assumptions and the ways they have been put into place. The value of guidance counselors in schools, of vocational programs for the handicapped, of parole supervision for released convicts, and of community health education for the prevention of disease is often taken for granted. Not only does the general public expect such programs to be provided as a matter of course, but involved advocates and employees (a significant proportion of the national labor force) have an investment in their continuation. Thus, the pressures to maintain them are strong.

At the same time, in many human resource sectors there are clearly programs that have outlived their usefulness, or at least represent poor human service "investments" as they are currently implemented. Either such programs should be modified or other available programs that yield greater benefits at comparable costs should take their place. Many outdated programs are rooted in values and intervention models that no longer are relevant; some have even lost their surface rationales and objectives over time.

As an illustration, take the delivery of ambulatory health services to the poor. Early in the history of medical care in the United States, both public and nonprofit hospitals developed outpatient clinics for treating the poor, because there were meager state and county funds available for their care or because no funds were available beyond the pittances the poor persons could pay themselves. In fact, in many communities, the hospitals that provided these services were called "charity hospitals." With the advent of Medicaid, a federal-state-supported initiative that provides payment for many of the basic health services for the poor, a number of community health centers developed that could treat low-income persons for the fees provided by Medicaid, with such desirable outcomes as lower rates of hospitalization (Freeman et al., 1982). Yet many hospitals have been slow to modify, reduce, and eliminate their outpatient programs. This is the case because the hospitals are reluctant to make changes in their programs, but also because the outpatient departments are used to train medical students and residents and are a source of inpatients, who are particularly valuable in the face of an oversupply of hospital beds in many communities.

Also, as we noted earlier, there is currently uneasiness in many quarters about the proliferation and redundancy of programs. Spiraling costs of established social programs and increased resource restraints, particularly on public funds, require that we make choices regarding what to support, and in what magnitude. Consequently, serious queries are raised by a variety of stakeholder groups about the extent to which programs operate efficiently and follow fiscal, legal, and operational requirements. Finally, constituencies and advocates of different programs are concerned with their impact and costs-to-benefits ratios in comparison to those programs with which they compete for sponsorship and funds. For all these reasons, policymakers responsible for resource allocations, program managers who must defend implementation, and concerned advocacy groups acknowledge the urgent need for evaluation of established programs. Exhibit 2-G describes, for example, the current questioning of alcohol education programs.

The Evaluability Perspective

The idea discussed in this section stems from the experiences of an evaluation research group at the Urban Institute, whose evaluation efforts led them to two related conclusions (Wholey et al., 1970; Wholey, 1979). First, they found it difficult, sometimes impossible, to undertake evaluations of public programs because managers and other stakeholders resisted, were uncooperative, or failed to grasp the purposes of the studies. Second, they found that too frequently evaluation results were not used to refine and modify programs. This led to the view that a systematic approach, which Wholey termed "evaluability assessment," should precede any typical evaluation effort.

Evaluability assessments, or "preevaluations," are designed to provide a climate favorable to future evaluation work and to acquire intimate acquaintance with an agency or program that would aid in the evaluation design. In addition, as systematic management consultation, such efforts may in and of themselves be utilized by program staff prior to further evaluation activities (Schmidt et al., 1978; Rutman, 1980). Evaluability assessments can also reveal whether or not implementation corresponds to the program as defined by those who created its policy and operational procedures; if not, any evaluation that is undertaken will probably be useless.

An evaluability assessment requires the commitment of program staff and, in many cases, sponsors and relevant policymakers to collaborate in explicating objectives, describing the program, and deciding on evaluation tasks. While it can be argued that program staff should, of their own accord, conduct the activities described as evaluability assessments, this is often not the case. Consequently, such assessments become an evaluator's responsibility, at least in terms of the leadership necessary to get the job done.

Conducting Evaluability Assessments

Evaluability assessments can be looked upon as a series of successive rounds of data collection conducted in order to gain as full an understanding as possible of the objectives, implementation, and management of a

Exhibit 2-G: Does Alcohol Education Prevent Alcohol Problems?

It has been considered a reasonable premise that the prevention of alcohol and drug problems among youth should begin by providing children and adolescents with a factual knowledge of the nature, use, and effects of those often abused substances. However, recent evidence has suggested that these education programs may actually augment rather than decrease pro-drug attitudes and drug use. Increasing criticisms of current drug and alcohol education efforts have led some to call for a moratorium on educational approaches to primary prevention.

The Ambiguous Effectiveness of Alcohol Education

Although educational institutions receive hearty endorsement as a primary preventive agent, as evidenced by the fact that virtually all states require instruction about alcohol in the public schools, actual implementation of instructional programs has often been neglected or given only superficial attention. It has been suggested that the present situation arose when the influence of temperance groups (e.g., the WCTU Department of Scientific Temperance) declined in importance. While the early efforts of these temperance groups had succeeded in making alcohol education a compulsory part of the public school curriculum, their educational materials were often criticized as distorted and based largely on appeals to fear. These criticisms, coupled with the advent and repeal of Prohibition, further damaged the status of the temperance approach and left most states with legal mandates requiring alcohol instruction, but no satisfactory message to replace that of the temperance forces. Faced with this dilemma, educators seem to have responded by avoiding the subject. The result has been an array of programs differing vastly in goals and methods. Materials presently used in public school programs are typically dominated by the topic of alcoholism education and the physiological and behavioral effects of alcohol, with little or no attention devoted to the important topic of adolescent drinking.

A clear statement of measurable objectives is a necessary way to start a program toward meaningful evaluation, yet several authors have pointed out the frequent lack of goals in alcohol education programs. Many programs operate without a clear-cut philosophy and this seems, in part, to be responsible for the absence of well-controlled studies of the effectiveness of such programs. It was reported in the 1960s that most alcohol education programs were without specific goals or evidence of impact and that little was being done to remedy the situation. These same problems exist today.

SOURCE: Adapted, with permission, from A. Mitch Cooper and Mark B. Sobell, "Does Alcohol Education Prevent Alcohol Problems? Need for Evaluation," *Journal of Alcohol and Drug Education,* Vol. 25, No. 1, 1979: 54-63.

program, and how it relates to other programs in the same social program domain. Evaluability specialists use each encounter with program staff to broaden their knowledge, identify new informants, verify information collected, and test various scenarios of future evaluative activities and alternative program options. The method is acknowledged to require considerable judgment on the part of the evaluability specialist. Efforts are made in various descriptions of the method (see Rutman, 1980) to codify procedures in order to render assessments reproducible by other assessors. In general, the following iterative steps are taken:

1. Preparing a Program Description. This description is based on formal documents, such as funding proposals, published brochures, administrative manuals, annual reports, minutes, and completed evaluation studies. It includes statements identifying program objectives and cross-classifying them with program elements or components. In other words, like the impact model discussed for innovative programs, the program description compares how the intervention is supposed to operate with how it actually works.

2. Interviewing Program Personnel. Interviews are conducted with key people in order to gather descriptions of the program's goals and rationales, as well as to identify actual program operations. From this information, models of both the intentions and the actual operations of the program are developed and subsequently verified with persons interviewed.

3. Scouting the Program. While evaluability assessments do not include formal research in the sense of large-scale data collection, they do generally include site visits to obtain firsthand impressions of how programs actually operate. These impressions are collated with information from documents and interviews.

4. Developing an Evaluable Program Model. From the various types of information obtained, the program elements and objectives to be considered for inclusion in evaluation plans are explicated.

5. *Identifying Evaluation Users.* The purposes of evaluation activities that are to be undertaken and the identification of the key stakeholders to whom they are to be directed are next identified. In addition, the ways decisions on changes would be made (e.g., administratively or through legislation) are decided.

6. *Achieving Agreement to Proceed.* The final step is the review of the evaluation plan with the various stakeholders. The process of information collection accomplished during the course of the evaluability assessment typically includes dialogue with key individuals and groups. Thus, at this point most components of the plan have been accepted. It is important before the plan is "signed off" by the various stakeholders, however, to reach explicit agreement on the following points:

   a. program components to be analyzed, the design of the evaluation, and priorities for undertaking the work;

   b. commitment of required resources and agreements on necessary cooperation and collaboration;

   c. a plan for utilization of the evaluation results; and

   d. a plan for efforts required from the program staff to strengthen the evaluability potential of program components not currently amenable to evaluation, and an approach for subsequently building them into the evaluation effort.

Some Observations on Evaluability Research Procedures

To a considerable extent, evaluability assessments make use of what are generically referred to as "qualitative" research procedures. In many ways the evaluability specialist operates like a field researcher in conventional qualitative field research studies. That is, the researcher seeks to describe and understand the program in terms of its participants' "social reality." He or she almost always begins with the conception of the program that is available from documents and "hearsay" information. But the investigator continually tries to see the program through the eyes of the stakeholders, program staff, and targets. The intent is to end up with a description of the program as it exists, to provide understanding of differences between how it is formally pictured and how it is actually conducted, and to explain the differences in the ways it is perceived and valued by the various parties involved (see Exhibit 2-H).

Certain parts of evaluability assessments are fairly standard, such as obtaining sufficient information to document the formal organizational structure and the informal or actual authority and influence structure, and to account for differences between the two. Also, certain statistical information is almost invariably obtained, including, for example, an accurate

Exhibit 2-H: An Inductive Approach

A qualitative research strategy is inductive in that the researcher attempts to make sense of the situation without imposing preexisting expectations on the research setting. Qualitative designs begin with specific observations and build toward general patterns. Categories or dimensions of analysis emerge from open-ended observations as the researcher comes to understand organizing patterns that exist in the empirical world under study. This contrasts with the hypothetico-deductive approach of experimental designs that require the specification of main variables and the statement of specific research hypotheses before data collection. A specification of research hypotheses based on an explicit theoretical framework means that general principles provide the framework for understanding specific observations or cases. The researcher must then decide in advance what variables are important and what relationships among those variables are expected. The strategy in qualitative designs is to allow the important dimensions to emerge from analysis of the cases under study without presupposing in advance what those important dimensions will be. The qualitative methodologist attempts to understand the multiple interrelationships among dimensions that emerge from the data without making prior assumptions about the linear or correlative relationships among narrowly defined, operationalized variables. In short, an inductive approach to evaluation research means that an understanding of program activities emerges from experience with the program. Theories about what is happening in a program are grounded in this program experience, rather than imposed on the program a priori based on hypothetico-deductive constructions.

SOURCE: Adapted from M. Q. Patton, *Qualitative Evaluation Methods*, pp. 40-41. Beverly Hills, CA: Sage Publications, 1980.

report on numbers and types of staff and targets. But, as in the data collection process in fieldwork, the evaluability analyst often finds it necessary to let each "discovery" lead him or her along whatever pathways are required in order to maximize opportunities for comprehending the program as it exists *in situ*. In the same sense, it is much more difficult to train fieldworkers than, say, survey researchers, for there are fewer "rules" that can be taught. Consequently, it is much harder to teach the art of evalua-

bility assessment than to provide guidance in how to undertake an experimental impact evaluation. Exhibit 2-I provides an illustration of an evaluability assessment.

At the same time, it should be stressed, as Wholey maintains, that many
formal impact evaluations are either not completed or superficial in their
findings, and of limited utility to program sponsors and staff because there
was too limited an understanding of the ways programs are actually
conducted and perceived. The inherent nature of evaluability assessments
often makes them appear—particularly to the "hard-nosed" quantitative
evaluator—as nothing more than "management consulting." However, as
in the case of the serious fieldworker, the evaluability analyst is as concerned as his or her quantitatively oriented peers with the replicability of
findings, even though such reproducibility is difficult to achieve. One of the
important efforts in the evaluability area is to codify procedures so that the
personalities and proclivities of the analyst influence the findings of the
assessment as little as possible.

One of the common outcomes of evaluability assessment is a recognition by program managers and sponsors that modifications are required in
their programs. It may be that a program's delivery system is identified as
faulty through its documentation as part of the evaluability assessment, or
it may be found that the program's target population is not well defined, or
that there needs to be a revision in the intervention procedures being
implemented. In such cases, fine-tuning of programs may occur prior to
undertaking either an assessment of the impact of the program or the
design and implementation of monitoring procedures.

This is not to say that an evaluability assessment makes it unnecessary
to undertake more conventional evaluation activities, such as an impact
assessment, at some later point in time. But in many established programs,
to leap in and perform such tasks at the outset is a waste of evaluation
funds and may result in an unusable product. Clearly it is wiser to make
modifications prior to rather than as a result of an evaluation.

Accountability and Monitoring Studies

A frequent evaluation activity in established programs, either as a
consequence of outside mandates or on the basis of an evaluability
assessment, is the planning and design of an accountability study. Accountability studies are directed at providing information about various aspects
of programs to stakeholders and program managers. They require monitoring one or more aspects of the ways programs are being implemented
and the conditions under which the intervention is taking place.

In order for the evaluator to develop an accountability study, he or she
must understand the objectives of the program, its rationale, the basis for

Exhibit 2-I: Appalachian Regional Commission

In the Appalachian Regional Commission (ARC), evaluators worked with managers and policymakers to achieve consensus on new program designs more likely to lead to demonstrably effective performance. Evaluability assessment of the Appalachian Regional Commission health and child development program began with collection of data on management's intentions and on program reality. In this evaluability assessment by the Urban Institute, the evaluators

- reviewed commission data on each of the 13 state ARC-funded health and child development programs;

- made one-day visits to five states to aid in selection of two states to participate in evaluation system design and implementation;

- reviewed approximately 40 pieces of documentation considered essential in understanding congressional, commission, state, and project objectives and activities (including the authorizing legislation, congressional hearings and committee reports, state planning documents, and project grant applications);

- reviewed 50 to 60 other pieces of documentation, including ARC contract reports, local planning documents, project materials, state documentation, and research projects;

- interviewed approximately 75 people on congressional staffs and in commission headquarters, state ARC and other state health and child development staffs, local planning units, and local projects; and

- participated in workshops with approximately 60 additional health and child development practitioners, ARC state personnel, and outside analysts.

Analysis and synthesis of the resulting data yielded a "logic model" that presented program activities, program objectives, and assumed causal links among program activities and objectives. The measurability and plausibility of program objectives were then analyzed, and possible redefinitions of the program design were presented. Here the evaluators moved beyond sterile critiques of program design and suggested how managers and policymakers could establish realistic, measurable objectives and use program performance data to improve performance.

The report presented both an overall ARC program model and series of individual models, each concerned with an identified objective of the program. The report outlined a series of information options, expressed in modeling terms, any one of which could be developed into a specific study or evaluation system. In reviewing the report, then, ARC staff had to choose explicitly among alternative courses of action. The review process used was a series of intensive discussions, with ARC and Urban Institute staff participating, in which we focused on one objective and program model at a time. In each session, we attempted to reach agreement on the validity of the flow models presented in the report, the extent to which the objective was important, and the extent to which any of the information options ought to be pursued.

This evaluability assessment was completed in approximately six months, at a cost of approximately $50,000. Another two months of work with the Appalachian Regional Commission and state local groups resulted in ARC decisions systematically to monitor the performance of all ARC health and child development projects and to identify and evaluate the effectiveness of "innovative" health and child development projects.

Twelve of the thirteen ARC states have since adopted the performance monitoring system voluntarily. Representatives of those states report that project designs are now much more clearly articulated and that they believe the projects themselves have improved.

SOURCE: Adapted from J. S. Wholey, "Using Evaluation to Improve Program Performance," pp. 92-106 in R. A. Levine et al. (eds.) *Evaluation Research and Practice: Comparative and International Perspectives.* Beverly Hills, CA: Sage Publications, 1981.

target selection, the appropriateness of procedures for selecting targets and securing their participation, the intervention elements of the program, the ways they are delivered, the monitoring procedures that are in place, and the current efforts to assess outcome and efficiency of the intervention. In one sense, in order to undertake monitoring activities, the evaluator must retrospectively "plan" the program. In another sense, it is necessary to undertake the types of activities described in the section above about conducting evaluability assessments. The details of undertaking accountability and monitoring are discussed in Chapter 4. Here, however, they are considered from the perspective of "planning" activities.

Sponsors, program staff, and a range of community groups may be concerned with all or some of the issues listed below. In addition, evaluators who are engaged in impact and efficiency evaluations often require these types of information. The following are the most common types of accountability information obtained:

1. *Impact Accountability.* Program managers and sponsors are concerned with impact, both for internal operating reasons and in order to justify programs externally.

2. *Efficiency Accountability.* Impact in relation to program costs is obviously important both internally, in terms of judging relative benefits and effectiveness against costs of different program elements, and externally, in competing for resources.

3. *Coverage Accountability.* The key questions here relate to the number and characteristics of targets, to the extent of penetration (that is, what portion of potential targets are served), to dropout rates, and so on.

4. *Service Delivery Accountability.* It is usually necessary to assess how the actual operation of a program conforms to program plans. For example, community mental health centers may include in their plans 24-hour emergency treatment; the accountability question is whether or not this is, in fact, provided. Also, many intervention plans specify the qualifications of providers; thus, the extent to which services are delivered by appropriately qualified staff is another accountability issue.

5. *Fiscal Accountability.* Programs have a clear responsibility to account for use of funds in their fiscal reports. However, in addition to what is strictly an accounting responsibility, a range of other costs questions may be pertinent. For example, costs per client and cost per service are data that may not be gleaned from a fiscal report. Incremental and marginal costs are also pertinent, because programs vary in size, different targets are included, and so on. Finally, costs may vary as a function of program site, time of year, and the initiation of competing programs.

6. *Legal Accountability.* All programs, public and private, require commitments in order to meet legal responsibilities. These include informed consent, protection of privacy, community representation on decision-making boards, equity in provision of services, and cost-sharing. In public programs, adequate compliance with legal requirements often is a prerequisite of continued funding.

The scope of a program's accountability activities is determined by both external and internal requirements. For example, many laws, including "sunset" legislation, require reports of program impact prior to approval of funding for subsequent years. Program managers and the executives to whom they report are concerned with accountability evaluations in order to improve and modify efforts and to administer their interventions efficiently. In many ways, evaluability assessments are seen as a means of developing an accountability strategy that meets current and future needs for information.

In developing accountability strategies, there are two important considerations: continuous versus cross-sectional evaluations and internal versus external assessments.

Continuous versus Cross-Sectional Evaluations

In planning accountability evaluations, a key decision is whether to implement a continuous or a cross-sectional effort. Many large programs employ monitoring and information systems, often referred to as *management information systems* (MISs), that allow them to assess on an ongoing basis the work and results of their programs. These systems record information on each encounter, on the delivery of the service, and on outcome and cost. Chapter 4 goes into more detail about management information systems; here it is important merely to understand the distinction between having a system or procedure that allows for regular collection and maintenance of information on such matters as the characteristics of clients, their problems or reasons for seeking treatment, and their outcomes in comparison with conducting "special" studies at single points in time. The latter type of study, referred to as a "cross-sectional" study, generally collects data around a small window of time, usually in conjunction with a specific evaluation activity, the evaluation of a change in a program or administrative procedure, or because of a specific need of the program manager or a request from an influential stakeholder.

Continuous systems are sometimes criticized for "overkill," and, given that they do represent a permanent commitment of resources, they need to be justified by their constant use. In recent years, however, both the reduced costs of computers and the availability of appropriate software have made it possible for many agencies to install MISs that allow them to oversee the conduct of programs, provide fiscal information, and track patients through their intervention programs. Some provide a ready data source for effectiveness and efficiency analyses.

At the same time, however, individual or cross-sectional studies undertaken from time to time may carry with them expensive start-up costs and may be resisted by program staff, because they are not perceived as part of routine operations. Further, they may not be timely and may have less utility for day-to-day administrative decisions. Again, there is no way to provide general rules that are valid for all programs; rather, a continual monitoring system must be judged on its own cost-to-benefit terms. Many programs use a mix of continual monitoring to assess process and cross-sectional evaluations to estimate their impact at various points and to estimate costs and benefits.

Internal versus External Evaluations

Accountability evaluations raise the issue of whether programs should undertake their own evaluations or contract with outsiders to do so. On the one hand, it is clear that in the case of these types of evaluations, the evaluator must know a great deal about program operations, both to design an evaluation and to engage in the consultation, education, and dialogue required to maximize its utility. On the other hand, there is the risk that the evaluator who is part of the program staff will be co-opted, and that sponsors and stakeholders outside the program staff will be suspicious of the authenticity of findings. In large programs, where evaluators can operate as a semiautonomous group, it is probably beneficial and economical for accountability evaluations to be internal. Smaller programs may be better served by outside assessments approximating the methods of fiscal audits. In some cases, a combination of the two, using consultants to provide both technical assistance and oversight, is advantageous.

In the end, the planning of evaluations of established programs is not qualitatively different from what occurs in innovative interventions. Perhaps the three key distinctions in style are (1) the increased emphasis on creating a program evaluation model from existing, ongoing program activities; (2) much more deliberate attention to stakeholders' views, responsibilities, and influence; and (3) recognizing that there may be important discrepancies between how programs are seen formally and how they are in fact undertaken.

FINE-TUNING ESTABLISHED PROGRAMS

Often, as we have noted earlier, there is a thin line between what are termed "innovative" interventions and the implementation of program refinements through fine-tuning. Likewise, fine-tuning evaluations often overlap with evaluations of established programs. Program managers, on the basis of ongoing evaluation information, may make day-to-day administrative and technical changes that are quite extensive and are subject to systematic evaluation. The core of fine-tuning, however, is program modification that has marked impact on intervention efforts. Its essence is captured by the term "initiative," which often is applied to fine-tuning efforts in national and other large-scale interventions.

Program fine-tuning typically occurs because program sponsors and staff are dissatisfied with either the effectiveness or the efficiency of their interventions, or with both. The basis for implementing such changes may be the findings of systematic evaluation studies of a monitoring or impact type, the outcome of evaluability assessments, or more impressionistic evidence of dissatisfaction with the way efforts are being conducted. Some illustrations are useful. In the mental health field, for example, community mental health centers in areas with predominantly Spanish-speaking populations have become aware of the barriers to access these persons face because of language problems. A variety of different approaches have been taken in order to increase access for persons of Hispanic background. One approach has been to increase the proportion of staff fluent in Spanish, and to employ persons of Hispanic background to contact key religious and voluntary groups in the Hispanic community. A second approach has been to establish satellite "feeder" programs in heavily Hispanic neighborhoods; here staff, materials, and interpersonal relations reflect the special cultural character of the residents, short-term diagnosis and treatment are available, and patients needing more extensive care are referred to the parent center. At issue, of course, is whether or not these approaches increase access for the target population, and which approach proves most effective.

Another example of fine-tuning concerns the large number of initiatives in connection with neighborhood community health centers, most of which initially exist as "freestanding" organizations. Here, government agencies and large foundations have adopted a variety of programs to link community health centers to hospitals and medical schools. While the basic character of medical care provided in the community health centers is not changed, the initiatives are seen as mechanisms that reduce undesirable overlap of services between hospital facilities and community health centers. Also, such affiliations may increase continuity of care for patients (Shortell et al., 1984). Similar types of efforts to reduce fragmentation of care have taken place: Single-neighborhood centers, for instance, offer welfare recipients and other persons of marginal income a variety of services that were previously available in separate offices at some distance from each other.

Fine-tuning basically requires, on the part of sponsors, program staff, and evaluators, three related sets of activities. We turn to these next.

Reappraising Objectives and Outcomes

Fine-tuning efforts, like innovative programs, are responses to existing conditions. In the case of fine-tuning, however, action focuses on conditions adhering to the program itself, rather than on a new and untreated problem. Often, awareness that a program has failed to meet community concerns requires some modification of the program's objectives and outcome criteria. Take our earlier example of community mental health centers and the Hispanic population. The original objective of the centers may have been to provide a range of diagnostic, emergency, and short-term treatment programs to the catchment-area residents. The objective, as originally stated, did not include special consideration for the ethnic and cultural backgrounds of the target population. Fine-tuning in the face of failure to provide access to persons of particular social and cultural backgrounds clearly would require a refinement of objectives. Likewise, the program affiliating community health centers with local hospitals reflects a refinement of objectives; it has redefined and operationalized its objective to include maximum continuity of care.

The need to redefine objectives often becomes apparent after program implementation, particularly as innovative programs stabilize and emerge as established ventures in the human service field. Sometimes, redefinition of objectives stems from the dialogue that almost invariably accompanies administrative and day-to-day working activities. Other times, evaluators undertake special studies, either as independent contractors or as staff members, to obtain data to aid program personnel in revising objectives. In some cases, evaluators and program staff have at their disposal (as described in our discussion of established programs) ongoing management and service information systems that provide data on issues surrounding current objectives and the extent to which they are being met. Increasingly, a number of formal approaches are being employed for continual auditing.

Reputability Assessments

We use the term "reputability assessments" to refer to systematic efforts to obtain from relevant stakeholders, particularly targets, opinions and experiential data on which to judge the extent of a program's success in meeting its objectives. Reputability assessments basically consist of obtaining "market" information on a program. Some programs provide questionnaires to clients in order to obtain information from them about their satisfaction with programs. This may be done through a special study or as part of an ongoing monitoring effort. The surveys would include questions on various aspects of treatment: waiting time, relations with practitioners, costs and fees, and the like. They may also seek expressions of desired services and unmet needs.

In addition, and particularly for larger programs, evaluators may survey providers of services. While persons rendering services, like clients, have their own biases and stakes in programs, they may nevertheless perceive gaps and deficiencies that can be corrected through fine-tuning. For example, regular and systematic data may be obtained from classroom teachers about the various types of special services offered by a school, such as counseling on emotional problems and vocational guidance. (See Chapter 4 for more on monitoring.)

Often, reputability assessments will point to fine-tuning efforts that are comparatively simple, such as providing feedback to teachers on what is being done for students, areas in which special programs are needed, and ways to collaborate effectively in order to deal with student problems. Other times, the information may highlight the need for considerable program modification. Less formal information includes the advocacy pressures exerted by stakeholders and community groups, and probing by persons in the mass media and in political life. When systematic reputability assessments are conducted in advance of these pressures, program management may be able to fine-tune interventions and avoid becoming subject to harassment.

Program Replanning and Redesign

Implementing refinements and fine-tuning, of course, requires a return to the various steps and activities discussed in some detail in the section above on evaluating innovative programs. It is necessary that the problem be well identified and described, that objectives be operationalized, that a revised impact model be developed, that the target population be redefined, that the delivery system be redesigned, and that plans be made for whatever revisions are required in monitoring impact and efficiency.

It should be stressed that not only are fine-tuning efforts much more commonplace than innovative interventions in the human service field, but the consequences of these efforts are extensive. For example, in many high schools, some students are prepared, on an informal basis, in such courses as English and mathematics, to take college entrance examinations. If it can be demonstrated that these students obtain higher scores on these examinations, formal preparatory sessions may be incorporated into the regular high school curriculum—particularly because maximizing students' opportunities for college education and selection of a college of their choice is an objective consistent with one of the general goals of high school education. At the same time, such curriculum modification may increase the gap between students with college aspirations and those without them, require that less emphasis be given to other aspects of the educational program, and interfere with teachers' course plans.

In terms of fine-tuning, then, the evaluator is involved in the following tasks:

1. reappraising objectives
2. identifying possible program modifications by drawing on the data of previous evaluations as well as information about program progress gathered as part of the service delivery

TABLE 2.1 Overview of Evaluation Activities

	Innovative Programs	Fine-Tuning	Established Programs
Conceptualizing	1. Problem Description	1. Identifying needed program changes	1. Determining evaluability
	2. Operationalizing objectives	2. Redefining objectives	2. Developing evaluation model
	3. Developing intervention model	3. Designing program modifications	3. Identifying potential modification opportunities
	4. Defining extent and distribution of target population		4. Determining accountability requirements
	5. Specifying delivery system		
Implementing	1. Formative research and development	1. RandD program refinements	1. Program monitoring and accountability studies
	2. Implementation monitoring	2. Monitoring program changes	
Assessing	1. Impact studies	1. Impact studies	1. Impact studies
	2. Efficiency analyses	2. Efficiency analyses	2. Efficiency analyses

3. undertaking reputability assessments
4. participating in program replanning and redesign
5. planning and implementing evaluation designs to monitor the program changes and their impact

LINKING EVALUATIONS TO PROGRAMS

In this chapter we have discussed how evaluation fits into the development of innovative interventions, into the conduct of established programs, and into fine-tuning and refining of programs. The primary lesson we would like to convey is that the evaluation must be tailored to the program (see Table 2.1).

In no way, of course, do we wish to downplay the importance of the technical and procedural evaluation activities that follow the conceptualization of studies. Indeed, that is what most of this book is about. Moreover, it is important to recognize that programs and evaluations are "dynamic" in the sense that additional program experience, preliminary evaluation feedback, and shifts in the political, economic, and social contexts in which programs and evaluations occur may require modification and adjustment to evaluation designs. At the same time, unless evaluations start strong and are congruent with program operations and requirements, successful systematic studies are unlikely to follow. While there are limits to how fully the process of tailoring can be explained formally—given that it involves not only the orderly formulation and refinement of ideas with data integration but also dialogue, discussion, and interaction with relevant stakeholders—our message should be clear. The evaluator's understanding and maximal involvement in fitting evaluations to programs is essential to the successful undertaking of systematic evaluations.

3

Diagnostic Procedures

As part of the development of evaluation activities and the application of social research methods to the human service area, systematic and reproducible approaches have been devised to identify problems and conditions that are untreated or insufficiently addressed by existing programs. These "diagnostic" procedures sometimes constitute the initial step in problem identification; other times they follow stakeholders' impressionistic and judgmental assessments of the need for purposive, organized social action programs. In either case, systematic documentation of program need must be undertaken in order to plan, refine, implement, and evaluate social action efforts.

KEY CONCEPTS

Incidence:

The number of new cases of a particular problem or condition that are identified or arise in a specified area during a specified period of time.

Indicators:

A measure reflecting a problem or condition on which time-series information is available.

Need Assessment:

Systematic appraisal of type, depth, and scope of problems as perceived by study targets or their advocates.

Population at Need:

Units of potential targets that currently manifest a given condition.

Population at Risk:

Segment of population with significant probability of having or developing a condition.

Prevalence:

Number of existing cases with a given condition in a particular area at a specified time.

Rate:

Occurrence or existence of a condition expressed as a proportion of units in the population (e.g., deaths per 1000 adults).

Sensitivity:

Proportion of target population correctly included in a population at risk.

Specificity:

Proportion of potential target population correctly excluded from a population at risk.

Survey:

Systematic collection of information from large study groups, usually by means of interviews or questionnaires administered to a sample of units in the population.

---

*I*f we were close to a utopian world, we would all live in good health almost forever. There would be no deviants. Full social equality, full political freedom for all, and ample opportunities for participation in occupational and social activities would exist. The human service programs in such a world would deal effectively and efficiently with individual, interpersonal, and community defects (which, of course, would be minor). Hence, few evaluations would be undertaken. Neither new programs nor fine-tuning of existing ones would be needed, and little monitoring of established efforts would be necessary. Evaluation can be seen, then, as a response to efforts to move toward a more perfect world. The myriad current and anticipated human and social problems, and the extensive pressure that persists to design, implement, and refine programs in order to mitigate and control these problems are what generate evaluation activities.

IMPETUS FOR INTERVENTIONS AND EVALUATIONS

In the overall shape of things, evaluators' contributions to the identification and ranking of human and social deficiencies and to the innovation and refinement of programs to address them are modest. Evaluation researchers must be humble about their influence on these matters in light of the weightier actions of political bodies, advocacy groups, investigative reporters, and charismatic personalities. The post-World War II attention to mental illness largely was related to the efforts of a single congressman; federal programs for the mentally retarded received a major boost during Kennedy's presidency because he had a retarded sibling; improved automobile safety can be credited to a considerable degree to Nader-led advocates; and efforts to control illegal and improper delivery of health and welfare services often come about because of exposés in the mass media and the activities of interest and pressure groups, including the organized efforts of clients themselves.

Nevertheless, evaluators do play an important role in identifying the parameters of the problems requiring attention and the deficiencies and limitations of current efforts to intervene. As we have noted, the initial impetus for attending to social problems most often comes from community advocates who have a stake, either personally or professionally, in dealing with a particular problem or condition. What the evaluator adds, however, by what we refer to here as "diagnostic procedures," are systematic and reproducible approaches to the identification of communal problems and the clarification of their scope.

The importance of diagnostic information cannot be overstated. Although speculation, impressionistic observations, and even overtly biased information may spur policymakers, planners, and funding organizations to initiate action, it is essential to have trustworthy and precise information on social problems, their corresponding potential program targets, and the context in which an intervention would operate before a program is designed and started. So, too, before fine-tuning an existing initiative or curtailing an ongoing program, the same information needs to be estimated. Here are a few examples of what happens when adequate diagnostic procedures are ignored:

- After a social intervention designed to prevent criminal behavior by adolescents was put in place in a midwestern suburb, it was discovered that very little crime could be attributed to young persons and virtually no juvenile delinquents were living in the community. The planners assumed that because juvenile delinquency was a general social problem, it would also be one in their particular community as well.

- Planners of many of the urban renewal projects undertaken during the 1960s assumed that persons living in "dilapidated" buildings regarded their housing as defective and thus would support the demolition of their homes and accept relocation in replacement housing. In city after city, residents of urban renewal areas vigorously opposed the urban renewal projects designed by city planners.

- Media programs designed to encourage people to seek physical examinations in order to detect early signs of cancer had the effect of swamping health centers with more clients than they could handle, since many hypochondriacal persons without any symptoms of cancer were stimulated by the media effort to believe they were experiencing warning signs.

- In an effort to improve the clinical identification of acquired immune deficiency syndrome (AIDS), which often afflicts homosexual males, community physicians were provided with literature about the details of diagnosing the syndrome among high-risk patients. Only after the materials had been disseminated was it recognized that few physicians take sex histories as a routine practice; thus there was little likelihood they could identify the population at risk and make use of their new knowledge, except by testing all their patients. This lead to an excessive amount of testing, at high cost and some risk to their patients.

- A birth control project was expanded to reduce the reportedly high rate of abortion in a large urban center. The program failed to attract many additional participants, and it was discovered subsequently that most of the potential clients were already being served. For the most part, it was discovered that the high abortion rate was caused by young women who came to the city from outlying areas to have abortions; a very high proportion of the urban residents already practiced contraception.

In all of the examples cited, diagnostic research might have provided information that would have prevented problems of program implementation. It should be noted that these are examples in which the intervention did not fail—it was simply not delivered, because the target population did not exist, did not seek the program provided, was incorrectly identified, or made demands the intervention was incapable of meeting.

ASSESSMENT OF INTERVENTION NEED

A critical step in the design of an innovative program is to verify that a problem either currently ignored or being treated unsuccessfully exists in sufficient degree to warrant a new or additional intervention. Further, justification of ongoing programs, and efforts to refine them, typically requires evidence of the persistence of unresolved defects in social conditions or of existing programs' ineffectiveness in dealing with the defects, either because of the ways the existing interventions are delivered or because of their limited efficacy. Verifying and mapping out the extent and location of a problem and identifying its attendant target population is called "needs assessment."

Needs assessments are necessary because it is often difficult to gauge the magnitude of a social problem. Those who are concerned about the issues involved often tend to exaggerate the extent of a problem. Professionals and community members, in their zeal to maintain and expand programs in which they have some self-interest, often may overestimate the size or character of the need. In some cases, although a problem—the prevalence of physical disabilities, for example—may be obviously serious and widespread enough to warrant an intervention, information on its distributional characteristics may be needed. Thus, if physical disabilities are predominantly a problem of older persons, arising from age-related infirmities, the treatment called for may be different from that for disabilities among younger persons. Needs assessments, then, are undertaken to estimate the number and program-relevant characteristics of targets.

What Is a Target?

Targets are often individuals, but they may be groups (families, work teams, firms, establishments, and so on), geographically and politically related areas (such as small communities in a particular region), or physical units (houses, road systems, and the like). Whatever the target, it is imperative at the outset of the diagnostic effort to define the unit of analysis clearly.

Definitional criteria vary. In the case of individuals, targets usually are identified in terms of one or more of the following: social and demographic characteristics; location; or targets' problems, difficulties, and conditions. Targets of an educational project in which individuals are pivotal might be specified as "male children between ages 10 and 14 who reside in a school district and who are between one and three years below their normal grade in school."

When aggregates (groups and organizations) are targets, they are often defined in terms of the characteristics of the individuals that constitute them—their informal and formal collective properties and shared problems. An organizational target might be elementary schools (kindergarten to eighth grade) with at least 300 pupils and in which at least 30 percent of the pupils come from households with incomes below the poverty line.

Direct and Indirect Targets

As we noted in Chapter 2, targets may also be regarded as direct or indirect, depending on whether treatments are delivered to the targets immediately (directly) or eventually (indirectly). Most programs specify direct targets. This is clearly the case in medical interventions, where persons with given afflictions receive medical treatment directly. In some cases, however, for either economic or feasibility reasons, programs are intended to affect target populations indirectly, by making their immediate targets a population or condition that will eventually have impact on those intended to receive benefits. In a rural development project, as an illustration, influential farmers are selected from small communities and provided with intensive training programs. Afterward, they are to return to their own communities and communicate their new knowledge to other farmers. Again, a project that identifies its direct targets as substandard dwelling units may be intended to have impact ultimately (but only indirectly) on the occupants of those dwellings.

If targets are defined as indirect, the effectiveness of a program depends to a large extent on the pathways leading from immediate to ultimate targets. The effectiveness of the project that uses influential farmers depends heavily on the abilities and motivation of those farmers to communicate their knowledge to other members of their communities. Similarly, if there is a strong relationship between housing quality and household health, investment in physical improvement of housing may be justified; if the correlation is low or essentially zero, however, such investment is likely to be wasteful and ineffective.

Specifying Targets

Specification of the size and distribution of targets may seem simple at first glance. But there are practically no human and social defects that can be estimated easily, merely by counting individuals or other units with a particular problem or condition.

Take a single illustration: What is the population of persons with cancer in a given community? First, it depends on whether or not one counts only permanent residents or includes temporary ones as well (an aspect that would be extremely important in certain cities, for example, in Miami Beach). Second, are "recovered" cases counted, or are those without a relapse for, say, five years eliminated from the estimate? Third, the estimate needs to take into account the purpose for which it is being used. If it is to be used in designing a special nursing-home program, persons with skin cancer should not be included, because their condition rarely requires inpatient services. An illustration of the considerations that go into specifying targets is provided in Exhibit 3-A, which is extracted from a landmark article that greatly influenced the development of the "poverty line" concept, a definition of poverty that is still employed today.

Target Boundaries

Adequate target specification establishes boundaries—that is, rules of inclusion and exclusion. One risk in specifying target populations is that of making the definition too broad or overinclusive. For instance, defining a "criminal" as anyone who has violated any law or administrative regulation is useless, because only the most saintly individuals have not in some way or another, at some time or another, violated a law or regulation, wittingly or otherwise. Stakeholders committed to alleviating poverty may describe their target population as "persons or households whose income cannot support a reasonable standard of living." Clearly, such a definition cannot be the starting point for a useful needs assessment or program design. It does not provide criteria specific enough to make determination of the relevant target group possible. An overinclusive definition, therefore, may result in overestimating need and thereby causing either uneconomical investment in an intervention the targets of which have little to gain from it or a watering down of the program in order to serve an excessively large target group.

Definitions may also prove too restrictive, or underinclusive—to the point where almost no one falls into the target population. For example, in a program aimed at the rehabilitation of released felons, the program designers decided to eliminate those who were drug or alcohol abusers. The prevalence of substance abuse was so great among released prisoners that, after substance abusers were eliminated from the target population, only one in ten was eligible to be included.

Feasibility

In addition, useful definitions are those that are feasible to apply. A specification that hinges on some characteristic of persons that is difficult to observe—for example, a favorable attitude toward evaluation research— may be virtually impossible to put into practice. Complex definitions

(text continues on page 112)

Exhibit 3-A: How Poverty Is Measured

Counting the poor is an exercise in the art of the impossible. For deciding who is poor, prayers are more relevant than calculation because poverty, like beauty, lies in the eye of the beholder. Poverty is a value judgment; it is not something one can verify or demonstrate, except by inference and suggestion, even with a measure of error. To say who is poor is to use all sorts of value judgments. The concept has to be limited by the purpose which is to be served by the definition. There is no particular reason to count the poor unless you are going to do something about them. Whatever the possibilities of socioeconomic research in general, when it comes to defining poverty, you can only be more subjective or less so. You cannot be nonsubjective.

Defining the Issue

In the Social Security Administration, poverty was first defined in terms of the public or policy issue: To how many people, and to which ones, did we wish to direct policy concern. Even when we bore this aim in mind, the level of living we used to separate the "haves" from the "have nots" could be understated so that everyone who was counted in the "have not" group really did not have enough. If we did the reverse, we ran the risk of counting some who should not be there. There is, in short, no one perfect scheme and no value-free scheme.

Since we were attempting to illustrate the level of public concern, we wanted to be sure that every family or consumer unit had its fair chance to be numbered among those who would be considered as needing attention. Indeed, it was precisely to ensure consideration of the needs of large families as well as small, and of young people as well as old, that we refined the initial standard developed by the Council of Economic Advisers. Their standard said that any family of two or more with less than $3,000 annual income, and any single person living alone with less than $1,500, would be considered poor for purposes of antipoverty program planning—but not for program eligibility. This original standard led to the odd result that an elderly couple with $2,900 income for the year could be considered poor, but a family with a husband, wife, and four little children with $3,100 income would not be.

Moreover, when we looked at the poor distributed demographically, by comparison with the total population, we made some unusual discoveries. For example, the percentage of the families classified as poor who had no children was higher than that for the population as a whole; and to make it even more unrealistic, the percentage of the poor families with four children or more was actually less than the representation of such families in the population. We did not think this was correct, so we tried to vary the poverty line—the necessary minimum of resources—with the size and composition of the family. The reason this had not been done by the Council is that no such data were available to them then.

Setting the Benchmark

A concept that can help influence public thinking must be socially and politically credible. We need benchmarks to distinguish the population group that we want to worry about. A benchmark should neither select a group so small, in relation to all the population, that it hardly seems to deserve a general program, nor so large that a solution to the problem appears impossible. For example, in the 1930s, President Roosevelt said, "I see before me one-third of a nation ill-clothed, ill-housed, and ill-fed." This fraction is now part of our history. No matter how we get our numbers today, if more than a third of the population is called poor, it will lose value as a public reference point.

At the Social Security Administration, we decided that we would develop two measures of need, and state, on the basis of the income sample of the Current Population Survey, how many and what kinds of families these measures delineated. It was not the Social Security Administration that labeled the poverty line. It remained for the Office of Economic Opportunity and the Council of Economic Advisers to select the lower of the two measures and decide they would use it as the working tool. The best you can say for the measure is that at a time when it seemed useful, it was there. It is interesting that few outside the Social Security Administration ever wanted to talk about the higher measure. Everybody wanted only to talk about the lower one, labeled the "poverty line," which yielded roughly the same number of people in poverty as the original $3,000 measure did, except that fewer families with more children were substituted for a larger number of older families without children.

Thresholds of Poverty

We have developed two poverty thresholds, corresponding to what we call the "poor" and "near-poor." These thresholds are set separately for 124 different kinds of families, based on the sex of the head, the number of children under 18, the number of adults, and whether or not the household lives on a farm. The threshold is defined as an attempt to "specify the minimum money income that could support an average family of given composition at the lowest level consistent with the standards of living prevailing in this country. It is based on the amount needed by families of different size and type to purchase a nutritionally adequate diet on the assumption that no more than a third of the family income is used for food." The two thresholds were developed from food consumption surveys that revealed that the average expenditure for food by all families was about one-third of income.

An assumption was made that the poor would have the same flexibility in allocating income as the rest of the population but that, obviously, their margin for choice would be less. The amount allocated to food from the average expenditure was cut to the minimum that the Agriculture Department said could still provide American families with an adequate diet. We used the low cost plan to characterize the near-poor and for the poor an even lower one, the economy food plan.

SOURCE: From M. Orshansky, "Perspectives on Poverty: How Poverty Is Measured." *Monthly Labor Review*, 92 (February 1969): 37-41. Reprinted by permission.

requiring much detailed information are just as difficult to apply in selection and should be avoided: It would be difficult, if not impossible, to accumulate the data required to seek out targets defined as farmers who have planted barley for at least two seasons and who have two adolescent sons who are members of a producers' cooperative. In general, the more criteria a definition has, the smaller the number of units that can qualify for inclusion in the target population. (The farmers satisfying the above criteria would be a small group indeed.) Complex specifications are therefore kin to narrow ones, and carry with them the same risks.

Varying Perspectives on
Target Specification

Another issue in the definition of target problems and populations arises from the potentially differing perspectives of professionals, policymakers, and the range of stakeholders involved—including, of course, the potential recipients of services. What is seen as a human or social problem by some persons and groups may not be perceived as such by others. Thus, the professional planners of a program concerned with improving the quality of housing available to poor persons may have a perspective on housing quality much different from the ideas of the people who will live in those dwellings. For example, in the Experimental Housing Allowance Project (Abt Associates, 1977; Struyk and Bendick, 1981), one of the building standards concerned the ratio of floor area to window area in bedrooms; housing in which the ratio was above 10 was considered inadequate. The perspectives of homeowners and renters who occupied the buildings were quite different, however; they regarded such housing as quite adequate.

Discrepancies also may exist between the views of policymakers and those of other groups. Congress may plan to alleviate the financial burden on the federal government by reducing special aid to victims of natural disasters. One means of doing so is to encourage states and local governments to invest in such disaster-mitigating measures as flood-plain land use management and building codes that lower risks of damage and injury. States and especially local governments, however, may object strongly to the plan, on the grounds that since floods seldom occur on their flood plains, such measures would burden them unfairly. Indeed, true to their name, 100-year floods occur in any one place only once in every century (on the average). However, from the federal perspective, 100-year floods may occur as often as once every few days, because the federal government must be concerned with all the flood plains in the United States (Wright et al., 1979).

While research obviously cannot settle the issue of which perspective is "correct," it can eliminate conflicts that might arise from groups talking past each other. Planning research may involve obtaining needs assessments from several perspectives. Exhibit 3-B describes a method of assessing community mental health needs by querying five stakeholder groups, each of which contributes its particular perspective. Exhibit 3-C provides an example for youth services, indicating that a variety of sources may be necessary to express the perspectives of agencies, youth, and parents.

Information collected about varying perspectives on needs may lead to a reconceptualization of the problem or the prospective intervention, or

(text continues on page 117)

Exhibit 3-B: Assessing Community Mental Health Needs

The consumer model presents the program planner with a method of assessing mental health needs using the consumer as the major source of input. The consumer is defined as any community member who resides within a given geographic area. The model supplies information on the priorities of need for additional services by target problem, age group, and geographic area. Within the model, five consumer groups are surveyed:

1. *Mental Health Agencies*—agencies and individuals that directly or indirectly treat people with mental health problems;

2. *Secondary Related Agencies*—agencies that make referrals to mental health services;

3. *High-Risk Individuals*—individuals who, because of past or present behavior, are using or have used mental health services;

4. *Community and Civic Groups*—groups within the community that are organized around a common goal or for a specific purpose;

5. *Community-at-Large*—a sample of area residents selected at random who may or may not be associated with any of the other four groups.

In order to determine the feasibility of using the model, consumer groups in the Kearny Mesa subregional area of San Diego County were surveyed. Of the 42 subregional areas in the county, Kearny Mesa was chosen because it closely approximated the sociodemographic characteristics of the overall county population.

Questionnaires and Interviews

Mental Health Agencies. Included were a school for the emotionally disturbed, a runaway and family crisis center, a private psychiatric hospital, a family services center, training centers for retardates, outpatient clinics, and a residential treatment facility for children. Of the 13 agencies that received the questionnaire, all 13 (100 percent) returned completed forms.

Secondary Related Agencies. Included were schools, the probation department, the coroner, Juvenile Hall, a general hospital, a convalescent home, a legal services center, a speech and hearing clinic, and an unemployment office. Of the 33 agencies that received a questionnaire, 22 (66.6 percent) returned completed forms.

The questionnaire asked both groups to rank the target problems that required the first, second, and third most immediate attention within three age groups: youth (under 18), adult (18-59), and geriatric (60+). In addition, information was sought regarding the quality and type of programs already existing in the Kearny Mesa area. Questions were asked about number of persons served, type of problems treated, waiting lists, and age, race, and geographic area served.

Community and Civic Groups. Included were women's auxiliaries of public agencies, a women's social club, a parent-teacher association, men's service organizations, a YMCA, and a boys' club. Of the ten groups mailed a questionnaire, five responded.

The questionnaire required the respondent to check the services that should be made available to a greater number of people in the Kearny Mesa area for the three age groups. In order to ensure a representative sampling across ethnic and socioeconomic groups, each group was asked to state the race, age, income level, and geographic level of members.

Community-at-Large. Questionnaires were mailed to a sample of residents selected at random from the Haines Directory of Locations, which lists all addresses by street and census tract. Two addresses were selected at random from each street. Because of the cost factor, only 594 households, 16 percent of the Kearny Mesa households, were surveyed. Of the 594 households, 53, or 8.9 percent, returned the questionnaire. The 53 households included 176 individuals, or 3.3 per household. The low response rate is one of the limitations of this needs assessment.

The questionnaire asked respondents to check the services that should be made available to a greater number of people in the Kearny Mesa area. The questionnaire also asked the consumer to indicate the race, age, income, living arrangement, and type of residence of the family members. One open-ended question was included, which asked the consumer to list the person or persons to whom he would go for help if he had a personal problem.

SOURCE: From A. T. Weiss, "The Consumer Model of Assessing Community Health Needs." *Evaluation,* Vol. 2 (1975): 71. Reprinted by permission.

Exhibit 3-C: Need Assessments of Youths

A comprehensive attempt to develop a methodology and instruments for need assessments of youths is the work by the Behavioral Research and Evaluation Corporation (BREC). The first stage of the recommended strategy is a "social area analysis," which provides information on the social, demographic, and economic characteristics of the community, with special emphasis on youth, and the structure and organization of the community. Here the available census data, police and court records, school data, welfare, unemployment, etc. are gathered and analyzed in order to understand the nature of the community and the extent to which broad categories of problems are present.

The "Youth Needs Assessment" that BREC has developed is intended to survey the needs of all the youth in a population, as opposed to youths who are receiving services. The suggested methodology involves simple random sampling in the schools, or cluster sampling in the schools or homes. Four types of items have been developed for the survey: (1) problems, difficulties, and needs, specifying frequency of their occurrence and perceived seriousness; (2) feelings, attitudes, and behavior regarding four factors—"(a) perceived opportunities for achieving personal goals and desired social roles, (b) perceived negative labeling by parents, teachers, and friends, (c) feelings of alienation and rejection, and (d) self-reported involvement in delinquent behavior"; (3) youths' perceptions and evaluation of available services and agencies; and (4) personal background and socioeconomic data of the respondents. In addition to uncovering needs, these measures also serve as baseline data for subsequent impact assessments.

The perceptions of agency regarding youth needs can be measured with the same instrument used for youths, where agency personnel are asked to estimate the percentage of all youths having the problem and to assess the problem's seriousness.

SOURCE: Summary, by permission, D. S. Elliott et al., *Research Handbook for Community Planning and Feedback Instruments*, Vol. 1 (rev.). Boulder, CO: Behavioral Research Institute, 1976.

may indicate the advisability of abandoning the program (especially if the different perspectives are highly contradictory and turn out to be intensely held by the different stakeholders). The consequences of proceeding under the illusion that there is consensus when in fact there is considerable conflict can be seen in the fate of the urban renewal program (Wilson, 1966). This program was predicated on presumed agreement regarding important criteria of housing dilapidation and obsolescence by planners, residents, and institutions. The criteria used by planners often did not correspond with those of residents. Consequently, urban renewal projects in city after city created rancorous conflict—so much that in many cases the programs were gradually abandoned.

CONCEPTUALIZING PROGRAM TARGETS

Estimating the nature of a target problem and the size of a target population and its characteristics is prerequisite to documenting the need for a program, its scope, and the special ways it must be designed to fit in with the characteristics of the target population. As program planning continues, it is necessary to decide on the procedures whereby the target population can be distinguished efficiently and economically from non-target units during project implementation. There are a number of different concepts that underlie target selection.

Incidence and Prevalence

A useful distinction is the difference between incidence and prevalence. *Incidence* refers to the number of new cases of a particular problem that are identified or arise in a defined geographical area during a specified period of time. *Prevalence* refers to the number of existing cases in a particular geographic area at a specified time. Again, the concepts are derived from health efforts, where the distinctions between the terms are sharp. For example, the incidence of influenza during a particular month would be the number of new cases spotted during the month. The prevalence of flu would be the number of people so afflicted at any time in a particular month. In planning projects in the health sector, one is generally interested in incidence when dealing with disorders that are of short duration, such as upper-respiratory infections and minor accidents. Prevalence is the important concept for those problems that cannot be eradicated quickly but require long-term management and treatment efforts. These include chronic diseases such as cancer and clinically observable long-term illnesses such as amoebic dysentery and severe malnutrition. In social problems, prevalence measures are useful for such chronic conditions as criminality, poverty, and low educational attainment.

The concepts of incidence and prevalence have been adapted to the area of social problems. Sometimes their uses are clear. For example, in studying the impact of crime on victims, the critical problem is the incidence of victimization—the numbers of new cases that occur per interval of time for a given area. In providing services for alleviating child abuse, again, new cases of child abuse per month for a city may be the best measure of the need for intervention into that problem. But in the case of poverty, the interest is generally in the prevalence of poverty, defined as the number of poor individuals or families in a community regardless of when they became poor.

For other social problems, it is often not clear whether one should define target populations in terms of prevalence or incidence. In dealing with the unemployment problem, it is important to know the numbers or proportions of the total population unemployed at a particular point in time. When the concern is more with the provision of financial support for the unemployed, however, it is not clear whether the focus should be persons who are unemployed at a particular time or or those who become unemployed in a given period. The principle involved centers on the issue of whether one is concerned with detecting and treating cases as they appear or with detecting existing cases in a population, whatever their time of origin.

Population at Risk

In the specification of targets, the public health concept of *population at risk* is helpful, particularly in projects that are preventive in character. The term refers to that segment of a population that is exclusively or largely subject, with significant probabilities, to developing a condition. Thus, the population at risk in fertility control programs is usually defined as women of childbearing age. Similarly, projects that are designed to mitigate the effects of typhoons and hurricanes may define targets as communities located in the typical paths of tropical storms.

A population at risk can be defined only in probabilistic terms. Thus, women of childbearing age may be the population at risk in a fertility control project, but a given woman may or may not conceive a child within a given period of time. In this instance, specifying the population at risk in terms of age results in overinclusiveness, that is, including many persons as targets who may not be in need of family planning efforts.

Estimating the target population poorly may have consequences for program implementation that are difficult or impossible to remedy. Underinclusion when estimating the population at risk may result in severe budget problems, too small a staff to undertake the intervention properly, inadequate physical space for the program, and so on. Failure to provide program services to the entire target population can alienate stakeholders so greatly that the program may be terminated. Overinclusion results in wasted expenditures of resources and, as will be discussed subsequently in this chapter, can limit the likelihood of the evaluation of a program yielding positive findings of impact. Thus, in identifying the target population in terms of population at risk probabilities, it is important to be concerned with both the sensitivity and the specificity of target estimation.

Sensitivity and Specificity

Sensitivity refers to the ability to identify correctly targets who should be included in a program because they have some disease or condition—that is, the ability to detect "true" positives. *Specificity* refers to eliminating correctly from the target population estimate (and any subsequent program) "false" positives—that is, persons or objects in the population who should not be included as targets. Both high sensitivity and high specificity are required ideally in estimating target population and in the future identification of targets for a program. (See Chapter 5 for a more extended discussion of "false positives" and "false negatives.")

In Exhibit 3-D, a test to screen developmentally disabled prekindergarten children is described. It is not regarded as a useful means of estimating the target population of children about to enter kindergarten because, while it is very accurate in correctly identifying children without developmental problems (specificity), it does not correctly classify as developmentally disabled a sufficient proportion of those who actually have disabilities.

Need and Demand

A *population at need* is a group of potential targets who currently manifest a given condition. For our earlier example of projects directed at alleviating poverty, one may define the target population as families whose income, adjusted for family size, is below a certain minimum. A population at need can usually be defined in absolute terms; that is, one can identify a precise criterion for including a unit among targets (e.g., a screening technique). For instance, there are reliable and valid tests for determining degree of literacy. These tests can be used to specify a target population of functionally illiterate persons.

Need must be distinguished from demand. As illustrated in Exhibit 3-D, although a fair proportion of new homebuyers need "warranty insurance" to protect them from defective dwellings, neither a mandatory nor a voluntary public program appears feasible because of both costs and homeowner disinterest (i.e., lack of demand).

Actually, some need assessments undertaken to estimate the extent of a problem and to serve as the basis for designing programs are "at-risk

Exhibit 3-D: Homeowner Warranties: A Study of Need and Demand

The decision to purchase a home often is made without complete information concerning the structural soundness of the dwelling or the condition of its mechanical systems.

Data on the nature and magnitude of unanticipated home-repair costs were obtained by a HUD-sponsored survey of some 1,800 households that purchased existing homes two years prior to the survey. The potential market demand for home inspection and warranty programs is estimated on the basis of data obtained from a second survey of approximately 1,800 recent home purchasers.

It is clear that unanticipated repair expenses pose a serious problem for some purchasers of existing homes, and a government-provided home inspection and warranty program could clearly be of considerable benefit to such purchasers. At the same time, however, many other home purchasers now escape serious unanticipated repair costs, and a mandatory program would result in increased housing expenses for this group without providing them with additional benefits. It also is apparent from the data at the present time a majority of home purchasers do not consider the benefits of home inspection and warranty services to be worth the cost. Making policy choices in the light of these findings, therefore, becomes a matter of judgment with regard to how appropriately to trade off the costs and benefits to the various individuals who would be affected. The analysts' judgment is that a mandatory program would not be a desirable policy initiative at the present time, because the benefits of such a program do not outweigh the substantial administrative costs and the loss of individual choice that a mandatory program would involve.

The analysts also believe that a voluntary government-run home inspection and warranty program should not be set up at this time. This judgment is based both on the low projected participation rates for such a program, noted above, and on the fact that a private market for such services seems to be developing.

SOURCE: Adapted, with permission, from J. Alan Brewster, Irving Crespi, Richard Kaluzny, James Ohls, and Cynthia Thomas, *Journal of the American Real Estate and Urban Economics Association,* Volume 8, No. 2, 1980: 207-215.

assessments" or "demand assessments" rather than true needs assessments, according to the definitions just offered. This is the case because it is either technically infeasible to measure need or impractical to implement a program that deals only with the at-need population. For example, although only sexually active females may require family planning information, the target population for most such programs is all fertile women, generally defined by an age span such as 15 to 50 (i.e., those assumed to be at risk). Again, while all nonliterate adults are the at-need group for an evening educational program, only those who are willing or who can be persuaded to participate can be considered the target population (i.e., those at demand). Clearly, the distinctions among populations at risk, at need, and at demand are important for estimating the scope of a problem, anticipating target population size, and subsequently designing, implementing, and evaluating the program.

Rates

In addition to estimating the size of a problem group, it is also important to know about the rate of a particular problem. Many times it is critical to be able to express incidence or prevalence as a rate: The number of new cases of unemployment or underemployment in an area experiencing a recession might be described per 100 or per 1000 of a population (e.g., 133 per 1000).

Rates or percentages are especially critical in identifying the characteristics of the target population. For example, in describing the number and characteristics of crime victims, it is important to have estimates by sex and age group. Although almost every age group is subject to victimization in some sort of crime incident, young people are much more likely to be the victims of robbery and assault, while older persons are more likely to have experienced burglary and larceny; men are considerably less likely to be victims of sexual abuse than women; and so on. The ability to estimate targets by various characteristics allows a program to be planned and developed in ways that maximize opportunities to include the most appropriate participants and to be tailored to the particular characteristics of sizable groups.

Estimates of target populations and their characteristics may be made at several levels of disaggregation. For example, illiteracy rates, calculated by dividing the number of functional illiterates in various age groups by the total number of persons in such age groups, allow one to estimate the target populations that can be reached by tailoring a project to specific age cohorts. More powerful statistical techniques may usefully be employed to take into account additional sociodemographic variables simultaneously.

In most cases, it is not only traditional but also useful to specify rates by age and sex. In communities in which there are marked cultural differences, variations in racial, ethnic, and religious background also become important denominators for the disaggregation of characteristics. Other variables useful in identifying characteristics of the target population include socioeconomic status, geographic location, and residential mobility. (See Exhibit 3-E for an example of crime victimization rates disaggregated by age, sex, and race.)

A final set of rates may refer to problems associated with ability to participate in the program and measures related to program implementation. Thus, it may be advantageous in various technical training programs to estimate rates for groups that require 15 minutes, one-half hour, or more than one hour to reach training centers.

SELECTING PROGRAM TARGETS

Programs are most efficient and effective when the targets reached are restricted entirely to units that need the intervention. That is, in the terms used in our section on target boundaries, there is neither overinclusion nor underinclusion. In terms of the population-at-risk concept, the effort should be to select the target population in a way that maximizes specificity and sensitivity.

Overinclusion

Especially in the case of projects for which resources are insufficient to cover all potential targets, selection is generally regarded as most efficient if treatment is given mainly to targets with the highest probabilities of successful outcome. Such an approach maximizes the likelihood of favorable costs-to-benefits ratios and the probability that positive impact can be demonstrated. For example, a program designed to strengthen the nutritional content of children's diets by providing school lunches at low cost would be inefficient if it reached a large proportion of children who already had adequate diets. This would be the case even if all children with nutritional deficiencies were also served by the program. Thus, if the program covered all children with nutritional deficiencies but 90 percent of those served did not suffer from that condition, a large proportion of the resources going into the program would be "wasted." Such overinclusion often results in highly uneconomical interventions.

However, the more precise and exacting the selection of targets becomes, the more expensive the selection procedures involved. A selection procedure for a project to combat functional illiteracy that specified targets by means of screening large numbers of persons through elaborate tests might cost a great deal for each case of illiteracy uncovered, thereby exhausting resources that could be used to provide services.

Exhibit 3-E: Crime Victimization Rates in 1981

Selected Crimes: Victimization Rates for Persons Age 12 and Over, by Race, Sex, and Age of Victims and Selected Crimes (rates per 100,000 persons in each group).

Race, Sex, and Age	All Assaults	Robberies
White		
Male		
12 to 15	5,494	1,418
16 to 19	7,893	1,549
20 to 24	7,540	1,516
25 to 34	4,498	734
35 to 49	2,142	611
50 to 64	1,019	361
65 and over	422	334
Female		
12 to 15	3,200	610
16 to 19	2,770	510
20 to 24	3,430	650
25 to 34	2,740	480
35 to 49	1,140	340
50 to 64	630	350
65 and over	220	310
Non-White		
Male		
12 to 15	5,754	3,162
16 to 19	7,253	3,538
20 to 24	6,082	2,944
25 to 34	3,113	2,135
35 to 49	2,484	1,167
50 to 64	947	1,421
65 and over	1,374	1,856
Female		
12 to 15	5,220	620
16 to 19	3,000	990
20 to 24	4,070	1,270
25 to 34	2,050	1,300
35 to 49	2,470	890
50 to 64	1,060	1,260
65 and over	730	610

SOURCE: U.S. Department of Justice, Bureau of Crime Statistics, *Sourcebook of Criminal Justice Statistics*. Washington, DC: Government Printing Office, 1984.

Overinclusion and Evaluation
of Program Utility

The consequences of inefficient target estimation and identification are often serious for the overall program effort. It is questionable in terms of costs, for example, to expose entire communities to educational, housing, medical, and cultural programs when only a small percentage of the community population is "at risk." Moreover, from the standpoint of estimating program impacts, failure to define the population at risk effectively lessens the chances of detecting positive effects. This is the problem of having too many "false positives" in the target group for an impact evaluation. Consider a program aimed at learning disabilities that covers all schoolchildren in a community in which only 5 percent of the children may have learning disabilities. If the program is effective only with the 5 percent, differences in learning from pretest to posttest are unlikely to be revealed (unless the population of schoolchildren is large), since the vast majority of children given treatment would not need it and thus could not be expected to benefit.

Underinclusion

Not only may underinclusion deny opportunities for program participation to targets at need or highly at risk, but there is also a trade-off between selection costs and the resources available for treatment delivery. It may be possible in a preventive health-care program to identify by laboratory tests those persons in a community who have not developed an immunity to polio and to provide only this group with vaccinations. Such a procedure, however, would be foolish, because the resources necessary to undertake the screening are greater than the costs of providing polio vaccinations to all community members. Similarly, a project in which a central water supply is piped to all dwellings in a community, including those that already enjoy potable water, may seem overzealous. However, costs of tailoring the project to skip certain housing units, the possible future contamination of currently potable water, and difficulties of obtaining community acceptance of a selective project present arguments against restricting the target households to those with contaminated wells.

There are also some psychological and political reasons for allowing a looser definition of the target population than necessary solely from a population-at-need or population-at-risk standpoint. First, efficient identification of target populations with a condition that may stigmatize them raises serious ethical considerations: Effective screening to locate mildly retarded children for a special project may result in invidious labeling by peers and teachers, with the consequences that any gains from a selective program are far overshadowed by the negative effects of the labeling process. Thus, it might be better to open the project to all children (or at least to those less likely to experience deleterious labeling effects).

Second, when programs include opportunities, goods, and services valued by all community members, and only those with particular characteristics or who live in particular circumstances are admitted, both policymakers and program staff may have to face considerable antagonism and loss of community support. This may explain why projects are underzealous in identifying target populations and selecting those with a definite, high probability of being at need or at risk.

PROCEDURES FOR TARGET ESTIMATION

A wide variety of techniques can be employed in order to estimate the scope of problems requiring new and refined intervention efforts, and to estimate the target population in ways that allow for the most effective deployment of available resources and staff. These techniques vary in their complexity and expense.

In selecting one or more techniques, the evaluator needs to be concerned with the trade-off between complexity and cost on the one hand and accuracy of the estimate obtained on the other. In selecting an approach, the evaluator must bear in mind the "good enough" theme we subscribe to and discuss at various points in this book. Take an extreme example: In African countries in which large numbers of persons living in confined areas can be seen to suffer from serious malnutrition, elaborate medical tests clearly are unnecessary. It is much more sensible to risk overidentification of the target population by simply counting the number residing in such camps and swiftly launching a program than to delay until such examinations are completed. In other instances, precise estimation may be called for before planning and implementing a program. For example, more precise estimation of the target population requiring hospital care in the United States could have avoided the surplus of general hospital beds found in most urban centers.

Several techniques for target estimation are discussed below. The procedures noted here are listed in ascending order of complexity and costs.

Key Informant Approach

The key informant approach is a simple and inexpensive informal survey technique that involves identifying, selecting, and questioning knowledgeable leaders and experts in order to construct estimates of target problems and populations. The technique provides a broad picture of the needs and services perceived as important and the characteristics of the population requiring them. It has the additional advantage of developing the support of community influentials, which may be necessary for project development and continuation.

The major limitation of the key informant approach is that it has the built-in biases of the individuals and organizations surveyed. It neglects the possibility that the characteristics of targets and the incidence and prevalence of the target problem may be perceived incorrectly by leaders and experts. Moreover, the perspectives of leaders and experts may be colored by their lack of intimate knowledge of all segments of what may be a complex society, and by their "interests." For example, a landlord's view of housing problems may be very different from the views of tenants.

The key informant approach works best when leaders and experts are asked for specific, concrete information. Thus, one is usually risking a biased perspective by asking leaders to list all the serious social problems in their communities. In contrast, asking an informant how many families are located within a block of public transportation lines usually will produce information less subject to upward or downward biases, especially if the person consulted is familiar with local public transportation services.

When using the key informant approach, it is good strategy to draw up a thorough list of potential interviewees prior to the start of interviewing. If the evaluators know the leaders and experts in a small community well, they might draw up a list of, say, 25 leaders. If they do not know the community sufficiently well, an alternative approach is to start with a smaller number of informants—say, 5 to 10—and to use a technique referred to as "snowballing." With this technique, the informant is asked at the end of the interview to provide the names of one or two persons who are also knowledgeable about the particular problem sector. Snowballing probably should not be carried beyond 50 interviews; after about this number, it is probably more cost-effective to undertake a community survey—a procedure to be discussed below.

The two main criteria for the selection of a key informant should be (1) knowledge of the community, its people, their needs, and the patterns of services already being received, and (2) leadership potential. The first criterion argues for interviewing local professionals and experts (teachers, doctors, nurses, local technical experts, civil servants, and the like) who, by virtue of their occupations, have contact with a range of persons, households, and conditions in an area. The second criterion is argued from the point of view of possible political benefit to the project. The use of leaders may provide project managers an opportunity to obtain their support, at best, and neutrality, at least. This may prove useful at the project implementation stage if the project meets with some potential opposition among the target population. Other criteria for the selection of a key informant may include his or her accessibility, whether he or she represents a particular subgroup or population, and whether he or she is a consumer or a potential consumer of the program.

With this technique, it is also useful to construct a data guide in advance—that is, a questionnaire that each informant is asked to complete or that is filled in after an informal discussion with the key informant (see Exhibit 3-F for an example). Using a data guide facilitates more rapid collating of the responses of the key informants and helps to standardize information from all informants. After all the informants have been contacted and interviewed, the information should be summarized and, if possible, put into tabular form. Sometimes it is valuable after the data are tabulated to provide feedback to the key informants, a step that allows checking the information and verifying the collated findings. It also provides a means of keeping the key informants involved in the planning and development of the program.

Unfortunately, there are few studies that compare different methods of obtaining diagnostic information. Deaux and Callaghan (1984) report a comparison of a random-digit dialed (RDD) telephone survey information on health-risk behavior (smoking, use of seat belts, and so on) of residents of New Mexico with similar information from key informants in the state. As summarized in Exhibit 3-F, they claim that the key informant approach has advantages over telephone surveys of residents.

Community Forum Approach

The community forum approach resembles an open town meeting—a gathering of members of a designated community organization or even an informal group. It is in part a technique to gain citizen involvement, but it is also a way to obtain estimates from a variety of individuals about the incidence and prevalence of particular problems and about the identifiable characteristics of the targets. The approach also can be used in gathering data on how well a delivery system is perceived to be working.

The utility of the community forum approach depends heavily on whether attendance at such open meetings constitutes a balanced representation of involved community members or targets, and whether participants feel free to express themselves openly. The technique may be superior to the key informant approach for obtaining valid information if the evaluators succeed in bringing together a cross section of the stakeholders. Often, this can be accomplished by having influential persons or respected organizations sponsor the meeting. Therefore, this technique is sometimes used as a follow-up to the key informant approach.

The forum approach is economical; it allows one to learn the perceptions and diagnoses of a large number of persons at relatively low cost. The limitations are fairly obvious, however. A forum may restrict the kinds of

Exhibit 3-F: Estimating Health-Risk Behavior

A statewide key informant survey of health-risk behavior was implemented in New Mexico at the same time that a random-digit dialed (RDD) telephone survey was conducted. The differences that were found to exist between the estimates made by the key informants and the self-reports of the telephone interviewees regarding health-related behavior reveal an apparent overreporting of positive—that is, healthy—behavior and underreporting of negative—that is, unhealthy behavior on the part of the telephone interviewers. Compared with key informants, a higher percentage of interviewees said that they always wore their seat belts; proportionately fewer reported being either over- or underweight; more, percentage-wise, claimed they participated in an active physical sport; a smaller proportion said they drove after too much to drink; and a small percentage said they smoked regularly. Through dissection of the findings and consideration of the direction of the differences, it became apparent that there were systematic response biases at play that account for the distorted results of the telephone survey.

In conclusion, the study has shown that the key informant approach, as implemented, produced prevalence estimates of health-risk behavior that are reliable and apparently more valid than those produced by a telephone survey. Additionally, the key informant approach involved one-third the number of respondents involved in the telephone survey. In the absence of a truly controlled experiment, in which the factual behavior of a sample is known and both types of estimates can be compared against objective measures, the authors conclude that the key informant approach is superior to the RDD telephone survey. It is recommended that it be used, particularly in instances where the behavior being assessed is inherently related to social values.

SOURCE: Adapted from E. Deaux and J. W. Callaghan, "Estimating Statewide Health-Risk Behavior: A Comparison of Telephone and Key Informant Survey Approaches," *Evaluation Review* 8 (August 1984): 467-492.

Exhibit 3-G: Suggested Interview Guide for Key Informant Approach to Assessing Community Mental Health Needs

Possible subjects to discuss with each person interviewed:

I. Community Problems (general)
   • In order of priority of importance.
   • Existing sources of help for each problem.
   • Unmet needs and problems, by groups.
   • Who gets most consistently left out of services?
   • Which problems are not visible?

II. Mental Health Problems
   • A priority listing of seriousness (including prevalence).
   • Existing sources of help for each problem.
   • Community attitudes toward use of public mental health services.
   • Groups that get most mental health services.
   • Groups that are most underserved.

III. Attitudes toward the CMHC
   (community mental health center)
   • Who gets to the CMHC for help?
   • What other mental health resources do people in the community use? Who uses them?
   • Who does not/will not go to the CMHC and why?
   • Which groups in need of mental health services get the least help? (Locate these as possible on a map of community.)

SOURCE: National Institute of Mental Health, *A Working Manual of Simple Program Evaluation Techniques for Community Mental Health Centers.* Washington, DC: Government Printing Office, 1976, p. 107.

information persons will reveal. It may also hinder expressions of views to those who are most likely to participate, and probably discourages individuals who perceive themselves as less powerful in the community from offering information and perspectives. A forum may become an arena in which local political cleavages are manifested, and thereby may lead to more rancor than data.

The forum technique is most effective when program objectives and delivery system operations can be stated explicitly in ways understandable to the forum group. Otherwise, the information received may prove to be valuable in terms of general need assessment but may not provide estimates of the extent of a particular problem and the characteristics of the targets. Sometimes, in order to obtain a wider cross section than one can expect from a general forum, an effort is made to develop several meetings of the same kind but with varying, carefully defined and selected populations. For example, in communities with several religious groups, separate meetings might be held at different places of worship under the sponsorship of local religious leaders.

The strictures on use applying to the key informant approach also apply to the community forum approach. The potential for biased estimates of need, size, and extent of target populations is considerable. This technique should be used only to supplement other methods, to build up supportive consensus for a program, or in the absence of enough resources to employ some of the better methods we describe in the following sections.

Rates under Treatment Approach

The commonly used rates under treatment approach estimates target populations via the services utilized for the same target problem in a similar community. The assumption underlying this approach is that the characteristics of the desired target population and its size will closely parallel the attributes of those who have already received treatment. Sometimes, particularly in communities where there have been no previous interventions, estimates may be derived from one or more geographical areas that resemble the proposed project site. If areas can be found in which the social and cultural properties of the individuals mirror those in the project areas, it is possible to derive estimates of target populations in terms of size and characteristics.

It is almost certain that estimates derived from the rates under treatment approach will be biased downward. Ongoing projects rarely attain full coverage of a target population; therefore, any given project's clientele will be a selected subset of the target population. The selection may be forced by the scarcity of funds or by the failure of target populations to make use of the services offered. It may make sense in certain circumstances to regard such estimates as the lower bounds of the estimated size of a target population and to adjust them accordingly.

For example, the Uniform Crime Reports, published by the Department of Justice, are based on crimes reported to the police. The figures are then transmitted to the Federal Bureau of Investigation. The crime rates printed in these reports are, in principle, "rates under treatment" indices, expressing "cases" that have received some treatment (i.e., investigation) by local police departments. When these rates are compared with crimes reported in victimization surveys (in which persons are asked about crimes they have experienced as victims), it becomes obvious that the Uniform Crime Reports significantly underestimate the total number of crimes in which a victim is involved. This underestimation occurs in part because some crimes are not reported to the police and in part because the police do not faithfully pass on to the FBI correct figures for all crimes reported to them. Actually, both the Uniform Crime Reports and victimization studies underestimate the "true" crime rate, for there is only partial overlap between the criminal encounters reported by means of each approach. Thus, if a precise estimate of the crime rate is required, it is wise to use multiple approaches to its measurement so that one can "triangulate" on the crime rate (Reiss, 1985).

In many ways, the use of service statistics and the opportunities to abstract information from records of treated populations appear to provide an attractive way to estimate target population. Rates under treatment are also used to estimate the extent of coverage of existing programs. For example, if unemployment information provides an estimate of 5000 unemployed persons between the ages of 18 and 25 in a particular community, but statistics reveal only 250 persons in this age range currently enrolled in the community's work training programs, it is clear that the programs must be modified.

A number of important cautions must be noted, however. In many interventions, the service records and statistics derived from them are unreliable. It is evident that some agencies regard the maintenance of records as a low-priority activity, particularly when there are strenuous demands for services. Also, because projects receive both economic and political support by demonstrating a large client population, there may be an effort to exaggerate the need for services and the extent of services rendered. Sometimes this is purposeful and other times it is generated more or less unconsciously from the enthusiasm of providers for their particular project.

Indicators Approach

Many federal, state, and community offices maintain relatively good statistical series that may be used as the basis for estimating target populations. Such series include data on trends in fertility, mortality, and the incidence of certain diseases; economic indicators of unemployment and personal and household income; and information on crime, poverty, and juvenile delinquency. In the United States, data are available on the population and housing composition of states, local political jurisdictions (cities, towns, counties), and census tracts within urbanized areas. They can be obtained as published summaries or in the form of computer tapes for public use. Myers and Rockwell (1984) provide valuable information on who produces data bases relevant to diagnosing problems, how to obtain them, and what they contain. In addition to their discussion of ways of locating time-series information, they identify and describe twenty of the most important federally sponsored statistical time series.

For social problems that are defined in terms for which census data are relevant, the decennial census can provide excellent information for need assessments and for the location of target populations. For instance, it is possible to use the census to obtain counts of persons and households by race, age, socioeconomic status, and condition of housing. For standard metropolitan statistical areas (SMSAs, defined as cities and surrounding counties with populations of 50,000 or more), data are available for census tracts—areas that average eight square miles and contain about 4,000 people. Exhibit 3-H describes the use of the census to produce estimates of the target population for the Upward Bound and Talent Search projects.

Whether or not one can use census data in either published or unpublished form depends on how quickly the data become obsolete over time and on how relevant the data series is. In areas that have experienced considerable growth and change in population through immigration, census data can become outdated within a few years, and hence may be useless for target population estimates.

Indicators do have another value, however. They are usually time series. Time-series data derive from observations made at regular intervals so that the trends of incidence and prevalence of particular problems can be assessed (Federal Statistical System, 1976). Sudden and sharp changes in these indicators often signal the emergence of phenomena that require action programs. For example, given that there is a known correlation between unemployment and suicide rates, and the time-series data on unemployment point to a sharp rise in the number of unemployed workers, it can be anticipated that, likewise, there will be a marked increase in the number of persons who may want the services of a suicide intervention unit.

Most of the data series of interest to persons dealing with social problems may be available only for very large geographic units—the nation as a whole, states, or SMSAs. Social indicator data for areas within cities or counties may have to be constructed by collating data from the agencies that collect such information (e.g., city health departments). Often the collation of such materials and the computation of rates for various peri-

Exhibit 3-H: Estimating the Target Population of Upward Bound and Educational Talent Search Programs with Census Data

The purpose of the study was to estimate the size of the UB (Upward Bound) and ETS (Educational Talent Search) target population, and to describe its composition with respect to personal and demographic characteristics. In this study the target population was defined to include all persons from 14 to 24 years old in 1970, whose highest grade attended in school was between grade 6 and grade 12, and whose family income in 1969 was below the poverty cutoff. Persons included in the target population were further classified according to the United States Office of Education (USOE) region and state of their residence, sex, ethnoracial background, and school enrollment status.

Data contained in the 1970 Census of Population records indicated that the UB and ETS target population contained 3,880,000 persons, or 2 percent of the U.S. population in 1970. The target population contained 2.1 million women and 1.8 million men and its ethnoracial composition included 54 percent whites, 36 percent blacks, 10 percent of Spanish descent, and less than 1 percent persons of other ethnoracial backgrounds. In 1970, 2.1 million persons in the target population were enrolled in school between grades 6 and 12, and 1.8 million were not enrolled in school. Geographically, the largest number of persons in the target population were in USOE Region IV, which contained 1,051,200 persons or 27 percent of the total target population, followed by USOE Region VI, with 627,200 or 16 percent of the total target population.

The target population was estimated from a 1-in-100 sample of the 1970 Census of Population basic records, but the aggregate estimates remain valid in terms of this study's objective, even though the size of the national target population declined 13 percent from 1970 to 1974.

SOURCE: Adapted, with permission, from D. H. Stuart and A. M. Cruze, *Estimates of the Target Population for Upward Bound and Talent Search Programs.* Research Triangle Park, NC: Research Triangle Institute, 1976.

ods is time-consuming and costly. Hence, unless time series are readily available in published form, the attempt to construct them for a particular local community may not be efficient or feasible.

In the past several years, concern has been expressed that federal time series are being suspended foolishly (Chelimsky, 1985). In part, this is a consequence of efforts to reduce research costs within federal departments. In part it is because some time series are outdated and, rather than undertake their modification, the departments involved have simply halted them. Evaluation researchers have a stake in maintaining—with appropriate modernization, of course—extant time series. Indeed, estimation of target populations and changes in the characteristics of these populations is crucial to diagnostic activities for planning, implementing, and evaluating the impact of large-scale—for instance, national—social programs.

Surveys and Censuses

The most direct and usually the most accurate data on target problems and populations can be obtained by conducting special censuses or sample surveys in which the best measurement techniques are used and estimates are derived under the most rigorous conditions. A *census* may be defined as a complete enumeration of a population of units (individuals, households, firms, and so on) in which relevant characteristics of the units are obtained. In contrast, a *sample survey* may be defined as measurements applied to a sample of units in a population, with the sample drawn in a way that minimizes bias in the selection of units. Clearly, there is a close relationship between censuses and sample surveys, since they share measurement problems and strive to provide estimates about populations.

Sample surveys are preferred to censuses for two main reasons: First, they are considerably less expensive; second, when properly conducted they provide estimates of population characteristics to any desired degree of accuracy within calculable limits of sampling error. In addition, surveys usually can be conducted with greater care, minimizing error of measurement. It should be noted that surveys need not be restricted to the study of individuals. Sample surveys can be conducted with households or larger organized groups as units, or with physical entities, such as dwellings, businesses, agricultural plots, and roads.

The science and art of sample survey research are well explicated (Rossi et al., 1982; Sudman, 1976). Methodologies exist for careful sampling and appropriate interview instrument construction. Surveys use standard measurements to determine the prevalence and incidence of certain problems. For example, a survey schedule might include a checklist measuring the quality of housing; or it may include items and tests to measure functional literacy of family members, the levels of health disabil-

Exhibit 3-I: National Childcare Consumer Study

The data gathered in this survey represent the most comprehensive examination to date of the current patterns of childcare use in the United States. The data were collected from a stratified national probability sample of approximately 4,600 households with children 13 years of age or younger. Nonwhite and low-income households were oversampled in order to guarantee their inclusion. The survey identifies the following nine modes of care: (1) in-home care by a relative; (2) in-home care by a nonrelative; (3) other home care by a relative; (4) other home care by a nonrelative; (5) nursery and preschool care; (6) daycare centers; (7) cooperative programs; (8) before-and-after-school care programs; and (9) Head Start. A distinction is also made between "market care," for which cash is paid or a government subsidy provided, and "nonmarket care," which is provided without a fee or in trade.

Nine out of ten households with children under 14 report using one of the forms of care listed here. It is worth noting that multiple arrangements for care are quite common. One in three households uses only one method of care, while the remaining two-thirds use at least two methods.

The National Childcare Consumer Study is particularly rich in enumerating the factors that influence a household's selection of its mode of childcare. The importance of various types of services provided by alternative modes—or, put in a demand framework, the characteristics of the good that influence choice—are discussed in some detail. The report is also properly circumspect in pointing out that consumer attitudes often lack concreteness, particularly when some of the questions are interpreted as hypothetical by some or all respondents. Given this caveat together with the fact that the data are not analyzed in a manner that holds other factors constant, it is worth noting that most consumers at least purport to select care for preschoolers for child-oriented reasons rather than their own convenience. The validity of this result remains questionable, but if confirmed by more vigorous analysis of the data, it—together with the result that most households use a nonmarket mode of care—will give us some insight into how preferences are formed and then exercised in the market for childcare.

SOURCE: Adapted, with permission, from UNCO, Inc., *National Childcare Consumer Study*, 1975.

Exhibit 3-J: Usefulness of the Denver Developmental Screening Test

The Denver Developmental Screening Test (DDST) was administered to 2500 children five to seven months prior to their starting kindergarten in September 1980 in a geographically well-defined community. The test was administered by trained public health nurses. At the end of the 1980-1981 school year, all 163 kindergarten teachers in the area completed a rating form for each child in their classes. The rating form obtained global ratings of (1) learning abilities, (2) classroom behavior, (3) amount of special attention required, and (4) referrals to special education services outside the classroom. The specificity of the DDST in predicting kindergarten teacher ratings was 99 percent for all areas. Test sensitivity varied from 5 percent to 10 percent in detecting problems in the four areas. These results based on kindergarten teacher ratings suggest that because of the low sensitivity, the DDST may be relatively inefficient to use in a school entry screening program in a general community population of children.

SOURCE: Adapted, with permission, from D. Cadman et al., "The Usefulness of the Denver Developmental Screening Test to Predict Kindergarten Problems in a General Community Population." *American Journal of Public Health,* Vol. 75 (October 1984): 1093-1097.

ity, and the like. These kinds of measures, along with characteristics such as length of residence and family income, allow estimation of target populations with considerable accuracy. Minimum requirements for an adequate sample survey include a sound sampling procedure, a well-prepared and pretested interview schedule or observation guide, and well-trained interviewers or enumerators who are familiar with the area being surveyed and who will not be perceived as intruders.

Surveys can be expensive and technically demanding. Hence, sample surveys should be undertaken only when there is adequate justification for the costs involved and when appropriately trained personnel are available. Most sample surveys, even of small populations, require months of preparation and, in order to provide important and useful predictive information, need to be large scale. In general, surveys of fewer than 1000 interviews or observations will rarely be useful; larger surveys are often

Exhibit 3-K: A Sample Survey for a Small Area

A sample of low-income families living in Brookline, Massachusetts, during 1964 who had at least one child in the local public or parochial high schools was drawn using health records kept in the schools in question. Preliminary selection of families was made on the basis of information in school records, and a final determination was made after interviews and sometimes credit checks verified the low-income status of the family and the occupation of household head. A sample of 806 households was drawn.

The purpose of the survey was to obtain a group of families that would be likely to use a public dental clinic. Interviews were undertaken with each family to ascertain the current patterns of dental care for members of the family. Dental examinations were made in school of those teenaged children in the family still attending school to ascertain the dental-care needs of the low-income families, assuming that the children involved reasonably represented the health-care status of the families from which they were drawn.

SOURCE: Summary, by permission, of C. Lambert, Jr., and H. E. Freeman, *The Clinic Habit*. New Haven, CT: The New College and University Press, 1967.

necessary to estimate the incidence or prevalence of relatively rare phenomena.

Exhibit 3-I illustrates the use of a sample survey conducted among families with children under 13 years old still living in the household. The purpose of the study was to estimate the need for child-care facilities as well as to estimate the usage of various types of child-care arrangements for households of this type in the United States as of 1975. While few evaluation researchers may need to estimate target populations for the United States as a whole, the same principles apply to sample surveys of smaller areas or even within institutions. Exhibit 3-K illustrates the use of sample surveys for smaller areas, in this case Brookline, Massachusetts.

The selection of target characteristics should be based on a combination of knowledge from previous research and practice, experience, and information obtained when determining the size of the population at need, demand, or risk. Often, after criteria are decided, additional procedures may be undertaken to check on the utility of such target selection characteristic decisions. For example, an educational project for literacy training may have as its definition of appropriate targets all community members between 16 and 60 years of age with less than four years of schooling. An estimate of 10 percent functional illiteracy for a community of 2000 adults may have come from a key informant survey. A sample survey would provide data on whether or not using a fourth-grade definition yields one potential target for each ten interviewed.

THE IMPORTANCE OF DIAGNOSTIC EVALUATIONS

It is clear that specification and selection of the target population need to be explicit and based on easily detectable and accurately measurable characteristics. From a program management viewpoint, without such specification it is virtually impossible to undertake a successful intervention. Further, unless diagnosis is well accomplished, neither monitoring nor utility evaluations are likely to be of use.

As every angler knows, there is little chance of catching fish—indeed, of selecting the right bait and tackle—unless one knows what kind of fish are running and the right depth at which to sink the line. So, too, the best intentions to better human conditions will do no good unless program staff and/or evaluators can specify the targets precisely and select them efficiently.

4

Program Monitoring and Accountability

The monitoring of programs is directed at two key questions: (1) whether or not the program is reaching the appropriate target population, and (2) whether or not the delivery of services is consistent with program design specifications. There are several reasons monitoring of programs is required. First, monitoring provides program managers with information on which to base judgment of the operational performance of their programs, so that they can make needed changes in the ways day-to-day activities are conducted. Second, monitoring information is required for accountability purposes; stakeholders and sponsors are continually concerned with the question, "Who is getting what, and how?" Third, monitoring evaluations generally are a necessary adjunct to impact assessments, since the failure of programs often is due to faulty or incomplete implementation of interventions rather than ineffectiveness of the treatments themselves. Fourth, monitoring information may be either the sole basis for judging program impact or a supplement to utility assessments; thus monitoring evaluations often are instrumental in decisions to continue, expand, or terminate ongoing programs.

KEY CONCEPTS

Access Strategy:	Plan for reaching and providing services to a target population.
Accountability:	The responsibility of program staff to provide evidence to sponsors and superordinate units of conformity to program coverage, treatment, legal requirements, and fiscal requirements.
Bias:	The extent to which a program is participated in differentially by subgroups of a target population.
Coverage:	The extent to which a program is reaching its intended target population.
Management Information System:	A system, usually computerized, that provides information on a routine basis about the delivery of services to specific clients; often includes information required for payment of services, social and demographic information, and treatment results.
Process Studies:	A general term referring to evaluation activities related to target identification and assessment of the appropriateness of services delivered.
Program Elements:	Identifiable and discrete intervention activities.
Service Delivery:	Procedures and organizational arrangements actually employed to deliver services to appropriate targets.

After signing a new bill, President Kennedy is reputed to have said to his aides, "Now that this bill is the law of the land, let's hope we can get our government to carry it out." If a president of the United States could express skeptical concern about the implementation of federal mandates, how much more uncertain is the carrying out of specific programs? Indeed, whether or not any program is carried out with full attention to the aims of its sponsors and program staff—reaching the population intended to benefit from the program and delivering the services that were mandated—is always problematic.

This chapter takes up the issues involved in monitoring implementation. By *program monitoring,* we mean the systematic attempt to measure both *program coverage,* the extent to which a program is reaching its intended target population, and *program process,* the extent to which the service being provided matches what was intended to be delivered. Together, program coverage and program process are often known as *program outputs,* that is, the products and services that are being delivered to the appropriate beneficiaries. Note that outputs are not to be confused with *outcomes;* the latter refers to the effects of outputs on targets, that is, impact. (For extended discussion of the problems of and research on implementation, see Williams and Elmore, 1976; Williams, 1980; Pressman and Wildavsky, 1973.)

THE USES OF MONITORING

The monitoring of program implementation is an activity that is undertaken at many different points in the development of programs and in the management of enacted programs. Program monitoring is particularly vital to the development process, when programs are tested and refined. Program designers need to know what problems are encountered in implementation so that changes may be made in program design to overcome such obstacles. No matter how well planned an innovative program may be, unexpected results and unwanted side effects often rapidly surface in the course of early implementation. For example, a medical clinic that is intended to help working mothers and is open only during daylight hours may discover that however much demand there may be for clinic services, such hours effectively screen out those who work during the day. A program predicated on the prevalence of severe psychological problems among acting-out children in school may quickly find that most such children do not have deep disorders but superficial ones instead; hence, the program needs to be modified accordingly.

The results of program monitoring are also essential in providing data for program diffusion. In order to be able to reproduce the essential features of an intervention in places other than where it originated, one must be able to describe the program in operational detail. Critical points in implementation must be identified, solutions to managerial problems outlined, qualifications of successful program personnel documented, and so on. Good program development includes producing manuals that detail administrative procedures, service delivery, necessary qualifications of personnel, and the like. The results of program monitoring at the development stage can be used profitably in the preparation of such manuals.

For programs that are beyond the development stage and in actual operation, program monitoring serves management needs by providing information on coverage and process, and hence feedback on whether the program is meeting specifications. Fine-tuning of a program may be necessary when monitoring information indicates that targets are not being reached, or that outputs cost more than initially projected, or that staff workloads are either too heavy or too light. Program managers who neglect to monitor a program systematically risk the danger of administering a program that is markedly different from its mandate.

Finally, without monitoring activities, it usually is not possible to satisfy program sponsors, who are obligated to defend the ways they allocate resources. For example, staff of private foundations require monitoring information so that they can explain and defend the ways funds have been allocated to their boards, and also to meet requirements of the Internal Revenue Service about the proper use of their monies. Then, too, stakeholders of programs also need to have their questions answered about the ways programs are implemented and delivered. In the case of federal programs, for example, the Freedom of Information Act requires public disclosure of such information. Stakeholders include the targets themselves. A dramatic example of this occurred when President Reagan called an artificial heart transplant patient to wish him well, and the patient complained, with all of the country listening, about not receiving his social security check.

CURRENT STATUS OF PROGRAM MONITORING

In previous periods, what might be referred to as monitoring for "outcome evaluation" purposes and monitoring for either "management" or "accountability" purposes were often thought of as discrete activities. Monitoring as part of outcome evaluation has as its main purpose to ascertain how a program was actually carried out in order to link program inputs to program outcomes. Monitoring for management and accountability purposes is directed at maximizing productivity and organizational effectiveness. In some cases, persons engaged in outcome evaluations insisted on doing independent monitoring, even though the program management staffs were deeply involved in their own monitoring activities. The reverse also has occurred: Program staff would not pay any attention to monitoring information provided by outside evaluation teams, even when it was freely provided to them in a timely fashion. These types of situations, in particular, occurred in innovative, experimental demonstration projects, in part as a consequence of the extensive mistrust between program staff and outside evaluators.

Today, there is much more convergence of activities and much less distinction between monitoring for management and outcome evaluation purposes. In part this is the case because evaluation has become a much more institutionalized, ongoing activity, and is typically accepted by program staff. In part it is related to the increased willingness of evaluators, particularly "inside" evaluators, to share their monitoring findings with program staff in order to effect program improvements.

An important reason for the convergence between the two types of monitoring efforts has been the adoption of the concept of management information systems, or MISs. As will be discussed in more detail below, these systems, usually computerized, routinely provide information on a client-by-client basis about services provided, staff providing the services, outcome of treatments, diagnosis or reasons for program participation, social demographic information, costs of treatment, and so on. Some of the systems may bill clients, issue payments for services to outside providers, and store other information, such as past history of treatment and current participation in other programs.

In terms of social program management, MISs provide systematic, continuing data on what is happening within a program, answering periodically or when queried such questions as the following: How many persons are being reached by the program and what are their characteristics? How many "units of service" are being delivered? How are funds being expended? How long do persons remain in the program? The purpose of a well-designed management information system is to provide program managers and staff with detailed, periodic reports on how well the program is functioning and to alert them to delivery problems as they arise so that corrective action may be taken. At the same time, of course, they can provide much of the information required to monitor interventions, with the objective of learning whether impact results can be attributed to target selection, program implementation, or both.

MISs were first implemented in large-scale programs involving a number of sites and large amounts of resources. Computer technology has advanced, however, to the point where fairly large social programs can make use of personal computers for their management information systems. Also, the costs of access even to large computers has been reduced considerably; in addition, software for the implementation of MISs has advanced greatly in recent years.

TYPES OF PROGRAM ACCOUNTABILITY

In today's world, program-monitoring information is critical for those who sponsor and fund programs—the levels above day-to-day program management. Are programs' funds being expended properly? Are the designated target populations being reached? How much of the intended service is actually being delivered? Indeed, it appears that for Congress, at least as far as national educational programs are concerned, program-monitoring information is often as important as or more important than information on program impact (Raizen and Rossi, 1981). Furthermore, stakeholders, in addition to funders and sponsors, press for program accountability. In the face of increased concern about the expenditures of public funds for social programs because of the personal stake of taxpayers in such expenditures, and in light of increased competition for all social program resources because of the cuts in available funding, concerned parties are constantly scrutinizing programs they support and those they do not in order to have an "edge" in seeking support. The marked emphasis on accountability activities in recent years has resulted in what Carter (1983) has termed the "accountable agency."

From a monitoring perspective, accountability takes several of the forms we have already listed in Chapter 2.

- *Coverage Accountability:* Are the persons served those who are designated as targets? Are there beneficiaries who should not be served?

- *Service Delivery Accountability:* Are proper amounts of outputs being delivered? Are the treatments delivered those the program is supposed to be delivering?

- *Fiscal Accountability:* Are funds being used properly? Are expenditures properly documented? Are funds used within the limits set by the budget?

- *Legal Accountability:* Are relevant laws being observed by the program, including those concerning affirmative action, occupational safety and health, and privacy of individual records?

The issues of fiscal and legal accountability are perhaps best left to professionals in these areas. Whether proper accounting procedures are being followed and whether the requirements of state and/or federal laws are being honored are issues requiring the know-how of the accounting and legal professions, and it is generally inadvisable for social research-trained evaluators to undertake such efforts by themselves. Typically, coverage and treatment accountability issues are most relevant to the monitoring of implementation from a social research perspective.

While management-oriented monitoring (including use of information systems) and program accountability studies often are concerned with the same questions, they are differentiated by the purposes to which their evaluation information is to be put. Management information systems typically are designed to detect, on an ongoing basis, faults that need to be corrected by program staffs. Accountability studies primarily provide information that decision makers, sponsors, and other stakeholders need to judge the appropriateness of program activities and to decide whether or not they should support having a program continued, expanded, or contracted. Accountability studies may use the same information base employed by program management staff, but they usually are conducted in a critical spirit. In contrast, management-oriented monitoring activities are concerned less with making decisive judgments and more with incorporating corrective measures as a regular part of program operations. In Exhibit 4-A, the importance of patterns of use—or, as they sometimes are called, client utilization studies—is elaborated by Landsberg (1983).

Some commentators on evaluation activities (Cronbach et al., 1980) hold that impact results are not so much a product of program management as they are a product of program design, which usually is not in the hands of program managers. Their view, therefore, is that program managers should be held responsible primarily for coverage, treatment, and fiscal integrity.

We agree that program managers should be accountable for delivery of services to the target population. We turn first to procedures for monitoring coverage and then to those that are used in the monitoring process.

TARGET POPULATIONS AND PROGRAM COVERAGE

As stated in the previous chapter, it is essential to define target populations carefully. But doing so is useless unless there also is a procedure for determining the extent to which the actual participation of targets takes place. This is particularly essential for the large number of interventions in which program acceptance and participation are voluntary. For example, community mental health centers designed to provide a broad range of services often fail to attract a reasonable number of persons who may benefit from these services. Even many patients recently discharged from

Exhibit 4-A: Program and Service Utilization Studies

Any service organization, especially in an era of shrinking resources, needs to evaluate its services and activities. Through these evaluative activities, an organization can develop and maintain the flexibility needed to respond to an ever-changing environment. It has been suggested that, even in an ideal world, an organization needs to be self-evaluating. Self-evaluation requires an organization to review its own activities and goals continuously and to use the results to modify, if necessary, its programs, goals, and directions.

Within the agency, the essential function of evaluation is to provide data on goal achievement and program effectiveness to a primary audience consisting of administration, middle management, and governing board. This primary audience, especially the administration and board, is frequently confronted with inquiries from important sources in the external environment, such as legislators and funding agencies. These inquiries often focus on issues of client utilization, accessibility, continuity, comprehension, outcome or effectiveness, and cost.

The building block of this information is the pattern of use or the client utilization study. The pattern of use study, whether it consists of simple inquiries or is highly detailed, sophisticated investigation, is basically a description. It describes who uses services and how, and it becomes evaluative when it is related to the requirements or purposes of the organization.

SOURCE: G. Landsberg, "Program Utilization and Service Utilization Studies: A Key Tool for Evaluation." *New Directions in Program Evaluation* 20 (December 1983): 93-94. Reprinted by permission.

mental hospitals, who have been encouraged to make use of the services of community mental health centers after discharge, often fail to contact the centers (Rossi, 1978).

Attracting Targets

In general, any intervention or treatment that requires participants to learn new procedures, change existing habits, or take instruction may encounter difficulties in attracting target groups. Hence, whether or not a program is reaching its target units, those with specified and appropriate characteristics, needs to be verified with monitoring evaluations.

The issue of the extent to which the target population is participating in a project concerns both project managers and program sponsors. Efficient project management requires accurate and timely information on target participation, especially for the many cases in which modification of project procedures may be required if target participation is not at the desired level. From the viewpoint of program managers, target participation is a critical measure of a project's vitality and ultimate effectiveness.

Target participation issues are often neglected in the development phase of new programs, when it is assumed that targets are necessarily motivated to participate. This may not be the case: In the Housing Allowance Demand Experiments (Kennedy, 1960; Struyk and Bendick, 1981), less than a third of the eligible families approached participated in one of the treatments, which required families to rent housing that met certain standards. Similarly, a program designed to provide information to prospective homebuyers might find that few persons seek the services offered. Hence, program developers need to be concerned with how best to motivate potential targets to seek out the program and participate in it. In some cases, this may require that outreach efforts be built into the program; in other cases, it might require special geographical placement of program personnel; and so on.

Coverage and Bias

The issues of target population participation consist of problems of coverage and bias. By *coverage,* we mean the extent to which a program obtains target population participation, as specified in program design. *Bias* is the degree to which subgroups of the designated target population participate differentially. A bias in the coverage of a program simply means that some subgroups are being covered more thoroughly than others. Bias can arise out of self-selection—some subgroups voluntarily participating more frequently than others. It can also derive from program actions: For instance, program personnel may tend to show favor to some clients and to reject others. One pressure commonly faced by programs is to select the most "success-prone" targets; this frequently occurs because of the self-interests of one or more stakeholders. A dramatic example of such "creaming" is described in Exhibit 4-B. Finally, bias may result from such unforeseen influences as the location of a program office, which may encourage greater participation by a target subgroup for which access to program activities is more convenient.

In testing programs, bias usually constitutes a serious threat to the validity of impact assessments. Especially critical is the differential participation of experimental groups receiving the new treatments and untreated control groups who are also observed in order to assess the impact of the intervention. In many impact assessments, control group members drop

Exhibit 4-B: "Creaming"

When administrators who provide public services choose to provide a disproportionate share of program benefits to the most advantaged segment of the population they serve, they provide grist for the mill of implementation research. The U.S. Employment Service (USES) offers a clear and significant example of creaming, a practice that has survived half a century of USES expansion, contraction, and reorganization.

It is hardly surprising that USES administrators, a generation after the establishment of the program, stressed the necessity rather than the desirability of an employer-centered service. Its success, by design, depended on serving employers, not the "hard-core" unemployed. As President Johnson's task force on urban employment problems noted some two weeks before the 1967 Watts riots, "We have yet to make any significant progress in reaching and helping the truly 'hard-core' disadvantaged."

SOURCE: Adapted from David B. Robertson "Program Implementation Versus Program Design." *Policy Studies Review*, Vol. 3 (May 1984): 391-405.

out more frequently than those receiving treatments in experimental groups. (See Chapter 6, where this issue of coverage in testing programs is discussed in more detail.)

Clearly, coverage and bias are related: A program that reaches all projected participants and no others obviously is not biased in its coverage. However, as few social programs ever enjoy total, exact coverage, bias is typically an issue.

It is usually thought desirable that a large proportion of intended targets be served by a program. The exception, of course, is when the resources of a project are too limited to provide the appropriate treatments to all potential target units. In this case, however, the target definition during planning and program development probably was not narrow enough. This problem can be corrected by sharper definition of the characteristics of the target population and by more effective employment of resources. For example, the establishment of a health center that provides medical services to persons without regular sources of care may result in so overwhelming a demand for services that limited resources and facilities make it impossible for many of those wanting to participate to receive care.

Under such circumstances, adding eligibility criteria that take into account severity of the health problem, family size, age, and income could reduce the size of the target population to manageable proportions.

The most common coverage problem in social interventions is that full target participation is not achieved, either because there is bias in recruiting participants from the specified group or because potential clients reject the treatment. For example, the Housing Allowance Experiments recently completed experienced low participation rates: Only 30 to 40 percent of the eligible groups have become involved, despite the apparently obvious advantages of participating in the experiment (Carlson and Heinberg, 1977; Struyk and Bendick, 1981).

However, there are examples of overcoverage: The *Sesame Street* program has consistently captured audiences that have far exceeded the number of originally intended targets, namely, disadvantaged preschoolers. Other audiences, including children who are not disadvantaged and even adults, have been attracted to the program. Fortunately, since these additional audiences are reached at no additional cost, this inappropriate coverage does not create a financial drain on the program. However, it also turns out that the advantaged children who view the program benefit more than do the disadvantaged viewers (Cook et al., 1975). Since one of *Sesame Street*'s goals was to lessen the gap in learning between advantaged and disadvantaged children, the program's success in reaching a much wider audience than intended has exacerbated one of the problems it sought to remedy.

In other instances, inappropriate coverage can be costly. The bilingual programs sponsored and funded by the Department of Education have been found to include many students whose primary language is English. School systems whose funding from the program depends on numbers of children enrolled in bilingual classes have been known to inflate attendance figures by registering inappropriate students (Raizen and Rossi, 1981). In some cases, it has been shown that schools have also used assignment to bilingual instruction as a means of ridding some classes of "problem children," resulting in bilingual classes with disproportionate numbers of disciplinary cases.

Measuring Coverage

Program staffs and sponsors need to be concerned with both undercoverage and overcoverage. *Undercoverage* is commonly measured by determining the proportion of the targets in need of a program that do not participate in it. *Overcoverage* is measured in two ways. Sometimes the number of program participants not in need is compared with the total number not in need in the designated target population. At other times, the number of participants not in need is compared with the total number of participants in a program. Generally it is the latter figure that is important; efficient use of program resources requires minimizing both the number served who are in need and the number not in need who are served. Efficiency of coverage may be measured by the following formula:

$$\text{coverage efficiency} = 100 \times \left[\frac{\text{number in need served}}{\text{total number in need}} - \frac{\text{number not in need served}}{\text{total number served}} \right]$$

The formula yields a positive value of 100 when the actual number served equals the designated target population in need and no inappropriate targets are served. A negative value of 100 occurs if only inappropriate targets are served. Positive and negative values between +100 and −100 indicate the degree of coverage efficiency. For example, if in a particular geographical area it is estimated that 100 targets need a program but in the actual group of 100 served only 70 are appropriate targets, the value obtained by the above formula would be +40. If 100 targets need a program, and only 10 of the 100 in it are appropriate targets, the value obtained would be −80.

The formula provides a means of estimating the trade-offs in a program including inappropriate as well as appropriate targets. A program manager confronted with a −80 value might impose additional selection criteria eliminating 70 of the 90 inappropriate targets and, by an extensive recruitment campaign, secure 70 appropriate replacements. The coverage efficiency value then would be +60. If the program was inexpensive or it was either politically unwise or too difficult to impose additional selection criteria to eliminate undercoverage, the manager might elect the option of expanding the program to include all appropriate targets. Assuming the same proportion of inappropriate targets are also served, however, the total number participating would be 1000!

The problem of measuring coverage is almost always the inability to specify the number in need or the magnitude of the target population. The activities described in Chapter 2, if carried out as an integral part of program planning, usually minimize this problem. In addition, three approaches may be used to assess the extent to which the appropriate target population has been served by a particular program: use of records, surveys of program participants, and community surveys.

Use of Records

Almost all programs are required to keep records on targets served. Such information is generally useful in accounting for the time of project staff and resources expended. There is great variation in the quality and extensiveness of records and in the sophistication involved in their storage and maintenance. Moreover, the feasibility of maintaining complete, ongoing record systems for all program participants varies with the nature of the treatment and available resources. Sophisticated computerized management and client information systems, for example, have been developed for medical and mental health systems (Gall and Norwood, 1977). Exhibit 4-C illustrates the use of records to describe participants in a food stamp program. A management information system for a small demonstration project is described in Exhibit 4-D. While this system was developed initially as an aid in describing project activities for the purposes of evaluation, project managers also used the results to retain service workers so that they could deliver outputs more appropriate to the problems presented by targets.

In measuring target participation, the main concern is that the data are accurate and reliable. A number of procedures can be undertaken to ensure accuracy. Perhaps the most important is to develop a record system that is simple enough not to become burdensome to program staff and yet comprehensive enough to meet evaluation needs. There is often as much risk in developing an overextensive record-keeping system as there is in having one that contains too little information. Failure to think through information requirements may result in a system that is partially ignored because it is cumbersome, tedious, or time-consuming to use.

On the other side of this coin, it is important not only that appropriate forms and other record-keeping instruments are constructed, but also that program staff receive adequate training in the skills and terms associated with their use. For example, if a participant's occupation at the time of program admission is an important criterion for defining the target population, then staff instruction on the recording of detailed occupational information is essential for record-keeping purposes. Moreover, continual training and retraining, as well as initial instruction, are usually necessary to keep staff apprised of developments affecting record-keeping and to maintain their skills. This may involve checking samples of records against their authoritative sources and noting errors of commission and omission.

Another procedure for ensuring reliability involves quality-control checks on a sampling basis. This may be done by having several project staff members complete the same set of records independently and checking the consistency from staff member to staff member of the information logged. Finally, information obtained from program records may be compared with other available data. For instance, a family planning program may compare its records with those of a local clinic or hospital.

Exhibit 4-C: Description of Food Stamp Program Participants

A national sample (over 10,500) was drawn from homemakers in the U.S. Department of Agriculture (USDA) Extension Service's Expanded Food and Nutrition Education Program (EFNEP). The goals of the program are to improve the nutrition knowledge and diets of poor families and to encourage program families to enroll in USDA food assistance programs.

Homemakers receiving food stamps had better diets, larger families, and higher incomes than those in the food distribution program or those eligible but not participating in a food assistance program.

Approximately 37 percent of EFNEP families participated in USDA food assistance programs in 1969. Twenty-three percent were enrolled in the food distribution program and 14 percent received food stamps. One in four EFNEP families were eligible but did not participate in either program. Twenty-eight percent were ineligible because of high incomes or small family size.

Socioeconomic characteristics were compared for families participating in the food stamp and food distribution programs, eligible nonparticipants, and ineligible nonparticipants during 1969. Families in all groups had low incomes, lived mainly in urban areas, had minority racial and ethnic backgrounds, and relatively low educational levels. About one-third of all families were on welfare. The groups with the largest proportions of black families and urban residents were nonparticipating eligibles. Educational levels were lowest (less than eight years of schooling) for food distribution and eligible nonparticipant homemakers. Welfare participation among assistance families was substantially higher than for nonparticipating families.

Average family income was about $200 per month for food stamp participants and $165 for both food distribution and eligible nonparticipating families. Although food stamp participants had larger family food expenditures, food expenditures per person equaled those of eligible nonparticipating families. Nonparticipating eligibles spent more than 40 percent of their income for food—a higher rate than for any of the other groups.

The income of ineligible families exceeded $300 per month. Only 7 percent were on welfare, and average family size was four members. Compared with other families, the ineligibles were more urban, had fewer blacks, and were less often on welfare. The economic advantages of these families were reflected in their higher incomes and food expenditures. Also, they spent a smaller proportion of family income for food and had better food consumption practices.

SOURCE: Summary of J. G. Feaster and G. B. Perkins, *Families in the Expanded Food and Nutrition Education Program: Comparison of Food Stamp and Food Distribution Program Participants and Nonparticipants.* Washington, DC: U.S. Department of Agriculture, 1973.

Exhibit 4-D: A Management System for a Small Program

A demonstration program designed to test the feasibility of training paralegal subprofessionals to identify the legal problems of mental health patients within state hospitals who have been deinstitutionalized, and to help patients to obtain their full legal rights, was financed by the National Institute of Mental Health to operate within the Western Massachusetts Mental Health Region. Paralegal workers (mostly college students) are trained to know the relevant portions of state and federal laws and regulations and are sent out to contact mental patients both within hospitals and in community treatment centers. In order to be able to identify the legal problems presented by patients (and hence to adjust training accordingly), a management information system was installed that provides close tabs on encounters between paralegal personnel and patients. After each encounter with a patient, the paralegal worker initiates a case file in which is recorded the complaint of the patient, what actions were taken by the paralegal personnel, dates, times, and cross-references to other files maintained on institutions and contact centers. Thus it was possible to identify areas of legal problems for which too much emphasis had been given in training and those in which too little emphasis had been given. In addition, the information system made it possible to compute the costs of service delivery.

SOURCE: John Hornik et al., *Technical Manual for Management Information System,* Mental Patients' Advocacy Project, Western Massachusetts Legal Services. Northampton, MA, 1981. Reprinted by permission.

It should be noted that all record systems are subject to greater or lesser degrees of unreliability. Some records will contain incorrect or outdated information and others will be incomplete. The extent to which unreliable records can be used for decision-making purposes depends on the kind and degree of their unreliability and the nature of the decisions in question. Clearly, critical decisions involving outcomes of considerable weight require better records than do trivial decisions. A decision to continue or discontinue a project should not be made on the basis of data derived from partly unreliable records, while a decision to change an administrative procedure may well be made based on data derived from such records. If administrative records are to serve an important role in decision-making on far-reaching issues, it is usually desirable to conduct regular audits of the records. Such audits are similar in intent to those conducted by outside accountants on fiscal records; for example, to test by sampling whether or not each target has a record, the completeness of the records, and whether or not "rules" regarding their completion have been followed. (See Chapter 5 for additional discussion of this point.)

Data from record systems—particularly from management information systems that have been developed by large-scale programs and human service institutions—can be used to estimate both program coverage and program bias. Information on the various screening criteria for a target population may be tabulated to determine if the units served are the ones specified in the program's design. For example, records of participants in a family planning program, the targets of which are women under 50 years of age who have been residents of a particular community for at least six months and who have two children under age 10, can be examined to see if the women actually served are within the eligibility limits, and the degree to which participants are under- or overrepresented in particular age or parity groups. Bias in program participation in terms of the eligibility characteristics, observed singularly and together, would be evident from such an analysis. Similarly, coverage and bias can be determined by hospitals, which normally maintain complete counts of persons admitted and patients' diagnoses, insurance coverage, and conditions of discharge. These data are tabulated and then consolidated by the American Hospital Association according to state and region. Many state welfare departments also have excellent management information systems.

Program coverage can also be estimated from record systems used in combination with other available information. A preschool program devised to meet the need for child care would be able to estimate coverage by the formula given above if a previous survey had estimated the number of preschool children in the program's region with both parents working away from home. Such calculations are important when the worth of a program depends partially on whether it provides services at a given level for persons in need (usually designated by area, socioeconomic level, ethnic background, and similar criteria). When programs are of long duration, as is true of many educational efforts and health interventions, it may be important to update records on a regular basis. Measures such as family size and composition, occupation, income, and place of residence change frequently, and estimates of target population, coverage, and bias must keep up with those changes. In sum, a useful record system must be both reliable and up-to-date.

Surveys of Program Participants

An alternative to using service and management records is to conduct special surveys of program participants. Sample surveys may be desirable when it is not possible to obtain the required data routinely as part of program activities, or when the size of the target group is large and it is more economical and efficient to undertake a sample survey than to obtain data on all of the participants (see Exhibit 4-C).

For example, a special education project conducted primarily by parents in a community may be set up in only a few schools. Children are tested in all schools and referred, but the project staff may not have time or training to administer appropriate educational skills tests. Rather, an evaluation group, probably on a sampling basis, could do so in order to estimate the appropriateness of the selection procedures and to assess whether or not the designated target population is being served by the project.

Community Surveys

When projects are not targeted at selected, narrowly defined groups of individuals but at an entire community, the most efficient and sometimes the only way to examine whether the presumed population at need is being reached is to conduct a community sample survey.

The evaluation of *Feeling Good* illustrates the use of surveys to provide data on national audience size and composition. This television program was an experimental production of the Children's Television Workshop, producers of *Sesame Street*. It was designed to motivate adults to engage in preventive health practices. Although the program was accessible to homes of all income levels, its primary purpose was to motivate low-income families to improve their health practices. Gallup conducted four national surveys, each of approximately 1500 adults, at different times during the weeks *Feeling Good* was televised. The data provide estimates on the viewing audiences as well as the demographic, socioeconomic, and attitudinal characteristics of viewers (Mielke and Swinehart, 1976). The major finding was that the program largely failed to reach the target group.

In addition to educational television, various types of health, educational, recreational, and other human service programs are often communitywide, although their intended target populations may be selected groups, such as delinquent youths, the aged, or women of childbearing age. Surveys are the major means of assessing whether targets have been reached.

To measure coverage of Department of Labor programs, such as training and public employment, the Department started a periodic national sample survey (Westat, Inc., 1976-1980). This large household survey, called the Survey of Income and Program Participation, ascertains through personal interviews whether or not each adult member of the sampled households was ever or is currently participating in each of a number of federal programs. By contrasting program participants with nonparticipants, the survey provides information on the biases in coverage of the programs. In addition, information on the uncovered but eligible target populations is also generated.

Program Utilizers, Eligibles, and Dropouts

Another way of assessing bias is to compare individuals who participate in a program with those who drop out, those who are eligible but do not participate at all, or both groups. In part, the dropout rate or attrition from a project may be an indicator of client dissatisfaction with intervention activities. It also may indicate conditions in the community that prevent persons from full participation. For example, in certain areas lack of adequate transportation may prevent participation of those who are otherwise willing and eligible.

It is important to be able to identify the particular subgroups within the target population who are not initial participants or who do not follow through to full participation. Such information not only is valuable in judging the worth of the effort but also is needed to develop hypotheses about how a project may be modified to attract and retain a larger proportion of the target population. Thus, the qualitative aspects of participation also may be important for subsequent program planning.

Data about dropouts may come either from service records or from surveys designed to find nonparticipants. Community surveys usually are the only feasible means of identifying persons who have not participated in a program. The exception, of course, is when there is adequate information about the entire eligible population prior to project implementation (as in the case of data from a census or screening interview). Comparisons with either data gathered for project-planning purposes or community surveys undertaken during and subsequent to the intervention may employ a variety of different analytical approaches, from the purely descriptive to very complex models.

In Chapter 8, we describe methods of analyzing the costs and benefits of programs to arrive at measures of economic efficiency. Clearly, estimates of the size of populations at need or at risk, the groups who start a program but drop out, and the ones who participate to completion are important for calculating the costs. Those data have also been the basis for estimating benefits. In addition, they are highly useful in judging the worth of a project for continuation and expansion in either the same community or other locations. Further, such information is essential for staff in meeting their managerial and accountability responsibilities. While project participation data are no substitute for knowledge of impact in judging either efficiency or effectiveness of projects, there is little point in moving ahead with an impact analysis without an adequate description of the extent of participation by the target population.

MONITORING DELIVERY OF SERVICES

Monitoring the delivery of services is important from the standpoint of decisions concerning program continuation and expansion. The extent to which program specifications actually are met in the delivery of the intervention obviously must be fully documented for policymaking (see Exhibit 4-D for an example of a project monitoring system). Additionally, research on service delivery is valuable in determining the levels of performance of staff members (see Exhibit 4-E for a report on the impact of a television program on teachers in El Salvador). Before all else, however, evaluators of service delivery seek to determine whether an intervention's actual outputs sufficiently approximate intended ones.

Why Programs Fail Through Delivery System Errors

Monitoring the delivery of services to evaluate the actual implementation of a program is undertaken for a number of purposes. A large proportion of programs that fail to show impacts are really failures to deliver the interventions in ways specified. There are three kinds of implementation failures: First, no treatment, or not enough, is delivered; second, the wrong treatment is delivered; and third, the treatment is unstandardized, uncontrolled, or varies across target populations. In each instance, the need to monitor the actual delivery of services and to identify faults and deficiencies is essential.

"Nonprograms" and Incomplete Treatments

Consider first the problem of the "nonprogram" (Rossi, 1978). McLaughlin (1975) reviewed the evidence on the implementation of Title I of the Elementary and Secondary Education Act, which allocated billions of dollars yearly to aid local schools in overcoming students' poverty-associated educational deprivations. However, local school authorities were unable to describe their Title I activities in any detail, and few activities could even be identified as educational services delivered to schoolchildren, although the funds had been expended. In short, little evidence could be found that a program existed.

Numerous other programs have been documented in the literature as failing to deliver services. Datta (1977) reviews the evaluations on career education programs and finds that the designated targets rarely participated in the planned program activities.

In a recent attempt to evaluate a program designed to motivate disadvantaged high school students toward higher levels of academic achievement, it was discovered that the program consisted mainly of the distribution of buttons or hortatory literature and little else (Murray, 1980). Although the program had received a great deal of publicity, few of the high school students in the participating schools who were supposed to be reached by the program knew of its existence, and even fewer had participated in any of the activities that were supposed to be part of the program.

Instead of not delivering services at all, a delivery system may dilute the treatment so that an insufficient amount reaches the target population. Here the problem may be a lack of commitment on the part of a front-line delivery system, resulting in minimal delivery or "ritual compliance" to the point of nonexistence (Rossi, 1978). Affirmative action laws, for example, have required businesses to advertise job openings to the public. Nevertheless, organizations often place public advertisements after positions have already been filled informally.

Wrong Treatment

The second category of program failures, namely, that the wrong treatment is delivered, can occur in two ways. One is that the mode of delivery negates the treatment. For example, to test an existing prisoner rehabilitation program in the California prison system, a randomized experiment was conducted to test the effectiveness of group counseling in prison. Mimicking the existing practices in the prison system, the experimenters used untrained and sometimes hostile prison guards as group leaders (Kassebaum et al., 1971). As can easily be imagined, the resulting group therapy sessions were usually parodies of group therapy practice.

In the Performance Contracting Experiment, in which private firms were contracted to teach mathematics and reading and were to be paid in proportion to the achievement gains of pupils, the companies faced extensive difficulties in operating the program. In fact, in some sites the school

Exhibit 4-E: Effect of a Program on Classroom Teachers

As part of the Educational Reform in El Salvador, a serious effort was made to retrain teachers so that they could work effectively with proposed new innovations. Teachers' attitudes toward the Reform therefore became an important aspect of the research and evaluation activities. Briefly, the findings are as follows:

1. Not unlike the student findings, there was a decline from high levels of enthusiasm in 1969 for ITV [instructional television] to less positive attitudes in 1971 and 1972. That is, teachers were more willing to be critical several years after the introduction of ITV and the reform program. Problems other than the presence of instructional television or the basic thrust of the Reform, however, were behind the teachers' negative attitudes.

2. In particular, teachers were not happy with their everyday working conditions because of increases in enrollment and the corresponding increases in teaching loads, with morning and afternoon classes from 7 a.m. to 6 p.m. becoming the norm. Despite this extra work, teachers' salary levels were not adequately improved and remained unattractive. Given these conditions, it was not surprising that two major teachers' strikes occurred within the initial years of the Reform.

3. There was also a general misunderstanding of the part played by the classroom teacher in the new system of student grading and promotion, and a sense of being inadequately prepared to use such a system well. This new system required classroom teachers to be better prepared for their classes and to invest precious out-of-class time in various evaluation activities. At the same time, the new grading system diminished the possibility that a student could be flunked for failure to perform adequately on a single end-of-year exam.

SOURCE: From H. Ingle, "Reconsidering the Use of Television for Educational Reform: The Case of El Salvador," in R. F. Arnove (ed.), *Educational Television: Policy Critique and Guide for Developing Countries*, p. 130. Copyright © 1976, published by Praeger Publishers, reprinted with permission of Holt, Rinehart and Winston.

system sabotaged the experiments, and in others the companies faced equipment failures and teacher hostility (Gramlich and Koshel, 1975).

Wrong treatment may also result from designing an overly sophisticated delivery system. There can be a considerable difference between pilot projects and production runs of sophisticated treatments. Thus, interventions that might work well in the hands of highly motivated and trained deliverers may end up as failures when administered by staff of a mass delivery system whose training and motivation levels are considerably lower. The field of education again provides an illustration: Teaching methods (e.g., computer-assisted learning, individualized instruction) that have worked well within experimental development centers have not fared as well in ordinary school systems.

The distinction made here between a treatment and its mode of delivery is not always clear-cut. For example, the difference is quite clear in income maintenance programs, in which the "treatment" is the money given to beneficiaries and the delivery modes may vary from automatic deposits in savings or checking accounts to hand delivery of cash to recipients. Here the intent of the program is to place money in the hands of recipients; the delivery, whether by electronic transfer or by hand, has little effect on the treatment. In contrast, staffing a counseling program may be handled by retraining existing personnel, hiring counselors, or employing certified psychotherapists. In this case the distinction between mode of delivery and treatment is fuzzy, since it is generally acknowledged that counseling treatments vary by counselor.

Unstandardized Treatment

The final category of program failures is due to unstandardized or uncontrolled treatment implementation, in some cases involving "planned variation" in treatments. The problem arises because program design often leaves too much discretion in implementation to the staff at individual sites, with the result that the treatment can vary significantly across them. Early programs of the Office of Economic Opportunity provide examples. The Community Action Program (CAP) left considerable discretion to local communities to engage in a variety of actions, requiring only "maximum feasible participation" on the part of the poor. Consequently, it is almost impossible to document what CAP programs accomplished (Vanecko and Jacobs, 1970). Similarly, Head Start provided funds to local communities to set up preschool teaching projects for underprivileged children. The centers across the country varied by sponsoring agencies, coverage, content, staff qualifications, objectives, and a host of other characteristics (Cicirelli et al., 1969).

Delivery System Concepts

Some programs are simple and straightforward, and evaluation of their implementation requires only minimal resources. Others, however, are exceedingly complex. A combination of evaluation methods usually must be employed to assess project implementation adequately. Before discussing various methodologies, it may be useful to review a set of concepts employed in the assessment of program delivery. During program planning, it is necessary to formulate hypotheses about these features of the delivery system. As part of the planning, testing of decisions on implementation may be advisable.

The delivery system for a program usually consists of a number of separate elements. As a general rule, it is wise to assess all the elements. However, there are instances in which previous experience with certain aspects of the delivery system makes the assessments of some elements unnecessary. The delivery system may be thought of as a combination of pathways and actions undertaken in order to provide an intervention (see Wholey, 1977). Exhibit 4-F lists the elements of a public human service program.

Access

Access refers to the structural and organizational arrangements that provide opportunities for and operate to facilitate program participation. All programs need to have a strategy for providing the services to the appropriate target population. In some instances, access may consist of simply opening an office and operating under the assumption that the designated participants will "naturally" come and make use of the intervention services provided at the site. In other instances, however, access may include active outreach campaigns to recruit participants, provision of transportation in order to bring persons to the intervention site, and efforts during the intervention to minimize dropouts.

A number of evaluation questions arise in connection with access, some of which relate only to the delivery of services, and some of which are directly relevant to or have implications for previously discussed issues of target participation. First, are the established access operations consistent with program design? Second, do participants remain in the program and terminate as planned? When dropout rates are excessive, not only are the targets minimally reached by the intervention, but costs per potential target may become excessive. Third, is there access for potential targets to the appropriate services? It has been observed, for example, that community members who originally make use of emergency medical care systems for appropriate purposes may subsequently utilize them for

Exhibit 4-F: A Simple Model of a Human Service System

Elements of the System	Function
Population Served	a group of community members in a specified geographic area receiving services from the system and having their needs and interests represented through governance;
Governance	a group of community members who represent the needs and interests of the population to be served;
Specification	a definition of needs of the population to be served stated in measurable terms;
Needs Audit Mechanism	a means of recording the extent to which the needs of the population to be served have been satisfied by the system;
System Manager	some individual or group who is accountable for the effects and costs of the system;
Client Pathway	a set of system functions through which clients pass from entry to discharge to have their needs met;
System Agent	a single point of accountability for client progress through the system;
Information System	a mechanism to provide delivery and management personnel with data to help clients through the pathway and enable corrective action to be taken if clients encounter difficulty.

SOURCE: Adapted from R. M. Bozzo, E. L. Kane, and S. Mittenthal, *Evaluation of the State of Delaware's Human Service Delivery System*. Washington, DC: National Institute for Advanced Studies, 1977, p. 32.

general medical care. Such misuse of emergency services may be overly costly and may hamper their availability to other community members (National Center for Health Services Research, 1977). Fourth, does the access strategy foster utilization by targets differentially from various social, cultural, and ethnic groups, or is there access with equity for all potential targets?

Finally, there are projects where it is important as part of access to evaluate participant satisfaction with the program. For example, if a pre-school project is viewed with dissatisfaction by the mothers of the children participating, it may fail to draw other children from these families in successive years or from neighboring families influenced by the mothers' reports.

Specification of Services

It is critical to specify in operational terms the actual services that are provided. The first task is to define each kind of service in terms of the activities and actions that take place and/or in terms of the types of participation by various providers. Exhibit 4-G provides guidelines on how to examine an educational program.

Units of services, or *program elements,* may be defined in terms of *time, costs, procedures,* or *products.* For example, program elements may refer to hours of counseling time provided in a vocational training project; in an effort to foster housing improvement, a unit of service may be defined in terms of amounts of building materials provided; in a cottage industry project, a program element may refer to an activity, such as training people to operate sewing machines; and in an educational program, an element may be specific curricular materials used in classrooms. In all these examples, what is important is that there is an explicit definition of what constitutes an element or unit.

There is a trade-off between specifying a large number of specific, simple program elements and having a few complex ones. For example, if a project providing technical education for school dropouts includes literacy training, carpentry skills, and a period of on-the-job apprenticeship work, it is advisable to separate these into three separate sets of services rather than to merge the activities. For purposes of estimating program costs for undertaking cost-benefit analyses, and for fiscal accountability, it is often important to attach monetary values to different program elements or units of services. This clearly is important when the costs of several programs will be compared and where the programs receive reimbursement on the basis of units of services provided.

Simple, specific elements are easier to identify, count, and record accurately and reliably. However, complex elements often correspond

Exhibit 4-G: Specifying the Elements of an Educational Program

When describing a program, one should begin by specifying the tangible features of the program and its setting:

- The classrooms, schools, or districts where the program has been installed.

- The program staff—including administrators, teachers, aides, parent volunteers, and secretaries.

- The resources used—including materials constructed or purchased, and equipment, particularly that purchased especially for the program.

- The students—including the particular characteristics that made them eligible for the program, their number, and their level of competency at the beginning of the program.

These context features constitute the bare bones of the program and must be included in any summary report. Listing them usually does not require much data gathering on your part, since they are not the sort of data that you expect anyone to challenge or view with skepticism. Unless there are doubts about the delivery of materials, that the wrong staff members or students may be participating, there is little need for backup data to support your description.

In addition to describing context features, however, it is necessary to devote some time to examining and reporting the activities in which program staff and participants took part. Describing important activities demands formulating and answering questions about how the program was implemented.

- Were the materials used? Were they used as intended?

- What procedures were prescribed for the teachers to follow in their teaching and other interactions with students? Were these procedures followed?

- In what activities were the students in the program supposed to participate? Did they?

- What activities were prescribed for other participants—aides, parents, tutors? Did they engage in them?

- What administrative arrangements did the program include? What lines of authority were to be used for making important decisions? What changes occurred in these arrangements or lines of authority?

Detailed means the list should include a description of the *frequency* or *duration* of activities and of their *form* (who, how, where) that is specific enough to allow you to picture each activity.

SOURCE: Adapted from L. L. Morris and C. T. Fitz-Gibbons, "How to Measure Program Implementation," Volume 4, in L. L. Morris (ed.), *Program Evaluation Kit.* Beverly Hills, CA: Sage Publications, 1978.

more closely to program goals. Hence, the strategic question is how to strike a balance, using program elements that can be identified and counted reliably and at the same time be meaningful as far as the goals of the program are concerned.

The specification of program elements or service units is also an aid in program management. Close monitoring of the actual distribution of service units delivered to participants can help program staff and administration to keep programs more closely aligned with original intents. For example, some types of service units may be more attractive to project personnel than others—simply providing income support payments may be easier than attempting to deliver a variety of supplemental social services—and project personnel may therefore tend, consciously or unconsciously, to favor the simpler service unit.

A description of project service elements in terms of activities and actions is preferable to a description in terms of the characteristics of the providers. An illustration of program elements is given in Exhibit 4-H. Of course, the scheme reported in this exhibit is very fine-grained, relating to each incident of interaction between teachers and students. Ordinarily, program elements would not be measured with this degree of refinement. The illustration is presented at this point to show the extent to which program element description may go, under appropriate circumstances. It is evident that to the extent concise and detailed description of elements can be offered, it is possible to expand and duplicate programs.

While descriptions of program elements in terms of concrete activities are preferable, in many projects the nature of the intervention allows wide choice in what takes place. In such situations, at least at the outset, it may be possible to describe elements only in terms of the general characteristics of the activities and in terms of the training and skills of the service providers. For example, master craftspersons may be located in a low-income community to instruct community members in various ways of improving their dwelling units. The activities in which the craftspersons engage may vary greatly from one household to another. They may advise

Exhibit 4-H: Measuring What Happens in Classrooms

In an effort to relate what happens in classrooms to the achievement of elementary school pupils, the investigators videotaped a number of individual classroom sessions in reading and math instruction. The videotapes were then coded to show the incidence of certain types of teacher/student interactions that were believed to be important in reading and math achievement. Listed below are a few of the codes developed for "instructional events," all involving actions taken by the teacher in question toward one or more students:

- individual management statements (statements by the teacher addressed to students to direct their behavior; e.g., "Please sit down!")

- individual cognitive statements (statements that contain some instructional materials addressed to a single student)

- whole-class cognitive statements (same sort of statement addressed to the whole class)

The total coding scheme contained literally scores of such categories. Once the videotapes had been coded, it was necessary to summarize the tapes for individual classes and for individual students and relate the resulting summary measures to the amount of learning taking place in the classes as a whole and among individual students.

SOURCE: Cooley, W. W. and Leinhardt, G., "The Instructional Dimensions Study." *Educational Evaluation and Policy Analysis* 2, January 1980. Copyright © 1980, American Educational Research Association, Washington, DC. Reprinted by permission.

one family on how to frame windows and in another case provide instruction on how to shore up the foundation of a house. In such cases, activities can be described only in general terms and by examples. It is possible, however, to describe the characteristics required of the providers. It can be stated that the persons selected for this activity should have a minimum of five years of experience in the construction and repair of homes and that they need to be knowledgeable about carpentry, electrical wiring, foundations, and exterior construction. Of course, during the project it is important to be able to document the actual activities and tasks the advisers undertook.

As a general guideline, monitoring is most successful when programs are kept as simple as possible. Programs that offer many different services and in which there is close tailoring of interventions to individual targets can be difficult to monitor, since it is a problem to unravel the particular intervention modalities that have favorable impact in terms of project goals. At the same time, it is evident that many programs offer alternative service elements because of individual target requirements, the contextual conditions under which the program is offered, or competence and expertise of program providers. Monitoring requires that alternatives be identified and specified as much as possible.

The planning phase includes refinement of delivery system concepts, development of operational specifications, and pretesting of the delivery system. During the program implementation, it is advisable for program management to undertake continual or periodic study of the implementation process (see Exhibit 4-I).

COLLECTING DATA FOR MONITORING

A wide variety of techniques may be used singly or in combination to gather data on program implementation. The particular approaches used must take into account the resources available and the expertise of the evaluator, as in all aspects of evaluation (Burstein et al., 1985). There are additional restrictions, however. One concerns issues of privacy and confidentiality. Program services that depend heavily on person-to-person delivery methods, particularly in such areas as mental health, family planning, and vocational education, are not readily amenable to direct observation of program activities because such observation violates the privacy of participants. In other contexts, self-administered questionnaires may be an economical means of studying program implementation, but functional illiteracy and cultural norms may prohibit their use.

There are four data sources that should be considered in the design of a monitoring evaluation: direct observation by the evaluator, service records, data from program staff who are service providers, and information from program participants or their associates. The actual data collection approach utilized and the analysis procedures overlap from one data source to the next.

Observational Data

In many programs, the preferable data collection approach for monitoring purposes is direct observation. Observational methods are feasible whenever the presence of an observer is not obtrusive.

Exhibit 4-I: Continuous Versus One-Shot Evaluation

If administrators consider evaluation to be one of their central responsibilities, they are apt to believe that evaluation should be a constant and continuous process. In practice, this has led to an emphasis upon input and process evaluation. In social programs the development of statistical systems—often quite sophisticated—and standardized tests are the most notable examples. Statistical systems reflect a desire and a need on the part of managers to know something about the clients being served by their programs and something, in an aggregated way, about what happens to these clients and how staff members spend their time. When such systems are reasonably well developed, they provide fairly detailed information about the demographic characteristics of clients, at least some indication of how clients happen to enter the program (e.g., source of referral), at least a categorical assignment of why the client entered the program (e.g., diagnosis), how staff time is expended among various types of activity (work/time analysis), and often what should be the next steps (disposition). Less often, but still with laudable frequency, such systems also provide information tracking the client through a system or program—services provided, transfers, and so on. Typically, a statistical system provides some of these types of information, depending upon the preferences of managers and the availability of resources. Statistical systems are probably the best developed and most widely used form of continuous evaluation of social programs.

One-shot evaluation is more apt to be a response to a perceived crisis, a particularly difficult policy decision, or possibly the receiving of a grant. Typically, evaluative research is one-shot in nature, because it usually involves a study. For whatever the reason, one-shot evaluation is aimed at answering a specific question about a particular program or program element at one point in time. The sources of crises are legion but usually result in the immediate need for information about a particular aspect of a program. There is a strong tendency, usually out of concern for credibility, to use outside evaluators in crisis situations, although what constitutes "outside" depends upon organizational level of the crisis. Consultants are often used in just such cases, and management consultant firms have multiplied in large part as a response to the frequency of such crises.

Periodic evaluation is a very useful midpoint between one-shot and continuous evaluation. Although many social phenomena change rapidly (e.g., public opinion and military situations), most do not. The changes wrought by many social programs are often slow in developing, or at least the impact is slow in emerging. This is particularly true for education and prevention programs. In addition, many of the instruments available for measuring change are sensitive only to gross changes. In many instances, particularly those requiring measurement of impact, long-term outcome, or prevention, neither continuous nor one-shot evaluation is adequate, but some type of periodic monitoring is possible, feasible, and necessary. Periodic evaluation permits some rest to the evaluators while they deal with other problems, and at the same time it does not compromise their or the program's ability to grow.

SOURCE: Adapted, with permission, from J. L. Franklin and J. H. Thrasher, *An Introduction to Program Evaluation.* New York: John Wiley, 1979, pp. 26-29. Copyright © by John Wiley and Sons, Inc.

It may be useful in some cases for observers to become, at least for a time, full or partial program participants. Reiss (1971), for example, placed in police patrol cars observers who filled out systematic reports of each encounter between the police and citizens in a sample of duty tours. A similar approach was used in the Kansas City Preventive Patrol Experiment (Kelling et al., 1974). Exhibit 4-J describes the use of observers in that study and some of the problems they encountered.

Investigators wishing to employ participant-observation methods usually find it possible to explain to program personnel and to other participants the purposes served by observation. However, the extent to which the presence of participant-observers may alter the behavior of program personnel, other participants, or the delivery system as a whole is not clear. Impressionistic evidence from the police studies does not indicate that observers affected the delivery system, since police in the patrol cars soon became accustomed to being observed. Nonetheless, participant-observation methods should be sensitive to the problem of observer effects.

An essential part of any observation effort is a plan for the systematic recording of observations made (see Schatzman and Strauss, 1973; Patton, 1980, for guidance on field research methods). Observers must be trained in how to make observations and how to record them uniformly.

Exhibit 4-J: The Participant Observer Program in the Kansas City Preventive Patrol Experiment

Trained observers were assigned to ride in patrol cars with officers in the experimental beats. It was felt that such observers would be valuable in observing and recording the unexpected consequences of such an experiment, that they could provide valuable feedback concerning the extent to which there was an experiment, that they could accurately record and provide data concerning those activities performed by officers while on routine preventive patrol (for the expenditure of noncommitted time analysis), and that they could serve as major mechanisms of data collection for the response time and police-citizen encounter portions of the experiment.

The first difficulty stemmed from task force objections to the use of observers. Several members expressed fears that police officers would automatically modify their behavior in the presence of observers, that they would be hostile to close, constant monitoring by nonpolice participants, and that because they would feel responsible for the observers, police officers might jeopardize their own safety in dangerous situations. Discussion eventually moved the task force from hostility to cautious openness and eventually to approval and interest, although the task force did reserve the right to discontinue the use of participant observers should they judge a discontinuance to be in the best interest of the experiment.

One major conflict concerned methods of data collection. The first step in observer data collection involved the gathering of phenomenological accounts (defined as a description sufficiently complete that a well-defined image of the event is generated in the mind of the reader, who is able to infer the moods of the participants from the behavior recorded). Over the course of the experiment this procedure moved toward a more highly structured means of data collection.

A second area of conflict involved the co-optation by the police of most of the participant observers. It should be noted that this problem was never confined to the observers, nor was it premeditated on the part of the police department. Police work has many aspects that are exciting, attractive, and alluring to those not directly engaged in it. As a result, laymen are often easily converted to a police point of view. Some of the observers were overly prepared to defend the police and were convinced that the information being gathered would eventually be used in an unprofessional manner by the police department, the Police Foundation, and individual staff members. Some observers began to insist that they and they alone should decide the degrees of sensitivity involved and, literally as protectors of the police, decide what information should and should not be gathered.

To deal with this problem, a variety of mechanisms were used. First, a police officer from the task force was selected to review regularly the information gathered by the observers and discuss with them the nature and sensitivity of the data. Second, regular meetings with the observers were held to discuss their work, their findings, and problems encountered in the field. And third, the observer portion of the experiment was put under the direct supervision of a full-time staff member to strengthen the administrative function and provide direct, ongoing managerial support.

The observers collected data of great value to the experiment, however, and there is much confidence in the quality of these data. Despite the problems experienced during the initial stages of this program, and the difficulties endemic to ethnographic research, there has been, and will be, a high level of return in terms of the data collected and their use.

SOURCE: Adapted, with permission, from G. Kelling et al., *The Kansas City Preventive Patrol Experiment: A Technical Report.* Washington, DC: Police Foundation, 1974, pp. 60-62.

There are three typical ways of making systematic observations. The first approach involves the least imposition of a set scheme for classifying events: The observer is simply asked to record events in as much detail as possible and in the order in which they occur. This is known as the narrative method. In its most extreme form, no guides are given to the observer about which events to record and which to ignore. Typically, however, it has been found useful to provide observers with a list of important types of activities to which their attention should be directed.

A second approach is to provide observers with a data guide—a set of questions for which answers are required to be given by observers from their observations. A data guide may resemble a survey instrument in which there are blank spaces between questions, which observers then fill in. For example, the data guide for observers attending technical training classes may have questions such as, "How did the instructor make use of available training aids? What were they and when were they used?" The use of a recording instrument such as a data guide simplifies analysis considerably. There is also greater likelihood of consistency of information across observers with this method than with narrative reporting. It presumes, however, much more specificity in program design and becomes unwieldy if there are a large number of alternative interventions to be applied to individual participants.

The third approach is to use a structured rating scheme. Some rating schemes are solely descriptive, such as checklists that specify the proportion of time devoted to different kinds of activities. Other rating schemes are normative or attitudinal, such as schemes to measure clarity of instructors' presentations or to assess the nature of encounters between participants and delivery systems.

Although direct observation methods appear to be attractively simple, they are not easily taught to untrained observers, they are highly time-consuming, and they produce data that are difficult to summarize and analyze. These problems are particularly troublesome the less structured the observation method used and the more complex the program services. Moreover, as noted, observation may change the behavior of program personnel and participants.

In some circumstances, it is possible to reduce observation problems by developing adequate sampling approaches, so that one or a few observers can record project activities in a more economical fashion. Such sampling is sometimes done by randomly selecting for observation a statistically adequate number of time periods. Another approach for projects involving individuals is to sample participants and then observe them as they interface with project activities.

It is sometimes practical and advisable to combine direct observation with other monitoring approaches; experience suggests that direct observation is difficult to accomplish with a high degree of reliability and is subject to the limitations described above.

Service Record Data

Record data were discussed in the section on measuring coverage. Just as characteristics of targets can be assessed from records, project service delivery can be monitored from them. (Exhibit 4-K describes the use of a medical chart review to evaluate the delivery of pediatric care.)

Service records vary. They can range from narrative reports to highly structured data forms on which project personnel check whether or not particular services were given, how they were received, and observable results (Cernea and Tepping, 1977). Their level of detail is related to the complexity of the project and to the number of alternatives that can be

Exhibit 4-K: Use of Records to Evaluate a Delivery System

The Watts Health Center is a family-oriented neighborhood health center in the predominantly black low-income community in Los Angeles. In operation since October 1967, it offers extensive ambulatory health services to approximately 35,000 people who live within the three-square-mile area and whose family income is below the federal poverty guidelines.

At patient registration, a permanent file is started for the client and all family members. This registration process, while it facilitates continuity of care, does not commit the registrant to utilize the center.

In December 1970, a 2.5 percent sample (244 families) of the entire registered population of 11,721 families was selected by use of a table of random numbers. With these families, the chart of every patient who was under 17 years of age when registered was studied by a pediatrician, and the information was recorded on a survey form.

"High-quality" pediatric care was presumed to be present when all of the following were recorded in the patient file: at least one comprehensive workup; immunizations appropriate for age according to the recommendations of the American Academy of Pediatrics; attention paid to all abnormal laboratory reports; and appropriate follow-up visits for all significant clinical conditions detected.

One-quarter of the children in these registered families had never been brought in for care at the center. Another 6 percent had been seen only in the dental clinic. Almost half (47 percent) had received medical but not dental attention. The remaining 22 percent had visited both a physician and a dentist.

Of the 339 children who had received at least some medical care at the center, 18 percent had appeared exclusively in the emergency room. Another 58 percent had visited another part of the health center, often in addition to an emergency room visit, but only on an episodic basis. Only 24 percent were adjudged as having received a comprehensive medical evaluation consisting of history, physical examination, and screening laboratory tests (as recommended by the American Academy of Pediatrics).

Thus, only 17 percent of the entire group of children had received all of the selected aspects of both preventive and curative high-quality pediatric care. An additional 11 percent were deficient only in immunizations, as recorded in the chart. The largest group, 58 percent, were receiving episodic care but all laboratory and clinical abnormalities had been noted and followed up. With the remaining 23 percent, at least one instance of inadequate follow-up had occurred whether or not the evaluation and immunizations had been complete.

SOURCE: Adapted, with permission, from H. M. Lieberman, "Evaluating the Quality of Ambulatory Pediatric Care at a Neighborhood Health Center: Creative Use of a Chart Review." *Clinical Pediatrics,* 13 (January 1974): 52-55.

specified in advance. (See Exhibit 4-L for a simple procedure in a nutrition evaluation.) Service records also vary in sophistication with respect to storage and access; in clinical contexts, for example, computerized information systems have been devised based on management science principles.

Many times, service record systems are simply too complex to be used properly for monitoring purposes (a problem, as we noted earlier, that plagues records on target populations). This occurs because they are designed primarily to serve the administrative and management needs of program staff. In such cases, record forms are often either not filled in completely or the parts that are believed to be irrelevant by project staff are completed haphazardly. On the one hand, there is a risk that adding monitoring components will overly burden program personnel, limit staff cooperation, and therefore render the resulting data incomplete and unreliable for monitoring purposes. On the other hand, record information is inexpensive and efficient. Clearly, its use depends on adequate training of program staff to maximize reliability, on providing motivation to staff, and on quality-control checks to ensure timely and appropriate completion.

As with records on target populations, a few items of data gathered consistently and reliably are generally much better for monitoring purposes than a more comprehensive set of information of doubtful reliability and inconsistent collection.

A second rule is that, whenever possible, it is useful to structure record forms as checklists so that program staff can check off various items rather than provide narrative information. Not only does such a procedure minimize the time required of project staff, but it is most convenient for subsequent analysis.

Exhibit 4-L: Program Implementation in a Nutritional Experiment

An example of a project in which there is precise measurement of the program variable is the Institute for Nutrition of Central American and Panama's (INCAP) evaluation of the impact of a high-calorie, high-protein supplement on physical growth and development and cognitive functioning of preschool children. In two villages the calorie supplement is provided twice a day at the same time periods to all villagers who receive it. The feeding spot is near the village school. In two other "control villages" a less fortified but still beneficial supplement is provided.

All persons entering have their names checked off from available census lists of village members. Each person receives the supplement in a standard cup and when they have drunk as much as they wish, the cup is returned to the project staff person, who can then measure the amount ingested, subtracting the total amount remaining in the cup. Since villagers are permitted as many cups as they desire, there is no reason for them to switch cups with one another, although they are carefully observed.

These daily logs are then brought back to INCAP and through a computerized system become part of the individual record for each mother and child who participates in the study.

SOURCE: Summary, by permission, of H. E. Freeman et al., "Relations Between Nutrition and Cognition in Rural Guatemala." *American Journal of Public Health* 67 (March 1977).

The third rule is that it is important to review completed records for consistency and accuracy as carefully and as soon as possible. Timely editing and quality-control procedures can catch omissions and inconsistencies.

Again, it is important to emphasize that there are risks in using service records as the only data source. Program staff, intentionally or unintentionally, may exaggerate the extent to which different program elements are being delivered to targets. Sometimes this is the result of an overzealous concern with maintaining appearances of efficiency and responsibility. At other times it may be because program staff are disenchanted with procedures for providing certain project services, although there is a formal requirement that they adhere to them. Finally, there are occasions on which project staff's interpretation of a particular intervention service differs from that of either the program designers or the evaluators.

Management Information Systems

Early in this chapter, we discussed the introduction of management information systems into the social program arena. In a sense, all record systems are management information systems. However, the concept is usually reserved for record systems that permit the organization of information, its cumulation and display in a variety of ways, and at specified periods and on demand. In other words, it is a record system that permits, on an ongoing basis, information for decision-making by program management, for reports (or "records," as they are technically termed) in order to meet stakeholders' needs and requests for information, and for data for use in effectiveness and efficiency evaluations. Davis (1984) characterizes viable systems as performing two functions: (1) information management—storing, retrieving, and reporting information in a format convenient to use; and (2) data quantification—condensing and analytically manipulating large bundles of data into a few indicators that extract the most relevant features of the information.

For example, a community mental health center may see 600 patients a week, have 5000 different clients, provide 15 different services, refer patients to 12 different providers outside the center, have patients treated within the center by 22 different professionals, some psychiatrists, others social workers and psychologists, and still others psychiatric nurses and vocational counselors. The patients range in age, sex, ethnicity, length and outcome of treatment, and diagnoses, among other things. It is conceivable that program managers are interested in knowing virtually all of the relationships among these different features of their program. For example, on a monthly basis they may want to know the average number of visits for patients with different diagnoses, ethnicity, sex, or age. They might also want to know what types of patients are being treated by personnel with different professional backgrounds, as well as what types of patients are receiving different services. The number of combinations and permutations of even these few measures is huge. Thus, management information systems are dependent upon computers for the storage and retrieval of data.

Typically, the MIS of a mental health center produces periodic tables— say, monthly—containing information of regular use to staff and management. A second set of tables may be produced quarterly to send to the county agency that provides their support, and an annual set of tables run for the National Institute of Mental Health in Washington. These tables may differ in the ways the data are accumulated, the summary statistics provided, and so on.

In addition, the MIS of the center may answer specific management and research questions. For example, the center's director may become uneasy about the proportion of patients who drop out of treatment and may want to see if they cluster by ethnicity, by which specific provider was treating them, and so on. As another example, a university-based clinical psychologist with research-demonstration funds may be developing an innovative program for depressive young adults and wants to include the center as one of the sites if they have a large enough target population. The MIS could provide information on diagnosis by age so that a decision could be made about the wisdom of including the center. Also, stakeholders, such as the local mental health association, may want information about whether elderly patients are provided with psychotherapy and rehabilitation services rather than simply given drug therapy. Again, the system could provide this information. Finally, if the center pays outside providers to whom it sends patients, the system could not only calculate the number of units of service each of these providers should be paid, but could actually issue the checks.

There are, of course, technical complications that should not be dismissed in the design and implementation of an MIS. Information systems for social programs may be more complicated than those used by, say, large airlines. However some of the software developed for existing systems can be transferred to others.

More difficult are two other aspects of management information systems. First, it is essential to conceptualize properly the information required by the program staff, program managers, sponsors and funders, stakeholders, researchers, and any other person or organization who may now or in the future have data requirements that are going to be filled by requests of the MIS. For example, if there is a need at some point to include information about physical illnesses of patients, then clearly this information needs to be entered into the system. There is more involved than simply identifying the information components, however. Each has to be operationally defined, and "rules" developed for entering and accessing information. For example, since 97 percent of the patients have only three or fewer diagnoses, the system may be required to store only three diagnoses per patient. But for the few patients with four or more diagnoses, a rule has to be set up to define which three would be entered. Until artificial intelligence is a much more developed activity, it must be recognized that the development of an MIS is dependent upon the conceptualization, definitions, and rules devised by those who operate the system. It is also important to recognize that each modification to an MIS has consequences for the utility of information already stored as well as the costs involved in making any changes.

Second, and perhaps the most critical consideration, is the need for program staff, whoever provides and enters data, to understand the utility of the system, the rules and definitions, and their responsibilities to collaborate in its implementation. It does no good to have the finest hardware and software and a sophisticated and well-conceptualized system if providers, for example, do not take the time to enter the data via the computer terminal after seeing each patient. If the provider waits until the end of the day and puts in what he or she remembers, it results in what many call a "gigo" system (garbage in, garbage out).

The combination of lack of training, apathy, fear of the system revealing negative information about a provider or unit in the organization, and sheer malice must be overcome in order for an MIS to function properly and for the organization to reap the benefits of it. Training, oversight, regular quality-control procedures, tender loving care, and sanctions are required if an organization is to realize the potential of management information systems. The time has come, however, when practically no human services program can afford to be without such a system. Its presence, in many ways, reduces the monitoring burden for both the program manager concerned with organizational performance and the evaluator concerned with appropriate program implementation in relation to evaluation of impact.

Service Provider Data

Rather than relying on information recorded in administrative and service records, program managers can require staff to provide special information for monitoring purposes. (Exhibit 4-M illustrates the use of staff to generate monitoring data for a Choctaw family education program.) Sometimes narrative reports are required of project staff in the form of diaries. Sometimes staff may be required to code or complete rating forms for the evaluator from diary information. Diaries generally are used only for backup information.

A compromise between a highly structured interview or questionnaire and a complete narrative is some form of semidirected interview or semi-structured questionnaire. This approach is analogous to the data guide discussed in the section about observational methods. It allows for some depth of information, but at the same time cuts down on the time and effort of program staff.

The most efficient approach is the use of a highly structured survey instrument that can be completed by interview or by the staff person alone. Structured instruments lend themselves readily to tabulation. As in the case of observation efforts, it is often wise to sample either time periods or target encounters in order to minimize work for staff. In doing so, it is

Exhibit 4-M: Home Visitors as Providers of Monitoring Information for a Family Information Project

The Choctaw Home-Centered Family Education Project demonstrates a workable early childhood model for a rural, reservation group. Specifically, one objective was to use the Choctaw home visitor to work with the mother or her surrogates in establishing an environment to stimulate the cognitive development of the Choctaw child from birth to 4 years of age.

The instructional home visit was the principal component used to maintain contact with the client families. In this approach, the interaction between mother and child was the central focus. The home visitor demonstrated the instructional techniques. Her behavior served as a model for those attitudes and practices being communicated to the mothers. The home visitor and mothers were encouraged to adapt the instruction to the household materials and individual style of the mother. The proposed cognitive stimulation occurred as a part of a program designed for the whole child: language, motor, sense, perception, social, and intellectual. The home visitors were given training in the stages and sequence for all these developmental areas in addition to community dynamics, early childhood instruction, behavior management, and learning. The home visitors planned, implemented, and evaluated the intervention for each family. Home visits were planned on a weekly basis at a time convenient for the mothers.

In addition to the functions and roles of the home visitor, the Choctaw home visitors were required to perform program evaluation functions. They were required to rate the home situation for its stimulation potential, to test the children, and to collect any additional information required by the evaluators to document or assess the project.

SOURCE: Adapted, with permission, from P. Quigley, L. Morris, and G. Hammett, *The Choctaw Home-Centered Family Education Demonstration Project*. Tucson, AZ: Behavior Associates, 1976, p. 8.

important that a representative sample be employed, leaving a choice of time periods or particular targets, as the subjects of inquiry may otherwise encourage project staff intentionally or unintentionally to bias accounts of project implementation.

Program Participant Data

The final approach to collecting monitoring information is to obtain data on program delivery from participants themselves. Such information is valuable not only because of the different perspectives from which it is offered, but because, among other reasons, it may be the only way to find out what was actually delivered. Participant data may be necessary for providers to know what is important to clients, including their satisfaction with and understanding of the intervention.

There may be disparities in many programs between services and interventions provided and those actually received or utilized, as the family planning literature has shown. For example, as part of a technical education program, participants may receive study guides, exercises, manuals, and equipment for additional extraclassroom use. While project staff may believe that these are employed as planned, it may well be that this is not the case. For such projects it may be critical to query participants to find out whether certain services were used or even received. Such participant data may also be generated by measures that indirectly test whether services were received, such as extraclassroom assignments consisting of calculating distances and converting them to standard values. In that case, not only could participants be interviewed regarding whether or not they used the services in the manner intended, but they could also be tested on whether they can perform reasonably on tasks the learning of which was supposed to be enhanced by the services in question.

The previous discussion on access pointed out that there are times when participant satisfaction with a program is a key indicator in monitoring program implementation. Clearly, here the participant is the appropriate and sole information source. (See Exhibit 4-N for an example of a study of client satisfaction with medical services.) In Exhibit 4-O we show the use of a community survey in the Kansas City Experiment to examine the effect of the experiment on the larger community.

Finally, Nicholson and Wright (1977) have shown that in interventions involving complex treatments, it is important to ascertain participants' understanding of such treatments, the program operating rules, and so on. In short, it is necessary to establish not only that designated services have been delivered, but also that they were received, utilized, and understood as intended.

Exhibit 4-N: Consumer Satisfaction with Prepaid Group Practice

Clients' satisfaction with the delivery of medical services in a prepaid practice plan, and comparative data from an alternative Blue Cross insurance plan, were obtained by means of household surveys. The results (showing the items asked) are summarized as follows:

Measures of Satisfaction	Blue Cross (N — 354) %	Prepaid Practice (N — 356) %
Proportion of respondents receiving services in past year	73	70
Percentage very satisfied among respondents receiving services in past year		
With amount of privacy in doctor's office	92	86
With the amount of time the doctor spends with you	82	74
With the doctor's concern about your health	85	70
With the doctor's warmth and personal interest in you	83	67
With the amount of information given to you about your health	81	64
With doctor's training and technical competence	93	78
With the doctor's friendliness	89	79
With friendliness of nurses, receptionists, etc.	84	81
With quality of medical care received	88	77
With adequacy of office facilities and equipment	93	84
With the doctor's willingness to listen when you tell him about your health	86	78

SOURCE: From R. Tessler and D. Mechanic, "Consumer Satisfaction with Prepaid Group Practice: A Comparative Study." *Journal of Health and Social Behavior,* 16 (March 1975): 99. Reprinted by permission.

Exhibit 4-O: Kansas City Community Survey to Determine the Effect of an Intervention

A random survey of households was designed to examine the six general aspects of the experiment's possible effects on the community:

1. citizens' perceptions of the likelihood of being victimized (by robbery, rape, assault, burglary, auto theft), violent crime, and general neighborhood safety;

2. the degree to which citizens protected themselves and their property along with the kinds of protective measures taken;

3. citizens' perceived need for police officers, random police patrol, and aggressive police patrol;

4. citizens' perceptions of police officers' reputations, police effectiveness, and citizens' respect for officers;

5. citizens' perceptions of police officers' behavior, fairness, and treatment of citizens; and

6. citizens' perceptions and satisfaction with police service.

SOURCE: From G. Kelling et al., *The Kansas City Preventive Patrol Experiment: A Technical Report.* Washington, DC: Police Foundation, 1974, pp. 240-241. Reprinted by permission.

Information from participants must necessarily be obtained by self-administered questionnaires or interviews. Participants may be sampled in some systematic way, or an entire census may be conducted.

ANALYSIS OF MONITORING DATA

In general, the analysis of monitoring data addresses the following three issues: description of the project, comparison between sites, and program conformity.

Description of the Project

An important question is the extent to which the program as implemented resembles in crucial details the program as designed. A description of the actual project derived from monitoring data would cover the following topics: estimates of coverage and bias in participation; types of services delivered and intensity of services given to participants of significant kinds; and reactions of participants to services delivered. Descriptive statements might take the form of narrative accounts, especially when monitoring data are derived from more qualitative sources. Of equal utility are quantitative analyses, specifically, the new and sophisticated analytic methods and measures that are being developed (see Miley et al., 1978; Heumann, 1979).

Comparison Between Sites

When a program includes more than one site, a second question concerns differences in program implementation between sites. Comparison permits an understanding of the sources of project diversity—such as staff, administrative, and target differences, or differences in the contextual environment of the program—and can also facilitate efforts to achieve standardization. In addition, between-site differences may provide clues to why projects at some sites may be more effective than those at other sites.

Program Conformity

The third issue, of course, is the one with which we began: the degree of conformity and convergence between program design and program implementation. Discrepancies between the two may lead to respecification of project design or to efforts to move project implementation closer to design. Such analysis also provides an opportunity to judge the appropriateness of an impact evaluation and, if necessary, opt for a more formative evaluation in order to develop the necessary convergence.

FEEDBACK FROM MONITORING

As we have noted, monitoring data have a number of uses, depending on who has sponsored the monitoring and the state of program development. When conducted as part of a more comprehensive evaluation, monitoring data provide guidance on congruence between program design and program implementation. Often it is recommended that they be collected prior to a firm commitment to undertake an impact analysis, although it may also be necessary that collection of such data be carried out parallel with an impact analysis, because a monitoring study undertaken in advance may not provide valid evidence of design conformity once the project is under way.

Monitoring evaluations undertaken for project managerial and accountability purposes are often fed back to project managers and staff on a continual basis. For an established project for which there is a continual set of evaluations undertaken, fluctuation and changes over time may allow one either to redesign or to fine-tune the programs and reassess the extent to which the pool of targets and project implementation need modification. Evaluators cannot assume, however, that merely providing information assures its use. Thus, as we discuss in Chapter 9, there is a need to be concerned with maximizing dissemination and utilization of monitoring—matters that in themselves call for evaluation.

5

Strategies for Impact Assessment

Impact assessment is directed at establishing whether or not an intervention is producing its intended effects. As is the case with all research activities, such estimates cannot be made with certainty, but only within limits of error and with varying degrees of plausibility. To reduce the size of such errors and to raise the plausibility of estimates of the effectiveness of social programs, impact evaluations need to be undertaken as systematically and as rigorously as practicality makes possible.

Ordinarily, the outcomes of social programs are assessed by comparing information about participants and nonparticipants, or by repeated measurements on participants, most commonly before and after an intervention, or by other methods that attempt to achieve the equivalent of such comparisons. The basic aim of an impact assessment is to produce an estimate of the "net effects" of an intervention, that is, an estimate from which the effects of other processes have been removed.

KEY CONCEPTS

Confounding Factors: Extraneous variables resulting in outcome effects that obscure or exaggerate the "true" effects of an intervention.

Design Effects: The influences of the methods used to estimate net effects on those estimates.

Generalizability: The extent to which an impact assessment's findings can be extrapolated to similar programs in other settings.

Gross Outcome Effects: Measured overall impact found by an evaluation, only part of which might be caused by the intervention.

Net Outcome Effects: Impact of an intervention, after confounding effects have been removed.

Proxy Measure: A variable that is used to "stand in" for one that is hard to measure directly.

Reliability: The extent to which scores obtained on measures used are reproducible in repeated administrations, provided all relevant measurement conditions are the same.

Reproducibility: The extent to which a research's findings can be reproduced by other researchers in replications.

Stochastic Effects: Measurement fluctuations attributable to chance.

Valid Measure: A measure for which there is evidence or a presumption that it reflects the concept it is intended to measure.

---

*T*he obstacles to impact assessments arise from several sources: First, the social world is complex, and most social phenomena have many roots and causes. With so many "moving parts," the severity of a social problem may be influenced by a number of causes in addition to those processes modified by a program. Second, because social science theories and empirical generalizations are weak and incomplete, it is difficult to develop models of social phenomena adequate for impact assessments. Third, social programs typically can be expected to have only modest impacts: No welfare program will eliminate poverty, and no criminal rehabilitation program will eradicate recidivism completely. More often than not, program effects are small and consequently difficult to detect. Finally, some social programs are especially hard to assess because they have been in operation for a long time. Ongoing programs covering vast target populations can be assessed only by making heroic assumptions that often tax credibility.

There are two points in the total evaluation process at which impact assessment is especially important. The first (and perhaps the most appropriate) is in the testing of new, proposed programs or proposed changes in existing programs. Coverage in these programs is frequently partial, and thus it is often possible to conduct evaluations that include comparing targets who experienced an intervention with those who did not, a strategy that can provide relatively definitive estimates of program effects.

The second point at which impact assessments are often undertaken is in reviewing the usefulness of existing, ongoing programs. Even when an established program appears to be either working well or at least not obviously failing, stakeholders or program staff often want plausible, precise estimates of how well the program is fulfilling its designated purposes. Policymakers may need impact evaluation results to justify expansion of what already may be widespread resource commitments, given the persistent competition for funds and the political pressures of various interest groups. Program managers may need impact results to learn how to fine-tune their programs and increase their efficacy and efficiency.

PREREQUISITES OF ASSESSING IMPACTS

As we outlined in Chapter 2, the prerequisites of assessing the impact of an intervention are as follows: First, either the project should have its objectives sufficiently well articulated to make it possible to identify measures of goal achievement or the evaluator must be able to establish what reasonable objectives are. Second, the intervention should have been sufficiently well implemented for there to be no question that its critical elements have been delivered to appropriate targets. It is obvious that it would be a waste of time, effort, and resources to estimate the impact of a program that lacks measurable goals and has not been implemented properly.

The task of explicating program objectives can be handled by one or several of the techniques described in Chapter 2. Discerning a set of objectives for a given program is not an impossible task, even when stakeholders are in disagreement over objectives or cannot explicate them. Often, as Chen and Rossi (1980) suggest, the perceptive evaluator, drawing on his or her general knowledge of the workings of our society and its organizations, can make rather reasonable inferences about what effects a program can be expected to have, given the working assumptions of the program and the relevant body of social science knowledge. The main point we make here, however, is that such objectives must be specified before impact assessment can be undertaken.

We cannot overstress the technical and managerial difficulties involved in undertaking impact evaluations. The targets of social programs are often persons and households who are difficult research subjects. In addition, as we will discuss in detail in Chapter 9, evaluation research is part of the political process. Hence, the evaluator must constantly culti-vate the cooperation of program staff and target participants, and meet the pressure to produce timely and unambiguous findings.

LINKING INTERVENTIONS TO OUTCOMES

The problem of determining the effectiveness of a program is identical to the problem of establishing that the program is the "cause" of some specified effect. Hence, establishing impact essentially amounts to estab-lishing causality. There are many deep and thorny issues surrounding the concept of causality that need not concern us here. Rather, we shall accept the view that the world is orderly and lawful and that "A is the cause of B" can be a valid statement.

Causal relationships are ordinarily stated probabilistically: Thus, the statement "A is the cause of B" usually means that if we introduce A, B is *more likely* to result than if we do not do so. The statement does not imply that B always results if A is introduced, nor does it mean that B occurs only after A has been introduced. The phrase "is more likely to occur" means that the probability of B, given A, is higher than the probability of B, absent A. In other words, a program designed to reduce unemployment is likely, if successful, to change the probability of being unemployed among participating targets. In addition, social progams have to compete with ongoing processes that also produce the desired outcomes. The unemployment rate is responsive to many factors, including labor market conditions, changes in the composition of work forces, and general trends in productivity.

The problems alluded to above may be best illustrated by the following example: The introduction of voluntary employment training projects for adults may reduce the amount of unemployment among the unskilled, at least in the short term. That is, if a program has an impact, unemployment will decline compared to not having a program. But no training program, no matter how well designed, will completely eradicate unemployment. Some target adults will simply refuse to take advantage of the opportunity offered; others will be unable to benefit for a variety of reasons, even though they are willing participants. Furthermore, unemployment levels are influenced strongly by job vacancies.

Moreover, a training program is not the only way in which the unemployment of unskilled workers can be reduced. Economic conditions may take a strong turn for the better, so that employers become more willing to take on new workers who have either little experience or poor work records. New firms with large needs for unskilled workers may start up. Furthermore, other social programs might be put into effect. Special incentives may be given to employers to hire the unemployed. On-the-job training opportunities can be made available, special "sheltered" jobs can be created to enable workers to gain experience while learning, and so on. Hence, the assessment of whether or not a specific employment training project can increase employment is complicated by the fact that employment trends are responsive to many factors, among which a specific training program is only one.

The critical issue in impact evaluation is, therefore, whether or not a program produces more of an effect, or outcome, than would have occurred either without the intervention or with an alternative intervention.

"PERFECT" VERSUS "GOOD ENOUGH" EVALUATIONS

There are many circumstances under which it can become extremely difficult, it not impossible, to conduct impact evaluations using the best possible designs. The choice left to the evaluator in such cases is either to use some less-than-perfect design or to conduct no assessment at all.

First of all, as we will explain later in this chapter, sometimes the best design cannot be applied because of the way the intervention is implemented, or because target coverage may not lend itself to its use. For example, the circumstances under which targets can be randomized and true experiments carried out are limited, and in these cases evaluators must use less powerful designs. Second, constraints of time and resources always present limitations. Generally, the most powerful designs are more costly in both respects than are less powerful designs. Third, the importance of using optimal designs varies with the importance of the intervention being tested. Other things being equal, an important program—one designed to remedy a very serious condition or employing a controversial intervention—should be evaluated more carefully than other programs.

We advocate using what we call the "good enough" rule in choosing research designs: The evaluator should choose the best possible design, taking into account practicality and feasibility. The application of this rule is discussed in greater detail at several points in later chapters. In this chapter, for didactic purposes, we will discuss research designs as if there were no "real-life" constraints on their choice. The reader should bear in mind that this perspective must be modified in practice.

GROSS VERSUS NET OUTCOME

The starting point for impact assessment is the identification of one or more outcome measures that represent the objectives of the program. Thus, in studying a program designed to increase adult literacy, the objectives of the program may be operationalized as increasing reading-level scores on a standard educational skills test. The program would be considered successful if, after exposure to the program, participants' scores are higher than would be expected without program participation.

A key distinction that must be made, however, is that between *gross* and *net outcomes*. Gross outcomes include *all* changes in an outcome measure that occur during and subsequent to program participation. The gross outcome measure in an adult literacy program might be defined as the increases (or decreases or no changes) in the participants' reading-level scores when scores taken before program participation are compared with postparticipation scores. Gross outcomes ordinarily consist of the differences between pre- and postprogram values on some outcome measure. In some cases preprogram measures cannot be obtained, and gross outcome changes consist of postprogram scores only.

Net outcomes are only those impacts that can reasonably be attributed to the intervention, free and clear of changes among targets due to the effects of other causal processes that may also have occurred. In symbolic terms, the relationship between gross and net outcomes can be expressed as follows:

$$\text{Gross Outcome} = \begin{bmatrix} \text{Effects of} \\ \text{intervention} \\ \text{(net outcome)} \end{bmatrix} + \begin{bmatrix} \text{Effects of} \\ \text{other} \\ \text{processes} \\ \text{(extraneous} \\ \text{confounding} \\ \text{factors} \end{bmatrix} + \begin{bmatrix} \text{Design} \\ \text{effects} \end{bmatrix}$$

Thus, an observed upward gain in literacy measured in before-and-after observations of a group of persons who participated in an adult literacy program (gross outcome) is composed of three parts: first, the effects of the program (net outcomes); second, the effects of "extraneous confounding factors" consisting of other events, experiences, and so on, that influenced literacy during the period in question (other processes); and, third, design effects, artifacts of the research process itself. Extraneous confounding factors include all other processes that affect the hoped-for objective of a program and hence may be regarded as confounding factors that originate within the subjects being studied or because of events that have occurred in the environment within which the program was implemented.

Gross outcomes also may include artifacts of the research effort itself, called here "design effects." Common design effects are errors of measurement, sampling variations, and data collection defects.

In the sections that follow, we will discuss first the problem of how to "remove" the effects of extraneous confounding factors. Later in the chapter, we turn our attention to an explication of design effects and how to counteract them.

EXTRANEOUS CONFOUNDING FACTORS

Given that gross outcome reflects not only the consequences of an intervention but also the effects of other processes occurring at the same time, the evaluator must "purify" gross outcomes by purging them of contaminating or confounding factors. That is, there may be extraneous "causes" that explain—in whole or in part—changes in the target problem or population that have occurred while the program has been in place.

Confounding factors vary according to the social phenomenon in question. Thus, we would expect that an intervention designed to improve the nutritional habits of families would compete with processes quite different from those affecting a program to improve the occupational skills of young people. Despite the idiosyncratic features of each program and the special characteristics of the particular target population it is designed to reach, certain processes are general enough to be identified as potentially competing with any intervention (Campbell and Stanley, 1966; Cook and Campbell, 1979). Some of the most important of these are outlined below.

Endogenous Change

Social programs operate in environments in which ordinary or "natural" sequences of events influence outcomes. For example, most persons who recover from acute illnesses do so "naturally," because typically ordinary body defenses are sufficient to overcome them. Thus, medical experiments testing a treatment for some pathological condition (say, influenza) must distinguish its effectiveness from the fact that many patients recover from influenza regardless of treatment.

Similarly, in testing for the net effects of a social intervention, one must take into account that the condition for which the intervention is seen as a remedy may change for reasons unrelated to the intervention. Thus, a program for training young people in particular occupational skills must contend with the fact that some people will obtain the same skills in ways that do not involve the program. Likewise, a program to reduce poverty has to consider that some families and individuals will become better off economically without help from the project.

Secular Drift

Relatively long-term trends in the community or country in question may produce changes in gross outcomes that enhance or mask the net effects of a program. Thus, in a period when a community's birthrate is declining generally, a program to reduce fertility in that community may appear to be effective because fertility trends are downward anyway. In such a case, gross outcomes indicate a reduced birthrate whether or not the program had any net effects. Again, a program to upgrade the quality of housing occupied by poor families may appear to be effective mainly because upward national trends in real income enable everyone to put more resources into their housing, thereby producing gross effects that appear to favor the program.

Such secular trends may also mask program impacts producing contrary gross effects that cancel out the positive net effects of an intervention: An effective project to increase crop yields may appear to fail, when only gross effects are observed, because weather conditions led to poor growing conditions during the program period. Similarly, a program to provide employment opportunities to released prisoners may appear to have no effects because it coincides with a depressed period in the labor market.

Interfering Events

Like long-term secular trends, short-term events may produce enhancing or masking changes. An earth tremor that disrupts communications and makes the delivery of food supplements difficult may interfere with a nutritional program. The threat of war with another nation may make it appear that a program to enhance local community cooperation has been effective, when it is actually the potential crisis that has brought community members together.

Maturational Trends

Programs that are directed toward changing persons in infancy, childhood, or adolescence (indeed, in any age-determined target population) have to cope with the fact that over time, maturational processes may be producing considerable changes in individuals that mimic or mask program effects. Thus, evaluation of an educational program designed to increase the language-handling capacities of small children has to compensate for the fact that such capacities naturally increase with age. Similarly, the effectiveness of a campaign to increase interest in sports among young adults may be masked by a decline in such interest that occurs when they enter the labor force. Maturational trends can affect adults also: A program to improve preventive health practices may seem ineffective because health declines with age.

Uncontrolled Selection

By "uncontrolled selection" we mean processes that are not under the control of the evaluator that lead some targets to be more likely than others to participate in the program under evaluation. Some person or agency may control selection of targets, but such selection is *uncontrolled* in the sense that the evaluator cannot materially influence who will or will not be a participant.

The most familiar uncontrolled selection process is target self-selection. For example, persons who volunteer for job training are likely to be more motivated to get jobs than those who do not volunteer. Hence, projects based on the voluntary cooperation of individuals, households, or other units are most likely to be affected by self-selection processes.

In some voluntary programs, self-selection may occur involuntarily from the viewpoint of participants, as a result of political or administrative actions. Consider a community that, through its municipal government, "volunteers" for a program to improve sewage disposal by installing an appropriate technical infrastructure. Although individual community members do not volunteer to participate, all persons living in the area are subject to the "treatment" and hence can benefit from the program. A community in which officials are more likely to "volunteer" its residents may be more progressive in other respects, or perhaps more affluent or different in some other respect that affects outcome results. Similarly, in the adoption of a new (and presumably improved) textbook for elementary schoolchildren, individual pupils ordinarily do not volunteer to use the textbook. The "volunteering" in this case is done by the school system.

There are similar processes at work, but in the opposite direction, that lead to differential attrition in program participation. It is seldom the case that participation in a treatment program is carried through to the end of a project, either by or for all participants. Dropout rates vary from project to project but are almost always disturbingly significant. Subjects who leave a program may be different in quite understandable ways from those who remain throughout. For one thing, those who feel they are benefiting from the intervention are likely to remain or be encouraged to do so, while those who find the project unrewarding or difficult are likely to drop out or be discouraged from remaining in the program. The consequence of attrition ordinarily is that the participants remaining through to the end of a program are those who may have needed the program least and were more likely to have changed on their own.

Although several evaluators have identified additional extraneous confounding factors (see especially Campbell and Stanley, 1966; Cook and Campbell, 1979), they are either primarily applicable to laboratory conditions or are encountered rarely. The extraneous confounding factors listed above are those to which an evaluator must be particularly alert in designing impact assessment research.

DESIGN EFFECTS

The obstacles to estimating net effects described above are a consequence of the nature of the social problem involved, the substance of the intervention, and its implementation. These confounding factors are neither equally nor uniformly distributed across all impact evaluations. Thus, one may not have to be much concerned about maturational effects in a study of the potential work disincentives of unemployment benefits, because such studies usually involve adults in the prime of their working lives and are relatively short in duration. Maturational effects are undoubtedly much more important in the study of impacts of programs directed at preschool children.

In contrast, design effects are always present and hence always threaten the validity of impact assessments. Fortunately, our knowledge about design effects is more complete than our understanding of extraneous confounding factors. Hence, it is possible to estimate and sometimes compensate for such errors, while adjusting for extraneous confounding effects is always problematic.

Stochastic Effects

The end result of any effort to measure effects is usually an estimate derived from observations of the size of such effects. For example, a carefully controlled study of the effectiveness of a teaching method may lead to findings that a class using that method increased its scores on an achievement test by 7.8 points more than a control group taught by conventional methods. Here the issue is whether or not 7.8 points is a large enough difference to conclude that the new teaching method is decidedly better.

Judgments about the size of differences are not easy to make, mainly for the simple reason that we can expect some differences between the experimental and control classes even if both were taught exactly the same way by the same teacher. Chance fluctuations can assure that in any pair of comparable student groups, differences between the two will be found. Just as samples from an urn in which there are exactly the same number of white and black balls will have either more or less than an even number of white and black balls, so any two classes may differ from each other in learning when measured at any one point in time. Of course, over many samples the proportion of black balls will average out to 50 percent; in a large number of tests of two comparable classes the differences in achievement scores also will average out to zero, even though on any one test there will be some differences in scores.

Given the inherent instability of measures taken on samples, how can we judge whether a given difference is big enough that we would be safe in believing that it is not the result of a chance fluctuation? Fortunately, there are adequate theories and models of sampling variation to help us make that judgment. Sampling variations are dependent on two characteristics of the observations made: First, the larger the sample, the smaller the sample-to-sample variation. Second, the more variable the individuals in a sample, the larger the sample-to-sample variation; that is, the more sampling variability, the larger the standard deviation (or variance).

For example, if the test used in the illustration given above had a standard deviation of 10 and the classes consisted of 100 pupils each, we can expect, on the basis of sampling theory, that two-thirds of classes of that size would show sampling variations that would lead to differences between the classes of +0.7 and –0.7. Furthermore, only one comparison in 1000 would show differences that are greater than +1.4 or lesser than –1.4. Given those considerations, it would be fairly safe to assume that a finding of 7.8 points difference between the two classes indicates an effect larger than may be reasonably attributed to chance. This line of reasoning is known as "statistical inference," inferring from what is known about the sizes of sampling variations.

But there is also the possibility that an impact assessment may characterize an intervention as ineffective when in fact it was effective. The concept of statistical power is useful in understanding the issues involved here. "Statistical power" refers to the likelihood that a given evaluation design will detect a net effect of a given size, taking into account the statistical properties of the measures used and the statistical procedures employed. For example, given an estimated value for the correlation between pre- and posttest scores for experimental and control groups, and given also sample size estimates, the probability of detecting a net effect of a given size can be calculated. This is known as the power of a statistical analysis. Conversely, calculating the statistical probability of results allows the estimation of appropriate sample size, given the use of a particular statistical procedure.

Setting the levels of statistical significance for a program evaluation involves making judgments about the relative importance of two types of error:

- *Type I error,* or false positives: Making a positive decision when the correct decision should have been negative; that is, concluding that a program has an effect when it actually does not.
- *Type II error,* or false negatives: Making a negative decision when the correct decision should have been positive; that is, failing to detect a real program effect.

The probability of making a Type I error is a consequence of the level of significance set for the test. One can minimize false positives by setting a very strict criterion for statistical significance, but that increases the probability of making a false negative error (or Type II). The two types of errors are inversely related, and it is possible to minimize both types of error simultaneously only at some increase in cost, usually by increasing the number of observations (sample size).

The calculation of the statistical power of a research is a fairly complicated procedure (Cohen, 1977) and can be accomplished only if one assumes a certain effect size. For example, if the evaluator anticipates that an intervention will produce a net effect of a given size, the power of a research design using a given level of significance and based on a sample of a given size can be calculated. The resulting coefficient, *beta,* is the probability that results of that size will be detected as statistically significant. Thus a beta of .80 indicates that 8 out of 10 studies with samples of that size will reveal that the intervention produces a statistically significant result if the .05 level is chosen.

In every evaluation project, one should decide a priori which of the two types of error is more important, and the study and particularly any statistical analysis should be designed accordingly. The judgment of whether it is more important to minimize false positives or false negatives is clearly one that should be based on the substantive area of the evaluation, not on theory or statistics.

Let us illustrate the circumstances under which false positives and false negatives dominate. In testing the equipment of an airplane for safety, it is clear that false positives are more serious than false negatives. In short, it is more important to avoid certifying as safe an airplane that might fail in use (i.e., avoid false positives) than it is to avoid rejecting as unsafe one that would not fail in use. One can make this judgment under the principle that preserving life is more important than developing and manufacturing airplanes inexpensively. Analogous decisions apply to medical interventions.

In contrast, the opposite situation may obtain in a relatively low-cost program such as an educational television intervention: Since effective educational programs of any type are difficult to design and the negative effects of adopting an ineffective project are not very serious (especially in the absence of other educational alternatives), it follows that in this case false positives are less costly than false negatives. It may be better to adopt a pool of educational projects that, in statistical terms, are problematic in their effectiveness in the hope that at least some actually are effective. Chapter 9 will take up the issue of judging evaluation results in greater detail. As we will see in that chapter, there are additional considerations, also based on value judgments, that should also be taken into account.

The general point of this section is that stochastic effects are designated as design effects because they can be minimized to some extent by modifications in design. If one anticipates small effects, then sample sizes can (and should be) enlarged so that the sampling variation will be smaller than the anticipated effects. Thus, if one anticipated, in the illustration used earlier, that the new teaching method would produce only average score gains between .5 and 1.0, then sample sizes would have to be several times larger than suggested in the illustration.

This is not the context in which it would be appropriate to introduce more than the barest minimum essentials of statistical inference. Any person planning to conduct evaluation research should be familiar with the main issues and methods of statistical inference, as may be found in Blalock (1979), Hanushek and Jackson (1977), Kmenta (1971), and other introductory textbooks on the uses of statistics in the social sciences.

Measurement Unreliability

Any measuring instrument, classification scheme, or counting procedure is subject to greater or lesser amounts of reliability. Measurement error, or the extent to which a measuring instrument produces results that vary from administration to administration when applied to the same (or comparable) object plagues all measurement, whether of physical or social objects.

A measure is reliable to the extent that in a given situation, it produces the same results repeatedly. Although all measurement is subject to reliability problems, measures have such problems to varying degrees. Thus, the measurement of height and weight in adults through the use of standard devices is regarded as more reliable than measurement of intelligence. That is, the use of measuring devices for height and weight in the hands of reasonably competent persons will produce less variability in measurement from one administration to another than will the repeated application of various intelligence tests. Similarly, IQ tests have been found to be more reliable than the measurement of household expenditures for consumer goods. In turn, the latter has been found more reliable than typical attitude scales.

For evaluators, a major source of unreliability lies in the nature of measurement instruments used, many of which are based on subjects' responses to written or oral questions posed to them by researchers. Colloquial language is inherently ambiguous. For example, many attitudinal scales that rely on subjects' agreement or disagreement with statements manifest some degree of unreliability because of the different meanings attributed to the same statements by different subjects. Furthermore, differences in the testing or measuring situation, observer or interviewer differences in measure administration, or even subjects' mood swings also contribute to unreliability.

The effect of the unreliability of measures is to dilute and obscure real differences when they exist. A truly effective intervention will appear to be less effective than it actually is if outcome measures have low reliability. To detect effectiveness, a larger sample is required than would be the case were a more reliable measure used.

An illustration of the effect of unreliability is shown in Table 5.1, where two measures of differing reliability are compared in a hypothetical example of an educational intervention designed to raise levels of cognitive achievement among children from a disadvantaged background. The "true" outcome of the hypothetical program is shown in Panel I. In the participating group, 40 out of 50 (80 percent) reached high achievement levels at the end of the program, but only 25 out of 50 (50 percent) of the nonparticipating or control individuals reached those levels. These "true" results would be observed if we had a perfectly reliable measure of cognitive achievement.

The reliability of two measures, A and B, is compared in Panel II: Measure A is less reliable than Measure B. Note that when a child is "truly"

**TABLE 5.1 A Hypothetical Example of Attenuation Effects of
Measurement Unreliability on Intervention Outcomes**

I. True outcome without measurement error:

	Participants	Nonparticipants
High Achiever	40 (80%)	25 (50%)
Low Achiever	10 (20%)	25 (50%)
	True Program Effect = 30%	

II. Comparison of percentages correctly classified on measures of achievement that vary in reliability:

	Observed Measurement for Measure A		Observed Measurement for Measure B	
	High	Low	High	Low
High Achiever	60%	40%	90%	10%
Low Achiever	40%	60%	10%	90%

III. Measured outcomes using Measure A and Measure B

	Measure A		Measure B	
	Participants	Nonpar-ticipants	Participants	Nonpar-ticipants
High Achiever	28 (56%)	25 (50%)	37 (74%)	25 (50%)
Low Achiever	22 (44%)	25 (50%)	13 (26%)	25 (50%)
Measured Effect =	6%		24%	

a high achiever, Measure A shows that individual to be correctly classified 60 percent of the time; when a child is truly a low achiever, Measure A shows that individual correctly as a low achiever only 60 percent of the time. In contrast, the corresponding figure for Measure B, the more reliable measure, is 90 percent. In short, Measure A makes mistakes in classification 40 percent of the time, while Measure B makes such mistakes only 10 percent of the time.

The different effects of the application of the two unreliable measures to the outcome of the hypothetical intervention are shown in the bottom panel of Table 5.1. On Measure A, we find 28 high achievers, or 56 percent of the participating group: (60 percent of 40 = 24) + (40 percent of 10 = 4), or 28. With Measure B, we would obtain 37 high achievers, or 74 percent of the experimental group: (90 percent of 40 = 36) + (10 percent of 10 = 1), or 37. Using Measure A, we obtain a difference between the nonparticipating and the participating groups of only 6 percent, while for Measure B the contrast is 24 percent. Clearly, Measure B, because it is more reliable, comes closer to showing the extent to which the program was effective.

Note that neither Measure A nor Measure B provides an accurate estimate of the hypothetical program's effects, both underestimating the true effects considerably. The problem is known as "attenuation due to unreliability" and is well documented (Bohrnstedt, 1982; Nunnally and Durham, 1975).

In most cases, it is not possible to eradicate unreliability completely, although it is possible to make adjustments in results that take it into account, if the degree of unreliability is known. The point of the example shown in Table 5.1 is to emphasize the importance of care in both the construction and the application of measurement devices.

There are no hard-and-fast rules about acceptable levels of reliability. Measures generally lose their utility, however, when their reproducibility falls below 75 to 80 percent; that is, when less than 75-80 percent of objects measured on two occasions with the same instrument are given the same scores. (See Blalock and Blalock, 1968; and Rossi et al., 1983, for ways to estimate reliability.)

Validity in Measurement

The issue of *measurement validity* is more difficult to deal with than the problem of reliable measurement. A measure is valid to the extent that it measures what it is intended to measure. While the concept of validity is easy to comprehend, it is difficult to test whether a particular instrument is valid, because for many, if not most, social and behavioral variables, no agreed-upon testing standards exist. For example, the validity of a measure of willingness to take business risks, if formulated as an attitude scale, ideally might require as a validity test some behavioral measure of the extent to which an individual is willing to take actions that might be profitable but also involve a good deal of risk. This would also have to be a scale that most researchers concerned with studying risk taking would agree is a valid measure. Although in principle it is possible to collect such behavioral data, doing so ordinarily is not practical in view of the time and costs involved. Furthermore, not all experts on the subject would accept that scale as an appropriate measure of risk taking, but would prefer, perhaps, a less direct measure—say, willingness to buy lottery tickets.

In practice, there are a number of ways such attitudes can be measured; that is, there are many different questions that could be asked that would be related, at least conceptually, to the idea of risk taking. If there were one way or a small number of ways that everyone could accept as the "best" method of measuring risk taking, then potential measures could be compared to the "best" measure. However, in the absence of a best measure, the question of whether a particular measure or set of measures is valid is usually a matter of case-by-case argument.

Clearly a useful measure must be both valid and reliable, in the sense of reliability that was discussed in the last section. Reliability is a necessary but insufficient criterion for selecting measures.

The validity of measures used for evaluations turns out to be a charac-teristic that depends very much on the widespread acceptance of the measures as valid among the appropriate stakeholders, including members of the scientific community. For example, there are several measures that are widely accepted as validly measuring "drunkenness," including "breathalyzer" test results, whether or not a person "blacked out," and blood alcohol level. Asking persons suspected of being drunk whether or not they are drunk is not regarded as a valid measure. Or, to take another example: There are many studies of "success" in marriage, but few widely accepted measures of marital success. Everyone will agree that a marriage that ends in divorce or separation was not a successful marriage, but there is no equivalent widespread acceptance of measures that are based on married couples' self-ratings of happiness in marriage.

The main criteria that must be met for a measure to be considered valid are as follows:

1. *Consistency with Usage:* A valid measure of a concept must be consistent with past work that has used that concept. Hence, a measure of "adoption of innovation" must not contradict the usual ways the term "adoption" has been used in previous studies of innovation.
2. *Consistency with Alternative Measures:* A valid measure must be consistent with alternative measures that have been used effectively by other evaluators. It must produce roughly the same results as other measures that have been proposed, or, if different, have sound conceptual reasons for being different.
3. *Internal Consistency:* A valid measure must be internally consistent. That is, if several data items are used to measure a concept, the several measures should be related to each other as if they were alternative measures of the same thing.
4. *Consequential Predictability:* Some measures implicitly or explicitly imply prediction of one kind of another. For example, a measure of "propensity to move" implies by its name alone that it predicts whether or not a person or household will move. For such a measure to be judged valid, it should in fact predict moving behavior. Although not all measures have such clearly implied predictability, many do, and such measures ought to be tested for an adequate degree of predictability.

It should be fairly obvious that the above criteria are a conservative force in the sense that they stress heavily the use of existing measures and discourage innovation in measurement. This conservative bent, however, is mitigated somewhat by the last criterion, consequential predictability. If a proposed new measure can be shown to be a better predictor than a previously accepted measure, it will tend to supplant the latter.

Measuring Outcomes Properly

A critical measurement problem in evaluations is the selection of the appropriate measure for assessing program outcome. A poorly conceptualized outcome measure may not properly represent the objective of the program being evaluated and may lead stakeholders to question the measure's validity, as well as the evaluation in general. An unreliable outcome measure is likely to underestimate the effectiveness of a program, and could lead to incorrect inferences about the program's utility.

For example, a family planning program might consider the following alternatives for measuring outcomes, each of which fulfills the four criteria outlined in the previous section:

- proportion adopting effective contraceptive practices
- average desired number of children
- average number of children born to completed households
- attitudes toward large families

These four possibilities do not exhaust all of the measures that can reasonably be viewed as relevant to the goal of reducing fertility. Furthermore, they vary in terms of ease of measurement and data collection costs. Thus, although a reduction in the average number of children born to "completed" families (i.e., those past childbearing) may be the best expression of the eventual goal of a fertility-reduction program, the use of that measure to define outcome implies a long-term evaluation of considerable complexity and cost. In contrast, it may be easy to measure attitudes toward large families, proceeding on the assumption that an effective fertility-reduction program is reflected in low approval of large families.

Alternative measures of outcome can be viewed as more or less direct expressions of program objectives. Given what is known about the often small and erratic magnitude of the relationship between attitudes and behavior, a downward shift in the average desirability of large families is likely to be a remote measure of the goals of a fertility-reduction program. Changes in such attitudes often may occur without a corresponding shift in fertility practices. The "consequential predictability" of such a measure is not likely to be very high.

In other words, a good outcome measure is one that may feasibly be employed, given the constraints of time and budget, and one that is more or less directly related to the goals of the program, and hence valid. Of the four alternatives listed for measuring reductions, shifts in contraceptive practices may be, on balance, the best choice as a measure. Contraceptive practices can be studied over relatively short periods of time; there are ample precedents for adequate measurements in previous research; and, in terms of what is known about fertility behavior, shifts in contraceptive practices are directly related to fertility. (See Exhibit 5-A for discussion of how a variety of outcome measures have been established for a program designed to improve the use of public health clinics in preventive children's health practices.)

Often, desired outcomes cannot be measured very directly or can be measured only at great expense. Under such circumstances, "proxy" measures—measures that stand in for objectives that are not measured directly—must be substituted. The selection of a proxy measure is clearly a critical decision. Ideally, a proxy measure should be closely related to the "direct" measure of the project objectives, but should also be much easier to obtain. In practice, it is often necessary to accept proxy measures that are less than ideal. While there are no firm rules for the selection of appropriate proxy measures, there are some guidelines.

First, for objectives that are measurable *in principle* but too costly to measure *in practice,* previous research may include studies that test the worth of alternatives. For example, one may be concerned with whether or not jobs obtained by persons completing training programs are better than those trainees might have found otherwise. In principle, the quality of jobs may be measured by some weighted combination of earnings, wage rates, steadiness of employment, working conditions, or other measurable job attributes. Several reasonable proxy measures can be employed instead of such a long and expensive procedure: Earnings and wage rates are good proxies, given that previous research has shown that such job attributes are highly correlated (i.e., better-paying jobs tend to have better working conditions, more employment security, and so on).

Second, objectives that are expected to be reached far in the future can be represented by proxy measures that are intermediate steps toward those goals. For example, while the objective of a project on family fertility is to reduce average family size, that goal can be measured definitively only after the women in those families have passed through their childbearing years. Proxy measures that center on the adoption of practices that will reduce completed fertility are reasonable surrogates (e.g., adoption of contraceptive practices and changes in expressed desired family size).

The "Hawthorne Effect"

In a famous experiment—an attempt to determine the effects of varying light intensity on the productivity of women assembling small electronic parts (Roethlisberger and Dickson, 1939)—it was discovered that *any* change in the intensity of illumination, either positive or negative, brought about a rise in worker productivity. The Hawthorne Effect (named after the site where the experiment was conducted) was interpreted by the experimenters as the result of experimenting, which included continuous observations of work-group members. Roethlisberger and Dickson reasoned that the workers took the fact that they had been singled out as an experimental group and given a lot of attention by the experimenters as a sign that the firm was interested in their personal welfare. Their response

---

Exhibit 5-A: Program Outcome Measures

In a program to increase the use of a public health clinic by young children for preventive health care rather than episodic care for emergency conditions, the outcome was measured in a variety of ways:

A. Measures of the success of the clinic's immunization program.
  1. Average age at which patient received each of seven different immunizations.
  2. The percentage of patients receiving their first polio immunization before 3 months of age.
  3. Percentage of patients receiving all of their immunizations before the age of 30 months.
B. Measures of the clinic's success in reducing accidents and illnesses.
  1. Percentage decrease (or increase) in acute episodes of accidents and illnesses from the first to second year of enrollment in clinic.
C. Measures of continuity of health care.
  1. Rate of broken appointments with clinic.
  2. On-time arrival rate.
  3. Rate of return of patients for follow-up visits after initial treatment.

SOURCE: Summary, by permission, of M. S. Augustin, E. Stevens, and D. Hicks, "An Evaluation of the Effectiveness of a Children and Youth Project." *Health Services Report,* 88 (December 1973): 942-946.

---

was to develop a high level of work-group morale and to increase their productivity. The measured outcome of the experiment was a combination of the intervention (increased illumination), the delivery of that intervention (apparent concern on the part of the management and the presence of experimenters in the workplace), and the constant observation.

The Hawthorne Effect is not exclusive to social experiments. It may be present in any circumstance in which there are human subjects. For example, in medical experiments, especially those involving pharmacological treatments, the Hawthorne Effect is known as the "placebo effect." Subjects may be as much affected by the knowledge that they are receiving treatment as by the treatment itself. Thus, the evaluation of the effectiveness of a new analgesic (painkiller) usually involves both a placebo control, consisting of a group of patients who are given essentially neutral medication (sugar pills), and a control given the "standard" pill commonly prescribed. The effectiveness of the analgesic is measured by how much more relief from the new drug is reported in comparison to that reported by those who received either the placebo or the standard pill.

A reanalysis of the Hawthorne experiment (Franke and Kaul, 1978), however, casts considerable doubt on whether the data actually demonstrated any Hawthorne Effect at all. This study underscores the fact that the effect may be less important than once thought.

Delivery System Contaminants

Another design effect stems from the fact that treatment is rarely delivered in a "pure" form. Thus, providing psychological counseling for juvenile delinquents usually involves not only a therapist but also other personnel (intake clerks, for example), a setting in which therapy is conducted, the reactions of those among the juveniles' peer group who know of the therapy, and so on. The intervention delivery system (including the physical plant, personnel, rules and regulations and the labeling of targets) affects the outcome of a planned intervention—indeed, so much so that monitoring the delivery of interventions is almost always a necessary adjunct to impact assessments.

Missing Values

No data collection plan is ever executed perfectly. For a variety of reasons, almost all data sets have gaps consisting of cases for which some portion of the required measures do not exist. In longitudinal studies, some respondents move away and cannot be located, others tire of participation and refuse to provide more information, others become too sick or disabled to participate; the result is that measures are often missing on some program participants or comparison group members. In addition, even for individuals who have consistently participated, some data are often missing: Interviewers forget to ask questions, or respondents inadvertently skip over items on questionnaires or simply refuse to answer questions that they regard as intrusive.

Were missing data randomly spread across observations, their main effect, as with unreliability, would be the obscuring of differences. But ordinarily that is not the case: Persons lost to an evaluation through attrition (dropping out) are often different from those who remain in ways related to treatment, outcome, or both. For example, in experiments on the effects of welfare payments, families in the control group who received no payments were more likely to drop out. Persons who refuse to answer questions are often different from those who answer. For example, more high-income persons than low-income persons refuse to answer questions about income.

Sample Design Effects

Most evaluation research is carried out on samples of potential or actual targets and controls. In order to generalize findings properly from such evaluations, it is essential that the sampling be designed properly and that the design be carried out with some degree of fidelity. The design of samples is a highly technical task and most evaluators faced with a sampling task of any magnitude would be well advised to enlist the aid of a sampling statistician.

The goal of a sampling strategy is selection of an unbiased sample of a relevant, sensible universe. The first task is the identification of a relevant, sensible universe—that is, a population including those units (persons, households, firms, or whatever) that are actual and/or potential targets of the program in question. Thus a program that is designed to provide benefits to young males between the ages of 16 and 20 should be tested on a sample composed of young men in that age range.

The second task is the selection of a sample from the identified universe in an unbiased fashion. An unbiased selection procedure is one that allows each and every unit in the universe a known, nonzero probability of being selected. In practice, this often means that every member of the universe has an equal chance of being selected. There are many ways of designing such a selection strategy; the interested reader is referred to standard textbooks on the sampling of human populations for additional details. (Good introductions to the problems of sampling of human populations can be found in Sudman, 1976, and in Rossi et al., 1983.)

The final task of a sampling strategy is the implementation of the selection strategy with fidelity; that is, persons who are supposed to be included in the sample should in fact be selected. Rarely, if ever, is a sample of noninstitutionalized humans carried out without some persons being missed. Indeed, most survey researchers are pleased when they are able to obtain cooperation from 75 percent or more of a designated sample.

The three main tasks of a sampling strategy also point to the three ways in which errors (or bad luck) in sampling can affect estimates of net impact. Errors (or bad luck) at each stage have very much the same effect, namely, producing samples of actual or potential targets that are biased in some potentially damaging way. For example, mistakes in identifying a relevant universe can produce estimates that are not relevant to the actual or intended target of a program. Thus, an impact assessment of a program for criminals convicted of minor offenses cannot be tested on a sample of persons on Death Row. A sampling strategy that permits biased selection can also have the effect of producing irrelevant estimates of net effects. For example, advertising for volunteers in local newspapers is almost guaranteed to produce a huge bias; those who volunteer are likely to be very different from the potential or actual target group.

Minimizing Design Effects

As suggested earlier in this chapter, design effects are technical deficiencies in research design the impact of which ordinarily is to diminish the power of a given research to discern net effects when they exist. Careful planning of evaluations is the remedy for design effects. In some cases, when evaluations are planned that involve, say, new measurement efforts, extensive pretesting may be advisable.

It is not possible to go into extensive detail here on the statistical or measurement issues involved in minimizing design effects. The interested reader is referred to good introductory texts on data collection strategies or on measurement issues (e.g., Bradburn and Sudman, 1982; Torgerson, 1958; Rossi et al., 1983). Statistical issues are dealt with extensively in Hanushek and Jackson (1977), Blalock (1979), and Cohen (1977).

DESIGN STRATEGIES FOR ISOLATING THE EFFECTS OF EXTRANEOUS FACTORS

A major strategic issue in impact assessment is how to obtain estimates of what the difference would be between two conditions: one in which the intervention is present and one in which it is absent. Ideally, the absent condition should be identical in all respects to the present condition, save for the intervention. There are several alternative (but not mutually exclusive) approaches that vary in effectiveness; all involve the establishment of "controls," groups of targets that represent the condition of being without the treatment. "Controls," then, are the method by which what would have happened, absent the treatment, is estimated. The several common approaches to establishing controls are sketched below, and will be discussed in detail in this and the following two chapters:

- *Randomized Controls:* Targets are randomly divided into an experimental group, to whom the intervention is administered, and "randomized controls," from whom the intervention is withheld.
- *Constructed Controls:* Targets to whom the intervention is given are matched with an "equivalent" group, constructed controls, from whom the intervention is withheld.
- *Statistical Controls:* Participant and nonparticipant targets are compared, statistically holding constant differences between participants and nonparticipants.
- *Reflexive Controls:* Targets who receive the intervention are compared to themselves, as measured before the intervention.

- *Repeated Measures Reflexive Controls:* A special case of reflexive controls in which targets are observed repeatedly over time. Also called "panel" studies.
- *Time-Series Reflexive Controls:* A special case of reflexive controls in which rates of occurrence of some events are compared before and after the start of some intervention.
- *Generic Controls:* Intervention effects among targets are compared with established norms about typical changes occurring in the target population.
- *Shadow Controls:* Targets who receive the intervention are compared to the judgments of experts, program administrators, and/or participants on what changes are "ordinarily to be expected" for the target population.

Full- versus Partial-Coverage Programs

The most severe restriction on design choice is whether or not the intervention in question is being delivered to all (or virtually all) members of a target population. For programs with total coverage (as in the case of long-standing, ongoing programs), it is usually not possible to identify a group that is not receiving the intervention and that is, in essential senses, comparable to the subjects who are beneficiaries. In short, it is not possible to define a control group. In such circumstances, the main strategy available is the use of reflexive controls and before-and-after comparisons. In contrast, interventions that are to be tested on a demonstration basis ordinarily will not be delivered to all of the target population. Hence, in the start-up phase, new programs are, by definition, programs with partial coverage.

In all likelihood, no program has ever achieved total coverage of its intended target population. Even in the best of programs, there are some persons who refuse to participate, others who are not aware that they can participate, and still others who are declared ineligible on technicalities. Nevertheless, many programs achieve almost full coverage. The Social Security Administration's retirement payments, for example, reach most of the eligible portions of the target population.

For purposes of the present discussion, we employ the following rule of thumb: When a program reaches as many as four of five eligible units, it is considered to have "full coverage." The smaller the proportion who are not reached, the greater the differences are likely to be between those who are covered and those who are not: For all practical intents, almost all children between the ages of six and fourteen attend school; those who do not suffer from temporary or permanent disabilities, receive tutoring at home from parents or private tutors, or are members of migratory worker families who move constantly from work site to work site. Hence, those children who at any point in time are not enrolled in school are likely to be so different from those who attend that no amount of matching or use of statistical controls will produce comparability of the kind needed for controls.

Fortunately for evaluation purposes, there are some programs with full coverage that are also *not uniform* over time or over localities. These differences over time and across administrative subdivisions provide the evaluator with some limited opportunities to assess their effects and hence the effects of variations in the program. Thus, one might not be able to assess what the net impact of elementary schooling is (as compared to no schooling at all), but one can assess the *differential* impact of various kinds of schools and of changes in schools over time.

These variations in ongoing, established programs occur in a variety of ways: Policies change over time, along with their accompanying programs. An intervention's administrators may institute modifications in order to meet some new condition or make administration easier. Thus, from time to time, social security benefits have been increased to take into account new conditions or to add new services (e.g., Medicare). Similarly, sufficient local autonomy may be given to states and local governments so that a program (e.g, Aid to Families with Dependent Children) may vary somewhat from place to place. With proper precautions, such "natural variation" may provide leverage for the estimation of program effects.

For partial-coverage programs, a larger variety of strategies are available. If the program is under the control of the evaluator (as may be the case in new or prospective programs), the ideal solution is the use of randomly selected controls: A set of potential targets, representative of those who might be served if the program goes into effect, are selected in some unbiased way and randomly sorted into an experimental group and a control group. This process of randomization assures probabilistic equivalence of the beneficiaries receiving the intervention (the experimental group) to others who are not (the randomized controls). When an evaluator cannot employ randomization in the formation of experimental and control groups or conditions, adequate constructed control groups often may be formed by uncovered target subjects, if proper precautions are taken.

A CATALOGUE OF
IMPACT ASSESSMENT DESIGNS

The simultaneous consideration of control strategies, intervention features, and data collection strategies produces the schematic classification of impact assessment research design shown in Table 5.2. Each of the research designs shown in the table will be discussed separately below.

Design I:
Randomized "True" Experiments

"True" experiments are applicable only to partial-coverage programs. The essential feature of true experiments is the random assignment of treatments to targets and the random withholding of treatment from targets, constituting, respectively, an experimental and a control group.

Randomized true experiments may vary greatly in complexity, as the following examples illustrate. (See also Boruch et al., 1978, for a relatively complete list of randomized social experiments.)

- To gauge the effectiveness of educational training films used in World War II, alternative versions of training films were shown to randomly selected troops whose understanding of the lessons was measured before and after viewing. The versions were then compared (Hovland et al., 1949).
- To test whether provision of limited amounts of financial aid would help prisoners released from state prisons to adjust to civilian life, 400 prisoners released from Maryland prisons were divided randomly into three experimental groups: one that received eligibility for 13 weeks of unemployment benefits, one that received 13 weeks of benefits and job placement help, and one that received job placement help only. A fourth group received neither benefits nor placements. The 400 persons were interviewed periodically over the years following release (Rossi et al., 1980).
- To assess whether reducing mothers' anxiety about minor surgery for their children resulted in better posthospital sequelae for their children, mothers were first randomized into experimental and control groups. The former received counseling and reassurance when their children were admitted; the controls received "usual" care (Skipper and Leonard, 1968).
- To test how best to handle cases of spouse abuse, a Minneapolis police precinct agreed to participate in a randomized experiment designed by the Police Foundation in which cases of spouse abuse reported to the police were handled randomly in one of three ways: The abusing spouse was arrested and kept in jail overnight; the abusing spouse was asked to leave the home and not to return for 16 hours; or the police attempted to conciliate the dispute between the spouses (Sherman, 1980).
- In the Experimental Housing Allowance Demand Experiment, a random sample of poor households in Pittsburgh and Phoenix were randomly placed either in one of twenty-three experimental groups or in a control group. The experimental groups were offered one of a variety of plans subsidizing the costs of housing. The plans varied in generosity and in the conditions under which payment would be made. Each of the participating families was followed for four years with periodic interviews and housing inspections (Kennedy, 1980).

Corresponding to complexity, the costs of the experiments described above varied widely, the most expensive being the Housing Allowance Demand Experiment and the least costly being the small-scale experiments conducted with World War II soldiers.

The most elaborate true experiments are longitudinal studies consisting of a series of periodic observations of experimental and control groups. Most of the large-scale field experiments undertaken over the past two decades to test proposed national programs have been longitudinal randomized experiments in which data on participants were collected over periods of years. For example, the several negative income tax experiments have all employed the same basic longitudinal design, varying one from the other in the kinds of treatments tested and in the length of time over which the intervention treatments were given, ranging from three to ten years.

The New Jersey Income Maintenance Experiment (Kershaw and Fair, 1976; Rossi and Lyall, 1976) was designed with eight experimental groups, each of which was offered a slightly different income maintenance plan, and one control group. Eligible families were randomly assigned to one of the nine groups. Each participating family was studied over a three-year period, through monthly income reporting requirements, and quarterly and annual interviews, in addition to special reviews of income tax returns. During the three-year period, the experimental group families were offered cash benefits as part of the income maintenance intervention, and both experimental and control families were paid fees for completing interviews.

Most randomized experiments are designed with pre- and postmeasurements of outcome, primarily because this makes it possible for the initial starting points of targets to be held constant in analyses of experimental effects. (The statistical reason for doing so is explained more fully in Chapter 6.) However, there are often circumstances in which preintervention measures are simply indefinable. For example, prisoner rehabilitation experiments that are designed to affect recidivism can be based only on postintervention measures, because, by definition, recidivism occurs only after release from prison. Similarly, intervention efforts designed to reduce the incidence of disease or accidents have undefined preintervention outcome measures. Several examples of post-only experiments are given in Chapter 6.

Design II:
Quasi-Experiments with Constructed
and/or Statistical Controls

A large class of impact assessment designs consists of nonrandomized "quasi-experiments," which have in common the strategy of comparing

TABLE 5.2 A Typology of Research Designs for Impact Assessment

Research Design	Intervention Assignment to Targets	Type of Controls	Outcome Data Collection Points	Applicability
I: "True" or randomized experiments	Researcher controlled random assignment	Random-ization often with statistical controls	Minimum—after intervention, usually before and after; often many measures during intervention	ONLY partial-coverage programs
II: Quasi-experiments with nonrandom controls	Uncontrolled selection: a nonrandom assignment	Constructed statistical, and/or generic	Minimum—after intervention, usually before and after; often many measures during intervention	ONLY partial-coverage programs
III: Regression-discontinuity	Controlled, biased, but known selection[b]	Statistical controls modeling known selec-tion bias	Minimum—before and after intervention	Partial-coverage programs
IV: Before-and-after studies	Uncontrolled selection	Reflexive	Minimum—before and after intervention	Partial- and full-coverage programs

V: Retrospective before-and-after studies	Uncontrolled selection	Retrospective reflexive	After intervention with retrospective measures of before state	Partial- and full-coverage programs
VI: Panel studies	Uncontrolled selection	Reflexive	More than two measures during intervention	Partial- and full-coverage programs
VII: Time series	Uncontrolled selection	Reflexive	Many measures before and after intervention	Partial- and full-coverage programs
VIII: Cross-sectional surveys	Uncontrolled selection	Statistical	After intervention only	Partial-coverage programs
IX: Judgmental assessments	Uncontrolled selection	Shadow controls	After intervention only	Partial- and full-coverage programs

a. In a few quasi-experiments, the control over who will receive the treatment is exercised by the researcher.
b. Selection process must be clearly stated and faithfully carried through.

"experimental" groups created out of targets who have elected in some fashion to participate in a program (or who have been selected administratively as participants), with "constructed controls" (groups of nonparticipants constructed to be comparable to participants in critical ways).

Closely related to constructed controls are net impact estimates obtained through statistical analysis. Persons who have not participated in a program are compared to those who have, using statistical techniques to adjust for known differences between participants and nonparticipants. Statistical controls are often used along with constructed control groups. Indeed, the combined use of constructed controls and statistical controls can often increase the power of a quasi-experiment considerably.

If statistical controls are used with post-only measures, the design is really a cross-sectional one. (See discussion of Design VIII.) In short, the line between nonrandomized experiments with constructed controls and one-shot surveys is often obscure. The important point, however, is that the reasoning involved in both is much the same: Both attempt to estimate net effects by creating control groups that presumably represent potential targets who were unexposed to the intervention.

Several examples of constructed controls follow:

- In order to estimate the effect of housing allowances on the supply of low-cost dwellings offered by builders and landlords, demonstration housing allowance programs were run in Green Bay, Wisconsin, and South Bend, Indiana. After several years of the demonstration, the prices of housing in those two cities were to be compared with prices in comparable cities in the Midwest (Struyk and Bendick, 1981).
- Students attending public high schools in a random sample of such schools were compared with students attending denominational or secular private schools, holding constant socioeconomic characteristics of the students. The comparison was made to see whether the type of school attended had any effects on average levels of achievement in critical subject areas (Coleman et al., 1981).
- Families who were selected for admission to public housing in Baltimore were matched with families who had applied but were not admitted to the units. Both the public housing families and the constructed controls were interviewed repeatedly over a five-year period (Wilner et al., 1962).

Some of these designs involve many measurements of outcomes made both before and after the interventions. For example, a recent study compared monthly crime rates in Boston, for a period several years before and for a year after the enactment of new gun-control legislation, with trends in comparable jurisdictions in nearby states in the New England region that did not experience any changes in gun-control legislation (Pierce and Bowers, 1979).

Another approach is to use generic controls, which usually consist of measurements purporting to represent the typical performance of targets or the population from which targets may be drawn. Thus, in an evaluation of the performance of schoolchildren enrolled in a new learning program, the participants' scores on a standardized achievement test may be compared with published national norms for schoolchildren of the same ages or grade levels. Generic controls are available for a range of common outcome measures—for example, IQ and achievement tests—but for many others are not readily obtained. In any event, as we will discuss in detail in Chapter 7, generic controls are rarely suitable mainly because target selection often is based on characteristics that differentiate the targets from the general population.

Design III:
Regression Discontinuity Studies

Some programs are administered using a definite and precise set of rules for selection of participants. For example, some college fellowship programs allocate fellowships on the basis of scores received on standardized tests (e.g., the National Merit Scholarship Test), and eligibility for food stamps is determined by family income. If such rules are followed with reasonable fidelity, it is possible to derive fairly good estimates of net effects of the program in question by statistical analyses that focus on persons who are at the cutting points used in selection. The analyses require that the rules of selection be administered uniformly and that valid and reliable measures of outcomes be employed.

Although this approach to studying impact is free of many of the problems associated with nonexperimental designs, it is of limited usefulness because participants in only a minority of programs are selected in a clear and precise fashion. In addition, the statistical analysis in a regression-discontinuity evaluation cannot be undertaken by persons with only an elementary knowledge of statistics. A more extended discussion of this design will be found in Chapter 7. (Detailed discussion of regression discontinuity designs is found in Trochim, 1984.)

Design IV:
Before-and-After Studies

Although few designs have as much intuitive appeal as before-and-after studies, they are among the least valid of assessment approaches. The essential feature of a before-and-after study is a comparison of the same targets at two points in time, separated by a period of participation in a program. Differences in scores from one point in time to the other are taken as an estimate of the net effects of the intervention. The main deficiency of such designs is that they ordinarily do not permit disentangling the effects of extraneous factors from the net effects of intervention.

Design V:
Retrospective Before-and-After Studies

The principal feature of this design is that it is based on retrospective reconstructions of the state of targets before an intervention along with postintervention measures. Typically, targets are located who have participated in a program and are asked to reconstruct what their circumstances were before participation.

For obvious reasons, this design yields estimates of the net effects of programs that are even less plausible than those yielded by straight before-and-after studies based on Design IV. In addition to the ambiguities of interpretation caused by uncontrolled-for extraneous events, this design also suffers from the problems of using fallible reconstructions of the situation before the intervention, relying as it does on possibly faulty recall. For these reasons, use of this design is not recommended.

Design VI:
Panel Studies

Although panel studies appear to be a simple extension of before-and-after designs through the addition of more data collection points, these studies enjoy a considerably higher standing in the order of plausibility of impact assessments. The additional time points, properly employed, allow the researcher to begin to specify the processes by which an intervention has an impact upon targets.

This design is especially important in the study of full-coverage programs. In Chapter 7 we will provide an example of how this design was used to study the impact of children's viewing of violence and aggression on TV programs on their own manifestations of aggression toward their classmates. Given the circumstances of almost universal television viewing among children, and hence the virtual impossibility of establishing controls who do not view, the best approach was to study how varying amounts of viewing violence and aggression affected the display of aggression at some subsequent point in time.

Design VII:
Time-Series Analyses

Time-series analyses may be regarded as an extension of panel studies. A time series provides repeated measures on an aggregate unit, such as a political jurisdiction, with adequate numbers of data points before and after intervention is introduced or substantially modified, so that the effect of the introduction can be identified by a change in the trajectory of the curve plotted from the measures obtained over time. By "aggregate" statistical series, we mean periodic measures taken on a relatively large population, as, for example, vital statistical series (births, deaths, migrations), usually defined as rates for fairly large populations.

Time-series analyses are especially important for estimating the net impacts of full-coverage programs, which present especially difficult problems in impact assessment because they lack uncovered target populations that might serve as controls or yield comparison observations. However, if extensive, over-time, before-program-enactment observations on outcome measures exist, it is possible to use the quite powerful techniques of time-series analyses. Thus, it may be possible to study the effect of the enactment of a gun-control law in a particular jurisdiction, but only if the evaluator has access to a sufficiently long-term series on gun-related offenses. Of course, for many ongoing interventions such long-term measures do not exist. For example, there are no long-term, detailed time series on the incidence of certain acute diseases, making it difficult to assess the impact of Medicare or Medicaid on them.

Although the technical procedures of time-series analyses are quite complicated, the ideas underlying them are quite simple. The trend before a treatment was enacted is analyzed in order to obtain a projection of what would have happened without the intervention. The trend after the intervention is then compared to the resulting projections and statistical tests are used to determine whether or not the postintervention trend is sufficiently different from the projection to justify the inference that the treatment had an effect. For example, time-series analysis can be used to study the effects of changing price policies on household water consumption: by plotting the consumption trends before pricing policy changes, projecting water consumption trends on that basis, and comparing actual consumption with the projections (Berk et al., 1981).

Some of the limitations of time-series analyses are detailed in Chapter 7. Perhaps the most serious limitation is that *many* preintervention time points are needed in order to model preintervention time trends accurately (more than 30 data points are recommended). For this reason, time-series analyses are usually restricted to outcome concerns for which government or other groups routinely collect and publish statistics.

Design VIII:
Cross-Sectional Surveys

Cross-sectional surveys are single censuses or sample surveys. They are cross-sectional in the sense of providing a set of measures as of a particular point or cross section in time. The typical cross-sectional survey used to provide estimates of net effects is usually a sample survey of some target population, part of which has received a treatment (or participated in a program) and part of which has not. In some cases, the cross-sectional survey is of target population members who have received differing amounts of a treatment or who have experienced several variations of the treatment. Targets who received the treatment are compared with those who did not on postintervention outcome measures, using statistical techniques to hold constant differences between the two groups. Although cross-sectional designs are among the less expensive ways to estimate impact, they are also among the more difficult to carry out rigorously. Therefore, they should be employed with all the cautions that will be discussed in Chapter 7.

When cross-sectional surveys are used with partial-coverage programs, they are to be considered a variant of constructed controls. However, their use to gauge the effectiveness of full-coverage programs that vary from place to place constitutes a unique application. Thus, there are several studies that attempt to gauge the effectiveness of gun-control legislation by contrasting levels of restrictions on licensing and gun use (Krug, 1967; Geisel et al., 1969; Seitz, 1972). In this case, the states constitute the units, with the observations being rates for various types of crime *in a particular year*. (The italics in the last sentence emphasize that these studies are not analyses of time series, but use rates at only one point in time.) Note that such impact assessments lead to estimates of how much of a net effect one variation in the treatment has compared to others. In the case of gun-control legislation studies, the variations being assessed are degrees of stringency in state laws.

A variant of the cross-sectional survey is a design that uses constructed controls with after-only measures. One of the best known of such studies is the controversial evaluation of Head Start (Cicerelli et al., 1969), which was based on a comparison of children in the first grade who had participated in Head Start at nursery-school age with first-graders of comparable background in the same or nearby schools who had not participated.

Whether or not a cross-sectional evaluation was carried out properly is a question that centers on the kinds of statistical controls employed—almost always a matter subject to disagreement. The issues involved in the proper design and analysis of one-shot surveys of existing, full-coverage programs with treatment that varies by site are especially complicated, and more will be said about them in Chapter 7.

Design IX:
Judgmental Assessments

The final design considered in Table 5.2 is one in which the judgments of presumed experts, program administrators, or participants play the major role in estimating net impact. In a connoisseurial impact assessment, an expert—or connoisseur—assesses a program, usually through visits to its sites, during which data are gathered informally and a judgment made. Such judgments may be aided by the use of generic controls—that is, existing estimates of performance of the population as a whole—or "shadow" controls—more or less educated guesses about what "normal" or exemplary performance is considered to be. Needless to say, connoisseurial assessments are among the shakiest of all—if not the pinnacle, then surely close to it.

Equally suspect are impact assessments the rely upon the judgments of program administrators. Because of the obvious self-interests involved, the judgments of such persons are far from disinterested and impartial.

In the assessment of some programs, participants' judgments of program success have been used. These judgments have some validity, especially for programs that have as their goals increasing participant satisfaction. But it is usually difficult, if not impossible, for participants to make judgments about net impact, because they do not have the appropriate knowledge.

We do not argue against all judgmental assessments: There are circumstances in which the evaluator has no other choice. And, although some might advise against undertaking any assessment in such cases, we believe that, more often than not, any assessment is better than none. Judgmental designs may be the only ones that can be used in circumstances in which either only small amounts of funds are available or the ways the program is implemented and the targets selected prevent use of stronger designs.

POOLING EVALUATIONS: META-EVALUATIONS

Strictly speaking, meta-evaluations are not a distinctive class of designs. They are an alternative to engaging in *de novo* impact evaluations. Advocates of meta-evaluations argue that it is often possible to cull from the extant body of evaluation studies more definitive evidence of the effectiveness or ineffectiveness of social programs than can be obtained by undertaking an additional impact assessment. Further, they suggest that meta-evaluations can put in perspective and provide summative findings about program impact that are missed unless the results of individual evaluations, which on the surface may appear contradictory, are examined systematically as a single body of evidence.

An illustration may be useful: By the early 1980s there were several hundred studies of the effectiveness of psychotherapy for increasing the functioning of patients. Some of the studies were done very carefully, others almost cavalierly, and a variety of different types of therapies were involved: Some of the studies employed adequate controls, others relied on shadow controls; some found the patients to have improved in subsequent functioning, others either found no improvement or, in some cases, actual deterioration.

In order to try to make sense out of this body of evidence, a group of researchers (Smith et al., 1980) decided to treat each of the evaluations as a case and to attempt a multivariate analysis in which the relevant characteristics of the research were held constant. Culling through the literature, the researchers found 475 evaluations in which groups of individuals who had undergone psychotherapy were compared with one or more control groups. Each of the 475 evaluation studies was coded on a number of dimensions, including the size of the sample, the types of controls employed, the method of psychotherapy used, the duration of treatment, and so on. Measures of the ways the evaluations were undertaken were included, for example, whether or not they were randomized experiments. Using the studies estimates of net effects as the dependent variable and the quality of the evaluations and their implementation effects as the independent variables, the researchers undertook multivariate statistical analyses to estimate the true net effect of psychotherapy (that is, net of the ways the evaluations differed from each other).

The results indicated that there was some substantial improvement in experimental groups who received psychotherapy, amounting to about .85 standard deviations. In other words, persons receiving psychotherapy improved to the point that they were better off than 80 percent of the controls. The researchers also found virtually no differences among therapy types.

Meta-evaluations of this sort have been undertaken in several other fields in which substantial numbers of evaluations have been published, including prisoner rehabilitation, vocational training, and surgical interventions. Although we cannot deal with this approach in great detail here, there are several monographs now available that can introduce the reader to this method (Glass et al., 1981; Light and Pillemer, 1984; Hunter et al., 1982).

MULTIMETHOD IMPACT ASSESSMENTS

The research designs described earlier may sometimes be used jointly, usually to the considerable enhancement of the credibility of conclusions. In some cases, an impact assessment's plausibility may be bolstered by bringing together consistent evidence from a variety of sources using a diversity of approaches, as in the unusual impact assessment using expert judgments, constructed controls, and other types of evidence described in Exhibit 5-B.

This impact assessment was undertaken in support of a lawsuit started by the survivors of a devastating flood in Buffalo Creek, West Virginia. The flood was caused by the failure of a dam built and maintained by a coal mining company. The plaintiffs asked for compensation for lasting psychological damages inflicted by the event. Note that this amounts to an assertion that there were net effects, hence making an impact assessment relevant in which the issue was the net effects of the disaster event on the survivors' mental health status.

The basic evidence presented to the court consisted of testimony by psychiatrists for the plaintiffs and defendants concerning the current mental health of the survivors. This testimony amounted to contradictory estimates of net effects, the plaintiffs' psychiatrist claiming that there was evidence of some enduring mental distress that could be traced to the flood event, and the defendants' psychiatrist acknowledging existing mental distress but attributing that distress to long-standing conditions that preceded the flood.

The research team hired by the plaintiffs' lawyers assembled several types of additional evidence that in effect tried to meet the challenges presented by competing explanations. The additional evidence attempted to refute charges of self-selection, provided evidence from constructed controls, and showed that the severity of the plaintiffs' symptoms varied with the "strength of the treatment," that is, how badly damaged they were in the flood. The evidence presented by the researchers was so compelling that the coal company settled out of court before the end of the trial.

Any one of the approaches used by the research team in this example would not have been convincing by itself. However, the fact that several approaches all led to the same conclusion was quite convincing to the court.

The general point made here is that the plausibility of an impact assessment can be enhanced considerably through the employment of several approaches, provided, of course, that those approaches yield results that are complementary and not contradictory.

TYPES OF DATA USEFUL
FOR IMPACT ASSESSMENT

The previous discussion of research designs has been almost exclusively concerned with quantitative studies. Whether the data collected should be qualitative or quantitative is a separate issue. Quantitative data can be

Exhibit 5-B: An Impact Assessment of the Long-Range Effects of a Man-Made Disaster

A tragic man-made disaster struck the small West Virginia town of Buffalo Creek when a dam built by a coal company above the town gave way after a torrential rain in the middle of the night. The released water wiped out the town, causing many deaths and injuries. A large group of survivors sued the coal company for negligence and claimed that the trauma had produced long-lasting effects on the mental health of the survivors. The survivors' suit claimed that the plaintiffs were suffering from depression, had elevated clinical symptoms, including high blood pressure levels, experienced recurring terrifying dreams, and had other psychological effects. The coal company's reply was that whatever mental health problems bothered the plaintiffs were not due to the disaster but had existed prior to it. Note that this is exactly the same sort of issue that is at the heart of impact assessment, namely, did the disaster produce net effects, above and beyond what one might expect had the disaster not occurred?

Both sides in the case employed experts to testify to their conflicting claims. The coal company's lawyers hired a psychiatrist to interview the survivors, and so did the plaintiffs' lawyers. Survivors were interviewed by both sets of experts. At least partially as a result of the evidence produced, the coal company settled out of court, providing a generous payment to the survivors to compensate them for their losses, including damages inflicted on their mental health.

After the settlement, a group of behavioral scientists at the University of Cincinnati obtained access to the evidence used in the case by both sides and analyzed those materials in considerable detail. In addition, data were collected to supplement the materials used in court. The objective of the analyses undertaken was to undertake an impact assessment. Although each part of the evidence collected by the research team was not in itself completely convincing, the fact that all the evidence pointed in the same direction was very convincing. First, the social scientists showed that the two psychiatrist experts who examined each of the survivors agreed on the assessments of individual survivors and also, in general, agreed that the survivors were showing low levels of mental health. The coal company's psychiatrist diagnosed the symptoms as "long standing" and existing before the disaster, while the survivors' psychiatrist testified to the opposite view of symptom etiology.

The social scientists collected data on patients in mental health clinics and showed that the survivors had scores similar to the clinical patients on tests of mental health. Second, the social scientists showed that the mental health problems were more severe the greater the trauma inflicted on the survivors; those who lost many members of their families showed more pathological symptoms than those who lost none. They argued that this pattern would not be evident if the mental health conditions of survivors existed prior to the disaster. Third, the social scientists showed that survivors who did not join in the suit as plaintiffs also showed symptoms of distress, indicating that malingering was not an issue. Finally, the social scientists collected data on the mental health of residents of other "comparable" West Virginia communities, showing that levels of mental health were considerably lower among Buffalo Creek survivors than in those "control" communities.

SOURCE: Adapted, with permission, from Goldine C. Gleser, Bonnie L. Green, and Carolyn Winget, *Prolonged Psychosocial Effects of Disaster*. New York: Academic, 1981.

defined as observations that lend themselves readily to numerical representations: answers to structured questionnaires, pay records compiled by personnel offices, counts of speech interactions among co-workers, and the like. In contrast, qualitative data, such as protocols of unstructured interviews and notes from observations, tend to be less easily summarized in numerical form. These distinctions are obviously not hard and fast; the dividing line between the two types of data is fuzzy. Furthermore, qualitative data may be transformed into quantitative data through content analysis (Miles and Huberman, 1984), while quantitative data may be treated as qualitative data by disregarding the numerical values (say, those given to responses to structured interviews, treating each interview schedule as a unit instead).

The relative advantages and disadvantages of the two types of data have been debated ad nauseam in the social science literature (Cook and Reichardt, 1979). Critics of quantitative data decry the dehumanizing tendencies of numerical representation, claiming that a better understanding of causal processes can be obtained from intimate acquaintance with people and their problems and the resulting qualitative observations (Guba and Lincoln, 1981; Patton, 1980). In response, the quantitative advocates reply that qualitative data are expensive to gather on an extensive basis, are highly subject to misinterpretation, and usually contain information that is not uniformly collected across all cases and all situations.

We cannot resolve here the debate surrounding data preferences. As we have indicated in previous chapters, qualitative observations have extremely important roles to play in certain types of evaluative activities, particularly in the monitoring of ongoing programs. However, it is true that qualitative procedures are difficult and expensive to use in many of the designs described in Table 5.2. It would be virtually impossible to meld a long-range randomized experiment with qualitative observations at any reasonable cost. Similarly, large-scale surveys or time series are not ordinarily built on such qualitative observations.

In short, while impact assessments of the structured variety shown in Table 5.2 could be conducted qualitatively in principle, considerations of cost and human capital usually rule out such approaches. Assessing impact in ways that are scientifically plausible and that yield relatively precise estimates of net effects requires data that are quantifiable and systematically and uniformly collected.

INFERENCE VALIDITY ISSUES
IN IMPACT ASSESSMENT

The paramount purpose of an impact assessment is to make possible valid statements about whether or not a program results in significant net effects. To accomplish this end, an impact assessment must have two desirable characteristics: (1) reproducibility and (2) generalizability. "Reproducibility" refers to the ability of the research design employed to produce findings that are robust enough to be reproduced with substantially the same results, if repeated by another researcher using the same design in the same setting. "Generalizability" refers to the relevance of the findings to the program in question, or to similar programs in comparable settings.

Reproducibility

The reproducibility of an impact assessment is largely a function of the power of the research design, the fidelity with which the design was implemented, and the appropriateness of the statistical models used to analyze the resulting data. Impact assessments using powerful research designs, with large numbers of observations, and analyzed correctly will tend to produce similar results no matter who conducts the research. In this regard, randomized controlled experiments ordinarily can be expected to have high reproducibility, while impact assessments conducted with cross-sectional surveys or using shadow controls can be expected to have low reproducibility characteristics.

Generalizability

In evaluation research, generalizability, or what is referred to as "external validity," is as important a characteristic as reproducibility. For example, a well-conducted impact assessment that tests a program under conditions that would not be encountered in its broad-scale operation may demonstrate that the program is effective under special conditions. But such findings may not be applicable when the program is implemented elsewhere. In practice, the problem of generalizability is an especially critical one in the assessment of a prospective program because such evaluations usually are conducted on a trial version of the program or at only some sites of an existing one.

The generalizability of an impact assessment is affected by a number of factors. First, the sample of units (people, organizations, households, and so on) should be an unbiased sample of the targets that will be (or actually are) the clients of the enacted program. Thus, it may make little sense to test a new method of teaching mathematics on classes consisting of especially gifted children when the program is being designed for use in classes of "normal" children. A method that produces fine results with gifted children may not work as well with children with lower levels of ability. Similarly, a program to help the unemployed that is tested with unemployed white-collar workers may yield findings that are inappropriate to other types of unemployed workers. Thus, the testing of gun-control measures in a state such as Massachusetts, where gun ownership in the general population is quite low, may not generalize to states such as Texas or Arizona, in which gun ownership levels are very high. Assessments of ongoing programs also may be faulty if the testing is undertaken on an inappropriate sample of targets.

Generalization issues also concern the variants of the programs being tested in an impact assessment. Results of a program administered by a dedicated and highly skillful staff may not be generalizable to programs administered by a large agency with workers who do not have the same levels of commitment and competence. For example, a randomized experiment run by a group of researchers to test the effectiveness of a prospective program providing limited unemployment benefit coverage to released prisoners produced results that were quite favorable to the prospective policy, while replications of the experiment in Georgia and Texas using state agencies to administer the payment program produced results considerably at variance with the earlier experimenter-run program (Rossi et al., 1980). The point is that the intervention programs tested in an impact assessment must be faithful reproductions of the programs that either are to be implemented or are being implemented in order for the impact assessment findings to be relevant.

Generalization issues also revolve around other aspects of impact assessments. Often, impact assessments are made in "settings" that may not resemble closely those that will characterize the enacted program. Evaluation of an income maintenance program in an extremely economically depressed community, and with a sample of extremely poor, long-term unemployed persons, may produce effects that are not generalizable to most communities and potential targets.

Whether or not an impact assessment will have high generalizability is always an issue in the assessment of prospective programs. A national program, when enacted, may bear only slight resemblance to the program that was tested; the coverage of a large program may emphasize the recruitment of clients who are markedly different from those studied in the evaluation. Changes of this kind can occur because legislators may formulate a program definition that will be supported by a variety of interests, and hence incorporate features or target populations that the evaluators did not study.

Some commentators on evaluation design issues (Campbell and Stanley, 1963; Cook and Campbell, 1979) have suggested that there is an inherent trade-off between reproducibility and generalizability. Powerful designs are expensive to implement and often cannot be conducted within reasonable cost on a large enough scale to meet high generalizability requirements. Evaluation researchers may often have to choose between reproducibility and generalizability, suggesting that the former is a more appropriate goal. Other evaluation experts (Cronbach, 1982), also acknowledge that there is a trade-off, but emphasize generalizability as most important for evaluations. Cronbach asserts that less rigorous impact assessment designs of high generalizability are more relevant for policy purposes than are very rigorous designs with low generalizability.

Our own inclination is to question whether or not the alleged trade-off is always a constraint in the design of impact assessments. We believe that the trade-off constraint varies with the kind of program being tested. An evaluator must assess in each case how strong the trade-off constraint is and make decisions accordingly. For example, a program that has a very robust treatment (e.g., transfer payments) need not be as concerned with the generalizability of the treatment being tested as a program of human services with treatments tailored to individual clients, a variety of treatment that tends to be much less robust. Reproducibility goals may be judged as more important for treatments that are controversial or that may have undesirable side effects (Berk and Rossi, 1978).

Perhaps the best strategy is to envisage the assessment of prospective programs as proceeding through several stages, the early stages stressing reproducibility and the later ones stressing generalizability. This strategy is based on the fact that it is initially important to identify programs that work, at least under some conditions. Having found such programs, it is then necessary to find out whether or not they will work under the conditions normally encountered under enactment.

THE "RIGHT" IMPACT ASSESSMENT STRATEGY

The overview of designs for impact assessments provided in this chapter has considered a range of strategies for examining the effects of social programs. At one extreme are randomized, "true" experiments, which provide the most rigorous means of establishing the net effects of social interventions. At the other extreme are judgmental evaluations, the results of which generally do not permit separation of net from gross effects.

Whenever possible, we advocate the use of randomized experiments; when such designs cannot be implemented, the evaluator must choose the evaluation strategy that provides the most plausible estimate of net effects. Some designs, such as quasi-experiments with adequate statistical controls or well-matched comparison groups, often can be used with considerable confidence. Still others, such as cross-sectional designs, generally are more problematic from the standpoint of isolating net effects.

But in this chapter and the two that follow on impact assessment, the underlying theme is that the choice of a design strategy cannot be made simply on the basis of rigor alone. There are many other conditions and circumstances that must be taken into account, including generalization potential, time, resources, human subject considerations, and the expertise of the evaluator. Thus, the evaluator must be practical as well as a proponent of rigor. The appropriate design is the one that provides the most plausible estimate of net effects, that stands the greatest chance of being carried out successfully, and that provides results most useful for administrative, planning, and policy purposes.

6

Randomized Designs for Impact Assessment

In this chapter we describe the use of randomized field experiments for the assessment of program impact. Randomized experiments are based on comparisons between equivalent groups of targets; equivalence is based on random assignment of the targets to two or more groups. As in many laboratory experiments, one group may be exposed to the "treatment" and the other left untreated. But this is the simplest design. In others, a number of groups of randomly assigned targets may be exposed to different types of interventions and compared to each other, or to each other and an untreated group.

The randomized experiment is presented in this chapter as the most rigorous evaluation design for assessing the net impact of an intervention. At the same time, we acknowledge that randomized experiments are limited in applicability, a theme advanced in the previous chapter.

KEY CONCEPTS

Control Group: A group of randomly selected untreated targets that is compared to experimental groups on outcome measures in impact evaluations. When the group to which the experimental group is compared receives an alternate treatment, rather than no treatment, it is often referred to as the "comparison group."

Experimental Group: A group of randomly selected targets to whom an intervention is delivered and whose outcome measures are compared with those of control groups.

Partial and Full Coverage: The extent to which a program reaches its potential targets.

Randomization: Chance assignment of potential targets in order to obtain equivalent treated and comparison groups.

Specification Error: Errors in impact estimation arising out of the use of an inappropriate model.

T his chapter provides an exposition of the basic ideas behind randomized experiments. This framework underlying randomized experiments is also important for examining many of the impact designs discussed in Chapter 7.

UNITS OF ANALYSIS

At the outset, a note on units of analysis is important: Social programs may be designed to affect a wide variety of targets, including individuals, families, communities, and formal organizations such as schools and business firms. In this and the next chapter, individual persons are used almost consistently as examples of program targets, but this should not lead the reader to believe that impact assessments are conducted only with individuals; we use them as examples because doing so facilitates our exposition. The reader is asked to keep in mind that, as we pointed out in Chapter 3, interventions may also be directed at households and families, neighborhoods and communities, business firms and other organizations, counties and states, and even nations.

The logic of impact assessment in general is not changed as one moves from one kind of unit to another, although the costs and difficulties of conducting field research may increase with the size and complexity of units. For instance, the confounding factors that affect individual students also influence classes. Hence, whether one works with individual students or classes of students as the targets of, say, an educational intervention, the same formal design considerations apply. However, the scale of field operations is considerably increased as one shifts from students as targets to classes as targets. The sample sizes in the two cases may be the same, composed, for example, of 200 students and 200 classes, respectively. However, gathering data on a sample of 200 students is usually easier and considerably less costly than accumulating similar data on the 200 classes, or even on half that number.

The choice of units of analysis is not arbitrary, but determined by the nature of the intervention involved. Thus, a program designed to affect communities through block grants to local municipalities requires that the units studied be municipalities. An impact assessment of block grants conducted by contrasting two municipalities has a sample size of two— completely inadequate for many purposes, even though observations may be made on a very large number of persons in the communities.

The evaluator must begin the design of an impact assessment by identifying the units designated as the targets of the intervention. In some cases defining the units of analysis involves no ambiguity; in other cases the decision may require careful appraisal of the intentions of program designers. Of course, interventions may be addressed to several types of targets: A housing subsidy program may be designed to upgrade both the dwellings of individual poor families and the housing stocks of local communities. Here the evaluator may require samples of individual households within samples of local communities, a design that is intended to estimate the net impacts of the program on individual households and also upon the housing stocks of the communities.

ASSESSING IMPACT OF PARTIAL-COVERAGE PROGRAMS

Randomized experiments and other comparative designs can be employed only to assess the impacts of partial-coverage programs. By "partial-coverage programs," we mean those that are to be tested on a trial basis or are reaching (for whatever reasons) only a modest proportion of their intended target populations. Generally, it is only under these circumstances that it is possible to make appropriate comparisons between groups of persons who are receiving the intervention and comparable persons who are not. Such comparative designs are not appropriate when the coverage of a program reaches a very large proportion (80 percent or more) of its target population.

The Concept of Control and Experimental Groups

One may conceptualize net outcomes as the difference between persons who have participated in a program and *comparable* persons who have not participated. Commonly, the contrasting group is called the "control" or "comparison" group, while those participating in the intervention are designated the "experimental" group. If perfect comparability is achieved, the same extraneous confounding factors would be present in both groups. That is, both would be subject to the same degree to endogenous change, secular drift, and the other extraneous confounding factors listed in Chapter 5. Depending on the ways in which data are collected from the experimental and control groups, design effects may also be identical for them. However, at least one of the design effects, stochastic effects, always causes some differences between the two groups. If the two groups are "truly" comparable, the only differences between the experimental and the control groups would be caused by the intervention and by design effects, of which stochastic effects are the most important.

On the basis of the formula developed in the last chapter, estimating a project's net effects in terms of control and experimental groups can be shown as follows:

$$
\text{Net Effects} = \begin{bmatrix} \text{Gross outcome} \\ \text{for an} \\ \text{experimental} \\ \text{group} \end{bmatrix} - \begin{bmatrix} \text{Gross outcome} \\ \text{for a} \\ \text{comparable} \\ \text{control group} \end{bmatrix} \pm \begin{bmatrix} \text{Stochastic} \\ \text{design} \\ \text{effects} \end{bmatrix}
$$

Since the effects of stochastic processes can be estimated through the use of appropriate statistical models, exactly comparable experimental and control groups (along with estimates of stochastic effects, and in the absence of other design effects) provide as close to perfect an approximation of an intervention's net effects as is possible.

A critical element in estimating net outcome is the identification and selection of *comparable* experimental and control groups. Comparability between experimental and control groups means, in ideal terms, that the experimental and control groups should be identical except for their participation or nonparticipation in the program under evaluation. In more specific terms, comparability requires the following:

- *Identical composition:* Experimental and control groups contain similar mixes of persons or other units.

- *Identical experiences:* Experimental and control groups should experience over the time of observation the same time-related processes (maturation, changes, "secular drifts" over time, and so on).

- *Identical predispositions:* Experimental and control groups should be equally disposed toward the project (i.e., self-selection tendencies should be identical in the two groups).

Implementing Control Group Evaluations

Ideally, in order to achieve comparability between experimental and control groups, each target in the former group should be matched with an identical one in the latter group. Experimental biologists sometimes try to do this by using incestuously bred animals from the same litter. However, even here the matching is imperfect, and certainly precise matching is not possible in program evaluations. There are no two individuals, families, or other units that are comparable in all respects—even twins are not identical in their lifetime experiences.

Fortunately, exact, one-to-one comparability is not necessary. It is important only that experimental and control groups be identical in aggregate terms, and in features that may modify, mitigate, or exacerbate effects of the program being evaluated. Thus, it may not matter at all in an impact evaluation that experimental and control group members differ in where they were born or vary slightly in age—as long as such differences overall between the groups are neither statistically nor substantively significant. Especially important are differences between experimentals and controls that are related to their selection for their respective groups. Any characteristic that is related to placement as an experimental or a control and is also related to the intended outcome of the intervention can cause incorrect estimates of net effect.

One of the important implications of this statement is that impact assessments require more than just a few cases. The larger the number of units studied (given the methods of selection discussed below), the more likely are experimental and control groups to be statistically equivalent. In short, studies in which only one or a few units are in experimental or control groups rarely, if ever, suffice for impact assessments. (Important exceptions to this last statement will be discussed in Chapter 7.)

While the discussion above has pictured control or comparison groups as consisting of targets who receive "no treatment," this is not always the case. More often, targets in control groups are receiving existing treatment programs or alternate treatments. For example, an evaluation testing the effectiveness of a nutrition program may have a control or comparison group consisting of persons who are following a variety of nutritional practices, some of their own devising and others directed by their doctors. All this means is that the effectiveness of the program under evaluation is estimated relative to whatever treatment or mix of treatments is being experienced by the controls or comparison targets.

Another design variation consists of comparing two or more programs in a systematic way. There may be several experimental groups, each of which is following a particular nutritional regimen, with the net effects of each of the "treatments" estimated relative to the others being tested.

A note to the reader: Some evaluators distinguish between the terms *control groups* and *comparison groups,* the former referring to groups formed through random allocation of targets and the latter to groups that are assembled of "matched" units so as to be comparable in important respects to an experimental group. We do *not* follow this usage in most of this chapter. The argument is developed here that the distinction is a matter of degree and thus not very relevant. Hence, we will use the term *control* group to refer to both control and comparison groups, making the distinction clear when it is important.

In the next few sections, we discuss randomized experimental designs in which there is only one intervention being tested for impact. As indicated earlier, this restriction is simply for convenience in exposition. The designs can be extended easily to involve the testing of several alternative interventions (or combinations of interventions) simultaneously. Indeed, there is much to be gained in the way of useful information for policymakers and project managers if evaluations of several interventions are undertaken comparatively, so that a given intervention is compared not only to the condition in which no intervention is made but also to alternative interventions. Multiple-intervention impact assessments provide important information on such issues as how best to modify treatments and maximize effects at a given level of funding; they are discussed in some detail in a later section.

RANDOMIZATION TO ESTABLISH COMPARABILITY

Randomly allocating members of a target population to different groups implies that whether a person (or other unit) is offered one treatment or another or is left untreated is decided by chance. It is important to note that "random" in this sense does not mean haphazard or capricious. On the contrary, random allocation of persons to experimental and control groups requires that extreme care be taken to ensure that every unit in a target population has the same chance as any other unit to be selected for either the experimental or the control group (Fisher, 1935; Riecken and Boruch, 1974).

Because the resulting experimental and control groups differ from one another only by chance, whatever processes may be competing with a treatment to produce outcomes are present in the experimental and control groups to the same extent, except for chance fluctuations. For example, given randomization, persons who would be more likely to seek out the treatment if it were offered to them on a free-choice basis are equally likely to be in the experimental as in the control group. Hence, both groups have the same proportion of persons favorably predisposed to the intervention. The confounding factor of "self-selection" has the same likelihood of being found in one group as in the other, and cannot affect whatever outcome differences are observed between experimental and control groups.

Randomization, therefore, is the surest way to obtain comparability between experimental and control groups. Of course, even though persons are allocated randomly, experimental and control groups will never be exactly comparable in any single instance. For example, chance fluctuations may place more women in the control group than in the experimental group. But if the random allocation were made over and over again, these fluctuations would average out to zero. In addition, the expected proportion of times that a difference of any given size will be found in a long series of randomizations can be calculated from appropriate statistical models. Any given difference in outcome among randomized experimental and control groups can be compared to what can be expected on the basis of chance (i.e., generated only by the randomization process). A judgment can thus be made on whether a specific difference is due simply to chance or whether it might represent the effect of the treatment. Since the treatment in a well-run experiment is the only difference other than chance between experimental and control groups, such judgments can become the basis for discerning the existence of a net effect. The statistical procedures for making such calculations are quite straightforward and may be found in any text dealing with statistical inference (e.g., Namboodiri et al., 1975; Hanushek and Jackson, 1977). They will also be discussed in relation to reflexive, generic, and shadow controls in the next chapter.

The Meaning of Randomization

It is important not to confuse randomization, as use in the sense above, with random sampling. *Randomization* means taking a set of units and allocating each unit to an experimental or control group, using some randomizing procedure. *Random sampling* consists of *selecting* units in an unbiased manner to form a sample from a population (Sudman, 1976; Kish, 1965). One may use random sampling to select a study group from a target population and then, by randomization, allocate each member of the resulting sample to experimental or control conditions on a random basis. Although the use of random samples to form a set of targets that is then randomized to form experimental and control groups is a highly recommended procedure, many randomized experiments are conducted using sets of targets that are not selected by random sampling (i.e., that do not necessarily represent a given population). This latter procedure, of course, may not be a sensible course to follow because of the potential loss of generalizability. (See Chapter 5 for a discussion of the issue of generalizability.)

Randomization Procedures

Randomization is technically easy to accomplish. Tables of random numbers are included in most elementary statistics or sampling textbooks.

Larger tables of random numbers are also available in published form. Many computer statistical packages contain subroutines that can generate random numbers easily. Even some of the better hand calculators have random number generators built into them. Flipping coins or rolling dice that are unbiased can also be used as randomizing devices. (See Riecken and Boruch, 1974, for a discussion of how to implement randomization; for alternative randomization procedures, see Conner, 1977; Goldman, 1977; Roos et al., 1977.)

A typical randomized experimental design can be represented by the following modification of our basic impact assessment formula:

$$
\begin{matrix} \text{Net} \\ \text{Effects} \end{matrix} = \begin{bmatrix} \text{Scores on outcome} \\ \text{measures after interven-} \\ \text{tion for randomized} \\ \text{experimental group} \end{bmatrix} - \begin{bmatrix} \text{Scores on outcome} \\ \text{measures after interven-} \\ \text{tion for randomized con-} \\ \text{trol (unexposed) group} \end{bmatrix} \pm \begin{bmatrix} \text{Stochastic} \\ \text{effects} \end{bmatrix}
$$

Note that the formula assumes only after-intervention measurement on outcome measures. Later in this chapter we will consider what is to be gained or lost by employing after-only measures or by having multiple measures before and after an intervention.

Table 6.1 presents a schematic diagram of a simple before-and-after randomized controlled experiment, indicating the logic behind the estimates of net effects that can be computed. Of course, the differences between the experimental and control groups, E – C, necessarily contain the stochastic effects described in Chapter 5. Hence, it would be necessary to apply tests of statistical inference in order to judge whether in any particular case, E – C can be viewed as so large that it is not likely to be stochastic error, that is, whether E – C is larger than one can expect in chance fluctuations when the true value of E – C is zero. Conventional statistical tests for before-and-after experiments include analysis of variance and t-tests.

Note that the schematic presentation in Table 6.1 defines effects as differences between pre- and postmeasures of outcome. While most evaluation experiments are designed in this fashion, obtaining both pre- and postmeasures is not essential. For some types of outcomes, a "preintervention" is not possible to define, as we have discussed earlier.

There are some statistical advantages to having pre- and postmeasures; greater precision in effect estimates can be attained when premeasures are used to hold constant each individual target's starting point before the intervention. The critical measurements, of course, are the postintervention outcome measures for both experimentals and controls.

TABLE 6.1 Schematic Representation of a Randomized Experiment

| | Outcome Measures | | |
	Before Program	After Program	Difference
Experimental Group	E_1	E_2	$E = E_2 - E_1$
Control Group	C_1	C_2	$C = C_2 - C_1$

Net Effects of Program $= E - C$

Where:

E_1, C_1	= measures of intervention goal *before* the program is instituted, for experimental and control groups, respectively
E_2, C_2	= measures of intervention goal *after* program is completed, for experimental and control groups, respectively
E, C	= gross outcome measures for experimental and control groups, respectively

NOTE: The stochastic component that represents randomization is always present and may introduce differences between experimental and control groups: i.e., $E - C$ may be nonzero, on the basis of chance. Statistical significance tests assess whether $E - C$ is too large to be generated by chance when the true value of $E - C$ is zero.

Stochastically generated differences between experimental and control groups depend almost entirely on the number of observations (i.e., targets) in the two groups and on the variability in outcome among the units involved. This means that the larger the number of units in the experiment, the smaller the stochastic effects and the more likely any true impact of the intervention will be detected. It also means that the more effects are uniform among all targets, the more likely it is that such effects will be detected.

Hence, for interventions that are likely to have small and/or variable effects, both experimental and control groups must be quite large. For example, in the TARP experiments testing the impact of unemployment insurance eligibility on recidivism among ex-felons, experimental groups contained close to 1500 and control groups nearly 2500 ex-felons (Rossi et al., 1980; see also Exhibits 6-D and 6-F). The very large samples of felons were used because it was expected (on the basis of previous evaluation evidence) that the effects of the intervention were going to be small and quite variable from individual to individual. (Standard statistical texts provide details on how to plan appropriate sizes of experimental and control groups; e.g., Namboodiri et al., 1975; Hanushek and Jackson, 1977.)

Exhibit 6-A provides a detailed description of a randomized experiment to test the effectiveness of a televised educational program for Mexican preschool children. The reader's attention is directed to several of the

Exhibit 6-A: A Randomized Controlled Experiment of the Effect of a Preschool Television Program in Mexico

In Mexico in 1971, a completely new production of *Sesame Street*, called *Plaza Sésamo,* especially adapted to Latin American culture, was developed. Educators, psychologists, psychiatrists, and other specialists cooperated in planning and conducting evaluative studies of a formative nature to assist the producers of *Plaza Sésamo* in developing the program.

These experiments were carried out with preschool children in day-care centers in Mexico City. A total of 221 children (3-, 4-, and 5-year-olds) from three different lower-class day-care centers were equally divided by age and sex and were randomly assigned to experimental and control groups. Children in the experimental groups watched *Plaza Sésamo* programs for fifty-minute periods, five days a week, until the entire series of 130 programs had been broadcast—a total of six months of continuous viewing. At the same time, children in the control group were viewing cartoons and other noneducational television programs on a different broadcast channel in a separate room.

Since *Plaza Sésamo* was a relatively new program, none of the control children had even seen it before. Strenuous efforts were made to prevent the control children from viewing *Plaza Sésamo* on another channel when it was broadcast each evening from 6:00 to 7:00 p.m. Further investigations toward the end of the experiment revealed that only a handful of control children viewed any *Plaza Sésamo* broadcasts when they were absent due to sickness. In no case did it appear that the experimental design had been compromised in any way.

The impact of *Plaza Sésamo* on the children who viewed it was evaluated by a series of individually administered tests given in both the experimental and control groups at three points in time: (1) pretest—immediately prior to the exposure to *Plaza Sésamo* or the control films; (2) during treatment—seven weeks after beginning the experiment; and (3) posttest—at the end of the experiment.

Dropouts were relatively few. Of 221 children in the initial sample, 173 completed the experiment. There was no discernible bias due to dropouts.

Nine individual tests were employed to measure the amount of learning for each child over the six-month period. Three of these tests—General Knowledge, Numbers, and Letters and Words—are criterion measures of skills specifically taught in the *Plaza Sésamo* programs. Five other tests—Relations, Parts of the Whole, Ability to Sort, Classification Skills, and Embedded Figures—are indirectly related to *Plaza Sésamo* but are not specifically criterion measures. The ninth test, Oral Comprehension, has no relation to the stated goals of *Plaza Sésamo*, although it measures an important cognitive ability related to school readiness among preschool children.

Statistical tests were carried out to see whether or not the *Plaza Sésamo* viewers did significantly better than the children who watched only cartoons. In general, children in the experimental group showed greater gains in test performance over the six-month period than those in the control group.

The main results can be summarized as follows:

1. Regardless of age-group, the children who watched *Plaza Sésamo* for six months did significantly better on at least four of the nine criterion tests than did the control children who only watched cartoons during this period.

2. The greatest increase for *Plaza Sésamo* viewers occurred on the three tests most closely related to the stated goals of *Plaza Sésamo*—General Knowledge, Numbers, and Letters and Words.

3. Oral Comprehension, the test unrelated to *Plaza Sésamo*, also revealed significantly greater gains for the *Plaza Sésamo* viewers than for the control children in all three age groups.

4. The 4- and 5-year-olds showed the greatest gains from watching *Plaza Sésamo,* while the 3-year-old experimental children failed to differ significantly from the control children on five of the nine tests. Test-retest correlations across the six months showed satisfactory stability (.41-.59) for four of the tests—General Knowledge, Numbers, Embedded Figures, and Oral Comprehension—but showed instability for the remaining five tests (correlations of .08 to .25). In spite of weaknesses in these five tests, positive results favoring the *Plaza Sésamo* viewers were obtained for them just as they were obtained for the more reliable tests.

5. Although the most rapid gains of the experimental children over the control groups occurred in the first seven weeks of viewing *Plaza Sésamo,* the gap between the experimental and control groups continued to grow throughout the six months.

6. Within the combined experimental group, the degree of attention to *Plaza Sésamo* correlated positively (as high as .49) in six of the nine posttest measures, indicating that children who regularly pay attention to the *Plaza Sésamo* program gain more than children whose attention wanders.

7. Experimental children with a large number of absences did less well on the posttreatment test battery than did children who attended regularly.

SOURCE: Adapted, with permission, from "Plaza Sésamo in Mexico: An Evaluation," by R. Diaz-Guerrero, Isabel Reyes-Lagunes, Donald B. Witzke, and Wayne H. Holtzman, in the *Journal of Communication*, Vol. 26, No. 2, pp. 145-154. Copyright © 1976 by the Annenberg School of Communications.

experiment's features. First, note that a number of output measures were employed, covering the multiple objectives of the educational project. Second, observe the care taken to ensure that control group children were not exposed to the television program. Third, statistical tests were used to aid in judging whether net outcome, in this case the experimental group's observed superiority in learning, was not simply a chance difference. Note also that outcome measures were taken in the course of the experiment, as well as before and after.

Exhibit 6-B contains a description of another randomized controlled experiment testing the effectiveness of group counseling as a rehabilitative measure in California prisons. Taking advantage of a prison that was about to open and be filled within a short period of time, the experimenters arranged to have entering prisoners randomly assigned to one of two programs or to a control group. The prison's architectural features facilitated the experiment; there were four relatively self-contained units (called "quads"), communications among which could be carefully controlled. Consequently, prisoners in each quadrangle could not communicate to those in the other quads the treatment they received. One quad was set aside for "behavioral problem" prisoners whom the prison authorities did not want to participate in the experiment.

In the example in Exhibit 6-B, the subjects of the experiment were in prison, and thus a high degree of control over their assignment to treatment groups was possible. Field experiments with noninstitutionalized populations as targets are more difficult to run, since they require voluntary cooperation and maintenance of experimental integrity over time. In addition, they are more subject to interference by outside events.

Exhibit 6-B: A Randomized Control Experiment Evaluating the Impact on Parole Success of a Group Counseling Intervention in a California Prison

In the 1960s the California Adult Authority (the agency in charge of prisons) had installed in most state prisons a voluntary group counseling program that attempted to help prisoners develop an understanding of their motivations for criminal activity through participating in weekly group counseling. Presumably the understanding gained would reduce adherence to peer-group norms within prison and enhance the ability to adjust successfully to civilian life and thereby succeed on parole.

Taking advantage of a new prison that was to be constructed, the authors received permission and encouragement from the California prison agency to run a randomized controlled experiment in the new prison. The prison in question was built in more or less isolated "quads." Two of the quads were designated to receive varying forms of counseling—small and large group counseling—a third quad was designated as a control to which no counseling would be given, and the fourth quad was reserved for special behavior-problem prisoners. As new prisoners were assigned to the prison when it was opened, random assignments among the first three quads were made of prisoners who were not assigned by the prison, for behavioral reasons, to the fourth quad.

When prisoners in both the control and the experimental groups were released on parole, their parole records for a period of two years beyond release were examined for evidence of adjustment to civilian life. No differences were found among the experimental and control groups. The group counseling interventions were judged to have failed.

SOURCE: Summary, by permission, of G. Kassebaum, D. Ward, and D. Wilner, *Prison Treatment and Parole Survival.* New York: Wiley, 1971.

Exhibit 6-C describes an experiment to determine the work disincentive effect of providing income support payments to poor, intact (i.e., two-spouse) families. The study was the first of a series of five, each of which varied slightly from the others, run by the Office of Economic Opportunity and the Department of Health, Education and Welfare (now the Department of Health and Human Services) to test various forms of guaranteed income and their effects on the work efforts of poor and near-poor persons. All five of the experiments were conducted over relatively long periods, the longest involving more than five years; all had difficulties maintaining the cooperation of the initial groups of families involved; and all found the income payments to create a slight work disincentive, especially for teenagers and mothers with young children—those in the secondary labor force (Rossi and Lyall, 1976; Robbins et al., 1980; SRI International, 1983; Mathematica Policy Research, 1983).

Despite their power in allowing valid conclusions about the net outcome of interventions, randomized experiments still account for a relatively small proportion of impact assessments. Political and ethical considerations may rule out randomization, particularly when interventions simply cannot be withheld without violating ethical or legal rules (although the idea of experimentation does not preclude delivering some alternative treatment to a control group). Despite the obstacles to randomized evaluation designs, there is a clear consensus on their desirability (Cook and Campbell, 1979), a growing literature on how to enhance the chances of success (Bennett and Lumsdaine, 1975; Riecken and Boruch, 1974), and increasing documentation of their feasibility (Boruch, 1975; Campbell and Boruch, 1975; Boruch et al., 1978; Basilevsky and Hum, 1984).

Some of the conditions that facilitate or impede the utilization of randomized experiments to assess impact will be discussed in a later section of this chapter.

Surrogates for Randomized Selection

Although randomization is the surest way of selecting equivalent experimental and control groups, there are other methods that also may satisfy the criterion of equivalence. The desirable feature of randomization is that it is a way of achieving unbiased selection of subjects into the experiment and control groups. Unbiased selection (not to be confused with bias as discussed in Chapter 4) requires that the probability of any individual target being selected for either experimental or control group membership be identical for all targets in the study. Correspondingly, biased selection occurs when some individuals have higher or lower probability of being selected for any group. Thus a biased selection procedure in constituting experimental and control groups from a population with equal proportions of men and women would be said to exist if, say, women were more likely than men to be selected as experimentals.

Systematic assignment from serialized lists can often accomplish the same end as randomization, provided that the lists are not constructed in some way that results in a bias. For example, in allocating high school

Exhibit 6-C: The New Jersey-Pennsylvania Income Maintenance Experiment

In the late 1960s, when federal officials concerned with poverty began to consider shifting welfare policy to provide some sort of guaranteed annual income for all families, the Office of Economic Opportunity (OEO) launched a large-scale field experiment to test one of the crucial issues in such a program. Economic theory predicted that the provision of such supplementary income payments to poor families would be a work disincentive (i.e., they would reduce the amount of work).

Started in 1968, the experiment was carried on for three years, administered by Mathematica, Inc., a research firm in Princeton, New Jersey, and the Institute for Research on Poverty of the University of Wisconsin. The experiment was aimed at a target population of intact families below 150 percent of the poverty level, whose male heads were between 18 and 58. The eight treatments consisted of various combinations of guarantees, pegged to what was then the current "poverty level," and the rates at which payments were taxed or adjusted to earnings received by the families. For example, for a family in one of the treatments with a guaranteed income of 125 percent of the then-current poverty level, if no one in the family had any earnings, the family would receive that guaranteed amount. However, if their plan had a tax rate of 50 percent, and someone in the family received earned income, payments would be reduced at the rate of $.50 for each dollar earned, until payments were reduced to zero. Other treatments consisted of tax rates that ranged from 30 percent to 70 percent, and guarantee levels that varied from 50 percent to 125 percent of the poverty line. A control group consisted of families who did not receive any payments.

The experiment was conducted in four New Jersey communities and one Pennsylvania community. A large household survey was undertaken to identify families who were eligible. Families identified were invited to participate; after agreement had been achieved, families were randomly allocated to one of the experimental groups or the control group. Families who were in the experimental group reported their earnings each month. If their earnings statement indicated eligibility for transfer payments, a check was mailed to the family.

Families were interviewed in great detail prior to enrollment in the program and at the end of each quarter over the three years of the experiment. These interviews generated data (among others) on employment, earnings, consumption, health, and various social-psychological measures. The data were then analyzed along with the monthly earnings reports to determine whether those receiving payments in any way diminished their work efforts (as measured in hours of work) in relation to the comparable families in the control groups.

Although about 1,300 families were initially recruited, by the end of the experiment 22 percent had discontinued their cooperation. Others had missed one or more interviews or had dropped out of the experiment for varying periods. Fewer than 700 remained for analysis of the continuous participants.

SOURCE: Summary, by permission, of D. Kershaw and J. Fair, *The New Jersey Income-Maintenance Experiment*, Vol. 1. New York: Academic, 1976.

students to experimental and control groups, it might be sensible to place all those with odd ID numbers into the experimental group and all with even ID numbers into a control group. As long as the numbers were not originally assigned to differentiate among students according to some characteristics (e.g., gender) by designating one type as "odd" and the other as "even" students, the result will be the same (statistically) as random assignment. However, if for some reason the school in question gave odd ID numbers only to female students, reserving the even numbers for males, this systematic bias would result in the experimental and control groups differing completely in sex composition. Hence, before using such systematic selection procedures, one must understand how the agency that generated the list accomplished serialization and judge whether the numbering process might produce unwanted systematic differences between various sections of the list.

Often, ordered lists of targets may have subtle biases that are difficult to detect. For example, an alphabetized list might tempt one to select, say, all persons whose last names begin with D as experimentals and those whose last names begin with H as controls. In a New England city, this would result in an ethnically biased selection; many French names begin with D (e.g., DeFleur), while very few Hispanic names begin with H. Numbered lists often reveal age biases: Because the federal government assigns Social Security numbers sequentially, those with low numbers generally are older than those whose numbers are higher. (See Sudman, 1976, for further precautions to be taken in systematic selection strategies.)

Occasionally, randomization occurs "naturally" for some unplanned interventions. Such situations can be regarded as equivalent to a randomized experiment. An example from a study of flood effects illustrates a fairly valid "natural" randomized experiment: Hydrologic engineers have marked off the flood plains of most American rivers into regions characterized by the expected return times of floods. Thus, the "ten-year flood plain" marks off those regions in a river basin in which floods are expected, on the average, to occur once in every decade. Although each year the areas within the ten-year flood plain have a one-in-ten chance of experiencing a flood, whether or not a flood occurs in a particular year in a particular spot can be regarded as a random event. Neighborhoods built on flood plains can be divided into "experimentals"—those in which floods actually occurred during, say, a two-year period—and "controls"—those in which no floods occurred. Given that both sets of neighborhoods had the same probabilities of experiencing floods, they constitute "natural" experimental and control groups. Growth trends in the two groups are then compared to obtain an estimate of the impact of floods on the growth of housing and population stocks.

Of course, floods are events that can be understood as outcomes of known natural processes. However, as those processes do not "select" some particular flood plains more than others, floods may be regarded for our purposes as random events. The validity of this approach depends heavily on whether or not the hydrologists marked out the ten-year flood plain correctly. Such maps are made partly on the basis of historical trends and partly on the basis of knowledge about how rivers behave in given terrains. The flood plain contours are still subject to some error.

Whether or not natural or unplanned events in fact provide adequate substitutes for randomized controls must be judged with close scrutiny of the circumstances of those events. Indeed, most circumstances that are called "natural experiments" cannot be regarded as such in the strict sense of the term. If there is any reason to suspect that the events in question were likely to affect some units (persons, communities, and the like) more than others, then the conditions for a "natural experiment" do not exist. For example, communities that have fluoridated their water supplies cannot be regarded as an experimental group to be contrasted with those who have not, because the act of adoption cannot be regarded as a random event in the sense used here. Similarly, households that have purchased townhouses cannot be regarded as appropriate controls for those who have purchased free-standing homes, because the very act of making such purchases is an indicator of other potential differences between the two groups.

DATA COLLECTION STRATEGIES FOR
RANDOMIZED EXPERIMENTS

Under some conditions, after-only measures are the only measurements of outcome that can be used (see Exhibit 6-B). However, it is generally the case that the more frequently measures of outcomes are obtained, the more definite the findings of an impact assessment. Ideally, repeated measurement is desirable both before and after an intervention is put into place. Multiple longitudinal measurements increase reliability and provide more information on which to build estimates of net outcomes. Measures taken before an intervention begins provide estimates of the preexperimental states of the experimental and control groups. These are useful for making adjustments for preexisting differences between the two groups, and for measuring how much of a gain the intervention effected. For example, preintervention measures of earnings for experimentals and controls in a vocational retraining project improve estimates of how much earnings will improve as a result of training and at the same time offer a variable to hold constant in the analysis of outcomes.

Periodic measurements taken during the course of an intervention are also useful; such series allow evaluators to construct useful descriptive accounts of how an intervention works over time. For instance, if a vocational retraining program produces most of its effects during the first four weeks of a six-week program, such a finding might lead to the suggestion that shortening the training period would cut costs without seriously curtailing the project's effectiveness. Likewise, multiple, periodic measurements can lead to a fuller understanding of how targets react to treatments. Some reactions may be slow-starting and then accelerate later; others may be strong initially but soon trail off to preintervention levels. For example, the response to the 55-miles-per-hour speed limit is reputed to have consisted of an initial slowing down of average vehicular speed, followed by a gradual return to higher speed averages. The ability to plot reactions to interventions allows evaluators to fine-tune treatments for fuller effectiveness.

For some types of interventions, only postintervention measures may be available (as, for example, in the California prison counseling experiment described in Exhibit 6-B). Likewise, a program designed to help impoverished high school students go on to college can be judged definitively only by whether experimentals go on to college more frequently than controls, a measure that can be taken only after the intervention. However, such cases aside, the general rule that can be drawn is that the more measurements made before and after the intervention, the better measured the estimates of net effects will be.

Thus, there are two compelling reasons for taking many measures before, during, and after an intervention: First, the more measures taken, the lower the unreliability of composite measures will be. Second, interventions can be expected to have their effects over time; hence longitudinal series (see Chapters 5 and 7) can allow evaluators to reconstruct the way an intervention works.

ANALYSIS OF SIMPLE RANDOMIZED EXPERIMENTS

The analysis of simple randomized experiments can be quite straightforward. Conducted properly, randomization produces experimental and control groups that are statistically equivalent. Hence, a comparison of outcomes in the two groups provides an estimate of net effects. A comparison of the experimental versus control groups' differences with chance expectation derived from a statistical model then provides a means for judging whether or not the differences are large enough that it is unlikely they were generated by chance fluctuations when there were really no differences due to the treatment or intervention involved. Exhibit 6-D provides an empirical example of the analyses conducted on a simple randomized experiment. In that exhibit, the results are analyzed first by a simple comparison between experimentals and controls, and then using a more complex multiple regression model.

COMPLEX RANDOMIZED EXPERIMENTS

Several of the examples given above (see Exhibits 6-B and 6-C) are tests of several treatments considered simultaneously, a strategy that enhances the value of findings considerably. In the New Jersey-Pennsylvania Income Maintenance Experiment, eight treatments were tested, each differing from the others in the amount of income guaranteed and in tax penalties on family members' earnings. The variation from treatment to treatment was included in the experiment in order to test the sensitivity of work effort to varying degrees of work disincentive effects that were believed to be embodied in different payment schemes. A critical evaluation question was whether or not the work response to payments would vary with the amount of payment offered and the extent to which earnings reduced the payments offered. Similarly, in the Housing Allowance Demand Experiment (Kennedy, 1980; Struyk and Bendick, 1981), seventeen experimental and two control groups were used (see Exhibit 6-E). Each group was offered a different subsidy, varying in ways that were deemed relevant to alternatives then in the policy space of Congress. Some subsidies required

(text continues on page 255)

Exhibit 6-D: Analysis of Simple Randomized Experiments: The Baltimore LIFE Experiment

The Baltimore LIFE experiment was designed to test whether provision of small amounts of financial aid to persons released from prison would aid them to make the transition to civilian life and to reduce the probability of their being arrested and returned to prison. The treatment was chosen to simulate unemployment insurance payments for which most prisoners are not eligible because they cannot accumulate work credits while imprisoned.

Persons released from the Maryland state prisons to return to Baltimore were randomly allocated to either an experimental group (who were told they were eligible for 13 weekly payments of $60 as long as they were unemployed) or a control group (who were told they were participating in a research project but were not offered payments).

Researchers periodically interviewed the released prisoners and monitored the arrest records of the Baltimore Police Department for a year beyond each prisoner's release date. The arrest records yielded the results over the postrelease year shown in Table 6-D.1.

The findings shown in Table 6-D.1 are know as *main effects* and constitute the simplest representation of experimental results. Since randomization has made experimentals and controls statistically equivalent except for the treatment, differences between experimentals and controls are due only to stochastic variability.

The substantive import of the findings is easily demonstrated by the last column on the right of Table 6-D.1. Here the differences between the experimental group and the control group in arrest experiences for various types of crimes are shown: 22.2 percent of the experimental group were arrested for theft crimes in the postrelease year and 30.6 percent of the controls were arrested on the same type of charges, leading to a difference of –8.4 percent, a difference that indicated a treatment effect in the desired direction. Of course, the issue then became whether 8.4 percent was within the range of expected chance differences given the sizes of the experimental and control groups. A variety of statistical models were available to settle this issue, chi-square, t-tests, and analysis of variance. The researchers used a one-tailed t-test, since the direction of the differences between the two groups was indicated by the expected effects of the treatment. Applying a one-tailed t-test to the findings showed that a difference of –8.4 percent or larger would occur by chance less than 5 times in every 100 experiments of the same size. The researchers then concluded that the difference was large enough to be taken seriously as indicating that the treatment had its desired effect, at least on theft crimes, reducing postrelease arrests more than could be accounted for by mere chance variation.

The remaining types of crimes did not show differences large enough to survive the t-test criterion. In other words, experimentals and controls were likely no different in arrests for "other" serious crimes or for minor crimes.

Of course, the question then becomes a substantive one: Are these differences large enough in a policy sense? In other words, would it be worthwhile to adopt the LIFE treatment as a social program? Would an 8.4 percent reduction in theft crimes justify the payments and accompanying administrative costs? In order to answer that last question, the Department of Labor conducted a cost-benefit analysis (discussed in Chapter 8) that showed that the benefits far outweighed the costs.

TABLE 6-D.1 Baltimore Life Experiment: Arrests During the First Year After Release: Experimental and Control Groups Compared (in percentages)

Arrest Charge	Arrests in Experimental Group	Arrests in Control Group	Difference (Experimentals – Controls)
Theft crimes (robbery, burglary, larceny, etc.)	22.2	30.6	–8.4
Other serious crimes (murder, rape, assault, etc.)	19.4	16.2	+3.2
Minor crimes (disorderly conduct, public drinking, etc.)	7.9	10.2	2.3
N =	216	216	

A more complex way or analyzing the same results is shown in Table 6-D.2, using multiple regression. The question posed is exactly the same question that motivated setting up Table 6-D.1, but in addition the multiple regression model takes into account that fact that many factors other than the payments also affect crime. The model holds those other factors constant while comparing the proportions arrested in the control and experimental groups.

In effect, comparisons are made between experimentals and controls within each level of the other variables used in the equation. For example, the unemployment rate in Baltimore fluctuated over the two years of the experiment: Some ex-felons were released at times when it was easy to get jobs and others were released at less fortunate times. Adding the unemployment rate at time of release to the equation reduces the variation among ex-felons due to that factor and thereby purifies the estimates of the effect of the treatment.

Note that all the variables added to the multiple regression equation of Table 6-D.2 were ones that were known from previous research to affect recidivism and/or chances of finding employment. The addition of these variables strengthened the findings considerably. The coefficient for being in the experimental group did not change: The b-coefficient indicates that being in the experimental group meant that an ex-felon's probability of being arrested for a theft crime over the postrelease year was lowered by 8.3 percent. But, because of the purifying effect of the other variables in the equation, the chance expectation of a coefficient that large or larger is much smaller, occurring only 2 times out of every 100 experiments. Hence the multiple regression results provide more precise estimates of net effects.

TABLE 6-D.2 Multiple Regression Analysis of Baltimore LIFE Experiment Results

Independent Variables	Arrests on Property-Related Charges	
	b	SE
Dummy variable for membership in experimental group	-.083*	.041
Baltimore unemployment rate at time of release	.041*	.022
Number of weeks worked in first quarter postrelease	-.006	.005
Age at release	-.009*	.004
Age at first arrest	-.010*	.006
Prior theft arrests	.028*	.008
Race (dummy: black = 1)	.056	.064
Education (years)	-.025	.022
Had prior work experience of 1 year or more	-.009	.008
Married	-.074	.065
Parole (dummy: paroled = 1)	-.025	.051
Intercept	.263	.185
$R^2 = .094*$		
$N = 432$		

SOURCE: Adapted from P. H. Rossi, R. A. Berk, and K. J. Lenihan, *Money, Work and Crime: Some Experimental Findings.* New York: Academic, 1980.

Exhibit 6-E: The Housing Allowance Demand Experiment

Perplexed by the problem of how best to provide decent housing to poor families and convinced of the inadequacies of previous policies that included direct buiding of public housing and providing subsidies to builders who built low-income housing, Congress in the late 1970s directed the Department of Housing and Urban Development to conduct experiments with direct money subsidies to poor families for the purpose of purchasing decent quality housing. Although many members of Congress were convinced that direct subsidies to poor families constituted a policy that would stimulate existing housing markets to provide such housing, other members were quite skeptical and feared that one response might be for landlords and builders to raise their prices and rents.

The Department of Housing and Urban Development funded three sets of experiments: (1) demand experiments, designed to judge whether direct subsidies would lead to occupancy of better-quality housing; (2) supply experiments, seeking to answer the question of whether housing markets would respond to subsidies by raising prices and rents; and (3) administrative demonstrations, the purpose of which was to see how efficiently local housing authorities could administer housing allowance programs.

The demand experiments were run by Abt Associates, a for-profit research firm, in Pittsburgh and Phoenix. Samples of households earning under 125 percent of the poverty level were recruited in those two cities to enroll in the program either as experimentals or as controls. 1001 families were recruited in Phoenix and 1240 in Pittsburgh. Within the demand experiment 17 distinct treatments were devised, along with 2 control conditions. The 17 treatments represented combinations of more or less generous payments and different forms and degrees of housing consumption requirements. (The 17 treatment and 2 control groups are described in detail in Table 6-E.1.)

The most basic distinction among the treatments was between those involving a "housing gap" formula for determining benefit payments and those involving a "percentage of rent" formula.

As its name implies, a housing gap formula calculates the housing allowance payments to which a household is entitled as the difference between what the household is presumed able to pay for housing and the presumed cost of adequate housing in that household's community. The formula is as follows:

$$P = C^* - bY$$

where P = maximum potential allowance amount;
     C* = estimated cost of acceptable quality housing for a household of a certain size and composition;
     b = fraction of the household's income the household is expected to contribute toward its housing costs; and
     Y = the household's income.

P is the maximum potential payment because households were never reimbursed for more than their actual expenditures for rent (plus utilities, if paid separately); hence a household's payment might be less than the payment specified by this formula. In the demand experiment, 12 of 17 experimental groups represented various forms of housing gap treatment. The variation among them involved alternative levels of benefits and alternative housing consumption requirements.

One way the level of benefits was varied was through the use of alternative values for C*, the estimated cost of acceptable quality housing. At each of the demand sites—Pittsburgh and Phoenix—a panel of local housing experts was convened to estimate the rental cost of standard housing units for households of different sizes. Three values of C* were used: 80 percent of C*, 100 percent of C*, and 120 percent of C*.

The variable, b, in the equation above was manipulated to vary the generosity of payments, being set at three different levels: 15 percent, 25 percent, and 35 percent. The lower this proportion, the higher the monthly allowance payment that a household would receive.

Of the 12 housing gap treatment cells, 11 offered allowance payments to households only as long as the household occupied a housing unit that met some sort of minimum housing consumption requirement. One set of these requirements, utilized in those treatment cells marked 1 through 5, required that the housing unit pass specific physical quality standards. These standards included such issues as the maximum allowable number of occupants, the presence of adequate light, heat, plumbing, and ventilation, and sound condition of walls, roof and floors. Conformity with these standards was monitored by inspection of the housing unit made at initial enrollment and periodically thereafter.

In contrast to these five minimum standards treatment groups, six minimum rent housing gap treatment groups used a more indirect method of ensuring minimum levels of housing consumption. Households in the minimum rent treatments were required to maintain at least a specified level of housing expenditures, under the assumption that housing units commanding certain levels of rent would automatically provide housing of certain levels of quality. Three of these treatment groups were required to spend at least 90 percent of C^* and the other three were required to spend at least 70 percent of C^*.

The final housing gap treatment cell, 12, was designated the unconstrained treatment group. Households in this group were free to choose whatever housing they wished to occupy.

Five treatment cells in the demand experiment received payments under a formula quite different from any of the housing gap programs described above. Households under this alternative approach received an allowance that was calculated as a fixed fraction of their actual rental payments, a plan known as the "percentage of rent" treatment. The fixed percentage was varied across the five groups, taking the values 20 percent, 30 percent, 40 percent, 50 percent, and 60 percent of rent.

The two control groups were differentiated from each other by whether or not housing information and counseling were offered by the experimenter. Of course, these two control groups differed from the other seventeen groups by not having any subsidies offered to them.

TABLE 6-E.1 Treatment Cells and Sample Sizes in the Demand Experiment

		A. Housing Gap Treatments ($P = C^* - bY$)		
			Housing Requirements	
b Value	C* Level	Minimum Standards	Minimum Rent Low = .7C*	Minimum High =
15% of income	100%	Cell 1 [81]		
25% of income	120%	Cell 2 [63]	Cell 6 [58]	Cell 9 [60]

TABLE 6-E.1 Continued

		A. Housing Gap Treatments ($P = C^* - bY$)		
			Housing Requirements	
b Value	*C* Level*	*Minimum Standards*	*Minimum Rent Low = .7C**	*Minimum High =*
	100%	Cell 3 [77]	Cell 7 [89]	Cell 1 [88]
	80%	Cell 4 [82]	Cell 8 [79]	Cell 1 [78]
35% of income	100%	Cell 5 [75]		

B. Percentage of Rent ($P = aR$)				
a = 60%	a = 50%	a = 40%	a = 30%	a = 20%
Cell 13	Cell 14	Cell 15	Cell 16	Cell 17
[49]	[190]	[179]	[176]	[11]

C. Controls (No Payments)	
With Housing Information	Without Housing Information
Cell 18	Cell 19
[296]	[307]

NOTE: Numbers in brackets indicate numbers of households in each treatment or control condition that were still actively participating in the experiments after two years.

SOURCE: Adapted from Raymond J. Struyck and Marc Bendick, eds. *Housing Vouchers for the Poor: Lessons from a National Experiment.* Washington, DC: The Urban Institute Press, 1981.

eligible families to obtain housing that met certain standards; some were simply rent rebates of up to 25 percent of family income; and others were rent rebates conditional on payment of rents at current market values or higher.

Complex experiments along these lines are especially appropriate for testing new policies, because it may not be clear in advance what exact form the new policy should take. A range of programs provides more opportunity to cover the particular policy that might be adopted and hence increase the generalizability of the impact assessment. In addition, testing variations can provide information to guide program construction toward effectiveness and economic efficiency. For example, it was shown in the Housing Allowance Demand Experiment that tying the allowances to occupancy of rental housing meeting certain building standards reduced participation greatly; consequently, only about one-third of eligible families actually received payments, the remaining two-thirds never occupying housing that met the quality standards tied to the payments.

This finding suggests that building standards should not be set so high that participation is unduly discouraged. Also, simple rent rebates (payments equal to some percentage of the rent paid) unfairly penalized those families who were careful (or lucky) housing shoppers and occupied "bargain" dwellings. The policy seemingly rewarded those who did not shop carefully in the housing market. The complex experiment described in Exhibit 6-E provided considerably greater amounts of information about the directions that policy might take than would a simple experiment incorporating only one of the alternatives tested in the Housing Allowance Demand experiment.

Under some circumstances, one might be concerned that the methods considered for administering a new program may seriously compromise the treatment being tested. For example, in the California group-therapy prison experiment (Exhibit 6-B), the evaluator might have anticipated that the use of prison guards as group-therapy leaders would seriously undermine the intervention's worth. This possibility might have been tested by adding an additional experimental treatment employing trained therapists recruited from outside the prison system, so that effectiveness of therapy administered by trained therapists could be contrasted with the therapy administered by prison guards. Indeed, had the design contained this component, the later criticism that the experiment did not address the issue of therapy effectiveness could have been avoided.

Similarly, the negative income tax experiments were criticized (Rossi and Lyall, 1976) for requiring monthly income reports from each of the participating families. Since the welfare system ordinarily does not require frequent income reports from families receiving payments, the experiment's stipulation appeared to critics to be a stricter "means test" than that required by ordinary welfare regulations, and hence as potentially more demeaning. Again, had the evaluators provided for an experimental group operating under the ordinary income-reporting rules, the criticisms would have been undercut.

Of course, one cannot proliferate experimental treatments endlessly to test every conceivable variation on a proposed program; a degree of restraint is required. Some evaluators have proposed the concept of "policy space" (Kershaw and Fair, 1976) as the basis for a rule for determining those program variations that should be subject to testing. Policy space, as we noted earlier, is that set of program alternatives likely to be politically acceptable, if the proposal is found to be effective and is then considered by policymakers or administrators for broad implementation.

Experiments should concentrate primarily on program variations that are clearly within the policy space defined by policymakers and administrators, perhaps extending a bit beyond, but not too far. In the income maintenance experiment, eligibility requirements ruled out families of full-time students on the grounds that Congress would be very unlikely to make that group eligible, even though their income level may have been well below the poverty line. Nor did it seem likely to the Housing Demand experimenters that homeowners would be made eligible for housing allowances.

ANALYZING COMPLEX EXPERIMENTS

As might be expected, complex randomized experiments require correspondingly more complex modes of analysis. Although a simple analysis of variance may be sufficient for obtaining an estimate of overall effects, the greater number of experimental groups allows more complicated forms of analysis, providing more precision in estimation of net effects and permitting the pursuit of analytical themes not ordinarily available in simple randomized experiments. Exhibit 6-F provides an illustration of how a complex randomized experiment was analyzed through analysis of variance and more complicated approaches.

LIMITATIONS ON THE USE
OF RANDOMIZED EXPERIMENTS

Randomized designs were initially formulated for use in laboratory or field agricultural research and can be adapted to social programs only with some difficulty: *First,* randomized experiments are not fruitful in the very early stages of program development. Under such circumstances it is often necessary to change features of a program for the sake of perfecting the treatment or its delivery. Although a randomized experiment can adapt to such changes, some degree of precision is lost, making it difficult in the final analysis to discern which of several treatments or combinations thereof produced the effects observed. For example, in a program that starts out providing group therapy and ends up giving individual counseling, it is difficult to tell whether one style of treatment or the other produced the observed effects. Hence, expensive, longitudinal field experiments are best reserved for tests of firmly designed treatments. A series of small-scale randomized experiments might be more suited to the development stage of a social program, as in the exemplary efforts of Fairweather and Tornatzky (1977) with respect to the development of halfway homes for discharged mental hospital patients.

Second, some persons have ethical qualms about randomization, seeing it as arbitrarily and capriciously depriving control groups of positive benefits. Often the reasoning of such critics runs as follows: If it is worth experimenting with a program (i.e., if the project is likely to help targets), it is a positive harm to withhold services from some units. To do so would be unethical. The counterargument is obvious: Ordinarily, it is not known

(text continues on page 261)

Exhibit 6-F: Analyzing a Complex Randomized Experiment: The Georgia and Texas TARP Experiments

Based upon the optimistic findings of the Baltimore LIFE experiment described in Exhibit 6-D, the Department of Labor decided to embark on a large-scale experiment that would use the existing agencies in two states to administer unemployment insurance payments to ex-felons. Of course, the objectives of the proposed new program were not changed: Unemployment insurance eligibility provided to ex-felons was intended to reduce the felons' needs to engage in crime in order to obtain income. The payments in that sense were intended to compete with illegal activities as a source of income and to provide for income during a transition period from prison life to gainful employment.

The new set of experiments, called Transitional Aid to Released Prisoners (TARP), were also more complicated in that they provided for varying lengths of eligibility for treatment and varying the "tax rate" applicable to payments (i.e., the amount of money by which payments were reduced for every dollar earned in employment).

The main effects of the treatments are shown in the analysis of variance in Table 6-F.1. (For simplicity's sake, only results from the Texas TARP experiment are shown.) The treatments had no effect on property arrests: The experimental and control groups differed by no more than one would expect by chance. However, the treatments had a very strong effect on the number of weeks worked during the postrelease year! Ex-felons receiving payments worked fewer weeks on the average than those in the control groups. In short, the payments did not compete well with crime but competed quite successfully with employment!

TABLE 6-F.1 Analysis of Variance of Property-Related Arrests in the Texas TARP Experiment

A. Property-Related Arrests
   During Postrelease Year

Treatment Group	Percentage Ever Arrested	Average Number of Arrests	N
1. 26 weeks payment: 100% tax	22.3	.27	176
2. 13 weeks payment: 100% tax	23.5	.30	200
3. 13 weeks payment: 25% tax	27.5	.43	200
4. No payments: job placement[b]	20.0	.30	200
5. Interviewed controls	22.0	.33	200
6. Uninterviewed controls[a]	23.2	.33	1000
ANOVA F value =	.70	1.15	
p value =	.63	.33	

B. Weeks Worked During
   Postrelease Year

Treatment Group	Average Number of Weeks Worked	N
1. 26 weeks payment: 100% tax	20.8	169
2. 13 weeks payment: 100% tax	27.1	191
3. 13 weeks payment: 25% tax	24.6	181
4. No payments: job placement	29.3	197
5. Interviewed controls	28.3	189
ANOVA F value =	6.98	
p value =	<.0000	

a. Control observations made through arrest records only. Hence no information on weeks worked.

b. Ex-felons in this treatment group were offered special job placement services (which few took) and some help in buying tools or uniforms if required for jobs. Few payments were made.

These inferences are based upon the F-ratio values along with their accompanying p values. Thus a value for p of .63 for the proportions who were arrested for property-related crimes means that in almost two out of three such experiments in which there are no effects the differences among the treatment groups shown would have occurred by chance. In contrast, the p values for the average number of weeks worked during the postrelease year shows that differences among the groups as great (or larger) than the ones shown would have occurred by chance in less than 1 in 100,000 experiments where there were no effects of the payments on the number of weeks worked.

In short, these results seem to indicate that the experimental treatment did not work in ways expected and produced undesirable effects as well. However, an analysis of variance of this sort is only the beginning of the analysis. The results suggested to the researchers that a set of counterbalancing processes may have been at work. It is well known from the criminological literature that employment for ex-felons is a strong predictor that the ex-felon will not be rearrested and subsequently returned to prison. Hence, the researchers postulated that the work disincentive effect increasing crime masked the positive effects of payments on reducing criminal activity. A model was constructed, as shown in Table 6-F.2, in which the effects of the payments were shown as increasing arrests through lowering work effort and reducing crime directly, the two effects canceling each other out and leading to the null results shown in Panel A of Table 6-F.1.

The coefficients shown in the diagram of Table 6-F.2 were derived empirically from the data using a statistical technique known as three-stage least-squares, and is too complex to discuss in detail here. The interested reader is referred to Kmenta (1974) or Hanushek and Jackson (1977) for further details.

A Texas estimates

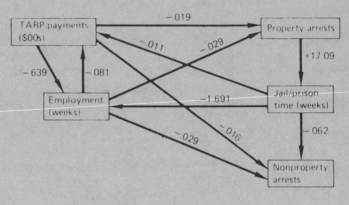

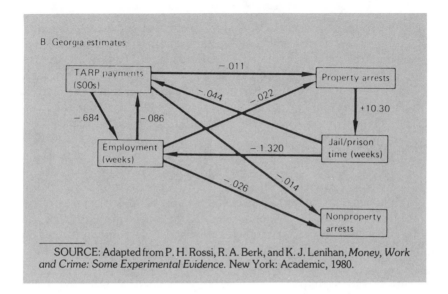

B. Georgia estimates

SOURCE: Adapted from P. H. Rossi, R. A. Berk, and K. J. Lenihan, *Money, Work and Crime: Some Experimental Evidence*. New York: Academic, 1980.

whether a treatment is effective; indeed, that is the reason one wishes to experiment. Hence, we cannot know in advance whether a treatment will be helpful or not. Another counterargument concerns the equity of randomness: If a treatment cannot be given to all who qualify, randomization is an equitable method for deciding who is to get the treatment because all targets would have an equal chance to receive it.

Sometimes an intervention may present some possibility of positive harm, and decision makers may be reluctant to authorize randomization on those grounds alone. In some of the utilities pricing experiments, for instance, there was a good chance that household utility bills would increase in some of the experimental groups. Experiment designers countered this argument by promising experimental households that any such overages would be reimbursed by the evaluators after the study was over. (Of course, this reimbursement changes the character of the treatment, possibly fostering irresponsible usage of utilities.)

Third, many of the major, large-scale field experiments used money payments as interventions (e.g., the negative income tax experiments and the housing allowance experiments). With such standardized and easily delivered treatments, one can be relatively certain that the experimental intervention will be similar to that of a fully implemented program, since there are only a limited number of ways that checks can be delivered. However, for more labor-intensive, high-skill interventions (job placement services, counseling, teaching, and the like), the treatments delivered in a field experiment are likely to be delivered with greater fidelity to designer intentions than when implemented as a program. Indeed, the very real danger of treatment deterioration in implementation is one of the reasons for monitoring programs, as advanced in Chapter 4. In addition, such possibilities argue for at least two rounds of experiments: a first round, in which treatments are tested in their purest form, and a second round, in which effective methods of service delivery through public agencies are tested and compared.

A good example of such a graduated series of experiments is the Department of Labor's two-stage experimentation with providing unemployment insurance benefits to released prisoners (Rossi et al., 1980; see also Exhibits 6-D and 6-F). In a small-scale first stage, social researchers ran an experiment in Baltimore with 432 prisoners released from the Maryland state prisons, selecting the prisoners before release, providing them with payments, and observing their work and arrest patterns for a year. First-stage results showed an 8 percent reduction in arrests over the postrelease period for experimental groups receiving unemployment insurance payments for thirteen weeks.

A much larger second-stage experiment was undertaken in Georgia and Texas with 2000 released prisoners in each state. In the second-stage experiment, payments were administered through the employment security agencies in each of the states and the tracking of the released prisoners over the postrelease year was accomplished jointly by the state prison systems and employment security agencies. The second-stage experiment was close to the system of administration that would have been put into place were the program enacted through federal legislation.

Fourth, randomized experiments are costly and time-consuming. Ordinarily, they should not be undertaken to test programs that will never be considered and that lie outside any conceivable policy space. Nor are experiments to be undertaken when information is needed in a hurry. To underscore this last point, it should be noted that the New Jersey-Pennsylvania Income Maintenance Experiment cost $34 million and took more than seven years from design to published findings (Kershaw and Fair, 1976). The Seattle and Denver income maintenance experiments took even longer, with their results appearing in final form (Office of Income Security Policy, 1983; SRI International, 1983; Mathematica Policy Research, 1983) long after income maintenance as a policy issue had disappeared from the national agenda.

Fifth, because randomized experiments require such tight controls on treatments and selection, they are likely not to have high generalizability or external validity. There has never been a field experiment evaluating some social program conducted using a sample of clients drawn from the entire population of the United States. The administrative complexities of running national experiments appears too severe a burden for designers to attempt.

In sum, large-scale, randomized field experiments are best reserved to test services that can be standardized and easily transferred to operating agencies and for which small local samples appear to be appropriate.

THE IMPORTANCE OF
RANDOMIZED EXPERIMENTS

Randomized experiments are the "flagships" of the evaluation field, because they allow evaluators to reach conclusions about impact or lack of impact with high degrees of certainty. Also, such evaluations make use of the same fundamental design strategy used in the physical and biological sciences and, when possible, in the social sciences to establish causal effects. Thus, the findings of randomized experiments are treated with a considerable degree of respect by policymakers and program staffs, as well as by the general public. Moreover, although other approaches to assessing programs generally do not ensure as definitive estimates of impact, randomized experiments are the conceptual underpinnings of most other designs for measuring the efficacy of social interventions.

7

Nonrandomized Designs for Impact Assessment

In this chapter we describe impact assessments that are undertaken without randomly assigned comparison or control groups. In the first part of the chapter, we discuss "quasi-experiments," evaluations that use comparison groups, albeit not ones selected by random assignment. Then we describe designs that do not rely on control groups at all, which, as a class, are called "single group" designs. They are especially relevant for full-coverage programs, when by definition it is not possible to use comparison groups. The first approach we discuss is the use of targets as their own controls, an option if participants have been observed for some period of time prior to the intervention. This class of designs is referred to as "reflexive-control" designs. An especially powerful type of reflexive-control design is time-series analysis, employing before-intervention trends to project what would have happened without the intervention. The final set of designs uses judgmental approaches and consists of having experts, program staff, or participants themselves assess program outcome.

KEY CONCEPTS

Constructed Controls: A group of untreated or differently treated targets selected by nonrandom methods to be as comparable as possible in crucial respects to the targets constituting the intervention groups.

Cross-Sectional Designs: Evaluations in which data are collected at only one time point.

Generic Controls: Established measures of social processes, such as published test norms, that are used as comparisons with the outcomes of interventions.

Matching: The construction of control groups by locating individuals who are identical in relevant respects to persons in experimental groups.

Reflexive Controls: Outcome measures taken before interventions on participating targets as control observations.

Shadow Controls: Expert judgments used to establish net impact.

Statistical Controls: Use of statistical techniques to hold constant differences between treatment and control groups.

Time-Series Analyses: Relatively long series of measurements on outcomes used to predict set of future outcomes.

Whether or not randomized experimental designs can be undertaken, evaluators are faced with the fundamental question: What would have happened without the intervention? Which of the alternatives to randomization is selected depends on the features of the program and the practical constraints that surround the conduct of the evaluation. The most common designs seek to approximate randomly selected control groups by constructing comparison groups or undertaking statistical analyses that in one way or another "tease out" net effects, or both.

QUASI-EXPERIMENTS

The reader should bear in mind that the term "quasi-experiment" does not imply that the procedures described are necessarily inferior to the randomized controlled experiment in terms of reaching plausible estimates of net effects. It is true that, without randomization, equivalence as described previously cannot be established with as much certainty. The possibility always remains that the outcome of a program is really due to a variable or process that has not been considered explicitly in the design or analysis. However, quasi-experiments, properly conducted, can provide information on impact that is free of most, if not all, of the confounding processes listed in Chapter 5. Indeed, the findings from a properly executed quasi-experimental design can be more valid than those from a poorly executed randomized experiment. Moreover, quasi-experiments may be the only feasible approach under many circumstances.

QUASI-EXPERIMENTS WITH CONSTRUCTED CONTROLS

In this approach, the evaluator attempts to identify and select a group of potential targets comparable in essential respects to those exposed to treatment. Several examples illustrate the use of such constructed control or comparison groups:

- In an attempt to assess the effects of nutritional supplements on intellectual functioning of children, nutritional supplements were given to all children in some villages while observations were also made on children in other villages to whom nutritional supplements were not given (Freeman et al., 1977).

- To assess the impact of manpower training for the unemployed, subsequent work histories of program participants were compared to those of relatives and neighbors of the participants who were also unemployed. The rationale for the use of unemployed friends of participants was that such friends were likely to share the same age, residential location, attitudes, and perhaps motivations of their participant friends and, hence, be similar to the participants in most aspects relevant to the manpower program (Main, 1968).

• In a study of the effects of attending church-related and -supported schools, Catholics who had attended such schools were compared with a control group of Catholics who had attended government-supported schools (Greeley and Rossi, 1966).

The basic formula for impact assessment, shown below, looks very similar, on the surface, to that shown earlier for randomized experiments, but there are important differences:

$$
\text{Net Outcome} = \begin{bmatrix} \text{Outcome for} \\ \text{program} \\ \text{participants} \end{bmatrix} - \begin{bmatrix} \text{Outcome for} \\ \text{constructed} \\ \text{control group} \end{bmatrix} \pm \begin{bmatrix} \text{Stochastic} \\ \text{error} \end{bmatrix}
$$

Whether or not this formula provides firm estimates of net effects depends largely on how closely the constructed control group resembles the intervention group in *all* essential respects.

A constructed control group of agricultural districts designed to match a set of districts participating in a program of increasing fertilizer use might differ from the program districts in a variety of ways that are difficult to detect. Although the constructed control group of districts might match with respect to average rainfall, average size of farm holdings, crops planted, and average amount of capital equipment per holding, there may be still other and perhaps unknown differences related to crop yield. Perhaps the districts in which officials have volunteered for the project might be more "progressive" in relation to innovations (or perhaps simply have a greater propensity to take risks). To the extent that project groups volunteer (or are volunteered by officials) to be in the project intervention group, self-selection processes may be at work that mask or enhance the effects of the project as computed through the above formula.

Target self-selection is not the only selection difference between an intervention group and its constructed controls. Administrators in charge of the program might bias target selection, thereby maximizing chances of showing positive program effects. They may try to do so by choosing districts that they know from their own experience are most likely to adopt the new agricultural practices enthusiastically. This practice is known as "creaming," and results from the all too understandable desire of program administrators to appear to run successful programs. An easy way for a program manager to do well is to choose participants who do well! A classic statement of this principle is the response made by former Governor Maddox (Georgia) to a question from reporters concerning his state's prisons. Maddox is reputed to have replied, "You can't reform the prisons of Georgia until we are able to attract a better class of prisoners!"

In evaluations in which target selection bias is at work, net effects would be overestimated by use of the formula shown above. Part of the differences between the experimental group and a constructed control group would consist of the stronger potential for positive change among the targets in the groups.

REGRESSION-DISCONTINUITY DESIGNS

The evaluator is not always at the mercy of self-selection or administrator-selection processes. Under some circumstances, the processes by which persons select themselves or are selected for participation is either known or can be investigated. Regression-discontinuity designs cover the special case in which selection procedures are explicit and known because participants are chosen according to some fixed procedure. This is the case when "contests" or eligibility tests that have been worked out in fine detail are the basis of target selection. For example, Berk and Rauma (1983), in an attempt to estimate the effects of an enacted program providing eligibility for unemployment insurance payments to released prisoners in California (modeled to some degree after the Baltimore LIFE experiment described in Exhibit 6-D), took advantage of the fact that program eligibility was contingent on the number of days worked during a felon's incarceration. Ex-prisoners had to have worked more than a certain number of days (652) in prison before becoming eligible for any payments and, if eligible, the amount of payments was made proportional to the number of days worked. The procedure for program inclusion and payments was quite explicit and presumably applied uniformly across the state. Comparison of the rearrest rates of those who were given payments with those who were not, holding constant the hours worked while in prison, provided an estimate of the net effects of the payments. Ex-prisoners who were given payments were estimated to have 13 percent fewer arrests.

Regression discontinuity designs, although powerful and virtually equivalent to randomized experiments, have not been applied often, mainly because there are few programs that have definite and precise enough selection rules. An exception is the use of this type of design to evaluate educational programs, although this has met with mixed success (Trochim, 1984).

Selection Bias Modeling

The general principles involved in regression-discontinuity designs have been elucidated in an attempt to apply the same reasoning to all circumstances in which participant selection processes are known. The general approach is known as "selection bias modeling." Although as yet there are few empirical examples based on applications to actual evaluations, this approach shows promise for evaluating programs in which randomized experiments cannot be undertaken. A few examples of possible applications follow.

In studying the outcomes of criminal justice procedures, in which accused persons proceed through a number of stages, each of which determines progression to the next stage, it is possible to develop a fairly accurate model of how cases move from one stage to another. For example, district attorneys seek indictments in robbery cases only when there are several witnesses. In this case, the selection process by which cases are brought to the indictment stage can be statistically modeled and incorporated into the design.

Another example of a circumstance in which the selection process can be modeled concerns tax return auditing procedures of the Internal Revenue Service. The IRS uses a set of algorithms based on information contained in returns to guide their selection of persons to be audited. An evaluation of the effect of being audited on subsequent tax reporting practices of individuals would be considerably improved if this information were used to construct a model based on the algorithms used by that agency of IRS auditing decisions.

The general rationale behind selection bias modeling was developed by econometricians (Cain, 1975; Heckman, 1980). Practical although technically complex procedures for such modeling are discussed by Barnouw (Barnouw et al., 1980) and Berk (1983; Berk and Ray, 1982).

**Practical Procedures for
Selecting Constructed Controls**

Devising an appropriate constructed control group is not a mechanical task (see Cook and Reichardt, 1976). The basis for such construction is prior knowledge and theoretical understanding of the social processes in question. It is such knowledge that guides the evaluator in determining the specific ways a constructed control group should resemble the experimental group. For example, we would draw on prior knowledge about the factors that affect crop yields to select agricultural districts for a constructed control group in an evaluation of a program to increase crop yields. Likewise, if we were interested in studying the effects of a program to increase the mathematics competence of secondary school students, prior knowledge about the characteristics of individuals and features of educational settings that affect learning would be used in constructing appropriate control groups (e.g., intelligence, parental background, sex, age, and size of class).

The prior knowledge necessary for constructing control groups may be found in the published literature of relevant substantive areas. An educational evaluator would consult the literature about circumstances known to affect, say, math learning; and the literature on fertility would be consulted in designing a study of a family planning campaign.

While one may be tempted to construct control groups using every factor mentioned in the relevant literature, some degree of restraint is advisable. Using more than a few variables for selecting constructed controls is neither very efficient nor necessary. In general, characteristics that are candidates for constructed control purposes tend to be highly intercorrelated. If parent's occupation is selected as a control characteristic in an educational intervention, then the groups are also equated to a considerable extent on parental income, because these characteristics tend to be closely related.

Matching

The procedures used in selecting constructed control groups are referred to as *matching*. Matching may be accomplished on an aggregate level, by locating groups to serve as controls whose characteristics parallel those of the group exposed to the program in their relevant features. For example, if children in a particular school are the targets of an intervention, a constructed control group might be the population of one or more schools whose demographic profiles of students mirror those of the participating school (see Exhibit 7-A).

An alternative is to select from one or more schools those children who are similar to the target participants. In doing so there are two options: *individual* or *aggregate* matching. In individual matching, the effort is to draw a "partner" for each target student from the unexposed pool of students. For example, if age, sex, number of siblings, and father's occupation were deemed the relevant matching variables, the roster of unexposed children would be scrutinized to locate the closest equivalent child for pairing.

The "closeness" of the match always needs to be adjusted in order to make matching practicable. For example, matching of the exposed and unexposed children on age may have to be done in terms of a six-month "window," though a smaller age difference in the selection of pairs is more desirable. (See Exhibit 7-B for an illustration of individual matching.)

With the use of computers, more elaborate forms of individual matching are possible. Westat, an applied social research firm, matched persons who entered the CETA (Comprehensive Employment and Training Act) programs in 1977 on an individual basis with persons included in the Current Population Survey of that year. A computer program was written

Exhibit 7-A: Use of Constructed Controls in the Education Voucher Demonstration

The Education Voucher Demonstration was designed to introduce free-enterprise concepts into the educational process. Under the voucher concept, parents freely select a school for their child and receive a credit or voucher equal to the cost of the child's education that is paid directly to the school upon enrollment. It was presumed that this form of financing education would foster competition among the schools and improve the quality of education by making schools more responsive to students' needs. An initial external evaluation at the conclusion of the first year found, however, a relative loss in reading achievement for students in six public schools that participated in the voucher demonstration. The purpose of this study was to reexamine these findings from the first year of the voucher demonstration.

A constructed control group design was devised as follows. Schools were divided into three groups: (1) voucher schools with a traditional academic orientation, (2) voucher schools with an innovative orientation, and (3) nonvoucher comparison schools. The comparison schools were selected from the same districts and were comparable in terms of ethnic and socioeconomic composition, welfare status, etc. Both gain-score analysis and analysis of variance were used to analyze the data. The results indicate that the deleterious reading effect of the voucher demonstration was confined to only a few schools with programs featuring nontraditional, innovative curricula.

SOURCE: Adapted from P. M. Wortman, C. S. Reichardt, and R. G. St. Pierre, "The First Year of the Education Voucher Demonstration: A Secondary Analysis of Student Achievement Test Scores," *Evaluation Quarterly* 2 (May 1978): 193.

that matched every one of 10,000 CETA participants with a closely comparable person from the national sample of 55,000 households drawn by the Bureau of the Census in order to estimate monthly unemployment rates. The program used a hierarchical matching algorithm that selected controls first on ethnicity/race, sex, and age, and then sought as close a match as possible on fifteen other factors. Wages reported to the Social Security Administration for the years prior to and after CETA participation were attached to records of CETA participants. CETA participants

Exhibit 7-B: An Evaluation of the Effects of Public Housing Using Constructed Controls with Individual Matching

This quasi-experiment was designed to assess the impact of moving into good-quality public housing from slum housing on family, health, student achievement, occupational attainment, and housing satisfaction.

Taking advantage of the opening of a new housing project in Baltimore, the authors chose families who could be matched on 26 different characteristics and who were admitted to the new housing project with families on the waiting list who were not to be admitted. A total of 396 families were admitted to the housing project and 633 families were constructed controls; the surplus control families were retained as part of the control group since a greater attrition rate was anticipated among control families.

All of the families were followed by eleven interviews between 1955 and 1958. Interviews covered inventories of illnesses experienced by the families, their social-psychological adjustment, and the school performance of school-age children. In addition, an initial interview before admission to the public housing project was undertaken with participating families and with control families.

Only minor differences were found between participants and controls: Those in public housing were more satisfied with their housing and liked their neighbors more, but there were few discernible effects on illness or the school performance of children.

SOURCE: Summary, by permission, of D. M. Wilner, R. P. Walkely, T. C. Pinkerton, and M. Tayback, *The Housing Environment and Family Life*. Baltimore: Johns Hopkins University Press, 1962.

were contrasted in their post-CETA wages to their matched controls (Bryant and Rupp, 1984).

The second approach is aggregate matching. In this case individuals are not matched, but the overall distributions on each matching variable are made to correspond for the experimental and control groups. The same proportions of children by sex and age would be found in the participating and comparison groups, but the result may have been obtained by including a 12-year-old girl and an 8-year-old boy to balance the aggregate distribution of the experimental group, which included a 9-year-old girl and an 11-year-old boy. (See Exhibit 7-C for an example of aggregate matching.)

Individual matching usually is preferable to aggregate matching. The drawbacks to individual matching are that it is more expensive, time-consuming, and difficult to execute for a large number of matched variables. One other possibility is matching on individual and aggregate characteristics, as illustrated in Exhibit 7-D. The methods employed for matching vary in complexity. Sherwood et al. (1975) describe a multivariate matching technique that improves the equivalence of matched experimental and control groups.

Individual matching can often result in a drastic loss of cases. If it is not possible to find matching persons for those included in an experimental group, those unmatched individuals have to be discarded as data sources. In some cases, the proportion of unmatched individuals can become so large, approaching 50 percent, that the experimental group becomes less and less representative of any population to which the intervention may be applied if enacted into a full-scale program.

Other shortcomings of matching designs for evaluation have also been identified as "upsetting statistical artifacts" (Campbell and Boruch, 1975; Campbell and Erlebacher, 1970). Essentially, inappropriate applications occur when matching is carried out on the basis of premeasures of the outcome variables used to assess impact. Particularly when scores on variables used as outcome measures taken prior to the start of the program are unreliable or otherwise fallible, the findings from the evaluation can be misleading or invalid, due to the shift in unreliable measurements obtained at the two time points (a phenomenon known as regression toward the mean). Thus, matching on the basis of variables other than outcome measures is the option of choice (Sherwood et al., 1975).

However matching may be done, there is always the possibility that some critical difference still remains between experimentals and controls that is related to both outcomes and selection into the experimental group. In an important methodological research, Fraker and Maynard (1984) compared estimates of the net effects derived from a randomized control group with those derived from control groups constructed by individual matching. The program in question was the Supported Work Experiment, in which unemployed youths, AFDC mothers, and some hard-core unemployed males were randomly allocated to treatments in which jobs were provided to experimentals. The control groups, constructed by individual matching, were drawn from the Current Population Survey files and matched by age, sex, and prior earnings. Since the randomized controls contrasted to the experimentals provide unbiased estimates of the net effects of the Supported Work intervention, the utility of matching con-

Exhibit 7-C: Evaluating Instructional Television in El Salvador Using Aggregate Matched Constructed Controls

As part of a project of educational reform, the El Salvador school system decided to introduce instructional television into grades 7-9.

To evaluate the effects of the project on learning, a joint team of researchers, from El Salvador and Stanford University, administered tests of general ability and reading achievement, as well as survey questionnaires (measuring such variables as occupational aspirations) to three samples of students, as described below. Students were tested and surveyed at regular intervals to track changes over time. The groups tested and surveyed were as follows:

Cohort A: 902 students who entered Grade 7 in 1969. 581 students (in twenty-eight classes) experienced a Reform curriculum including television instruction; and 207 students (in nine classes) received the traditional curriculum (pre-Reform). The first two groups were chosen by the Ministry of Education, while the third was chosen at random from among a large pool of classes.

Cohort B: 707 students (in twenty-nine classes) who entered the seventh grade in 1970, all of whom experienced the Reform curriculum. 482 students (in eighteen classes) experienced television instruction, while the remaining 225 students (in eleven classes) did not.

Cohort C: 600 students in twenty-three classes experiencing the Reform curriculum. 467 students in eighteen classes experienced educational television, while 133 students in five classes did not.

Comparisons were made among cohorts and within cohorts, depending on experience with educational television. Differences among groups in background (sex, place of residence, socioeconomic status of families) were held constant statistically.

Results indicated that students experiencing the Reform curriculum gained more in general ability than those experiencing the "traditional" curriculum, and those who received televised instruction did better than those who did not. Comparisons were made over a period of two years for cohorts A and B. However, results for achievement tests measuring knowledge acquired in specific subjects were less favorable to television instruction: Television classes gained more in the initial year of exposure, but subsequent years showed no clear pattern of differences.

SOURCE: Summary, by permission, of J. K. Mayo, R. C. Hornick, and E. G. McAnany, *Educational Reform with Television: The El Salvador Experience.* Stanford, CA: Stanford University Press, 1976.

Exhibit 7-D: A Nonrandomized Experiment with a Constructed Control and Before/After Survey Measures

The Dacca Family Planning experiment was a comparative evaluation of family planning programs directed at both males and females. The primary purpose was to analyze differential changes in birth control practices resulting from three educational approaches to family planning—direct education with husbands only, direct education with wives only, and direct education with both. The effectiveness of each of these educational approaches was to be measured by comparing each to a fourth group, who received birth control services but no educational experimental program (the control).

The study populations were chosen from the four housing colonies maintained by the Central Government of Pakistan for its employees in Dacca. The type of housing provided was based on the salary of the employees, ranked into five classes. The study groups were defined as those having low levels of position in the government (Class III and IV workers ranging from sweepers to low-level clerks) and living in separate but similar housing colonies. Couples within the study groups were then screened to exclude ineligibles on the following criteria: one spouse not usually residing in the area at the time of the Before Survey; couples who could not understand Bengali (the language to be used during the interview); husbands with more than one wife at the time of the Before Survey; couples who had been married for less than two years; couples with wives over 50 years of age; couples in which either spouse was sterilized.

Data were gathered through the Before Survey and the After Survey and through clinic records and home visit records. Both spouses in the three experimental groups were interviewed in both the Before and After surveys. The control group was interviewed only in the After Survey. The Before and After surveys contained questions on the following topics: demographic characteristics; fertility; knowledge of birth control; intended future fertility; the use of birth control; and attitudes toward learning about and future use of birth control.

This study concluded that certain educational approaches are more effective than others in meeting multiple goals among many types of target populations. The educational approach aimed at both males and females had, by far, the greatest impact in increasing knowledge about family planning. The program directed at both sexes was superior for almost all criteria of program success, including improving the attitudes regarding the acceptance of other people using family planning. This approach also had the greatest clinic attendance and acknowledged use of contraceptives. Only in the cases of older women, upper-class women, and younger men did the program directed at only one sex have a greater impact. (In these instances, the program directed at the females had greater impact.) It appears that educational efforts aimed at both sexes may be the most effective in achieving the broadest range of cognitive, attitudinal, and behavioral changes in family planning.

SOURCE: Summary, by permission, of L. W. Green et al., *The Dacca Family Planning Experiment*. University of California, Berkeley, School of Public Health, 1972.

trols can be judged. Several methods of making individual matches were employed, but all gave estimates of net effects that were wide of the mark. At least in this research, matching proved far inferior as an alternative to randomized controls.

Still a third way of constructing a control group is to select a sample of individuals from a population from which the experimental group has been selected and to control the relevant differences statistically. This method is described in detail under the heading of statistical controls and discussion of this approach will be postponed until that section.

Selecting Constructed Controls

As we have noted, appropriate matching requires intimate knowledge of the substantive area involved if one is to identify the important matching

TABLE 7.1 Characteristics Useful in Devising Constructed Control Groups

I. Characteristics of Individuals:
    Age
    Sex
    Educational attainment
    Socioeconomic status (income, wealth, property ownership)
    Tenure (land and/or home ownership)
    Marital status
    Occupation (occupational prestige)
    Ethnicity (race, cultural group, language group, national origin)
    Intellectual functioning (IQ, cognitive ability, knowledge)
    Labor force participation

II. Characteristics of Families (or households):
    Life-cycle stage
    Number of members
    Number of children
    Socioeconomic status (household income or earnings, wealth, occupations
        followed, etc.)
    Housing arrangements
    Ethnicity

III. Characteristics of Organized Units (schools, classes, unions, etc.):
    Size differentiation
    Levels of authority
    Number of subunits
    Number of distinctly different roles (occupations)
    Industry class
    Growth rate
    Budget

IV. Characteristics of Communities (territorially organized units):
    Industry mix
    Governmental organization
    Population size
    Territorial size
    Growth rate
    Population density
    Location in relation to other territorial units (part of metropolitan area, independent
        city, town, etc.)

characteristics. However, whenever there is very little a priori knowledge about the substantive area of an intervention, some general guides may be followed, based on what social scientists have found over the past several decades to be generalized features of individuals, families, communities, or other units that affect many areas of human behavior. A brief list of such "standard" variables is given in Table 7.1.

Note that the characteristics shown in the table are "nested." That is, characteristics of individuals may also be used to characterize higher units by forming averages, measures of dispersion, or other aggregate-descriptive measures. An individual may be characterized by his or her calendar age, a family by the average age of its members, a factory by the average age of its employees (or the proportion between certain ages), and a city by the average age of its inhabitants (or by the proportion of persons who are in the economically productive age group).

Perhaps the best way to use the characteristics shown in Table 7.1 is to regard them as a "checklist" designed to remind the evaluator of characteristics that are likely candidates for consideration in constucting control groups. In assessing the impact of an antismoking educational campaign directed to preadolescent schoolchildren, an experimental group of schools could be matched with a constructed control group of schools, ones comparable in parental socioeconomic status, student intellectual functioning, city size, and location.

The characteristics in Table 7.1, however, are no adequate substitute for a priori knowledge directly relevant to the phenomenon being studied. For example, a program that is designed to lower rates of fertility among unmarried adolescents is best evaluated using constructed controls chosen on the basis of some theoretical understanding of adolescents' motivations for allowing themselves to become pregnant, engage in sexual behavior, and so on.

Data Collection Strategies for Constructed Control Designs

The strategic considerations that enter into data collection for designs with constructed controls are not essentially different from those discussed in connection with randomized experiments. The general recommendation made in Chapter 6 is the more before-and-after intervention measures of outcome, the better. The two reasons for this recommendation discussed in the case of randomized controls apply here as well: First, the more measures, the more reliable the readings that can be made on pre- and postoutcomes. Second, the process by which the intervention may work can be tracked more carefully over time.

THE USE OF GENERIC CONTROLS IN ASSESSING IMPACT

All of the approaches discussed in Chapter 6 and the first part of this chapter are based on the use of observations undertaken especially for the purpose of estimating what would have happened without the intervention being tested. These procedures are stressed because, in most intervention situations, we rarely have firm knowledge about what ordinarily happens in the course of social action. In contrast, many of the physical sciences (e.g., chemistry) publish large handbooks that provide standardized values for wide varieties of physical processes. For example, it is not necessary for the industrial chemist to ascertain *de novo* typical BTU values for various fuels, because there are several handbooks in which such values are listed, based on the pooled experiences of perhaps scores of investigators. For the social researcher, however, there are few comparable compilations. We do not know, for instance, the typical experiences of persons on urban labor markets. Even more important, we do know that such "typical" experiences change from season to season and from year to year, fluctuating with the business cycle and with the mix of workers on the market.

Despite the general lack of standardized values in the social sciences, there are a few areas of human behavior in which such generic controls are available. As discussed in Chapter 5, generic controls are measures of social and human processes generally recognized as well established. Existing generic controls include measures of vital processes (e.g., death rates, birthrates, sex ratios, proportions of persons in various labor force categories) and derivatives of these measures. In addition, there are published standards or norms for various psychological tests (including tests of intelligence, achievement of various skills, personality, and the like). The information provided by generic controls, with proper safeguards, can be used to estimate what would ordinarily happen without an intervention.

For example, the effects of fluoridated water on dental caries were discovered when researchers noted that the incidence of dental disorders varied among localities, and that such variation was correlated with the amount of fluorides naturally found in the drinking water. This correlation was discovered because dental epidemiologists had a fairly firm notion of the normal rates of caries formation. Similarly, the detection of epidemics rests heavily on the epidemiologist's knowledge of ordinary incidence rates for various diseases. Likewise, the efficacy of occupational health measures is judged against expected death rates from various causes in the general population.

Another example from the field of public health is that of comparing death rates from cancer for persons who have been in occupations with high exposures to suspected carcinogenic substances with those of persons in other occupations. For example, it is suspected that high levels of exposure to formaldehyde among workers in medical pathology laboratories account for the high death rate among such workers from brain cancers. Expected death rates for persons of roughly the same age and sex in the general population are compared to death rates from the same condition for workers in medical pathology labs. The latter have been found to be several magnitudes higher than expected on the basis of the general rates of death from brain cancer.

In considering educational interventions, it is tempting to use the norms of achievement-test publishers as generic controls. But doing so may result in serious errors; there is so much variance in achievement associated with socioeconomic level, ethnic background, and similar factors that published norms are usually too general to be useful. Thus, in evaluating whether or not a new teaching program in education is effective, it is probably not appropriate to compare the gain in achievement-test scores of a sample of inner-city children against the published norms of the test constructor. The ordinary rates of learning for such children are likely to differ greatly from such general norms. Similarly, it is probably a mistake to compare the earnings of 34-year-old males as reported in the Census Bureau's Current Population Survey to those of 34-year-olds who have just completed a vocational training course. Generic controls, in short, are usually unavailable in sufficient detail for evaluators to be confident that the standards in question are appropriate for a particular use.

Absolute standards are a special form of generic controls, sometimes applied in circumstances in which goals are very explicit. For example, a goal for an income maintenance program may be to see that every person over the age of 18 receives a minimum monthly income of $500. Such a specific goal may be viewed as a "generic control," and a program can be assessed by whether or not that goal is achieved. Similarly, the objective of a prisoner rehabilitation program may be to reduce recidivism to zero, also a measurable attainment. However, few programs are willing to commit themselves to such absolute goals, nor is it likely that any goal so specific can be achieved by an intervention.

A variant on generic controls is the use of existing data sets to provide disaggregated measures on individuals who can then be used as controls in constructed control groups. The public use tapes of the U.S. Census have been used in this fashion, as well as public use data sets of the Current Population Survey and the NORC General Social Survey. Such data sets can be useful if it is possible to select the appropriate controls, a procedure that is highly dependent on knowledge about relevant comparisons, good measures of the outcome in question, and appropriate time matching. Given that, in many social programs, targets are persons who constitute a very small proportion of the general population, matching persons are correspondingly rare in general samples of the population, making the use of these data tapes somewhat problematic.

We wish to stress that in general generic controls should be used only under circumstances in which other types of controls are not available. It is tempting to consider their use in other evaluation contexts. Certainly, generic controls are inexpensive and take virtually no time to collect, especially in comparison to the expense involved in using randomized or constructed controls. However, even when randomized, constructed, or statistical controls cannot be employed, generic controls should be used only with the utmost caution, with intense scrutiny of whether or not the generic controls in question are comparable to participants in every critical way.

THE USE OF STATISTICAL CONTROLS IN ASSESSING IMPACT

Impact assessments using randomized controls or constructed control groups employ a strategy in which participants in a program are matched in designated ways with nonparticipants. In contrast are efforts to equate or adjust statistically for differences between program participants and nonparticipants. As we have discussed, both constructed controls and statistical procedures may be in the same evaluation.

Cross-Sectional Surveys

First, we will address the strategy in which only postintervention measures are used. Cross-sectional surveys, in which all measurements are made at one point in time, permit post hoc comparisons between participants and nonparticipants, providing a high degree of comparability between the two groups that can be established by removing selection biases.

For example, in estimating the effects of childhood attendance at Catholic schools on adults, evaluators contrasted those who had attended parochial schools with Catholics who had not (Greeley and Rossi, 1966; Greeley et al., 1976). In this case it was possible to use constructed controls because there were many parishes without parochial schools, and some Catholics therefore did not have the opportunity to attend such schools. Since the authors were concerned with measuring occupational attainment in adulthood (among other outcomes), only postintervention measures (occupational attainment as measured in a sample survey of Catholic adults) were available.

Of course, there were a number of additional ways in which the parochial-school attendees could have differed from their secular-school counterparts. Attendance at parochial schools might have represented a stronger commitment to Catholicism among the parents of such adults, a commitment expressed by settling in parishes that had parochial schools. The parents of the parochial-school attendees may have been more affluent as well, since usually only parishes with sufficient revenues can afford to establish schools, and only relatively well-off parents can afford to pay the tuition charges. We know from numerous studies that economic status is related to school achievement. These possible differences in family wealth must be taken into account in the application of appropriate statistical controls.

Essentially, cross-sectional impact assessment depends heavily on the use of statistical methods to factor out the differences between persons who have experienced an intervention and those who have not. A cross-sectional study, then, is one in which observations are made at a single point in time, contrasting program participants with nonparticipants (or those who have participated to varying degrees). Usually, the target population is sampled and a survey administered to gather information on a large number of possible confounding variables. Differences between levels of exposure to an intervention are observed, holding constant through statistical analyses other relevant differences between participants and nonparticipants.

It should be noted that impact assessments with constructed controls and those using statistical controls are identical in conceptualization. The main difference lies in screening for nonparticipant targets through deliberate selection (constructed controls) as opposed to screening targets through statistical techniques (statistical controls). Both methods are used to obtain comparability between participants and nonparticipants and both depend heavily on a priori knowledge about what characteristics might distinguish the two groups.

Whether one conducts an impact assessment with constructed controls or with statistical controls may hinge on the distribution of target participants and nonparticipants in the population under study. To cite an obvious example, it makes little sense to attempt to use surveys of the general population to find participants and nonparticipants in prison rehabilitation programs, because persons who have been in prison and therefore might be targets would be relatively rare in any general population survey. Hence, general population surveys do not represent an efficient tool for estimating the impact of any program that is aimed at a very narrowly defined set of targets.

An additional consideration is whether or not it is possible to obtain before-and-after measures. If for one reason or another it is not possible to obtain or collect before measures on both experimental and constructed control groups, the use of surveys may be an efficient way to proceed. For example, to gauge the effects of the GI Bill's tuition-financing programs on veterans of the Korean War, it is probably not possible to do anything more than survey surviving veterans, in the hope that it will be possible to hold constant the potential differences between those who used their benefits and those who did not.

The identifying characteristic of a cross-sectional survey is that all its measurements are taken at a given point in time. However, some of the measurements may be retrospective, that is, referring to a previous time. For example, measuring an adult's educational attainment in reality measures previous behavior, that is, school attendance during childhood and early adulthood. Similarly, asking a person his or her age is an implicit request for date of birth. These two examples deal with measures that are not likely to be subject to recall bias. However, there are many recall measures that are likely to be subject to such biases. For example, if we ask adults how eager they were to participate in a program at the time they entered that program, there is likely to be some significant degree of rationalization of previous attitudes so that they are in line with present assessments of the program.

It is tempting to regard a cross-sectional survey's ability to obtain measures of past behavior as a substitute for the before measures and to use such studies to simulate before- and after-research designs. For most impact assessments this use of cross-sectional surveys is not recommended, unless the measures happen to be known to be reliable under conditions of recall.

Successive Statistical Adjustments

The logic of holding variables constant is illustrated in Table 7.2, which presents a hypothetical impact assessment of a vocational training program for unemployed men between the ages of 35 and 40. The program is designed to upgrade the job skills of participants in order to enable them to obtain better (i.e., higher-paying) jobs. The program was evaluated by taking a sample of 1000 participants and interviewing them one year after they completed vocational training. In addition, another 1000 men from the same age brackets were sampled from the general population of the large metropolitan area in which the program was operating. Since the program was small, almost none of the men approached for interviews in the general sample had participated in the program. Both samples were asked for information about earnings, and hourly wage rates were computed for both groups.

In Panel I of Table 7.2, the average wage rates of the two groups are compared. Those who had participated in the project were earning, on average, $3.75 per hour; for those who had not participated, the corresponding average was $4.20. Clearly, those who had participated were earning considerably less than those who had not (their wage rate was only 89 percent of that of nonparticipants). However, these unadjusted comparisons are quite misleading, because participants and nonparticipants could have differed on a number of earnings-related variables other than their participation in the project.

Panel II of Table 7.2 takes one such difference into account, by presenting average wage rates separately for two educational levels: those who

TABLE 7.2 Illustrations of Statistical Adjustments in a Hypothetical Evaluation of the Impact of an Employment Training Project

Outcome Measure = Average hourly wage rates 1 year after completion of training program

I. Gross comparison between men 35-40 who have completed training program with sample of men 35-40 who did not attend training program:

	Participants	Nonparticipants
Average Wage Rate	$3.75	$4.20
N =	(1,000)	(1,000)

II. Comparison after adjusting for educational attainment:

	Participants		Nonparticipants	
	Less than High School Completion	Completed High School	Less than High School Completion	Completed High School
Average Wage Rate	$3.60	$4.10	$3.75	$4.50
N =	(700)	(300)	(400)	(600)

III. Comparison adjusting for educational attainment and employment at start of training program (or equivalent date for nonparticipants):

	Participants		Nonparticipants			
	Less than High School	Completed High School	Less than High School		Completed High School	
	All Unemployed		U	E	U	E
Average Wage Rate	$3.60	$4.10	$3.50	$3.83	$4.00	$4.60
N =	(700)	(300)	(100)	(300)	(100)	(500)

NOTE: U denotes unemployed; E, employed.

had not completed high school and those who had. Note that 70 percent of those who had been participants had not completed high school, as opposed to 40 percent of the nonparticipants. When we compare the wage rates of persons of comparable educational attainment, the hourly wages of participants and nonparticipants approach one another: $3.60 and $3.75, respectively, for those who had not completed high school, and $4.10 to $4.50 for those who had. Obviously, holding educational attainment constant diminishes the differences between wage rates of participants and nonparticipants.

Panel III takes still another difference into account. Given that all participants were unemployed at the time of enrollment in the training program, it is appropriate to compare participants with those nonparticipants who were also unemployed around the same time. In this panel, nonparticipants are divided into those who were unemployed and those who were not. This time, those who participated in the project earned more at each educational level than those who did not participate and were unemployed around the same time: $3.60 and $3.50, respectively, for those who did not complete high school, and $4.10 and $4.00 for those who did.

Note that the introduction of successive statistical adjustments (controls) was not a haphazard procedure. There was justification for introducing each control based on a priori knowledge about the determinants of earnings. In any real example, of course, additional controls would have been entered—perhaps for previous occupations held, marital status, number of dependents, and race—all factors known to be related to wage rates. Again, the worth of impact assessments made through statistical controls is heavily dependent on such a priori knowledge.

It also should be noted that this evaluation design is ordinarily unable to account fully for the effects of self-selection and to remove such effects from estimates of net program impact. In the hypothetical example presented in Table 7.2, unemployed persons who participated were by that very fact differentiated from those who did not—perhaps by higher levels of motivation, a difference that is not possible to measure retrospectively with any strong degree of confidence.

The adjustments made in Table 7.2 were accomplished in a very simple way in order to illustrate the logic of successive statistical controls. More complex and sensitive statistical methods are available to take a number of adjustments into account simultaneously. Especially appropriate are the techniques of multiple regression and analysis of covariance, as well as multiple discriminant function analysis and log-linear models. (Advanced texts should be consulted; e.g., Hanushek and Jackson, 1977.)

Similarities Between Constructed Controls and Statistical Controls

Despite differences in specific procedures, there are many important similarities between the method of constructed controls and the use of statistical controls. The figures shown in Table 7.2 are identical in critical respects to ones that might have been generated by an evaluation using constructed controls. Each of the successive statistical controls introduced had the effect of isolating comparable groups of persons in the experimental group and in the general survey. The numbers of persons in each of the comparable groups are not identical, as would be the case had constructed controls been used, but that is not important because percentaging within each group compared holds numbers constant.

The comparisons in the bottom panel of Table 7.2 are, in principle, identical to those that would have been found had constructed controls been used with matching procedures employing the variables shown in that table as matching variables. Indeed, if we discarded randomly from the bottom panel all surplus matches in the population survey, the numbers in each of the groups being compared would be identical also. In short, constructed and statistical controls are equivalent ways of proceeding, but some superior qualities reside in statistical controls, arising out of the retention of observations that might have to be discarded under matching procedures.

Complex Multivariate Methods

The use of more complicated multivariate methods is illustrated by Exhibit 7-E, which shows the result of an analysis designed to estimate the net impact of parole on postrelease employment of ex-felons released from Texas prisons during the first six months of 1976. The equation shown in the table expresses the number of weeks from date of release to date of first employment for ex-felons during the first year after release, as a function of parole and a number of variables that can be viewed as affecting either work or receiving parole.

The coefficients shown in the column marked "b" are unstandardized regression coefficients expressing the net number of weeks to first employment for each unit of each of the independent variables. The coefficient for having been released on parole is –3.45 weeks, meaning that persons released on parole found their first job 3.45 weeks sooner than other persons, holding constant all the other variables in the equation. In effect, the regression coefficient for parole is an estimate net effect for parole status, indicating that persons released on parole went to work sooner than those who were released unconditionally.

The remaining variables in the equation were entered because there were good reasons to believe that the conditions they represent affected employment or parole status. Thus age, sex, race, education, marital status, having a physical handicap, having arranged a job prior to release, and being returned to Houston (a prime labor market in Texas at the time) were entered into the equation. All were variables available in the data set and all were expected to affect how quickly the released felons obtained employment. Indeed, we see that some of them were useful: Males were likely to go to work much more quickly than females (about 14.5 weeks sooner); the physically handicapped took longer to begin working; those who returned to Houston got work faster in that very good labor market; and those who had arranged for a job prior to release also went to work sooner.

Another set of variables was entered, to hold constant the tendency to be granted parole and hence to represent the selection process used by

Exhibit 7-E: Regression of Number of Weeks Postrelease to First Employment on Selected Prerelease Characteristics and Parole Status for Texas Prison Releases

Independent Variables	Dependent Variable Is Number of Weeks Before First Job in Postrelease Year	
	b	*SE*
Released on parole	−3.45**	1.25
Age (years)	.01	.08
Male	−14.45***	2.72
Black	4.45**	1.53
Chicano	4.33***	2.07
Education (years)	−.16	.34
Married	−.01	1.89
Number of previous convictions	.08	.09
Gate money ($00's)	.00	.00
Handicap prison classification	7.36**	2.25
Released to Houston	−4.67**	1.44
Job arranged before release	−.20**	.06
Expected number of weeks between release and first job	2.81***	.76
Prison Behavior Code	−.03	.02
Constant	16.68*	6.50

$$R^2 = .25***$$
$$N = (397)$$

*statistically significant at .05
**statistically significant at .01
***statistically significant at .001

NOTE: The regression results shown above are computed from the control group in one of the TARP experiments. Note that because the table above is concerned only with members of the control group, the table, in effect, describes a cross-sectional survey and is equivalent to having drawn a random sample of all persons released from the state prisons of Georgia over a six-month period in 1976. (The details of the experimental treatment used in the TARP experiments are described in Exhibit 6-N.)

SOURCE: Unpublished tabulations from TARP experiment control group in Texas. (See P. H. Rossi, R. A. Berk, and K. J. Lenihan, 1980, for full description of study.)

the Texas parole board: the number of previous convictions, and a prison behavior code (actually, a sort of point system in which each incident of misbehavior in prison led to a score increase).

The worth of the analysis presented in Exhibit 7-E depends largely on how thoroughly the variables used capture (or model) the nonparole factors involved in going to work quickly and the kinds of factors taken into account in the granting of parole.

Examples of Statistical Control Use

Exhibits 7-F, 7-G, and 7-H illustrate varying levels of statistical sophistication in the analysis of cross-sectional data to assess impact. Exhibit 7-F is of mainly historical interest, as it was undertaken very early in the development of social research, before computers made it possible to make many calculations easily and cheaply. It is a study of the impact of desegregation in the U.S. Army during the Korean conflict in the early 1950s. Assessing impact consisted of comparing soldiers in racially integrated units with those who served in segregated units. Elaborate statistical controls were not practical, because it was difficult to apply the appropriate statistical techniques in that period and because self-selection was scarcely a factor (the army placed soldiers in their units, and for them to switch voluntarily from one to another was very difficult).

Exhibit 7-G describes an attempt to discern whether currency exchanges in Chicago pursued different pricing policies in black as opposed to white neighborhoods. Using service charges of currency exchanges as an outcome variable and census data characterizing the racial and socioeconomic compositions of the tracts in which the exchanges were located as statistical controls, the analysis sought to detect consistent price differences indicative of a discriminatory pricing policy among the currency exchanges.

Exhibit 7-H presents an elaborate attempt to discern whether federal family planning programs had an impact on fertility. Taking advantage of the existence of a survey of all family planning clinics in the United States that included measures of the services delivered in each unit, the researchers linked that information to vital statistics for the same areas. Modeling the fertility rates and adding enrollment in the family planning units as an element in the model, they discerned a significant impact of family planning units on fertility by counties. The impact they found is proportional to the level of activity of the family planning units in question.

Note that this fertility study was an evaluation of a full-coverage program. Under the relevant federal legislation, all areas of the country were eligible for funds that would support family planning clinics. For one reason or another, some areas elected not to participate, and there was some

Exhibit 7-F: The Effects of Integration in U.S. Army Units in Korea

The authors were commissioned by the U.S. Army in the early 1950s to assess the impact of integrating blacks into previously all-white army units serving in Korea during the Korean "conflict." The study was based on qualitative interviewing with officers and enlisted men as well as self-administered questionnaires from a large sample of soldiers. Impact was evaluated by comparing responses given by each of the following four groups: whites in all-white units, whites in integrated units, blacks in all-black units, and blacks in integrated units. The analysis is illustrated by the following table, in which soldiers in quartermaster corps units are compared in their responses to a question of how they viewed the future of race relations in the United States.

How Quartermaster Troops Answered the Question, "As time goes on, do you think that white and colored people in the United States will get along better together than they do today, not as well as they do now, or about the same as now?"

EXHIBIT 7.F: The Effects of Integration in U. S. Army Units in Korea

	Whites in All-White Units	Whites in Integrated Units	Negroes in Integrated Units	Negroes in All-Negro Units
Answers:				
They will get along better together	13%	68%	85%	82%
They will get along about the same as now	65	23	13	15
They will not get along as well as now	22	7	1	2
No answer	0	2	1	1
N (100%) =	(68)	(99)	(73)	(144)

In general, both whites and blacks in integrated units were more favorable to members of the other race, leading to the conclusion that actual experiences serving in integrated units led to more favorable attitudes.

SOURCE: From L. Bogart, *Social Research and Desegregation of the United States Army*. Chicago: Markham, p. 176. Reprinted by permission of the author.

variation in effort among participating local government units. This variation provided the opportunity to discern the effects of such clinic efforts. Of course, one must assume that the factors held constant in the statistical analysis also hold constant local variations in willingness to start up fertility clinics (i.e., the self-selection processes).

All the studies cited above required researchers to have a priori knowledge of the intervention in question and the phenomenon concerned. For Bogart and his colleagues (see Exhibit 7-F), it was essential to know that soldiers had little choice about the units in which they served. For Bridges and Oppenheim (Exhibit 7-G), it was important to conceive of the currency exchanges as largely responsive to their customers' socioeconomic levels; this enabled the evaluators to adjust service rates in order to discern whether or not the racial composition of their clientele was also a factor in pricing policies. Finally, Cutright and Jaffe (Exhibit 7-H) drew on their knowledge of how demographic and socioeconomic variables influence fertility.

Note that Cutright and Jaffe did not use a sample survey in the traditional sense. It is cross-sectional in that it is composed of one-shot measures of fertility and program services. It uses the results of a survey of service agencies, but melds that survey with census data and vital statistics.

In sum, statistical control is an excellent procedure to apply when one can enter as control variables measures that reflect competing explanations of program outcomes. The procedure is especially important when addressing problems for which it is not possible to undertake randomized experiments, or even to envisage them.

Limitations on the Use of Cross-Sectional Studies

Cross-sectional approaches to impact assessment have some advantages and some limitations. On the positive side, cross-sectional studies usually can be accomplished quickly and are therefore highly cost-effective methods for estimating net project effects. The approach is also useful if one is unwilling or unable to take the time necessary to make

Exhibit 7-G: Racial Discrimination in Chicago's Storefront Banks

The main objective of Chicago currency exchanges is to serve residents in areas of the city so poor that they cannot attract a bank. Currency exchanges, for the most part, charge 1 to 2 percent of the face amount to cash checks and write money orders and $.20 to $.30 to remit utility payments. The purpose of this study was to evaluate the extent and form of price differentials in Chicago currency exchanges according to the racial or ethnic composition of the areas they serve.

A sample of forty-three exchanges was selected from the Yellow Pages of the telephone directory (every tenth exchange was chosen). The racial composition of census tracts in which exchanges were located was obtained by dichotomizing the census tracts into two groups: "3 percent or less" and "7 percent or more." Multiple regression analysis was used to analyze the data. Service charge, the dependent variable, was regressed on amount of service, percentage black in census tract, percentage Spanish-speaking in census tract. The latter also was analyzed as a squared term: interaction of percentage black and amount of service, and interaction of percentage Spanish and amount of service.

It was found that each percentage change in the racial composition from white to black results in an increase in service charge of $.0016. Although this seems to be a trivial amount, it translates into a 20 percent added surcharge for a mostly black area. The authors conclude that exchanges are exploiting Chicago's residential race segregation by charging higher prices to blacks, although they caution that their findings are exploratory.

SOURCE: Summary of W. Bridges and J. Oppenheim, "Racial Discrimination in Chicago's Storefront Banks," *Evaluation Quarterly* 1 (February 1977): 159-171.

before-and-after measurements. Under some circumstances, especially when randomized experiments or quasi-experiments are completely out of the question, cross-sectional studies may be the only employable approach in impact assessment. One should be aware, however, that cross-sectional studies rely heavily on a priori knowledge of the processes involved.

Exhibit 7-H: Impact of United States Family Planning Programs on Fertility

The primary objective of U.S. family planning clinic programs in 1968-1969 was "to enable Americans freely to determine the number and spacing of their children, with priority for serving low-income persons." This study evaluated whether these programs had a significant impact on the fertility of those who participated in them. Sources of data were the 1970 census, National Center for Health Statistics, and Alan Guttmacher Institute (program service statistics). Units of analysis were called "statistical analysis units" (SAUs), which were either a county or a number of small counties. There were 778 "white" SAUs (each SAU had at least 20,000 white women) and 237 "black" SAUs (each had at least 10,000 black women).

The main program variable was enrollment in the family planning clinics (from the service records), and the outcome variable was fertility rate (from the census, measured in different ways). Statistical controls were introduced for population density, education, migration, marital status, in-school status, race, labor force, age, and parity in a linear, additive, multiple regression model.

The authors found that the program had strong negative effects on the fertility rates of both white and black married women in all subgroups defined by age and socioeconomic status, after controlling for the other factors. (A cost-benefit analysis of the program produced favorable ratios. That analysis is summarized in Exhibit 8-C.)

SOURCE: Summary, by permission, of P. Cutright and F. S. Jaffe, *Impact of Family Planning Programs on Fertility: The U.S. Experience.* New York: Praeger, 1977.

On the negative side, cross-sectional studies are very vulnerable to "specification errors" (to use the econometric term). Specification errors are mistakes made in specifying the appropriate theoretical structure that can rule out competing explanations. For example, in the analysis of the effects of parole on subsequent recidivism (shown in Exhibit 7-E), if the analysts have failed to take into account an important factor in how parole boards judge whether or not prisoners are eligible for parole, the analysis presented in that table may simply be wrong. To be more specific, if it turns out that parole boards released only prisoners who undertook vocational training in prison, the effects that are claimed for parole in Exhibit 7-E may simply reflect the fact that parolees were better prepared to obtain jobs, and, hence, parole effects simply mask vocational training effects that have nothing to do with parole per se.

Perhaps the most common specification error made in cross-sectional analyses is to have an inadequate model of the process of self-selection. The risk is particularly great in any cross-sectional study in which beneficiaries have exercised the option of participating or not participating in the program.

Cross-sectional designs can be used for both partial-coverage programs and some types of full-coverage programs—namely, those in which the treatment was varied in some known way. The family planning center assessment conducted by Cutright and Jaffe (Exhibit 7-H) is a good example of a full-coverage program that varied in activity from area to area, including some regions where the activities of family planning clinics were essentially zero. By estimating the effects of differing levels of clinic activity, the evaluators were able to estimate how much of that activity was associated with how many averted births.

In the same way, several attempts have been made to estimate the effects of state gun-control legislation on gun-related crime rates (e.g., assaults with firearms and murders with firearms). Because the states vary in the extent to which guns are regulated through systems of permits and registrations, a group of investigators (see Exhibit 7-I) attempted to relate the level of regulation to relevant crime rates. It turned out that the results are extremely sensitive to specification errors, some studies finding some effects and others finding none. The main differences among studies were the characteristics of states held constant in the analysis, illustrating dramatically the dangers of specification error inherent in cross-sectional designs.

Among the better-known cross-sectional studies of full-coverage programs is the Coleman Report (Coleman et al., 1966), in which variations among a set of schools in staffing levels, finances, student composition, and physical plants are assessed for impact on student learning. Coleman's original assessment was that differences in these variables among U.S. schools in the early 1960s were not related very strongly to student achievement. Holding such variables as student background constant, he found that students achieved no more in schools spending a great deal per capita on public education than those whose expenditures were considerably less. Similar findings hold for student-to-teacher ratios, the adequacy of physical plants, and the training of teachers.

The Coleman Report was not universally acclaimed as a definitive assessment, however. Many educators and educational researchers dis-

**Exhibit 7-I: Using Cross-Sectional Studies of
Interstate Variations in Gun-Control Legislation
to Discern the Effects of Gun-Ownership
Restriction on Crime Rates**

For a variety of historical reasons, the fifty states vary widely in the extent to which there are gun-ownership registration laws and in the restrictions placed on both the ownership of weapons and their use. Since whether or not such legislation affects crime rates is a matter of some considerable controversy, several analyses have been undertaken to estimate the net effects on crime rates of variations in such legislation, as follows.

Geisel et al. (1969) attempted to relate a set of crime, accident, and suicide rates that involved the use of firearms to a combined index that expressed the extent to which each of the state's legislation in force in 1960 restricted the sale and ownership of guns. A regression model was devised that took into account state average per capita incomes, median educational attainment of adult residents, the sex ratio, police per 1,000 residents, proportion black in each state, population density, median age, and licensed hunters per capita in that state. The dependent variables consisted of gun homicide rates, gun assault rates, gun accident rates, and gun suicide rates. The resulting coefficients for gun accident regulations purportedly showed that the stricter were the regulations, the lower were the rates of each of the gun-related incidents. The authors further estimate that if each state's legislation were brought up to the strictness of New Jersey's laws, several hundred deaths per year could be averted.

In a study that disputes the findings of Geisel and his associates, Murray (1975) addressed himself to the same problem, using much the same data. However, an alternative specification of the regression model is used: State legislation is measured by the presence or absence of specific regulatory provisions, rather than an overall restrictiveness measure; 1970 Census data and 1970 crime, accident, and suicide rates are used; and additional state characteristics are used, including percentage unemployed, percentage of the population below the poverty line, and the proportion of the population who were immigrants. Murray's regression analysis did not yield significant coefficients for state gun-control legislation, from which finding Murray argues that gun-control legislation does not affect gun-related crimes, accidents, and suicide.

SOURCE: J. D. Wright, P. H. Rossi, K. Daly, and E. Weber-Burdin, *Under the Gun: Weapons, Crime and Violence in America*. New York: Aldine, 1983.

puted Coleman's findings. A two-year-long seminar led by Mosteller and Moynihan (1972) produced a spate of reanalyses, all testing alternative specification models on the same data. The vulnerability of one-shot surveys to criticisms on grounds of specification errors is again illustrated.

Hence, cross-sectional studies of impact share with quasi-experiments a built-in vulnerability to criticism. Since one can make only a persuasive, not a definitive, case for having correctly specified the analysis to account for potentially competing explanations of program effects, cross-sectional studies are always open to the criticism that alternative analyses would lead to different results.

SUPPLEMENTARY USE OF STATISTICAL CONTROLS

Although a randomized experiment or a quasi-experiment using constructed controls may be analyzed properly only by straight comparisons between experimental and control groups, evaluators frequently also use statistical controls in their analyses. Much is to be gained by doing so.

Sometimes programs may be more effective with some types of beneficiaries and less so with others. Hence, separate analyses of, say, males and females may find that the program has been differentially effective with the two sexes. For example, in the TARP experiment (Rossi et al., 1980), a separate analysis was made of female ex-felons in the expectation that the very different situations of the two sexes (men and women are typically imprisoned for quite separate kinds of offenses and return to equally distinct home circumstances) would lead to differential impacts from the experimental intervention of unemployment insurance eligibility upon release from prison. It was found in this experiment that the benefit eligibility had a stronger work disincentive effect for women ex-felons because they were more responsible for dependent children and apparently preferred caring for their children to working, given unemployment benefit eligibility.

The use of statistical controls in randomized experiments also helps to increase the statistical power of such experiments. By holding constant preintervention factors related to the outcomes of interest, the intervention effects are estimated with less measurement error. In statistical terms, the error sum of squares is thereby reduced, resulting in smaller standard errors for intervention estimates. For example, although the comparison of a straight control group to an experimental group in the LIFE experiment (see exhibit 6-D) showed that the experimental group experienced 8 percent fewer arrests than did the control group, this difference hovered at the .05 level of significance. A regression analysis in which a number of pre-experiment characteristics of the released prisoners were employed led to a lowering of the standard error for the intervention and a decrease in the associated level of significance, to .02.

A final advantage of using statistical controls in randomized experiments is the potential for detecting interaction effects. In an analysis of a criminal justice intervention (Exhibit 7-J), for example, it was found that the program simultaneously produced two effects that tended to counteract each other—a finding that was completely obscured in the straight, one-way comparison between experimental and control groups.

The use of statistical control techniques in cross-sectional studies, quasi-experiments, or randomized experiments clearly requires both an intimate understanding of the substantive processes underlying the intervention and its presumed outcome and a thorough mastery of multivariate statistical methods. While a general understanding of the logic behind statistical controls can be attained by almost anyone, proper employment of the techniques involves considerable technical training, substantive knowledge, and access to high-capacity computers.

REFLEXIVE CONTROLS

As noted in Chapter 5, using before-intervention outcome measures of participant targets instead of a control or comparison group is known as using "reflexive controls." The term is simply a way of describing the use of targets as their own controls.

Before-and-After Studies

For full-coverage programs in which it is impossible to define randomized or constructed control groups or to locate nonparticipants through surveys, the use of reflexive controls may be the only approach available. This is the case in many programs directed at all residents of a geographic area; for example, efforts on a communitywide basis to increase access to health care by establishing new types of ambulatory care centers (Aday et al., 1984). In other evaluation circumstances, the use of reflexive controls may be an economical first step, especially if there is no reason to believe that targets' scores on outcome measures would have changed without the intervention. For example, in evaluating the outcome of a nutrition

Exhibit 7-J: A Mixed Randomized Experiment and Statistical Control Approach to the Analysis of a Criminal Justice Intervention

Two identical randomized experiments were designed to test the impact on recidivism of providing eligibility for unemployment insurance payments to released prisoners, each with 2,000 released prisoners, conducted in Georgia and Texas. Prisoners released from state prisons during the period January 1976 to June 1976 were randomly assigned to experimental groups (which offered eligibility for thirteen or twenty-six weeks of unemployment insurance benefits) or to control groups (which were simply followed through the year beyond release). The outcome measure was arrests on property-related charges over the year after release.

Direct comparisons between experimentals and controls led to the conclusion that the treatment had no discernible effect on subsequent arrests on property-related charges. The addition of statistical controls, however, brought to light a fairly complex process at work. The payments had both a direct positive effect, reducing arrests, and a negative indirect effect on arrests, reducing employment and thereby increasing arrests. These two effects canceled each other out, leaving the experimental groups with the same arrest rates as the controls.

The introduction of statistical controls to this randomized experiment's results led to an important policy discovery, namely, that policies providing modest financial support to released prisoners would reduce recidivism if they did not at the same time create a work disincentive. Since unemployment insurance benefits are usually made only to those who are unemployed as a condition of eligibility, this procedure, if modified, might lead to a program with positive benefits in the reduction of property crimes.

SOURCE: Summary of P. H. Rossi, R. Berk, and K. Lenihan, *Money, Work and Crime.* New York: Academic, 1980.

education program testing participants' knowledge of nutrition before and after participation in a three-week set of lectures, the use of reflexive controls is likely to provide a good measure of the impact of the course, because knowledge of nutrition is unlikely to change spontaneously over such a short period of time.

The essential justification for using a reflexive control design is that in some circumstances it is reasonable to believe that targets remain identical in relevant ways before and after participation. In other words, in such circumstances one can assume that without the intervention the preintervention and postintervention outcome scores would have been the same; hence, if any changes show up after the intervention, such changes would be directly attributable to the intervention (i.e., net impact would equal gross impact).

It should also be obvious that reflexive control designs are highly vulnerable to incorrect estimation of net effects. The major problem with targets as their own controls is that, by definition, the reflexive groups are observed at different points in time. Preintervention observations are made on units that are younger than they will be when the intervention is completed. To the extent that the outcome variables are either age-related or influenced by the extraintervention experiences these units undergo during or after program exposure, the use of reflexive controls is not advised.

The danger of relying upon reflexive designs for age-related behavior is demonstrated in the following illustration. Consider the evaluation of a program designed to lower fertility addressed to women of childbearing ages. The evaluation attempts to show that participation in the program lowers the probability of conceiving, compared to the ten-year period previous to program participation. Such comparisons would be misleading, because fertility behavior at one point in time is not independent of prior fertility behavior. Some women will have completed their fertility at the point of program participation and would not have had any more children in any event. Others may be beginning their families and may not have had children previously, so that any children born to them would appear to indicate failure of the program. The processes at work producing fertility vary from age group to age group; hence, a reflexive design would be inappropriate.

For many processes, however, maturational effects are not very important, especially over short periods of time. For instance, a ten-week educational campaign to change adults' beliefs about the nutritional components of certain types of foods is not likely to compete with maturational processes. Sometimes, time-related changes are quite subtle: For example, in studying the impact of job training programs, reflexive controls are likely to be misleading. One of the main reasons that targets choose to enter job training programs is that they are unemployed and are experiencing difficulties obtaining employment. Hence, at entry into a job training program most participants have depressed incomes. Any change in income is likely to be upward; thus, a job training program will appear to be successful if only reflexive controls are used in its evaluation.

A second problem with reflexive controls arises out of potential changes in secular trends between the two periods involved. If observations of a reflexive control group of farmers are made during a period of depressed crop yields, a comparison with crop yields during a project period of more normal yields would be misleading. Similarly, a program to reduce crime will appear more effective if it coincides with other efforts to increase policing; or an employment training program will appear ineffective if it is accompanied by a prolonged period of rising unemployment and depressed economic conditions.

A third problem results from differences in interfering events between the two time periods. An interfering event, as defined previously, represents an unusual, one-time occurrence that affects outcome measures. Examples include serious natural disasters, political crises, and health epidemics. Any event that might affect output measures could interfere with the proper use of reflexive control observations.

An unusual example of the use of reflexive controls is shown in Exhibit 7-K. Shlay and Rossi (1981) obtained data on a sample of census tracts in the Chicago metropolitan area to assess the effects of zoning regulations on population and housing growth in the tracts. They used zoning laws and regulations applicable to each of the tracts in 1960 to form a measure of how restrictively each tract was zoned. Using the relevant 1960 population and housing census measures to predict by regression analysis what the population and housing stock would be in 1970, and entering the zoning restrictiveness measures in the regression, Shlay and Rossi arrived at estimates of the effects of zoning restrictions on the growth of housing and population in the census tracts.

Note that the analysis shown in Exhibit 7-K depends heavily on the existence of variation from census tract to census tract in the 1960 zoning regulations. Hence, each tract serves as its own control in predicting growth in the intercensal period, and tracts are contrasted according to the number of restrictions placed on land uses in each. The "maturational trends" in tract growth, like age-related changes in individuals, are taken into account by estimating such trends for the entire set of tracts and by considering zoning the cause of deviations from such maturational trends, as represented by predicted 1970 values of housing and population stocks.

Before-and-after studies of full-coverage interventions are relatively rare, mainly because before-intervention measures of full-coverage programs are, unfortunately, usually unavailable and because proper analysis depends heavily on treatment variation, usually by political subjurisdiction (as shown in Exhibit 7-K). Full-coverage programs with constant treatments more often tend to be assessed using generic or shadow controls, as we will discuss in a later section of this chapter.

Exhibit 7-K: Estimating the Effects of Zoning Regulations on the Growth of Housing and Population Stocks in the Chicago SMSA, 1960-1970

Using samples of census tracts drawn from within the city of Chicago and from within the rest of the Chicago SMSA, Shlay and Rossi ascertained from local municipal records the zoning regulations in force in each of the census tracts in 1960. A set of indices were constructed for each tract reflecting the extent to which the zoning regulations restricted residential use of tract land, ranging from the most exclusionary use pattern, in which only single-family homes on large tracts were permitted, to the least exclusionary usage, in which any type of land use, including industrial and commercial uses, was permitted.

Using 1960 and 1970 Census values for housing and population characteristics, a regression equation was run that predicted 1970 characteristics of Chicago area suburban tracts on the basis of 1960 values and the zoning index, as illustrated in Table 7-K.1. The investigators found that zoning regulations did change the growth rates from what would have been expected on the basis of normal growth, and affected the nature of the tract populations' socioeconomic and life-cycle distributions. Table 7-K.1 shows the regression equation used to study the effect of zoning restrictiveness on the density of housing units in suburban Chicago tracts. Note that it is a reflexive analysis in that the 1960 housing density of the tracts is held constant by including that variable in the equation. Thus, what is being studied by the equation is the difference between actual 1970 density and what one might have expected on the basis of the 1960 density measures. The other independent variables are all measures of the zoning regulations that govern land use in the tracts as of 1960. The more extensively a tract was zoned, the less its density grew in the period between 1960 and 1970. In short, zoning restricted the growth in density in suburban tracts over and above what would be expected on the basis of their density in 1960.

TABLE 7-K.1 The Effects of 1960 Zoning Restrictiveness on Changes in Housing Density 1960-1970 for a Sample of Chicago Metropolitan Area Suburban Tracts

Independent Variables	b	SE
1960 housing units per square mile	.95*	.03
Exclusionary zoning index[a]	−253.01*	50.61
% tract zoned for business	−52.18*	3.93
% tract zoned for manufacturing	−4.18	2.93
Intercept	2325.74*	413.58

$$R^2 = .94$$
$$N = 144$$

NOTE: Dependent variable is 1970 housing units per square mile.

a. An index based on the extent to which a tract is zoned to restrict the use of land for high-density, multiple-dwelling units, and favors single units on large tracts of land. Index was constructed by reading relevant zoning regulations for the jurisdiction in question.

*Indicates coefficient with p value of .05 or smaller.

SOURCE: A. Shlay and P. H. Rossi, "Keeping Up the Neighborhood: Estimating Net Effects of Zoning." *American Sociological Review,* December 1981. Reprinted by permission.

Reflexive Studies Using Panels

Panel studies that involve repeated periodic measurements on the same group over a period of time can often be used productively to estimate the effects of treatments that vary in their coverage. Exhibit 7-L describes an elaborate attempt (Milavsky et al., 1982) to estimate the impact of viewing television programs that contain episodes of aggression and violence on the subsequent aggressive behaviors of children.

In this study, elementary and high school students from samples of schools in two cities, Forth Worth and Minneapolis, were surveyed repeatedly concerning their television viewing of programs that showed violence and were rated at those times by their classmates on their aggressiveness. The analysis centered on determining how aggressiveness at a later point in time was related to exposure to programs showing violence.

The advantage of panel studies, thoroughly exploited in the work of Milavsky and his colleagues, is that the measures of the treatment and of outcomes (TV viewing and aggressiveness, respectively) are related to each other through time lags and are not cross-sectional correlations. Thus the aggressiveness at time 2 is shown as a function of viewing patterns measured at time 1.

Exhibit 7-L: Measuring the Effects of Viewing Violence on TV on the Aggressive Behavior of Young Children

In an attempt to provide rigorous answers to public concern about whether the viewing of TV programs that depict violence and aggression affected the aggressive behavior of children who viewed such programs, the National Broadcasting Company (NBC) sponsored an elaborate panel study of young children, measuring aggressiveness and TV viewing repeatedly over several years.

In the main substudy, samples of elementary school classes, grades 2 through 6, drawn from Fort Worth and Minneapolis schools, formed the base for a six-wave panel study, in which 400 male children in 59 classes were interviewed six times in the period 1970 to 1973. (Additional substudies were conducted with female elementary school children and with samples of high school students in the same cities.) At each interview wave, the children in the classes were asked to rate each other on aggressiveness using questionnaires including such items as "Who is likely to punch and kick another child?" In addition, at each interview, each child was asked to check those programs he had watched recently on lists of programs shown locally. The programs previously had been rated by media experts according to the amount of violence depicted in the programs. The questionnaires also picked up information about the socioeconomic backgrounds of the children. Additional interviews were made with teachers and the parents of the children. To check on the accuracy of recall, several nonexistent program names were placed on the checklists.

The analyses undertaken related the viewing of violence on TV at one interview time with rated aggressive behavior on subsequent interview times, holding constant the initial level of aggressiveness. (Note that this analysis method is formally identical to that used in Exhibit 7-K.) The results estimated the additional amount of aggressiveness that seemingly resulted from exposure to high levels of viewing violence on TV programs. The results indicated that while the direction of effects indicated that a small increment in aggressiveness was associated with high levels of viewing of TV violence, the increment was not statistically significant.

SOURCE: A partial summary of J. Ronald Milavsky, Ronald C. Kessler, Horst H. Stipp, and William S. Rubens, *Television and Aggression: A Panel Study*. New York: Academic, 1982. Used by permission of the authors.

Panel studies are especially appropriate as designs for impact assessments of full-coverage programs in which dosage varies over individuals. Thus, in the case of TV viewing, all the children participated in the sense that virtually all viewed some TV; nevertheless, some viewed more of the programs that were regarded as showing high levels of violence. Self-selection was to some degree controlled by holding constant the initial level of aggressiveness of the boys under study.

It should be noted that the researchers considered using randomized experiments to estimate the effects of viewing violent programs on subsequent aggressiveness, but that design was rejected as introducing an artificiality that would undermine the generalizability of the findings. It would be difficult, if not impossible, to recruit schoolchildren for experimentation, randomly allocate them to experimental and control groups, and then somehow prevent the controls from viewing any programs containing aggressive or violent behavior. An experiment along these lines might be conducted for a very short period of time, on the order of a few days, but it would be extremely difficult to carry out such an experiment over the length of time needed to show the expected effects on children exposed to violence and aggression in television programs. In other words, the researchers opted for a less-than-optimal design of lower reproducibility but of higher generalizability.

Time-Series Analyses of Full-Coverage Programs

For many phenomena that are of public concern (e.g., fertility, mortality, and crime) or of administrative concern (e.g., proportions of college students dropping out at the end of their first year), there are often extensive time series—measures of outcomes taken weekly, monthly, quarterly, or at longer intervals. Such time series provide relatively firm bases upon which to build estimates of what would have happened in the absence of an intervention.

When a relatively long time series of preintervention observations exists, it is often possible to model long-standing trends in the target group, projecting those trends through time of the intervention and observing whether or not the postintervention period shows significant deviations from them. The use of such general time-trend modeling procedures as ARIMA—Auto Regressive Integrated Moving Average (McCleary and Hay, 1980; Pyndyck and Rubinfeld, 1976; Cook and Campbell, 1979; Hibbs, 1977)—can identify best-fitting trends by taking into account long-term secular trends and seasonal variations. One must also allow for the degree to which any value or score on a measure is necessarily related to previous ones (technically referred to as "autocorrelation"). It should be noted, however, that the procedures involved are highly technical and require a fairly high level of statistical sophistication.

Exhibits 7-M and 7-N illustrate the use of existing time series in evaluations to assess the impacts of a gun-control law and of a water conservation project. Note that in both cases the evaluation is made possible by the existence of relatively long series (with approximately 120 time points) of measures on outcome variables. Thus, Exhibit 7-M uses information collected over several years on violent crimes reported to the police—homicide, assault, and armed robbery—to establish an expected trend for such crimes in the absence of the gun-control law that went into effect in 1975. Comparison of the rates experienced after enactment with the expected rates provides a measure of net outcome. Exhibit 7-N illustrates the same procedures, employing water usage rates before and after the enactment of fairly stringent regulations designed to lower water consumption. It should also be noted that both studies use a priori knowledge about the factors that affect the outcome measures in order to rule out possibly competing explanations.

It should be noted that the units of analysis in time-series analyses as applied to social programs are usually highly aggregated. Exhibit 7-M deals essentially with one case, the city of Boston, where crime rates are constructed by aggregating crimes over the entire jurisdiction and expressing the crime rates as crimes per 100,000 persons. A single unit, although much smaller in total size, was also used in Exhibit 7-N in analyzing water usage in the Goleta water district.

As in the case of other types of statistical controls, time-series analyses are vulnerable to specification error. For example, the analysis presented in Exhibit 7-M has been disputed by Hay and McCleary (1979), who claimed that the model used by Deutsch and Alt was incorrect. Applying an alternative model, Hay and McCleary found that some of the effects of the Massachusetts gun law assessed by Deutsch and Alt disappeared when a "more correct" model was applied. (See also Deutsch, 1979, for a continuation of this debate.) The point to bear in mind is by now an old refrain to the reader: Statistical controls, either those of cross-sectional analyses or those used in modeling time-series trends, are no better than the a priori thinking that goes into their construction.

Simpler methods of examining time-series data before and after an intervention can provide crude but useful clues to impact. If the confounding influences on an intervention are known, and there is considerable certainty that their effects are minimal, time series are useful for establishing net program effect.

The chart shown in Exhibit 7-O presents auto accident rates in Great Britain before and after the enactment and enforcement of drastically

Exhibit 7-M: A Time-Series Analysis of the Effect of the Massachusetts Gun-Control Law

In April 1975, the state of Massachusetts formally put into operation a gun-control law that mandated a one-year minimum sentence on conviction of carrying a firearm without a special license. This study evaluated the deterrent effect of the law. Gun-related offenses of homicide, assault with a gun, and armed robbery for the city of Boston were examined for shifts or changes in their levels in time periods prior to, concurrent with, and after the enactment of this law.

Multiplicative empirical-stochastic models with an embedded shift parameter were employed to analyze the time-series data of the monthly occurrences of homicide, assault with a gun, and armed robbery for the city of Boston from January 1966 through October 1975.

The authors found that the gun-control law has effected a statistically significant decrease in both armed robbery and assault with a gun in the time period. However, no statistically significant changes in the homicide rate were observed. The authors attributed the lack of effect on homicide to the large proportion of residential homicides and to the fact that future impact of gun control on homicide in general may not show up for several years, if ever.

SOURCE: Summary of S. J. Deutsch and F. B. Alt, "The Effect of Massachusetts' Gun Control Law on Gun-Related Crimes in the City of Boston," *Evaluation Quarterly* 1 (November 1977): 543-567.

changed laws dealing with the treatment of persons involved in accidents and in the penalties for driving while under the influence of alcohol. The chart indicates that the legislation had a discernible impact: Accidents declined after it went into effect, and the decline was especially dramatic for accidents occurring over the weekend. (Statistical analyses verified that the clearly apparent effects were also significant.)

Time-series approaches are not necessarily restricted to single cases, however. When time series exist for interventions at different times and in different places, more complex analyses can be (and should be) undertaken. In the study on water conservation districts described in Exhibit 7-N, Berk and his associates (1981) employed a multiple time series of water consumption to compare the relative efficacy of pricing policies

Exhibit 7-N: A Time-Series Analysis of the Impact of a Water Conservation Campaign

In 1972 the Goleta Water Board declared a moratorium on new water hookups in an effort to maintain the level of demand within the limits of supply until alternative sources for water could be assessed. In addition, other conservation measures were taken to reduce water consumption, including the enactment of local laws to prohibit waste and an educational campaign. The purpose of this study was to assess the effectiveness of the Goleta County Water District's program to decrease water consumption.

The effectiveness of the program was measured by two dependent variables: domestic and commercial sales, and production. In order better to assess program impact, in addition to the moratorium, rainfall, season, and population were also treated as exogenous variables in a regression model. Monthly data for these variables were available from 1966 to 1976.

By holding other relevant variables constant, the authors were able to illustrate that the presence of the moratorium had a statistically significant influence on water use. The findings indicated an average 15 percent reduction in water consumption for the three years following the implementation of the moratorium.

SOURCE: Summary of J. E. Maki, D. M. Hoffman, and R. A. Berk, "A Time Series Analysis of the Impact of a Water Conservation Campaign," *Evaluation Quarterly* 2 (February 1978): 107-118.

versus educational campaigns in reducing domestic and commercial water consumption.

Time-series analyses are powerful designs for estimating the effects of constant-treatment, full-coverage programs. We strongly recommend them for circumstances in which appropriate statistical series exist, with the caveat that such analyses are vulnerable to specification errors.

Time-Series Analyses of Changes in Individuals

The time-series analyses discussed in the last section use highly aggregated data such as rates computed over large jurisdictions. The general logic of time-series analyses, however, can also be applied to highly disaggregated data, as in the analysis of treatments administered to single cases

Exhibit 7-O: An Analysis of the Impact on Traffic Accidents of Compulsory Breathalyzer Tests for Drivers Involved in Accidents

In 1967 the British government enacted a new policy that allowed police to give breathalyzer tests at the scenes of accidents. The test measured the presence of alcohol in the blood of suspects. Heavier penalties were also instituted for drunken driving convictions. Considerable publicity was given to the provisions of the new law, which went into effect in October 1967.

The chart below plots the vehicular accident rates by various periods of the week before and after the new legislation went into effect. Visual inspection of the chart clearly indicates that a decline in accidents occurred after the legislation, which affected most times of the week, but had especially dramatic effects for weekend periods. (Statistical tests also verified what can be seen from visual inspection.)

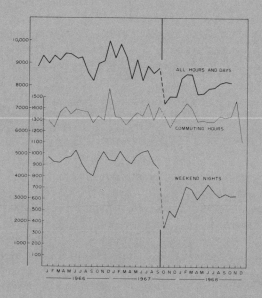

SOURCE: From H. L. Ross, D. T. Campbell, and G. V Glass, "Determining the Social Effects of a Legal Reform: The British Breathalyzer Crackdown of 1967." *American Behavioral Scientist,* 13 (March/April 1970): 500.

whose behavior is measured a number of times before and after a treatment has been undertaken.

Therapists concerned with evaluating the impact of courses of treatments on individuals have used time-series designs for the purpose of making impact assessments. For example, the performance of a child on some achievement test may be measured periodically before and after a new teaching method is used with the child; or the drinking behavior of an adult may be measured before and after therapy for alcohol abuse is administered to that adult. The logic of time-series analyses is the same when applied to a single case, although the statistical methods appear to be quite different because the issues of long-term trends and seasonality usually are not as serious for individual cases (Kazdin, 1982).

JUDGMENTAL ASSESSMENTS

For some social programs, it is difficult to find ways of either comparing persons with and without program experience or employing changes over time to estimate net impact. In such cases, about all one can do is have faith that identifiable groups can make judgments that estimate net impact with some degree of plausibility. There are persons with expertise in various human service areas on whose judgments it may be possible to rely for determining whether or not a program has had an effect. Also, some program administrators may be able to divorce themselves from their self-interests to assess program impact with a fair degree of objectivity. Finally, it is sometimes possible to obtain assessments from program participants themselves of whether or not a program has affected them significantly. Judgmental assessments involve the use of what we have called shadow controls, a term that reflects their typical lack of substantial evidential basis.

Despite the fact that shadow controls ordinarily can be used only with extreme caution, there are some circumstances in which their use is justified. One such circumstance is the case of an extraordinarily successful program, as the following example illustrates.

One may find that a two-month-long vocational training program to produce drivers of heavy-duty trucks has enabled 90 percent of its participants (selected from among persons without such skills) to qualify for appropriate drivers' licenses. Such a finding suggests that the program has been quite successful in reaching its goal of imparting vocational skills. We can make this judgment because it seems highly unlikely that so large a proportion of any group of previously unskilled persons who wanted to become truck drivers would be able to qualify for such licenses in a two-month period on their own. The worth of this judgment depends heavily on the judges' knowledge of truck-driving and the special skills required to be proficient in it, plus some knowledge of the driver's license tests. A priori knowledge of high validity is clearly important in such judgments.

The obverse outcomes could also lead to firm judgments. If all of the truck-driving program's participants failed the license examination, that finding would be fairly clear evidence of program failure. But even this judgment cannot be made by someone without some knowledge about truck-driving and the licensing tests. It may well be that all applicants fail on the first try, and that the crucial test is whether or not there is success on the second try.

Of course, it is likely the outcome results would be more ambiguous: It may well be that only 30 percent pass the licensing examinations. The typical finding raises the question of whether or not a comparable group receiving no training would have done as well. Usually, simple before-and-after measures on target participants only serve to document the fact that a project is having a gross impact on participants that is consistent with project goals. But this is hardly definitive proof of net impact. Hence, for typical program results, the use of shadow controls is always risky.

Connoisseurial Assessments

If expert judgments are to be used as shadow controls, their worth depends greatly on the skills and knowledge of the experts in question. Those familiar with the field of adult vocational education and the typical outcomes of intervention projects in that field might be asked to draw on that background to judge whether the 30 percent outcome described previously is greater or less than is ordinarily the outcome of successful adult vocational training. Clearly, the usefulness and validity of such judgments, and hence the worth of an evaluation using them, depend heavily on the judges' expertise and the development of firm knowledge in the field.

If expert judgments (or any shadow controls) are to be used, it is essential that their use be made explicit; that is, the bases upon which the expert judgments are made should be described as completely as possible. If an expert makes a judgment based on his or her own direct experiences, the extent of such experiences and the variations from instance to instance should be revealed. When possible, explicit references to other evaluation studies should be given, so that it is possible to check on whether or not the circumstances of the other interventions are comparable to those of the one under judgment.

Often, the shadow control is a conclusion or construction based on an expert's understanding of the processes involved. Thus, to an expert in criminology, it may "stand to reason" that a given intervention with ex-prisoners will be effective, because it follows closely the leading paradigms in the field concerning the rehabilitation of ex-prisoners. However, although the judgment of an industrial engineer concerning the effectiveness of a production process may be quite enough upon which to base action, the judgment of a criminologist about rehabilitation simply does not command the same standing. Unfortunately, the very reason we must employ rigorous impact assessment designs in the area of social programs is that the state of knowledge in the appropriate fields is inadequate. Although it "stands to reason" that many programs will succeed, they often do not pass the more rigorous tests of the better impact assessment designs.

The actual procedures employed by expert connoisseurs to arrive at shadow controls may vary considerably. Typically, a well-known expert (or experts) in a relevant field is hired as a consultant and sent to visit the site of a program to examine its workings closely in order to write a report summarizing his or her experiences and to render assessments. (Exhibits 7-P and 7-Q provide typical examples of such judgmental assessments.) Visiting experts may examine project records; observe the project in operation; conduct interviews with participants; talk to project managers, staff, and other officials; and conduct interviews with former participants. In short, all of the means of informal social research may be employed.

The worth of an expert's judgmental assessment depends on the following factors: First, one must consider the general state of knowledge in the substantive fields relevant to the program. In a field where knowledge of how to achieve a particular outcome is quite advanced, an expert's appraisal may be very accurate. If little is known about an area (e.g., how to rehabilitate criminals), an expert's judgment of a particular project's effectiveness may not be worth more than that of any other person.

Second, one must consider how well grounded the expert is in the substantive field. An expert should be knowledgeable about the area in question and should have demonstrated that knowledge in actual accomplishments. Experts should also be familiar with the findings of other evaluations, including more systematic ones, of similar programs. For example, an expert asked to judge whether or not a community treatment center for released prisoners helps ex-felons obtain employment should be familiar with the many studies on the employment rates for ex-felons during the months following release. Similarly, knowledge that few studies show much influence of classroom size on achievement, although it has strong positive effects on teachers' satisfaction ratings, should make one

**Exhibit 7-P: The Use of Expert Judgment to
Evaluate the Impact of Citizen Participation
on Urban Renewal**

Using interviews with major participants as well as data from the
membership lists of a citizen's organization, the authors assessed the
effectiveness of attempts to use a participatory process in the design
of an urban renewal plan for the area around the University of
Chicago. The assessment took several forms: First, planners were
asked to identify those features of the completed plan that were
affected by the participatory process; second, documentary records
were examined for accounts of meetings between planners and
citizens; and finally, detailed case studies were made of specific plan
features, in an attempt to discern how the final plans were formed.

A specific provision in the urban renewal plans was judged to have
been influenced by citizens' organizations if the provision was
changed from those originally proposed by planners in the directions
suggested by citizens' organizations and both planners and citizens'
group leaders believed that the change was made in response to the
citizens' groups suggestions. Essentially, an assessment of positive
net impact of a citizens' group's influence was made if the changes
were congruent with citizens' requests and there was consensus
among major figures in the planning process that influence had taken
place. Instances in which there was contradictory testimony were
resolved by developing a category called "possible influence."

SOURCE: Summary, by permission, of P. H. Rossi and R. A. Dentler, *The Politics
of Urban Renewal.* New York: Free Press, 1961.

skeptical that a program based largely on such strategy is likely to do much
for student achievement (although it may please the teachers).

Finally, because experts often must rely on "guided" field visits to
program sites, and often have more contact with program staff than with
program operations or program participants, it is essential to be skeptical
about judgments based too heavily on program staff reports. After all, one
must realize that it is only natural for a project administrator to attempt to
present his or her project in the best possible light. Thus, one can expect
the state of a project at the time of an announced visit to be better than at
other periods, in ways ranging from the neatness and cleanliness of the

Exhibit 7-Q: Judgmental Expert Assessment Using Before-and-After Project Administrative Statistics

The Integrated Family Life Education (IFLE) Project in Ethiopia is an attempt to educate adults in appropriate practices in health, nutrition, agriculture, family planning, and civics. Adult education classes are the medium used, with many instructional materials carefully constructed and pretested, especially for the target population in question.

An outside evaluator, John Pettit, conducted a field visit to the project sites for a period of three weeks. Using administrative statistics derived from before-and-after measurements of literacy, subscription to proper sanitary practices, etc., he was able to show that significant advances had been made by program participants. Interviews were undertaken with participants, community leaders, and staff workers on the project. The before-and-after measurements were made primarily to provide feedback information to project workers, but were also useful for evaluation purposes. For example, in one small village, participants using appropriate family practices were 5 percent at the start of the program and 32 percent at the end of a training cycle.

SOURCE: Summary, by permission, of C. D. Crone, "Evaluation: Autopsy or Checkup?" *World Education Reports*, 15 (October 1977): 3-13.

headquarters to possibly well-rehearsed laudatory statements from participants. A skillful expert bases judgments on data obtained from many sources.

Because in many circumstances connoisseurial assessments by experts are the only kinds of impact assessments that can be made, it is important that such experts be selected very carefully, with attention to their ability to surmount barriers to communication and their mastery of the state of knowledge in the discipline involved. At minimum, experts should consider the following sources of data:

1. *Administrative records.* Experts should collect information from administrative records (or have such tabulations made) on such topics as:
   a. size of project
   b. type of participants recruited

    c. attrition experiences with participants
    d. postproject experiences of participants
    e. project costs per participant who completes program
    f. before-after measures of participant changes relevant to project goals

2. *Observations of project operation.* Projects that call for active work with participants (e.g., household visits, classroom sessions, media presentations) should be directly observed by the visiting experts.

3. *Interviews with participants.* Informal interviews with participants and/or former participants, at least some of which are spontaneous, can take up such issues as:
    a. recruitment of participants
    b. motivation of participants
    c. participant satisfaction with project
    d. participant progress toward attaining project goals

4. *Interviews with relevant context.* Informal interviews with local officials, administrators of competing programs, administrators of important local institutions (e.g., school superintendents, police chiefs), and local powerful individuals or representatives of local powerful institutions (e.g., large landlords, bankers, political officials) should cover the following topics:
    a. worth of project
    b. extent to which project is viewed as help or threat to community
    c. interest in continuing project when demonstration period is over

Despite the weaknesses of connoisseurial assessments, there are circumstances in which this approach may be the only one that can be used. This is certainly the case for full-coverage, constant-level interventions of long standing. Also, the urgency of the need for impact assessment may force evaluators to rely on expert judgments; a lack of resources may prohibit the mounting of a relatively expensive, full-scale impact assessment using control groups or a cross-sectional approach. Moreover, other controls may be feasible in principle but prohibitively tedious to put into practice.

In addition, when funds allocated to evaluation are inadequate for a full-scale impact assessment, researchers may resort to connoisseurial judgments on the grounds that any kind of assessment may be better than none at all. This may be the case particularly when the program in question is on a small scale and it would appear somewhat incongruous if the impact assessment cost a large fraction of the program costs. Under these circumstances the "good enough" rule propounded in the last chapter may be invoked. Of course, a responsible connoisseurial evaluation would warn the reader of the judgmental basis for findings.

Exhibit 7-R presents an unusual evaluation in which the time elapsed since program enactment is more than three decades. Salamon (1974) assessed the efficacy of a 1930s land-reform policy by examining land titles to see if the people who settled in the 1930s were still holding the land. Finding that there was some continuity over time, Salamon concluded that the policy was effective in creating a landed black middle class.

Of course, this conclusion is a result of his judging whether the proportion of settlers or their descendants still remaining on the land was greater or less than could be expected from the general tendency of landholdings to shift from generation to generation. That any of the original settlers or their descendants still remained is evidence of some gross impact, but the issue is whether this impact is any different from what would have happened in any event over the intervening three decades or more.

Salamon's case for impact of the New Deal land-reform programs would have been strengthened considerably if he had been able to show that similar parcels of land in the same parts of the South did not show a comparable shift to black ownership over the period, and/or that nonprogram black-owned land tended to shift to white ownership. Undoubtedly, difficulties in ascertaining the races of parcel owners 35 years ago hindered the employment of this strategy.

Program-Administrator Judgments

Project administrators routinely are asked to assess their progress toward fulfilling project goals. In most cases it is doubtful that much reliance can be placed on such impact assessments, for fairly obvious reasons. First, it is difficult to undertake a judgmental impact assessment under the best of circumstances. But the weakest point of the use of program administrator judgments is that it is too much to expect administrators to apply the appropriate attitude of skepticism toward their own work that is necessary for them to make hard judgments. A properly conducted impact assessment takes as its guiding hypothesis that the project has no effects, a stance that runs exactly counter to the principle that should guide the administration of a project, namely, that the intervention does have important effects on participants. To expect ordinary mortals to hold both hypotheses simultaneously is unrealistic. Furthermore, program administrators who have day-to-day responsibilities for the conduct of a project, often coupled with a lack of appropriate technical qualifications, simply cannot devote a great deal of time and care to an impact assessment. In addition, there is an understandable tendency for administrators to want to put their projects in the best of all possible lights, a motivation that may act to downplay or actively suppress negative information on effectiveness.

About the best one can expect from an administrator's judgmental assessment is reasonably accurate descriptive statements about operational procedures. One is entitled to expect that administrators can pro-

---

Exhibit 7-R: An Analysis of the Long-Range Effects of a New Deal Land-Reform Program

In the 1930s during the New Deal, a series of agricultural reforms were enacted, most of which were short-lived. One of the reforms involved purchasing land and selling it to small farmers for home-steading purposes at very favorable prices and financing terms. A few of the specific projects were started before protests from establishment agricultural interests brought about a cancellation of the program.

In the 1970s the author conducted an "evaluation" of the New Deal Land-Reform program by examining the current owners of parcels of land that were sold to black tenant farmers in eight land-resettlement projects in five states. Landownership records were searched to determine whether the land in question remained to any degree in the hands of persons related to or descended from the families to whom the parcels were originally sold in the 1930s.

Salamon concludes that the project was successful in creating a permanent, black middle class, since much of the land was still in the hands of the original settlers and their descendants.

SOURCE: Summary, by permission of John Wiley and Sons, Inc., of L. M. Salamon, "The Time Dimension in Policy Evaluation: The Case of the New Deal Land-Reform Experiments." *Public Policy,* Vol. 27, No. 2 (Spring 1979).

---

vide reliable statistical, descriptive statements about a project, based on a well-kept set of administrative records. The kinds of records necessary have been described earlier in this chapter and in Chapter 4. Table 7.3 also lists administrative records useful to impact assessments. Clearly, portions of these records are not appropriate to all projects, and therefore Table 7.3 should be regarded as a checklist of suggested rather than essential records.

Participants' Judgments

Because the participants in social programs are the recipients of services, one may be tempted to look to participant accounts of how well they were served by a program as approximations of net impact. While participants can tell us many useful things, it is overly optimistic to hope to obtain from them what it takes a highly skilled social researcher considerable

TABLE 7.3 Administrative Records Useful for Project Description and as Aid in Impact Assessment

I. Participant Records:
   1. Socioeconomic data on participants:
      age, sex, location, household composition, income, occupational data.
   2. Critical dates:
      date of entry into project, attendance record, dates of leaving project.
   3. Treatment records:
      exposure of participants to project, aid given, etc.
   4. Follow-up data:
      addresses of participants, including future addresses and contacts to aid in follow-up beyond participation.
   5. Critical event records:
      records of meetings with participants, important events in participants' lives (e.g., births, deaths, residential shifts, job changes).

II. Project Records:
   1. Critical events in project history:
      dates of startup for important segments of project, encounters with helpful or hostile officials, important segments of program suspension.
   2. Project personnel:
      biographical data on project personnel, shifts in personnel, instances of personnel training.
   3. Changes in project implementation:
      problems encountered in project implementation changes instituted in project operations (including dates).

III. Financial Records:
   No attempt to describe such records will be made here, since one can assume that the typical local fiscal procedures required by project sponsors would be employed. The main issue to be emphasized is that financial records should be kept in a way that will facilitate cost-effectiveness or cost-benefit analyses, as described in Chapter 8.

effort to obtain. The problem is that it is difficult for any individual to assess what would have happened to him or her if some specific event had not occurred. That is why individuals' accounts of how they "chose" their spouses or careers usually appear to be reports of strings of "chance" events. Individuals simply do not have the varied experiences to be able to construct for themselves the appropriate "controls" or to "hold constant" their particular social and psychological characteristics. Note that this is not a view of human beings as somehow naive and deficient, but a recognition that assessing net impact is a comparative task and that most persons simply do not have either the breadth of experience or perceptual competence necessary to make such comparisons.

Participants ratings of satisfaction with a program or with services, however, are interesting and important in their own right. In the first place, some programs stipulate participant satisfaction as one of their goals. Fine-tuning is often designed to rid programs of the "bugs" that irritate

Exhibit 7-S: An Analysis of Client Satisfaction with Agency Performance

As part of a study of urban service delivery systems in fifteen metropolitan areas, samples of residents were asked whether they were currently on welfare and, if so, their level of satisfaction "with the way you are treated by welfare workers or officials." In addition, caseworkers in local welfare agencies were interviewed concerning their attitudes toward clients, and information was obtained on their caseloads and other aspects of their jobs.

Considerable variation was found among the cities in the levels of satisfaction expressed by welfare clients toward their local welfare departments. Particularly interesting was the finding that welfare clients were most satisfied with their welfare departments in departments in which caseloads were very high and in which caseworkers, as a consequence, had infrequent contact with their clients. The correlation across the fifteen cities was .66, possibly indicating that frequent contact with caseworkers was a source of irritation to clients.

In the same study, ratings were also obtained from black residents concerning police maltreatment. An index of maltreatment complaints (insulting remarks, unfair arrests, etc.) had a high correlation with police self-reports of potentially abrasive actions frequently undertaken. These findings suggest that client assessments of services may turn out to be an important source of evaluation of urban services.

SOURCE: Summary, by permission, of P. H. Rossi, R. A. Berk, and B. K. Eidson, *The Roots of Urban Discontent*. New York: John Wiley, 1974.

participants: Retirement benefit programs attempt to deliver retirement income in a way that is most satisfying to beneficiaries, including automatic bank deposits or special pickup provision. Public service programs may be particularly concerned with client satisfaction as an index of service-unit functioning. Exhibit 7-S provides a summary of a study conducted for the Kerner Commission of Urban Disorders. The study attempted to find out how blacks in big-city ghettos related to the police and welfare departments of those cities, testing those levels of satisfaction as reasons for the urban disorders of the 1960s.

In the second place, participant surveys may provide clues on how to increase target involvement, especially when program participants are contrasted with program dropouts. Participant assessments of programs offer useful information, but they cannot replace impact assessments conducted according to the research designs described in Chapter 6 and in this chapter.

We have devoted as much space as we have in this chapter to the use of shadow controls in impact assessment because this approach is used fairly often, and the reader should be aware that evaluations using such controls are fraught with danger. In evaluating social programs, it is doubtful that experts can do more than establish gross outcomes. Net impact estimates made by experts appear to be fragile and greatly subject to error. In short, we do not recommend this approach; it is almost always second-best.

A NOTE ON APPLICABILITY

The approaches discussed in this chapter vary widely in their rigor. Impact assessments using constructed controls or reflexive controls may be as useful in providing knowledge of net impact as the randomized approach described in Chapter 6. In contrast, the use of shadow controls to estimate net impact provides only uncertain estimates. Indeed, the latter types of evaluations should be used only when other approaches are either impossible or the evaluation so constrained by the demands of time and budget that the choice is really between doing nothing at all or using judgmental methods.

8

Measuring Efficiency

Knowledge of the extent to which programs have been implemented successfully and the degree to which they have had the desired outcomes is indispensable to program managers, stakeholders, and policymakers. In almost all cases, however, it is just as critical to be informed about how program outcomes compare to their costs. In fact, whether by formal means or impressionistically, as we do in making everyday life decisions, one of the important considerations when deciding upon the expansion, continuation, or termination of social programs is that of their costs compared with their benefits.

Efficiency assessments (cost-benefit and cost-effectiveness analyses) provide a frame of reference for relating costs to program results. In cost-benefit analyses both inputs and outcomes are measured in monetary terms; in cost-effectiveness analyses, inputs are estimated in monetary terms and outcomes in terms of actual impact (for example, number of disability days or improvements in reading scores). Cost-benefit and cost-effectiveness analyses provide information for making decisions on the allocation of resources; in addition, they are often useful in gaining the support of planning groups and political constituencies who determine the fate of social intervention efforts.

The procedures employed in both types of analyses are often highly technical, and their applications will be described only briefly in this chapter. It is not possible for a comprehensive text to ignore these procedures, however, because implicit in all impact evaluations is the issue of the cost or effort required to achieve a given magnitude of desired change. At least at a conceptual level, all program evaluators must understand the ideas embodied in efficiency analyses.

Cost-benefit and cost-effectiveness studies may be undertaken during the program-planning phase. Such *ex ante* efforts have great utility, although the required information and estimates necessary to undertake them often may not be fully available or may be imprecise. In such cases it is either impossible to conduct ex ante analyses or their results must be used cautiously.

While opportunities to conduct ex ante analyses are limited by the availability of the required data, it is often feasible to undertake either cost-benefit or cost-effectiveness analyses as part of the assessment of project outcomes. These *ex post* analyses are important and powerful inputs into planning and decision-making processes.

KEY CONCEPTS

Accounting Perspectives:	Perspectives underlying decisions on which categories of goods and services to include as costs or benefits in an analysis.
Benefits:	Net project outcomes, usually translated into monetary terms. Benefits may include both direct and indirect effects.
Benefit-to-Cost Ratio:	The total discounted benefits divided by the total discounted costs.
Costs:	Inputs, both direct and indirect, required to produce an intervention.
Cost-Benefit Analysis:	The economic efficiency of a program expressed as the relationship between costs and outcomes, usually measured in monetary terms.
Cost-Effectiveness Analysis:	The efficacy of a program in achieving given intervention outcomes in relation to the program costs.
Discounting:	The treatment of time in valuing costs and benefits; that is, the adjustment of costs and benefits to their present values, requiring a choice of discount rate and time frame.
Ex Ante Analysis:	Analysis undertaken prior to program implementation to estimate net outcome in relation to costs, usually undertaken as part of program planning.
Ex Post Analysis:	Analysis undertaken subsequent to knowing net outcome effects.
Internal Rate of Return:	The calculated value for the discount rate necessary for total discounted program benefits to equal total discounted program costs.

Net Benefits: The total discounted benefits minus the
                       total discounted costs (also called *net
                       return*).

Opportunity Costs: The value of opportunities forgone because
                       of an intervention project.

Shadow Prices: Imputed or estimated costs of goods and
                       services when these goods and services are
                       not valued in the current marketplace.

• Policymakers must decide which to emphasize among a variety of educational programs: basic primary education for young children, secondary education for adolescents, or vocational education for adults. All these have been shown to have substantial net impact in completed evaluations. How should the nation's educational resources be allocated?

• A government agency is reviewing national disease control programs currently in operation. If additional funds are to be allocated to disease control programs, which programs would show the biggest payoffs per expenditures?

• Evaluations in the criminal justice field have established the effects of various alternative programs aimed at reducing recidivism. Which program is most cost-effective to the criminal justice system? Given the policy choices, how would altering the current pattern of expenditures maximize the efficiency of correctional alternatives?

• Members of a private funding group are debating whether to promote a program of low-interest loans for home construction or to initiate work-skills training for married women to increase family income. How do they decide?

These are examples of some common resource allocation dilemmas faced by planners, funding groups, and policymakers everywhere. Over and over again, they must choose how to allocate scarce resources in order to put them to their optimal use. Consider even the fortunate case in which two or more pilot projects of programs have shown them all to be effective in producing the desired net impacts. To decide which to fund on a larger scale, one needs to take into account the relations between costs and outcomes of each. While other factors, including political and value considerations, come into play, the preferred program often is the one that produces the most impact on the most targets for a given level of expenditure. This simple principle is the foundation of cost-benefit and cost-effectiveness analyses, techniques that provide systematic approaches to resource allocation.

PERSPECTIVES ON RESOURCE ALLOCATION ANALYSIS

The basic procedures and concepts underlying resource allocation analysis stem from work undertaken in the 1930s to establish decision-making criteria for public investment activities. In the United States, early applications were to water resource development, and, in England, to transportation investments. After World War II, stimulated by the World

Bank, cost-benefit analysis was applied to both specific project activities and national programs in lesser developed as well as industrialized countries.

Cost-benefit and cost-effectiveness analyses in the social program area have their analogue in the world of business, where costs are constantly compared with profits. A computer company may be concerned with the relationship of costs to profits of making microcomputers compatible with those of a major competitor; a small restaurant owner is concerned with whether to provide dinner music or promote a "happy hour" in order to increase profits.

The idea of judging the utility of social intervention efforts in terms of their efficiency (profitability, in a business sense) has gained widespread acceptance. However, "correct" procedures for actually conducting cost-benefit and cost-effectiveness analyses remain an area of considerable controversy. Since their conception, methods and procedures of such analyses have undergone continual refinement, but the area is still referred to as an "emerging field." Evaluators undertaking cost-benefit or cost-effectiveness analyses of social interventions must be aware of the particular issues involved in applying efficiency analyses to their particular field, as well as the limitations that characterize the use of cost-benefit and cost-effectiveness analyses in general.

Program Efficiency

As we have indicated, cost-benefit and cost-effectiveness analyses can be viewed both as conceptual perspectives and as sophisticated technical procedures. It bears emphasis that in many evaluations, formal, complete efficiency analyses are either impracticable or unwise.

First, the required technical procedures may be beyond the resources of the evaluation project, may call for technical sophistication not available to the project's staff, or may be unnecessary, given either the very minimal or the extremely high efficacy of the intervention. Second, political or moral controversies that would result from placing economic values on particular input or outcome measures could obscure the relevance and minimize the potential utility of an otherwise useful and rigorous study. To some minds, these considerations may deny the wisdom of undertaking an efficiency study. Third, expressing the results of evaluation studies in efficiency terms may require that different costs and outcomes be taken into account, depending on the perspectives and values of sponsors, stakeholders, targets, and evaluators themselves, again obscuring the relevance and utility of evaluations.

Furthermore, in some cases the requisite data for undertaking cost-benefit calculations are not fully available. Even the strongest advocates of efficiency analyses acknowledge that often there is no single "right" analysis (Thompson, 1980; Stokey and Zeckhauser, 1978). In the case of some social program areas, the work done has been found to be so faulty or questionable in the assumptions made as to bring into question the totality of their findings. For example, using a large number of studies on rehabilitation, Noble (1977) has been able to document inadequate analytic and conceptual models, insufficiency of existing data, and the extreme sensitivity of cost-benefit results to their underlying but untested assumptions. Consequently, sensible policy priorities simply cannot be based on the cost-benefit calculations in the field of rehabilitation that existed when Noble undertook his review.

At the same time, the pertinence of efficiency analysis is undeniable. While we want to emphasize that the results of cost-benefit and cost-effectiveness analyses should be examined with a proper amount of caution, and at least some efficiency analyses treated with a fair degree of skepticism, they do provide a reproducible and rational way of estimating the efficiency of programs. While advocates of efficiency analyses rarely argue that such studies should be the sole determinant of decisions about programs, they are a valuable input into the complex mosaic from which decisions emerge.

Social programs, almost without exception, are conducted under resource constraints. They almost invariably operate under circumstances where maintaining continuing support depends on convincing policymakers and funders that the "bottom line" (i.e., dollar benefits or the equivalent) justifies the program. Often, choices between competing programs are, at least in part, based on relative payoffs in economic terms. Even when efficiency studies are not undertaken, program decisions that take into account evaluation findings often are framed in terms of presumed output-to-input results.

Even if specific applications and conclusions of the approach can be questioned, the strength of efficiency analysis lies in the discipline it forces on the evaluator, policymaker, planner, and manager to articulate economic considerations that might otherwise remain implicit.

The Uses of Efficiency Analyses

The employment of cost-benefit and cost-effectiveness techniques may be appropriate at two pivotal points in program efforts. In the planning and design phases, *ex ante* cost-benefit analyses may be undertaken on the basis of anticipated costs and benefits of programs. Such analyses, of course, must presume a given magnitude of positive net impact, even if this value is solely a conjecture. Likewise, the costs of providing and delivering the intervention must be estimated by one means or another. In some cases, estimates of both the inputs and the magnitude of impact can be made with considerable confidence, either because there has been a pilot program—or a similar program in another location—or because the program is fairly simple in its implementation. Nevertheless, since ex ante analyses in whole or part are not based upon empirical information, they run the risk of seriously under- or overestimating the ratio of costs to benefits or effectiveness. Indeed, the issue of the accuracy of the estimates of both inputs and outputs is one of the controversial areas in ex ante analyses.

Ex ante cost-benefit analyses are most important in cases where there is no way to abandon or great difficulties in abandoning programs once they have been put into place. For example, the decision to increase recreational facilities by putting in new jetties along the New Jersey shore would be difficult to overturn once the jetties had been constructed; thus, there is a need to estimate the ratio of costs to benefits of such a program compared with other ways of increasing recreational opportunities or of the wisdom of increasing recreational opportunities compared with the ratio of costs to benefits of allocating the resources to another social program area.

There is, however, an insufficient use of ex ante analysis in general. Many social programs are initiated or markedly modified without attention to their practicality in cost-benefit or cost-effectiveness terms. For example, if the application of a particular dental treatment that prevents cavities costs $50 per child annually, and it is estimated that it reduces caries among children by one-half cavity per year, it is not likely to gain acceptance, even if it works—after all, this is four or five times as much as a dentist would charge for filling the cavity. A cost-effectiveness analysis in such a case might easily dissuade decision makers from implementing the program.

Most commonly, efficiency analyses in the social program field take place after the completion of an impact evaluation, when the net impact of a program is known. The focus of ex post cost-benefit and cost-effectiveness assessments may be on examining the efficiency of a program in either absolute or comparative terms.

In both cases, the analysis is undertaken to assess whether the costs of the intervention can be justified by the magnitude of net outcomes. In absolute terms, the idea is to judge whether or not the program is worth what it costs by comparing costs to benefits or to outcome in substantive terms. For example, a cost-benefit analysis may reveal that for each dollar spent to reduce shoplifting in a department store, two dollars are saved in terms of stolen goods, an outcome that clearly indicates that the shoplifting program would be economically beneficial.

In comparative terms, the issue is to determine the differential "payoff" of one program versus another; for example, comparing the reduction in arrest rates for drunken driving of an educational program with a program that consists of paying for taxis to take people home after they have imbibed too much. In ex post analyses, costs and outcomes are based on studies of the types described in previous chapters on planning, monitoring, and impact evaluations.

The Concepts of Cost-Benefit and Cost-Effectiveness

A cost-benefit analysis requires estimates of the benefits of a program, both tangible and intangible, and the costs of undertaking the program, both direct and indirect. Once specified, the benefits and costs are translated into a common measure, usually a monetary unit. Obviously, many factors besides economic efficiency are brought to bear in policy-making, planning, and program implementation, but considerations of economic efficiency are almost always critical, given universally scarce resources.

Cost-benefit analysis requires the adoption of a particular economic perspective; in addition, certain assumptions must be made in order to translate program inputs and outputs into monetary figures. As noted, there is considerable controversy in the field regarding the "correct" procedures to utilize in converting inputs and outputs into monetary values. Clearly the assumptions underlying the definitions of and the measures of costs and benefits strongly influence the resulting conclusions. Consequently, the analyst is required, at the very least, to state the basis for the assumptions that underlie his or her analysis. Often analysts do more than that: They may undertake several different analyses of the same program, varying the assumptions made. For example, later we will discuss the need to take into account inflation (or deflation) in valuing costs and benefits that occur at different periods of time. The analyst could undertake a single study and state that an annual inflation rate of 10 percent was assumed; or the analyst could provide findings based on rates of 5, 10, and 15 percent. An important advantage of formal efficiency studies over impressionistically gathered information about costs in relation to outcomes is that the assumptions and procedures are open to review and checking.

Cost-benefit analysis is least controversial when applied to technical and industrial projects, where it is relatively easy to place a monetary value on benefits as well as costs. Examples include engineering projects designed to reduce the costs of electricity to consumers, highway construction to facilitate transportation by means of roads, or irrigation programs to increase crop yields. However, estimating benefits in monetary terms is frequently more difficult in social programs, where only a portion of program inputs and outputs reasonably may be valued in monetary terms. For example, it is possible to translate future occupational gains from an educational project into monetary values. The issues are more complex in such social interventions as fertility control programs or health services projects, because one must ultimately place a value on human life in order to monetize program benefits fully (Zeckhauser, 1975).

In general, there is much more controversy about converting outcomes into monetary values than inputs, as in the case of how much a day of life is worth. Because of the controversial nature of valuing outcomes, in many cases cost-effectiveness analysis is seen as a more appropriate technique than cost-benefit analysis. Cost-effectiveness analysis requires monetizing only program costs; benefits are expressed in outcome units. For example, the cost-effectiveness of distributing free textbooks to rural primary schoolchildren could be expressed as follows: Each 1000 project dollars increased reading scores by an average of one grade level.

For cost-effectiveness analysis, then, the outputs, or benefits, are expressed in terms of the costs of achieving magnitudes of substantive outcomes. That is, the efficacy of a program in attaining its goals is assessed in relation to the monetary value of the resources or costs put into the program. For example, alternative educational interventions may be analyzed by measuring educational gains, measured by test scores, and relating them to program costs. An educational program that makes use of computer-assisted instruction, for example, may raise scores on a reading test an average of 10 points per student, with a per student cost of $200. This might be compared with a program based upon providing students with individual, face-to-face instruction. The latter program might have an average per student cost of $400, but if it raised scores an average of 25 points on the same test, it would probably be a better "investment." Often programs that cost more per target may in fact turn out to be the program of choice in terms of efficiency.

A cost-effectiveness analysis allows comparison and ranking of choices among potential programs according to the magnitudes of their effects relative to their costs. Put differently, the comparison is stated in terms of units of effectiveness for achieving particular outcomes. Actual program operations and impact—and hence inputs and outputs—replace, to a considerable extent, estimates and assumptions. Moreover, retrospective analyses can yield useful insights and experiences, or methodological procedures that can be applied to future programs.

Efficiency analyses, at least ex post analyses, can be considered an extension of, rather than an alternative to, impact evaluation. It is impossible to engage in cost-benefit or cost-effectiveness calculations for programs in which impacts are entirely unknown and unestimable. It also is senseless to do so for ineffective programs—that is, when impact evaluations discover no significant net effects.

When applied to efficacious programs, efficiency analyses are useful to those who must make policy decisions regarding the support of one program over another, decide in absolute terms whether the outcomes of a program are worth its costs, or review the utility of programs at different points in time. Moreover cost-benefit analysis can be useful in the determination of the degree to which different levels or "strengths" of interventions produce different levels of benefits (Shortell and Richardson, 1978).

ESTIMATING COSTS AND BENEFITS

A program's benefits are its net outcomes, both tangible and intangible. For example, the benefits of a public health project may include reductions in illness and mortality, and increased economic productivity; the benefits of a vocational training project may include increased future earnings and economic productivity for participants, as well as the value of work done during training; and the benefits of a housing project may include increased quantity and quality of housing, and reduced health hazards.

Costs are the program inputs, both direct and indirect—that is, the resources required to conduct the program. Program costs include expenditures for personnel, administration, equipment, facilities, supplies or materials, and any other labor and operating costs incurred. As we shall discuss in more detail subsequently, however, which specific components should be included in the calculations and how to value them depend on the accounting perspective taken. In other words, the preceding "list" of project costs is an oversimplification of the calculations actually required.

A summary of the costs and benefits of an Upward Bound study is reproduced in Exhibit 8-A. A list of such costs and benefits is usually made as the first step in undertaking an efficiency analysis.

Important to the determination of project costs is the economists' notion of opportunity costs, or the value of forgone opportunities. From the target's point of view, participation in a program (e.g., vocational training) often means forgoing regular earnings, and is therefore treated as a cost.

Opportunity Costs

The concept of opportunity costs reflects the problem of limited resources, when individuals or the community must choose only some of

Exhibit 8-A: List of Costs and Benefits for the Upward Bound Evaluation

Upward Bound was a program of remedial education at the high school level, developed in the 1960s. The purpose was to identify high-potential disadvantaged youths who would not be likely to go to college and to provide them with special college-preparatory education. A cost-benefit analysis was based on data from a large evaluation of the postprogram experiences of students who had entered the program over a number of years. The evaluation data also included information on nonparticipant older siblings of participants. From the point of view of the participants, the benefits and costs were defined as follows:

Benefits

1. Increased after-tax lifetime incomes, measured on the basis of expected ultimate educational attainment of participants and their nonparticipant siblings.

2. Stipends paid to participants during the program.

3. Increase in scholarships and college attendance grants to Upward Bound students.

Costs

1. Additional tuition costs required of Upward Bound students because of higher rates of college attendance.

2. Additional expenses of Upward Bound students while in college.

3. Earnings forgone by Upward Bound students while in college.

4. Transfer income over the lifetime forgone by Upward Bound students (e.g., unemployment and welfare).

SOURCE: Adapted, with permission, from W. I. Garms, "A Benefit-Cost Analysis of the Upward Bound Progam." *Journal of Human Resources, 6* (Spring 1971): 206-220.

the existing alternatives. The cost of the choice can be measured by the worth of the forgone options. While this concept is relatively simple, the actual estimation of opportunity costs often is complex. For example, a police department may decide to pay the tuition of police officers who want to go to graduate school in psychology or social work on the grounds that this will improve their job performance. In order to have the money to do so, the department might have to keep its police cars an extra two months each. The opportunity costs could in this case be estimated by calculating the additional repair costs to the department's automobiles, which they would have to undertake if they offered tuition to the police officers and replaced the patrol cars later. Since in many cases opportunity costs can be estimated only by making assumptions about the consequences of alternative investments, it is one of the controversial areas in efficiency analyses.

Costs and Benefits

After as exhaustive a list as possible is made up of all the program benefits and costs, the next step is to attach monetary values to them. In cost-benefit analyses, the changing value of at least some of the costs and benefits over time must be taken into account. For example, because of inflation, the value of equipment and buildings may change considerably. The technique for determining the changes in value is known as *discounting*, which will be discussed later.

The final step consists of comparing total costs to total benefits. How this comparison is made depends to some extent on the purpose of the analysis and on the conventions in the particular program sector. The most direct comparison can be made simply by subtracting costs from benefits. For example, a program may have cost $185,000 and its benefits are calculated at $300,000. Thus the positive benefits (or profit, to use the business analogy) is $115,000.

When using cost-benefit analyses to compare the efficiency of one program with another, frequently the ratio of benefits to costs is calculated. Thus the benefit-to-cost ratio in the example used above would be $300,000/$185,000, or 1.62. This value could then be compared to a program that cost $400,000 and the benefits of which were calculated at $600,000 (or a benefit-to-cost ratio of 1.50). Benefit-to-cost ratios are similar to the ratios of prices to earnings shown in newspapers to make it possible for investors to compare one stock with another in terms of common units. Another way of conceptualizing the benefit-to-cost ratio is the benefit gained for each dollar invested in a program: Thus, a benefit-to-cost ratio of 1.50 means that the program yields $1.50 in benefits for each dollar invested.

The results of cost-benefit analyses can be expressed in other ways as well. For example, the rate of return, like the percentage of profit in the business world, can be calculated by subtracting costs from benefits and then dividing the net benefit (which of course can be negative or positive) by the costs. For example, if the cost of a program was $800,000 and its benefits are calculated to be $1,600,000, the rate of return would be 100 percent. Correspondingly, if the benefits were only $400,000 in this case, the rate of return would be a negative 50 percent. In a sense, all "bottom lines" obtained from cost-benefit studies provide fundamentally the same information, although one set of calculations may have more meaning to some stakeholders than to others (see Thompson, 1980: chap. 5).

In discussing the comparison of benefits to costs, we have noted the similarity to business decision-making. The analogy is real: In particular, some large private foundations, in the process of deciding upon which programs to support, actually phrase their decisions in investment terms. They may want to "balance" a high-risk venture (that is, one that might show a high rate of return but has a low probability of success) with a low-risk program (one that probably has a much lower rate of return but a much higher probability of success).

Sometimes, of course, programs yield negative cost-benefit ratios or negative values for other summary measures calculated. This means that the costs of a program outweigh its benefits. It bears noting that sometimes programs that yield negative values are nevertheless important and should be continued. For example, there is a communal responsibility to provide for severely retarded persons, and it is unlikely that any program designed to do so will have a positive cost-benefit ratio. But even in such cases, one may want to compare the costs to benefits of different programs, such as institutional care compared with home care. (See Exhibit 8-B for an illustration of a cost-benefit study for a family planning program.)

Having reviewed the framework underlying analyses of costs to benefits in particular and of economic efficiency in general, we turn to certain technical issues and an elaboration of the concepts.

METHODOLOGY OF COST-BENEFIT ANALYSIS

In order to carry out a cost-benefit analysis, one must first decide which perspective to take in calculating costs and benefits. What point of view should be the basis for specifying, measuring, and monetizing benefits and costs? In short, costs to and benefits for whom? Benefits and costs must be defined from a single perspective, because mixing points of view results in confused specifications and overlapping or double accounting. This is not to say that cost-benefit analyses for a single program cannot be undertaken from various perspectives. Separate analyses based on different perspectives often provide information on benefits to costs as they affect relevant stakeholders.

Accounting Perspectives

Three accounting perspectives may be used for the analysis of social projects: those of (1) individual participants or targets, (2) program sponsors, and (3) communal aggregates, or the society involved. The *individual* accounting perspective takes the point of view of the unit that is

---

Exhibit 8-B: The Costs and Benefits of a Family Planning Program: Cost-Benefit Ratios and Net Return Summaries

An analysis of the family planning program in the United Arab Republic estimated the benefits and costs of a prevented birth as follows.

Benefits

1. The main effect—the consumption expenditures that would have been required for an averted birth and which are now available to the households involved.

2. The wage productivity effect—the increase in output resulting from better nutrition of smaller-size families.

3. The increase in total public savings resulting from the diversion of resources that would have been required to educate the averted birth.

Costs

1. The magnitude of the loss of output resulting from a smaller labor force as the result of the long-term effects of lower fertility.

2. The costs of averting a birth through the provision of family planning services.

The final summary table is reproduced here. When two figures appear in a column, they reflect alternative assumptions made in the calculations.

	Egyptian Pounds per Prevented Birth	
	10% Discount Rate	15% Discount Rate
Benefits		
Consumption	222-351	109-206
Wage productivity effect	16-21	9-14
Public savings effect	37	24
Total	275-409	142-244
Costs		
Productivity	79-91	24-31
Family Planning Services	4-20	4-20
Total	83-111	28-51
Difference between		
benefits and costs		
(row 4 minus row 7)	164-326	91-216
Benefit-cost ratios		
(row 4/row 7)	2.5-4.9	2.8-8.7

SOURCE: From G. C. Zaidan, *The Costs and Benefits of Family Planning Programs*. Washington: World Bank, 1971, pp. 2, 45. Reprinted by permission of the copyright holder.

the program target—that is, the persons, groups, or organizations receiving the intervention or services. Cost-benefit analyses using the individual target perspective often produce higher benefit-to-cost ratios than those using other perspectives. In other words, if the sponsor or society bears the cost and subsidizes a successful intervention, the individual program participant benefits the most. For example, an educational project may impose relatively few costs on participants. The cost to targets may be primarily in time spent in project participation, since books and materials used are furnished. Furthermore, if the time required is primarily in the afternoons and evenings, there may be no income loss to participants. Benefits to the participants may include improvements in earnings as a result of increased education, greater job satisfaction, and increased occupational options, as well as transfer payments received while participating in the project.

The *program sponsor* accounting perspective takes the point of view of the funding source in valuing benefits and specifying cost factors. The funding source may be a private agency or foundation, a government agency, or a for-profit firm. From this perspective, the cost-benefit analysis most closely resembles what frequently is termed "private profitability analysis."

The program sponsor accounting perspective is most appropriate where there are clear policy choices involving alternative programs that a government or other sponsor may fund, and under fixed budgetary conditions—that is, when new revenues will not be generated to fund additional projects. From the program sponsor's point of view, for example, benefits from an educational project in terms of local, state, and federal governments are decreases in expenditures that no longer have to be made, such as public assistance subsidies or other forms of direct government spending. Another major sponsor (government) benefit is that of increased revenues as a result of participants' improved earnings subsequent to the training (i.e., if trainees obtain better jobs and earn more, they will pay more in taxes). The costs to government are for operation, administration, instruction, supplies, facilities, and any additional subsidies or transfers paid to the participants during the training. Exhibit 8-C shows a cost-benefit calculation of short-term benefits to the government in terms of births averted by family planning programs.

The *communal* accounting perspective takes the point of view of the community or society as a whole, usually in terms of total income. It is therefore the most comprehensive perspective, but also the most ambiguous and difficult to apply. Taking the point of view of society as a whole implies that special efforts are being made to account for secondary project effects. A program will ordinarily have effects on groups not directly involved with the intervention, and these are taken into account when calculations are made based on a communal accounting perspective. Moreover, in the current literature, communal cost-benefit analysis has been expanded to include equity considerations, or the distributional effects of programs among different subgroups. For example, from a communal standpoint, every dollar earned by a minority member who had been unemployed for six months or more may be seen as a "double benefit" and so entered in the analyses. Exhibit 8-D lists the communal costs and benefits of Upward Bound, which can be compared to the list in Exhibit 8-A showing individual costs and benefits.

Although the components of a communal cost-benefit analysis appear to include most of the costs and benefits that also appear in calculations made from the individual and program sponsor perspectives, the items are valued and monetized differently. For example, communal costs for a project include opportunity costs in terms of alternative investments forgone by the community in order to fund the project in question. These are obviously not the same as opportunity costs incurred by an individual as a consequence of project participation. Communal costs also include

Exhibit 8-C: Cost-Benefit Analysis of Family Planning Programs

A recent national evaluation of government-provided family planning programs aimed at low-income women in large population centers in the United States was carried out to assess the effects on fertility rates from 1970 to 1975. The evaluation linked data enrollments at the family planning clinics to census data. An impact assessment showed that there was a significant reduction of fertility among groups served by the program, net of other relevant variables such as age, race, and marital status.

As a final step in the study, benefit-cost ratios were estimated from the point of view of the government and based on unwanted and unintended births averted. All the cost and benefit figures reflect expenditures and savings to the government in terms of births averted.

The calculations used to establish program impact suggest that during the six years in question, participation in the family planning clinics resulted in a total of almost 1.1 million births averted. These amount to the direct effects of the program for women served, and do not include possible secondary effects of unserved persons who also might have benefited.

Available data were used to measure the following benefits to the government, which are listed as costs saved to the government by averting unwanted births: (1) medical care associated with pregnancy and birth, which is borne by all sorts of multilevel government programs for the low-income population; (2) public assistance during the first year for children born to women already on public assistance; and (3) selected social services for public assistance recipients and their newborn for one year. The authors argue that these costs seriously understate savings in short-term costs of unwanted births, such as additional forms of public assistance and social services, and public housing, as well as opportunity costs consisting of income lost due to the mother's giving up employment during portions of the pregnancy and early child-rearing periods. These categories were excluded because data were not available to allow specifying the proportions of low-income women who would fall into each category and the resulting government expenditures.

Estimates of national costs of public assistance for the three categories listed above took into account the fact that during the period in question, 16 to 19 percent of the patients in family planning clinics under evaluation were receiving public assistance. Estimated savings were $1,076 million ($1.1 billion), a figure that therefore represents total benefits.

Costs were simply the federal appropriations for family planning clinic services, readily available from government records, and which amounted to $584 million in total (ranging from $33 to $160 million during the six-year period).

The benefit-cost ratio or total estimated savings to total costs for the program 1.8 (1,076/584). This is interpreted to mean that one dollar invested by the federal government in family planning in one year saved federal, state, and local governments approximately $1.80 a year later. These savings are in addition to long-term savings, and the health, social, and demographic benefits to government and individuals from the prevention of unwanted and unintended births.

SOURCE: Summary, by permission, from P. Cutright and F. S. Jaffe, *Impact of Family Planning Programs on Fertility: The U.S. Experience.* New York: Praeger, 1977.

outlays for facilities, equipment, and personnel, usually valued differently than they would be from the program sponsor perspective. Finally, these costs do not include transfer payments, because they would also be entered as benefits to the community, and the two entries would simply cancel each other out.

Table 8.1 shows some of the basic components of cost-benefit analyses for the different accounting perspectives. (In the illustration, the program sponsor is a government agency.) The list is not to be taken as complete, but as an illustration only. Specific items included in real analyses vary.

Table 8.2 provides a simplified, hypothetical example of benefit-cost calculations for a training program from the three accounting perspectives. Again, the monetary figures are gross oversimplifications; a real analysis would require far more complex treatment of the measurement issues involved. The example is intended merely to illustrate the previous discussion. Note that the same components may enter into the calculation as benefits from one perspective and as costs from another, and that the result of the calculation (in this case the ratio of benefits to costs and the difference between benefits and costs, or net benefit) will vary, depending on the accounting perspective used.

Although we have offered a three-way classification of accounting perspectives, actually it may be necessary for the analyst to undertake a

Exhibit 8-D: Communal Costs and Benefits of Upward Bound

Benefits

1. Increased before-tax lifetime incomes for program participants. (Before-tax incomes are used to reflect societal productivity.)

Costs

1. Direct cost of the Upward Bound Program to the government, including all resources expended, except student stipends.

2. Direct cost of program to participating colleges.

3. Extra costs of education incurred by society because of the higher rate of college attendance by Upward Bound students.

4. Extra living costs required by college attributable to the program.

5. Before-tax earnings forgone by Upward Bound students while in college.

SOURCE: Adapted, with permission, from W. I. Garms "A Benefit-Cost Analysis of the Upward Bound Program." *Journal of Human Resources*, 6 (Spring 1971): 206-220.

number of analyses. For example, if a government group and a private foundation jointly sponsor a program, separate analyses are required for each to judge the return on its investment. Also, one might want to calculate the costs and benefits to different groups of targets, such as the direct and indirect targets of a program. For example, many communities offer tax advantages to industrial corporations if they build their plants there; the intent is to provide employment opportunities for residents. Costs to benefits could be calculated for the employer, the employees, and also the "average" resident of the community, whose taxes may rise to take up the slack resulting from the tax break to the factory owners.

Measuring Costs and Benefits

The specification, measurement, and valuation of costs and benefits—procedures that are central to cost-benefit analysis—raise two distinct problems: first, the identification and measurement of all program costs and benefits; second, the expression of all costs and benefits in terms of a common denominator, that is, their translation into monetary values.

TABLE 8.1 Components of Cost-Benefit Analyses for Different Perspectives

	Individual	Program Sponsor	Communal
Benefits	Increase in earnings (net of taxes)	Increase in tax revenues	Increase in earnings (gross of taxes)
	Additional benefits received (e.g., direct transfers, fringe, and noneconomic benefits)	Decrease in expenses of public assistance, and other subsidies Value of work done within the project	Increase in other income (e.g., fringe benefits, excluding direct transfers) Decrease in expenses of alternative projects no longer applicable Value of work done
Costs	Opportunity costs (earnings forgone net of taxes) Loss of direct subsidies no longer applicable (alternative projects) Extra costs related to participation (e.g., fees, materials)	Taxes lost Project costs (e.g., capital, administrative, instructional, direct subsidies)	Opportunity costs (gross of taxes) Project costs excluding direct subsidies or transfer payments)

The problem of identifying and measuring costs and benefits is most acute for ex ante appraisals, where there are scanty or imprecise data available. However, data often are limited in ex post cost-benefit analyses as well. For many social interventions, the information from an evaluation (or even a series of evaluations) may in itself prove insufficient for a retrospective cost-benefit analysis to be carried out. Thus, evaluations often provide only some of the necessary information, and the analyst frequently must use additional sources or judgments.

The second problem in many social programs is the difficulty of translating benefits and costs into monetary units. Social programs frequently do not produce results that can be valued accurately by market prices. For example, many would argue that the benefits of a fertility control project, a literacy campaign, or a program providing training in improved health practices cannot be monetized in ways acceptable to the various stakeholders. Exhibit 8-E exemplifies the problems of measurement for a methadone program. For example, what value should be placed

TABLE 8.2 Hypothetical Example of a Training Project Cost-Benefit Calculation from Different Accounting Perspectives

Benefits/Costs[a]

1. Earnings improvement of trainees (before taxes) — $100,000
2. Earnings improvement of trainees (after taxes) — 80,000
3. Value of work done in training period — 10,000
4. Project costs for facility and personnel — 50,000
5. Project costs for equipment and supplies — 5,000
6. Trainee stipends (direct transfer payments) — 12,000
7. Earnings forgone by trainees (before taxes) — 11,000
8. Earnings forgone by traineees (after taxes) — 9,000
9. Taxes lost: (7) minus (8) — 2,000

	Individual	*Program Sponsor*	*Communal*
Benefits	(2) 80,000	(1)-(2) 20,000	(1) 100,000
	(6) 12,000	(3) 10,000	(3) 10,000
	92,000	30,000	110,000
Costs	(8) 9,000	(4) 50,000	(4) 50,000
		(5) 5,000	(5) 5,000
		(6) 12,000	(7) 11,000
		(9) 2,000	
	9,000	69,000	66,000
B/C Ratio	$\dfrac{92,000}{9,000} = 10.22$	$\dfrac{30,000}{69,000} = .44$	$\dfrac{110,000}{66,000} = 1.67$
Net Benefit	83,000	− 39,000	44,000[b]

a. Assume that these figures represent present values; see subsequent section.
b. Note that net social benefit can be split into net benefit for trainees plus net benefit for the government, which in this case is negative: $83,000 + (-39,000) = 44,000$.

on fear and anguish (Item 1)? In such cases, cost-benefit analysis might be a reasonable alternative, because such analysis does not require that benefits be valued in terms of money, only quantified by outcome measures.

Because of the advantages of expressing benefits in monetary terms, a number of approaches have been specified for monetizing outcomes or benefits (Thompson, 1980: 140-151).

Money Measurements. The least controversial approach is the estimation of direct monetary benefits. For example, if keeping a health center open for two hours in the evening reduces targets' absence from work (and thus loss of wages) by an average of 10 hours per year, then, from an individual perspective, the annual benefit can be calculated by multiplying the average wage by 10 hours by the number of employed targets.

Market Valuation. Another relatively uncontroversial approach is the monetization of gains or impacts by valuing them at market prices. If crime is reduced in a community by 50 percent, benefits can be estimated in

Exhibit 8-E: Measuring the Benefits of a Methadone Treatment Program

The Direct Benefits of Methadone Treatment

1. *Benefits to Potential Victims*

    a. decrease in private protection expenditures

    b. decrease in the value of damage to victim resources

    c. decrease in the value of forced transfers

    d. decrease in the negative value placed on fear and mental anguish

2. *Benefits to Taxpayers*

    a. decrease in criminal justice expenditures

    b. decrease in medical expenditures for narcotic-related illnesses

3. *Benefits to Methadone Patients*

    a. decrease in expenditures on heroin

    b. increase in legal earnings, minus the decrease in illegal earnings

*The Empirically Measurable Direct Benefits
of Methadone Treatment*

1. decrease in criminal justice expenditures

2. decrease in medical expenditures for narcotic-related illnesses

3. decrease in expenditures on heroin

4. increase in legal earnings

SOURCE: From T. Hannan, "The Benefits and Costs of Methadone Maintenance," *Public Policy*, 24 (Spring 1976): 200, 201. Reprinted by permission.

terms of housing prices through adjustment of current values on the basis of such prices in communities with lower crime rates and similar social profiles.

Econometric Estimation. A more problematic approach is the estimation of the presumed value of a gain or impact in market terms. For example, the increase in tax receipts from greater business revenue due to a reduced fear of crime could be determined by calculating relevant tax revenues of similar communities with lower crime rates, and then estimating the tax returns that would ensue to the community in question. Such an estimation may require complex analytical efforts and problematic assumptions, making such pricing tentative at best.

Hypothetical Questions. A still more problematic approach is the estimation of the value of intrinsically nonmonetary benefits through direct questioning of the targets. For instance, a program to prevent dental disease may decrease participants' cavities by an average of one at age 40; thus, one might conduct a survey on how much people think it is worth to have an additional intact tooth as opposed to a filled tooth. Such estimates presume that the montary value obtained realistically expresses the worth of an intact tooth. Clearly, hypothetical valuations of this kind are open to considerable skepticism.

Observing Political Choices. The most tentative approach is the estimation of benefits on the basis of political actions. If state legislatures are consistently willing to appropriate funds for high-risk infant medical programs at a rate of $50,000 per child saved, this figure could be used as an estimate of the monetary benefits of such a program. But, given that political choices are complex, shifting, and inconsistent, this approach is generally very risky.

In summary, for the results of a cost-benefit analysis to be valid and reliable and reflect fully the economic effects of a project, all relevant components must be included. When important benefits are disregarded because they cannot be measured or monetized, the project may appear less efficient than it is; if certain costs are omitted, the project will seem more efficient. The results may be just as misleading if estimates of costs or benefits are either too conservative or too generous.

Pricing Methods

Benefits and costs need to be defined and valued differently, depending on the accounting perspective used. For many programs, however, the outputs simply do not have market prices (e.g., the reduction of pollution or the work of a housewife), yet their value must be estimated.

The preferred procedure is to use "shadow prices," also known as "accounting prices," to reflect better than actual market prices the real costs and benefits to society. Shadow prices, in other words, are derived prices for goods and services that reflect their "true" benefits and costs. Sometimes it is more realistic to use shadow prices even when actual prices are available. For example, suppose an experimental program is implemented that requires a director who is knowledgeable about every one of the building trades. For the single site, the sponsors may be fortunate to find a retired person very interested in the program and willing to work for, say, $30,000 per year. But if the program was shown to be a success through an impact evaluation and a cost-benefit analysis was undertaken, it might be best to use a shadow price of, say, $50,000 for director's salary, because it is very unlikely that five persons with the nonmonetary interests of the first director could be found (Levin, 1983).

Distributional Considerations

Traditionally, the effectiveness of social interventions is predicated on the notion that an effective intervention makes at least one person better off and nobody worse off. But this may be very difficult to achieve in social programs that rely on income transfers. Lowering the minimum wage for teenagers, for instance, may increase their employment at the cost of reducing work opportunities for older adults.

The basic means of incorporating equity and distributional considerations in the cost-benefit analysis involves a system of weights whereby benefits are valued more if they produce the anticipated positive effects. If a lowered minimum wage for teenagers increases total family incomes of the most disadvantaged households but decreases the family incomes of the moderately disadvantaged, the dollars gained and lost could be weighted differently, depending on the degree of disadvantage to the families. Some accomplishments are worth more to the community, both for equity reasons and for the increase in human well-being, and should therefore be weighted more heavily.

The weights to be assigned can be determined by the appropriate decision makers, in which case value judgments will obviously have to be exercised; they may also be derived through certain economic principles and assumptions. There are a number of formal approaches, including Guttentag's decision theoretic approach (discussed in Chapter 3). In any case, it is clear that weights cannot be applied indiscriminately. Analysts will undoubtedly develop further refinements as they continue to deal with the issue of distributional effects.

An intermediate solution to considerations of equity in cost-benefit analyses is to make calculations for separate subgroups of the society instead of calculating a single aggregate measure. Disaggregation has been done for income groups (e.g., Hansen and Nelson, 1976) and levels of achievement (e.g., Wolfe, 1977). A great deal of attention has been devoted to such distributional issues in analyses of the effects of schooling, particularly because the costs of subsidized education are in part borne by taxpayers who do not have children in school, and the benefits are received by those who are less well off (Ribich and Murphy, 1975). Finally, it has even been suggested that intergenerational considerations must be taken into account in resolving the equity of returns to education (Conlisk, 1977).

Secondary Effects (Externalities)

Projects may have external or "spillover" effects, that is, side effects or unintended consequences that may be either beneficial or detrimental. Given that such effects are not deliberate outcomes, they may be omitted inappropriately from cost-benefit calculations if special efforts are not made to include them. A secondary effect for a training program, for example, might be the spillover of the training to relatives, neighbors, and friends of the participants. Among the more commonly discussed negative external effects of industrial or technical projects are pollution, noise, traffic, and destruction of plant and animal life.

For many projects, two secondary effects are likely: displacement and vacuum effects. For example, an educational or training project may produce a group of newly trained persons who enter the labor market, compete with workers already employed, and displace them (i.e., force them out of their jobs). Project participants may also vacate jobs held previously, leaving a vacuum that other workers might fill.

Externalities or secondary effects may be difficult to identify and measure (see Klarman, 1974, for a review of the difficulties of specifying indirect and intangible benefits of health services), but, once found, should be incorporated into the cost-benefit calculations.

Discounting

The last major element in the methodology of efficiency analyses concerns the treatment of time in valuing program costs and benefits. The technique is known as *discounting*, and consists of reducing costs and benefits that are dispersed through time to a common monetary base, or adjusting them to their present values.

Intervention programs vary in duration, and successful ones in particular produce benefits that are derived in the future, sometimes long after the intervention has taken place. The effects of many programs are expected to persist through the participants' lifetimes. Often the evaluator has to extrapolate into the future to measure impact and ascertain benefits, especially since program benefits are gauged as projected income changes for participants. But costs are usually highest at the beginning of an intervention, when many of the resources must be expended; they either taper off or cease when the intervention ends. Even a fixed cost expended at different time points, or a constant benefit derived at various times, cannot be considered equivalent at different time points. Ex ante appraisals often extrapolate into the future in carrying out a complete analysis. Otherwise, the evaluation would be based only on the restricted period of time for which actual program performance data are available.

Costs and benefits occurring at different points in time must be brought into a common measure, or made commensurable. In other words, the time patterns for costs and benefits of a program must be taken into account. Instead of asking, "How much more will my investment be worth in the future?" standard economic practice is to ask, "How much less are benefits derived in the future worth compared to those received in the present?" The same goes for costs. The answer depends on what we assume to be the rate of interest, or the discount rate, and the time frame chosen. Exhibit 8-F provides an example of discounting.

The choice of time period on which to base analysis depends on the nature of the program and whether the analysis is ex ante or ex post. All else being equal, a program will appear more beneficial the longer the time horizon chosen.

The choice of discount rate is related to the accounting perspective. There is no authoritative approach. One choice is to fix the rate on the basis of the opportunity costs of capital, that is, what an amount can be expected to gain if invested elsewhere in the private market or in the public sector. Another approach, under the communal perspective, is to use the social discount rate, which presumably reflects a community's time preference. Also, a program sponsor such as a government group might make an administrative decision on a given rate to be used for all calculations. Recent manuals recommend that a more sophisticated accounting rate of interest be computed that is linked to the shadow wage rate (Little and Mirrlees, 1974) or that takes distributional impacts into account (Squire and van der Tak, 1975).

The results of a study are thus particularly sensitive to the choice of discount rate. In practice evaluators usually resolve this complex and controversial issue by carrying out discounting calculations based on several different rates. Finally, instead of applying what may seem to be an arbitrary discount rate or rates, one may calculate the program's internal rate of return, or the value that the discount rate would have to be for program benefits to equal program costs.

When to Do Ex Post
Cost-Benefit Analysis

Much earlier in this chapter, we discussed the importance of undertaking ex ante analyses in developing programs that result in irrevocable or almost irrevocable commitments. We also indicated that many more ex ante analyses are called for in the social program arena; too often it is only

Exhibit 8-F: Discounting Costs and Benefits to Their Present Values

Discounting is based on the simple notion that it is preferable to have a given amount of capital in the present rather than in the future. All else equal, capital can be saved in a bank to accumulate interest, or can be used for some alternative investment. Hence it will be greater in the future. Put differently, a fixed amount payable in the future is worth less than the same amount in the present. Conceptually, discounting is the reverse of compound interest, since it tells us how much we would have to put aside today to yield a fixed amount in the future. Algebraically, discounting is the reciprocal of compound interest, and it is carried out by means of the simple formula:

$$\text{Present Value of an Amount} = \frac{\text{Amount}}{(1 + r)^t}$$

where r is the discount rate and t stands for the number of years. Hence, the total stream of benefits (and costs) of a program expressed in present values is obtained by adding up the discounted values for each year. An example of such a computation follows:

A training program is known to produce increases of $1,000 per year in earnings for each participant. The earnings improvements are discounted to their present values at a 10 percent discount rate and for five years.

YEAR	1	2	3	4	5
	$\dfrac{\$1{,}000}{(1 + .10)^1}$	$\dfrac{\$1{,}000}{(1 + .10)^2}$	$\dfrac{\$1{,}000}{(1 + .10)^3}$	$\dfrac{\$1{,}000}{(1 + .10)^4}$	$\dfrac{\$1{,}000}{(1 + .10)^4}$
	$909.09	$826.45	$751.32	$683.01	$620.92

Over the five years, total discounted benefits equal $909.09 + $826.45 + ... + $620.92, or $3,790.79. Thus, improvements of $1,000 per year for five years are not worth $5,000, but only $3,790.79. At a 5 percent discount rate, the total present value would be $4,329.48. In general, benefits calculated using low discount rates will appear greater than those calculated with high rates, all else being equal.

after programs are put in place that policymakers and sponsors realize that their costs compared with their benefits make them impractical to implement on a permanent basis.

In terms of ex ante analyses, it is important to consider a number of factors in determining whether to undertake a cost-benefit analysis. In some evaluation contexts, the technique is feasible, useful, and a logical component of a comprehensive evaluation; in others, its application may rest on dubious assumptions and be of limited utility. Optimal prerequisites of an ex post cost-benefit analysis of a program include the following:

- The program has independent or separable funding. This means that its costs can be separated from other activities.

- The program is beyond the development stage and it is certain that net effects are significant.

- Program impact and magnitude of impact are known or can be estimated validly.

- Benefits can be reduced to monetary terms.

- Decision makers are considering alternative programs, rather than simply whether or not to continue the existing project.

COST-EFFECTIVENESS ANALYSIS

Cost-benefit analysis allows the comparison of the economic efficiency of program alternatives, even when the interventions are not aimed at common goals. After initial attempts in the early 1970s to use cost-benefit analysis in social fields, however, some evaluators became uneasy about directly comparing cost-benefit calculations for, say, family planning to health, housing, or educational projects. As noted, sometimes it is simply not possible to obtain agreement—for example, on the monetary value of a life prevented by a fertility control project, or of a life saved by a health campaign—and then compare the results.

Cost-effectiveness analysis does not require that benefits and costs be reduced to a common denominator. Instead, the effectiveness of a program in reaching given goals is related to the monetary value of the resources going into the program (Levin, 1975). In cost-effectiveness analyses, programs with similar objectives are evaluated and the costs of alternative programs for achieving the same goals are compared. One can compare programs aimed at lowering the fertility rate, different educational methods for raising achievement levels, or various interventions to

Exhibit 8-G: Cost-Effectiveness Analysis Concepts for Corrections Programs

Any correctional program is made up of these major components: First, there are tasks or activities performed on a day-to-day basis within the program. Second, there are outputs or intermediate products or subgoals that result from the daily activity in the program. Finally, there are outcomes, or final products or goals, which represent what a program seeks to achieve. In a prison, for example, the major day-to-day activity is "taking care of" inmates. An output or intermediate product is "treatment," which begins when an inmate enters the facility and is regarded as completed when the inmate leaves. But treatment is not an end in itself. Treatment is provided in order to achieve a goal or outcome, which in this article is assumed to be reduced recidivism. The following table outlines alternative ways of conceptualizing the distinction between inputs, outputs, and outcomes.

| | Focus of Analysis | | |
	How	What	Why
Alternative Conceptual-izations	Activity, task, inputs	Objectives, subgoals, intermediate products, outputs	Goals, final products, outcomes
Example	Group counseling, food and clothing, recreation	"Treatment" or "rehabilitation"	Reduced recidivism
Cost Measure	Input cost	Output cost	Outcome cost
Example	Cost per day	Cost per case	Cost per reduced arrest

SOURCE: From C. M. Gray, C. J. Conover, and T. M. Hennessey, "Cost Effectiveness of Residential Community Corrections: An Analytical Prototype," *Evaluation Quarterly* 2 (August 1978): 378.

reduce infant mortality. Exhibit 8-G summarizes the concepts used in cost-effectiveness analyses of corrections programs.

Cost-effectiveness allows comparison and rank-ordering of programs in terms of their costs for reaching given goals, or the various inputs required for different degrees of goal achievement. But, because the benefits are not converted to a common denominator, one can neither ascertain the worth or merit of a given intervention nor compare which of two or more programs in different areas produces better returns. One can compare the relative efficiency of programs' goals only with respect to each other, where efficiency is a function of minimal costs. Exhibit 8-H summarizes a cost-effectiveness analysis of correctional program alternatives in terms of cost per reduction in recidivism.

Cost-effectiveness can be viewed as an extension of cost-benefit analysis to projects with multiple and noncommensurable goals. Cost-effectiveness is based on the same principles and utilizes the same methods as cost-benefit analysis. The assumptions of the method, as well as procedures required for measuring costs and discounting, for example, are the same for both approaches. Therefore, the concepts and methodology introduced previously with regard to cost-benefit analysis can also be regarded as a basis for understanding the cost-effectiveness approach.

Exhibit 8-I shows the use of cost-effectiveness analysis to compare an experimental educational television program with a proposed reform of an existing formal school system. It shows in simple terms the use of cost-effectiveness ratios to compare alternative projects in terms of costs to produce measured cognitive gains.

SUMMARIZING A COMPLEX FIELD

In this chapter we have provided an overview of cost-benefit analysis by examining its logic, assumptions, concepts, and procedures. Cost-benefit analysis requires that program costs and benefits be known, quantified, and transformed to a common measurement unit; that they be projected into the future to reflect the lifetime of a program; and that future benefits and costs be discounted to reflect their present values. Cost-effectiveness analysis has been suggested as a feasible alternative to cost-benefit analysis in the many instances where benefits cannot be calibrated in monetary units. Also, we have stressed that ex post analyses are more appropriate than ex ante studies for evaluating human service programs.

In terms of ex post efficiency estimation, cost-benefit and cost-effectiveness analyses should be viewed as components of a comprehensive evaluation, since solid evidence of net impact is the basis for the formulation of benefits and effectiveness. Competent analysis can provide

(text continues on page 356)

Exhibit 8-H: Cost-Effectiveness of Residential Community Corrections

An analysis of the relative cost-effectiveness of a community corrections program for adult and juvenile offenders, in comparison with traditional probation and incarceration methods, is based on the reduction of recidivism. Different measures of recidivism are employed, as well as duration. The results are summarized in the following table:

Correctional Alternative	Cost per Client Treated		Net Offense Reduction Due to Treatment		Cost per Reduced:		Cost per Reduction in:	
					Offense Sustained	Nonstatus Offense	Seriousness of Offenses	Severity of Offenses
Juvenile Probation								
Very short run	$ 504	÷	4.3	=	$ 117	$ 180	$ 4	$ 81
Short run	504	÷	4.3	=	117	180	4	81
Long run	661	÷	4.3	=	154	239	4	107

Residential Clients—								
No Prior Institutionalization								
Very short run	739	÷	4.2	=	176	352	14	101
Short run	836	÷	4.2	=	199	398	16	114
Long run	3,649	÷	4.2	=	869	1,738	68	500
Residential Clients—								
Prior Institutionalization								
Very short run	1,132	÷	6.2	=	183	1,415	25	166
Short run	1,281	÷	6.2	=	207	1,601	28	188
Long run	5,592	÷	6.2	=	902	6,990	123	822
Juvenile Institutions								
Very short run	621	÷	6.3	=	99	222	8	65
Short run	2,597	÷	6.3	=	412	928	34	412
Long run	12,641	÷	6.3	=	2,006	4,515	165	1,317

SOURCE: From C. M. Gray, C. J. Conover, and T. M. Hennessey, "Cost Effectiveness of Residential Community Corrections: An Analytical Prototype," *Evaluation Quarterly* 2 (August 1978): 394.

Exhibit 8-I: Cost-Effectiveness Analysis of Educational Television and Educational Reform Projects

Data from an experimental evaluation of educational television (ETV) and an educational reform program introduced in El Salvador by AID allow a cost-effectiveness comparison of the two alternatives for expanding basic schooling (in this case at the seventh-grade level). Educational gains were measured by means of standard achievement tests administered at the beginning and end of the school year in 1972. Educational reforms involved expanded curriculum and materials and retrained teachers, with and without ETV. Actual costs for the reform and ETV programs were calculated: The annual cost per student in the program without ETV was $16, and the cost of ETV alone was $22. The following table summarizes the results of the cost-effectiveness analysis:

	Gain	Gain Over Traditional
Mathematics		
Gain for traditional classes	1.95	—
Gain for experiment ETV class	5.70	3.7
Gain for experiment control group (reform but no ETV)	5.20	3.2
Science		
Gain for traditional classes	1.34	—
Gain for experiment ETV class	4.20	2.9
Gain for experiment control group (reform but no ETV)	5.10	3.8
Social Studies		
Gain for traditional classes	2.61	—
Gain for experiment ETV class	6.40	3.8
Gain for experiment control group (reform but no ETV)	3.10	1.6

The cost-effectiveness ratios for the different subjects are the following:

	ETV	Reform Only
Math	3.7/$22 = .17	3.2/$16 = .20
Science	2.9/$22 = .13	3.8/$16 = .24
Social Studies	3.8/$22 = .17	1.5/$16 = .10

Only in social studies is the cost-effectiveness ratio for ETV larger than for reform only. Therefore, the author argues for investing in the curriculum and teaching reforms, and not installing ETV.

SOURCE: Reprinted from M. Carnoy, "The Economic Costs and Returns to Educational Television," in *Economic Development and Cultural Change*, 23 (1975), 237-238. By permission of the University of Chicago Press. © 1975 The University of Chicago.

Exhibit 8-J: Effects and Costs of Day-Care Services for the Chronically Ill

Long-term, adult day-care settings not now covered by Medicare were studied in a randomized experiment to test the effects on patient outcomes and costs of using these new services. This article reports findings for day care. Patients' physical, psychosocial, and health functions were assessed quarterly, and their Medicare bill files were obtained. Medicaid data were obtained on most patients, but few used many Medicaid-covered, long-term care services. Multi-stage analysis was performed to mitigate effects of departures from the randomized design. Day-care patients showed no benefits in physical functioning ability at the end of the study, compared with the control group. Institutionalization in skilled nursing facilities was lower for the experimental group than for the control group, but factors other than the treatment variable appeared to explain most of the variance. There was a possibility that life was extended for some day-care patients. The new services averaged $52 per day, or $3,235 per year. When costs for existing Medicare services used were added, the yearly cost of the experimental group was $6,501, compared with $3,809 for the control group—an increase of $2,692, or 71 percent.

SOURCE: Adapted, with permission, from William Weissert, Thomas Wan, Barbara Livieratos, and Sidney Katz, "Effects and Costs of Day-Care Services for the Chronically Ill: A Randomized Experiment," *Medical Care.* Vol. 18, No. 6, 1980: 567-584.

extremely valuable information about a program's economic efficiency and is important in program planning, implementation, and policy processes. As shown in Exhibit 8-J, cost-benefit and -effectiveness analyses often provide important information not available from impact assessments alone.

We have provided only a general overview of the efficiency approach. As should be apparent, considerable technical sophistication charac- terizes much of the work surrounding it. As a style of thinking about program results, however, it has great value for the evaluation field.

9

The Social Context of Evaluation

In the preceding chapters, we have been concerned mainly with the technical aspects of conducting systematic evaluations. From the outset, however, we have tried to convey our view that evaluations involve more than just the use of appropriate research procedures. Evaluation research is a purposeful activity, entered into to affect policy development, to shape the design and implementation of social interventions, and to improve the management of social programs. In the broadest sense of politics, evaluation is a political activity.

There are, of course, intrinsic rewards for evaluators, who may derive great pleasure simply from satisfying themselves that they have done as nearly perfect a technical job as possible—like artists whose paintings hang in their attics and never see the light of day, and poets whose penciled foolscap is hidden from sight in their desk drawers. But that is not really what it is all about. Evaluations are a "real-world" activity. In the end, what counts is the degree of critical acclaim with which an evaluation is judged by peers in the field, and the extent to which it leads to modified policies, programs, and practices—ones that, in the short or long term, improve the human condition.

KEY CONCEPTS

Conceptual Utilization:	Incorporation into the general knowledge base of the ideas and findings of an evaluation concerning a social problem.
Direct Utilization:	Utilization of ideas and findings of an evaluation in modifying social policies or programs.
Policy Significance:	The significance of an evaluation's findings for policy (as opposed to the statistical significance of those findings).
Policy Space:	The set of policy alternatives existing at a given point in time that are within the bounds of acceptability to policymakers.
Primary Dissemination:	Dissemination of the detailed full set of findings of an evaluation to sponsors and technical audience.
Secondary Dissemination:	Dissemination of summarized and simplified findings to lay audiences composed of stakeholders.

---

*N*ow, as in the past (and undoubtedly in the future as well), evaluators must remain humble about the potency of their efforts. Even the strongest proponents of the evaluation enterprise realistically acknowledge that its potential contributions are constrained by many factors: the range of competencies and self-interests of both the persons who undertake evaluations and those who are consumers of them; the diversity in styles of work and organizational arrangements in the field of evaluation; and the political contradictions and economic constraints that mitigate all efforts at planned social change.

Evaluators, then, are confronted with the same frustrations, feelings of impotence, and lack of self-esteem felt by all groups whose efforts almost always fall short of their aspirations. Their response has been the same as well: a great amount of introspection, a concerted effort to shift the blame to others, and a literally endless outpouring of verbal and written commentaries about the dismal state of affairs—especially about the futility of evaluation as an agent of social change.

We concur that neither the world nor the world of evaluation resembles Utopia. At the same time, however, the contributions of the evaluation enterprise should not be dismissed out of hand. There is considerable evidence that the findings of evaluations often influence policies, program planning and implementation, and the ways social programs are administered—sometimes in the short term, and other times in the long term.

In this final chapter, we try to provide a balanced view of the current status of the field, to stress its accomplishments without neglecting the strains and tensions that persist in it, and to offer ideas about how to maximize the utility of evaluations while acknowledging that there are many practical considerations for which no general advice is possible. The chapter is based on an admixture of our own experiences and the writings of colleagues who have addressed the various interpersonal, political, and structural issues that surround evaluation studies.

THE PURPOSEFULNESS OF EVALUATION ACTIVITIES

Evaluation activities fall within the rubric of "applied" social research. While the boundaries are not always perfectly clear, there are qualitative differences between "basic" or "academic" research and applied research (Freeman and Rossi, 1984). We have discussed some of these differences earlier, such as the idea that evaluations should be conducted so that they are "good enough" to answer the questions under study. (In contrast, basic researchers typically strive for the "best" methodology that can be used in carrying out their research.)

There are three additional important distinctions between applied and basic research. First, basic researchers generally have a single disciplinary orientation, most often make use of a narrow band of methodological procedures, and address a limited substantive domain from one study to the next. For example, a sociologist might use participant observation as his or her primary method of choice, and may devote most of his or her career to the study of professional education. Or an economist may focus on the costs of health care, and may consistently apply econometric modeling procedures.

In contrast, during his or her career an evaluator usually moves back and forth from one program area to another, and the evaluation questions posed in the different studies undertaken typically require use of a range of methods. The difference in careers between basic researchers and evaluators raises a number of issues about the training and outlook of the latter group—indeed, more generally about the profession of evaluation.

Second, basic research typically is initiated to satisfy the intellectual curiosity of the investigator, and to contribute to the knowledge base of a substantive area, one of interest to the researcher and his or her peers. In contrast, applied work is undertaken because it might contribute to the solution of a practical problem. In the evaluation field, most often the impetus for undertaking work does not come from the evaluators themselves but from persons and groups who, for one reason or another, are concerned with a particular social problem (later in this chapter we will discuss the range of these stakeholders in more detail).

Sometimes this interest in a particular social problem comes from the highest levels: Congress may mandate evaluations of major national initiatives, as it did in the case of compensatory education programs (St. Pierre, 1983a), or the president of a large foundation may insist that all of the foundation's large social action programs be evaluated, as in the case of the national health initiatives of the Robert Wood Johnson Foundation (Aiken et al., 1980). At other times, evaluation activities are initiated in response to requests from managers and supervisors of various operating agencies and focus on administrative matters quite specific to them (Oman and Chitwood, 1984). Still other times, they are undertaken in response to the interests of individuals and community groups who are concerned with a particular social problem and with the planned or current efforts to address it.

In undertaking these evaluation activities, evaluators usually find that they are confronted by individuals and groups who hold competing, and sometimes combative, views on the appropriateness of their evaluation work, and whose self-interests are affected by the outcome of their efforts. In order for evaluators to conduct their work effectively, and for their activities to contribute to the resolution of the issues at hand, they must understand what we refer to as the "social ecology" of the arena in which they work—the set of relationships with stakeholders. This is the second major topic considered in this chapter.

Third, there is a major difference in the audiences for basic and applied work, and in the criteria for assessing its utilization. Conventional researchers are most concerned with their peers' responses to their studies; they judge utilization by the extent to which their research stimulates work by others and by the acceptance of papers in prestigious journals. Applied researchers judge themselves, and are judged by the sponsors of their studies, by how much of a contribution they make to the resolution of social problems and to the development and implementation of policies and programs. Utilization of evaluation results and ways to maximize that use are the last topics considered in this chapter.

THE PROFESSION OF EVALUATION

There is no roster of persons who identify themselves as evaluators, and no way of describing their backgrounds or the range of activities in which they are engaged. An educated guess is that there are some 50,000 persons engaged in evaluation activities full or part time. We have arrived at this estimate by adding the number of federal, state, county, and city governmental organizations that are engaged in social program development and implementation to the total number of school districts, hospitals, mental hospitals, universities and colleges in the United States, all of which usually are obligated to undertake one or more types of evaluation activities. We do not know, in fact, the actual number of persons engaged in evaluation work in these groups, for we have no way of estimating how many university professors, persons affiliated with nonprofit and for-profit applied research firms, and so on do evaluations. In fact, the actual number of full- and part-time evaluators may be smaller than or double or triple our estimate of 50,000.

It is clear that there is a wide variation in the social program areas in which evaluators work, and that persons in the field devote varying amounts of their working time to evaluation activities. At best, the role definition of the evaluator is blurred. At one extreme, persons may undertake evaluations as an adjunct activity. Sometimes, their evaluation activities are undertaken simply because they must conform to legislative or regulatory requirements. This apparently is the situation in many local school systems. In order to comply with state or federal funding requirements, usually a condition for receiving funds, they must have personnel designated as "evaluators." A school may comply by appointing someone on the teaching or management staff as an "evaluator." Often, the person appointed has no particular qualifications for the assignment, either by training or by previous experience. Indeed, sometimes it is someone not regarded very highly as either a teacher or an administrator.

At the other extreme, within university evaluation institutes and departments, and within applied social research firms in the private and nonprofit sectors, there are full-time evaluation specialists. These persons are highly trained and have years of experience working at the frontiers of the evaluation field.

Indeed, the common labeling of persons as evaluators or evaluation researchers conceals the heterogeneity, diversity, and amorphousness of the field. Evaluators are not licensed or certified, so the identification of a person as an evaluator provides no assurance that he or she shares any core knowledge with another so identified. The proportion of evaluators who interact and communicate with each other, particularly across social program areas, probably is infinitesimally small. For example, the Evaluation Research Society, the major "general" organization in the field, has only a few thousand members, and the most widely read cross-disciplinary journal, *Evaluation Review*, has only a few thousand subscribers as well. Within program areas, likewise, there are only weak social networks of evaluators; most are unaffiliated with national and local professional organizations that have organized evaluation "sections."

In brief, evaluation is not a "profession," at least in terms of the formal criteria that sociologists generally use to characterize such groups. Rather, it can best be described as a "near-group," a large aggregate of persons who are not formally organized, whose membership changes rapidly, and who have little in common in terms of the range of tasks undertaken, competencies, work-sites, and shared outlooks. It is this feature of the evaluation field that underlies much of the discussion that follows.

Intellectual Roots

All of the social science disciplines—economics, psychology, sociology, political science, and anthropology—have contributed to the development of the field of evaluation. Persons trained in each of these disciplines have made contributions to the conceptual base of evaluation research and to its methodological repertoire. In addition, contributions have been made by persons trained in the various human service professions with close ties to the social sciences—medicine, public health, social welfare, urban planning, public administration, education, and so on. Finally, the applied mathematics fields of statistics, biometrics, econometrics, and psychometrics have contributed important ideas on measurement and analysis.

Cross-disciplinary borrowing has been extensive. Take the following examples: Although economics traditionally has not been an experimentally based social science, economists have designed and implemented a large proportion of the major large-scale field randomized experiments of the past two decades, including the well-known income maintenance, housing allowance, and national health insurance experiments. Sociologists and psychologists have borrowed heavily from the econometricians, notably time-series analysis methods and simultaneous equation modeling. In turn, sociologists have contributed many of the conceptual and data collection procedures used in the monitoring of organizational performance. Psychologists have contributed the idea of regression discontinuity designs to time-series analyses. Psychometricians have provided some of the basic ideas underlying all fields' theories of measurement, and anthropologists have provided some of the basic approaches used in qualitative fieldwork. Indeed, the vocabulary of the field is a mix from all of these fields. The list of references at the back of this book is testimony to the multidisciplinary character of the evaluation field.

In the abstract, the diverse roots of the field constitute one of its attractions. In practice, they confront the evaluators with the need to be general social scientists and with the need to be lifetime "students" if they are even to keep up, let alone broaden their knowledge bases. This diversity in the field also accounts for some of the questionable choices of research design made by evaluators; it is clearly impossible for every evaluator to be a scholar in all of the social sciences and an expert in every methodological procedure.

There is no ready solution to the need to have a broad knowledge base and a broad range of competencies—two things ideally required by the "universal" evaluator. It means that evaluators must at times forsake opportunities to undertake work, because their knowledge bases may simply be too thin; it means that evaluators may have to use an "almost good enough" method rather than a more appropriate one because they are unfamiliar with the latter; and it means that sponsors of evaluations and managers of evaluation staffs must be highly selective in deciding upon contractors and in making work assignments. It also requires, at times, heavy use of consultants and solicitation of advice from peers.

In a "profession," a range of opportunities are provided for keeping up with the state of the art and for expanding one's repertoire of competencies: for example, the peer learning that occurs at regional and national professional meetings, along with the didactic courses that are often offered there. At present only a few thousand of the many thousands in the field participate in these organizations and enjoy the opportunities they provide. There are liabilities to overprofessionalization, as we know from the state of many of the practicing professions. But the "near-group" character of the field and its diverse roots have their consequences as well, and they are exacerbated by the different ways in which evaluators are educated.

The Education of Evaluators

There are few in evaluation who have achieved responsible posts and rewards by working their way up from lowly jobs. Most evaluators have some sort of formal graduate training, in either social science departments or professional schools. One of the important consequences of the multi-disciplinary character of evaluation is that appropriate training for full participation in it cannot be undertaken adequately within any single discipline. In a few universities, interdisciplinary evaluation programs have been set up that include graduate instruction in a number of departments. In these programs, a graduate student might be directed to take courses in test construction and measurement in a department of psychology, econometrics in a department of economics, survey design and analysis in a department of sociology, policy analysis in a political science department, and so on.

Such interdisciplinary training programs are neither common nor very stable. In the typical graduate training and research-oriented university, the traditional departments are powerful units. The interdepartmental coalitions of faculty that form interdisciplinary programs tend to be short-lived, because departments typically do not reward participation in such ventures very highly and faculty drift back into their departments as a consequence. The result is that too often graduate training of evaluators is primarily unidisciplinary, despite the clear need for it to be multi-disciplinary.

Moreover, even within academic departments, applied work is often downgraded. As a consequence, training in evaluation-related competencies is often limited. Psychology departments may provide fine courses on experimental design, but fail to give much consideration to the special problems of implementing field experiments in comparison with laboratory studies; sociology departments may teach survey research courses but not deal at all with the data collection problems involved in interviewing the special populations that are typically the targets of social programs. Moreover, the low status accorded applied work in graduate departments often is a barrier to undertaking evaluations as dissertations and theses.

If there is any advice to be given, it is that the student interested in an evaluation career must be assertive: He or she often must take the initiative in organizing a special program that includes course offerings in a range of departments, must be insistent about undertaking an applied dissertation or thesis, and should seize on any opportunities within university research institutes and in the community to supplement formal instruction with relevant apprenticeship learning.

The other training route is the professional school. Schools of education train evaluators for positions in that field, programs in schools of public health and medical care produce persons who engage in health service evaluations, and so on. In fact, over time these professional schools, as well as MBA programs, have become the training sites for many evaluators.

These programs have their limitations as well. One criticism raised about them is that they are too "trade-school" oriented in outlook. Consequently, some of them fail to provide the conceptual breadth and "basic" education that allows graduates to move back and forth across social program areas and to grasp technical innovations when they occur. Moreover, particularly at a master's degree level, many professional schools are obliged to have a number of required courses because their standing and sometimes funding depend upon accreditation by professional bodies who see the need for common training if persons are going to leave tagged as MSWs, MPHs, MBAs, and the like. Since many programs in professional schools leave little time for electives, the amount of technical training that can be absorbed is limited. Increasingly, the training of evaluators in these schools has moved from the master's to the doctoral level.

Also, in many universities both faculty and students in professional schools are viewed as second-class citizens by those located in social science departments, and this pseudoelitism often isolates professional school students, so that they cannot take advantage of course offerings in social science departments and, where they exist, apprenticeship training opportunities in their affiliated social science research institutes. Students trained in professional schools, particularly at the master's degree level, often trade off opportunities for intensive technical training for substantive knowledge in a particular program area and the benefits of professional certification. The obvious remedy is either to engage in further graduate work or to seize opportunities for additional learning of technical skills while pursuing an evaluation career.

We hold no brief for one route over the other. Each has its advantages and liabilities. Increasingly, it appears that professional schools are becoming the major suppliers of evaluators, at least in part because of the reluctance of graduate social science departments to develop appropriate applied research programs. But these professional schools are not homogeneous in what is taught or, particularly, in the methods of evaluation they emphasize; differences between them, as well as among the programs of graduate social science departments, contribute to the continued diversity of the field.

Consequences of Educational Diversity

The many educational pathways to becoming an evaluator constitute a major reason for the lack of coherence in the field. They account, at least in part, for the differences in the very definition of evaluation and the different outlooks regarding the "appropriate" way to evaluate a particular social program.

Some of the differences are related to whether the evaluator is educated in a professional school or in a social science department. For example, evaluators who come out of professional schools such as social work or education are much more likely than those trained in, say, sociology to see themselves as part of the program staff and to give priority to tasks that help program managers. Thus, they are likely to stress "formative" evaluations that are designed to improve the day-to-day operation of a program.

The diversity is also related to differences among social science departments and among professional schools. Political scientists frequently are oriented to "policy analysis," an activity designed to aid legislators and high-level executives, particularly government administrators. Anthropologists, as one might expect, are predisposed to qualitative approaches, and are unusually attentive to targets' interests in their evaluations. Consonant with their discipline's emphasis on small-scale experiments, psychologists often are concerned more with internal than external validity; in contrast, sociologists are often more concerned with generalization potential and are more willing to forsake some degree of internal validity to achieve it. Economists are likely to work in still different ways, depending on their body of microeconomic theory to guide their evaluation designs.

The same is true among those educated in different professional schools. Evaluators trained in schools of education may focus on educational competency tests in measuring the outcome of early childhood education programs, and social work graduates on the children's emotional status and parental reports of their behavior. Persons coming from schools of public health may be most interested in preventive practices, those from medical care administration programs in frequency of physician encounters and duration of hospitalization, and on and on.

It is easy to exaggerate the different outlooks that each discipline and profession manifests in approaching the design and conduct of evaluations, and there are many exceptions to the preference tendencies just described. Nevertheless, disciplinary and professional diversity has produced a fair degree of conflict within the field of evaluation. Perhaps the deepest rift is the one that divides the advocates of qualitative methods from those who favor more structured approaches.

Qualitative and
Quantitative Evaluations

A rich, although somewhat pointless, literature has developed around this controversy. On one side, the advocates of qualitative approaches stress the need for intimate knowledge and acquaintance with a program's actual operations as necessary to the attainment of valid knowledge about a program's effects. Qualitative evaluators tend to be oriented toward making a program work better by feeding information on the program to program managers. In contrast, quantitatively oriented evaluators view the field as one primarily concerned with impact assessment and with cleanly measuring net impact, as we discussed in Chapter 5.

Often the quantitative/qualitative polemics obscure the critical point, namely, that each approach has utility, and the choice of approaches depends on the evaluation question at hand. We have tried in this volume to identify the appropriate applications of each viewpoint. As we stressed in Chapters 2 and 3, qualitative approaches can play critical roles in program design, and are important means of monitoring programs. In contrast, quantitative approaches are much more appropriate in net impact estimation as well as in assessing the efficiency of social program efforts.

It is fruitless to raise the issue of which is the better approach without specifying the evaluation questions to be studied. The complementarity of approach and research purposes is the critical issue: To pit one approach against the other in the abstract results in a foolish dichotomization of the field.

Working Arrangements

The diversity of the field is also manifest in the variety of settings and bureaucratic arrangements under which evaluators work. There are two contradictory theses about working arrangements: One position is that evaluators are best off when their positions are as secure and independent as possible from the influence of project management and project staff. The other is that evaluators' work is enhanced by sustained contact with policy and program staff, for it provides understanding of organizational objectives and activities and inspires trust in and thus increased influence for the evaluator.

Inside versus Outside Evaluations

In the past, some experienced evaluators went so far as to state categorically that adequate evaluations could rarely, if ever, be undertaken within the organization responsible for the administration of a project. Hence, outside evaluations were to be preferred. One reason "outsider" evaluations may have seemed desirable was that there were differences in the levels of training and presumed competence of insider and outsider evaluation staffs. These differences have narrowed. The career of an evaluation researcher typically has taken one of three forms. Until the 1960s, a large proportion of evaluation research conducted on health, social, rehabilitation, education, and welfare services was done either by university-affiliated researchers or by research firms. Since the late 1960s, public service agencies in these program areas have been hiring researchers for staff positions to conduct more in-house evaluations. Also, the proportion of evaluations done by private, for-profit research groups has increased markedly. As research positions in both types of organizations have increased and the academic job market has declined, more persons well trained in the social and behavioral sciences have gravitated toward research jobs in public agencies (Polivka and Steg, 1978) and for-profit firms.

The current evidence is far from clear. In a study of correlates of evaluation quality, Bernstein and Freeman (1975) found that there was a somewhat greater likelihood for insider than outsider evaluations to be high quality, a finding attributed to the greater ability of insiders compared with outsiders to influence the conduct of the intervention efforts studied.

In the discussion in Chapter 2, we noted the likelihood that accountability has the most utility if undertaken internally. Recent studies in the Netherlands of external and internal evaluations suggest why internal evaluations may have a higher rate of impact on organizational decisions. According to van de Vall and Bolas (1981), insider evaluations were more successful in influencing social policy because inside researchers and policymakers communicate more easily and frequently, and apparently develop greater consensus over substantive and methodological issues. "In operational terms," according to van de Vall and Bolas (1981: 479), "this means that social policy researchers should seek equilibrium between time devoted to methodological perfection and translating results into policy measures." Their data suggest that in-house social researchers are in the more favorable position for achieving these instrumental goals than are external researchers.

Given the increased competence of staff and the visibility and scrutiny of the evaluation enterprise, there is no longer any reason to favor one organizational arrangement over another. Nevertheless, there remain many critical points during an evaluation when there are opportunities for work to be misdirected and consequently misutilized (Cook et al., 1980).

Organizational Roles

Certainly evaluators, whether insiders or outsiders, need to cultivate clear understanding of their relationships to sponsors and program staff. Evaluators' full comprehension of their roles and responsibilities is one major element in the successful conduct of an evaluation effort. Again, the heterogeneity of the field minimizes generalizations on how to develop and maintain appropriate working relations.

One common mechanism is to have advisory groups of one or more consultants to oversee evaluations and provide some validation of the authenticity of their findings. The ways such advisory groups work depend on whether an inside or an outside evaluation is involved, and on the levels of sophistication of both the evaluator and the program staff. For example, large-scale evaluations undertaken by federal agencies and major foundations often have advisory groups that meet regularly and assess the quality, quantity, and direction of work. Some public and private health and welfare organizations with small evaluation units have consultants who provide technical advice to the evaluators, advise agency directors on the appropriateness of the evaluation units' activities, or both. Sometimes, these advisory groups and consultants are mere window-dressing. (We do not recommend the use of consultants or advisory groups if providing window-dressing is their only function.) At other times they truly work, and are particularly useful in adjudicating disputes between program and evaluation staffs, and defending evaluation findings in the face of concerted attacks by those whose self-interests are threatened.

Of course, increased professionalism in the evaluation field would mitigate many of the strains in relations among evaluators, program staffs, and sponsors of evaluations. A major effort in this direction is the *Standards for Evaluation Practice* adopted by the Evaluation Research Society (Rossi, 1982). While neither perfect nor complete, the standards provide a valuable set of guidelines on a wide range of areas, from negotiation of evaluation agreements to communication and dissemination of results. Also, the Joint Committee on Standards for Educational Evaluation has issued a set of standards of particular relevance to educational evaluations, and the General Accounting Office (which, in addition to conducting its own evaluations, has oversight over all the evaluations conducted by federal agencies) has published a special set of standards for impact evaluations.

Moreover, the management of evaluations, a previously uncharted field, is now receiving considerable attention. A recent issue of *New Directions for Evaluation,* for example, was devoted to the management

Exhibit 9-A: Efficient Evaluation Teams

Evaluation teams consisting of many staff members each contributing small proportions of their time, complex subcontracting arrangements in which the division of labor between the prime contractor and subcontractors is unclear, and banks of consultants with ambiguous roles who participate primarily through large group meetings are not organized to do good evaluation research. Such teams are unwieldy and fragmented. In contrast, the most efficient evaluation team is the one with the fewest moving pieces—the one in which staff members work full time on the study, in which all the work is concentrated in one organization (or if a subcontractor is involved, the division of labor is clear-cut), and in which consultants are used in a structured manner.

SOURCE: Robert G. St. Pierre, "Management of Federally Funded Evaluation Teams," *Evaluation Review* 6 (February 1982): 94-113.

and organization of program evaluations (St. Pierre, 1983). As we have noted, the different types of organizational arrangements in the field and the various tasks emphasized in individual evaluations make it difficult to offer generalizations on the most effective managerial structure for their conduct. The conclusions of St. Pierre, drawn from his examination of federally funded evaluation groups, however, have considerable general relevance, at least for large evaluation projects (see Exhibit 9-A).

Major Evaluations

In reviewing the profession of evaluation, it should be noted that a small group, perhaps no more than a thousand evaluators, constitutes an "elite" in the field by virtue of the scale of the evaluations on which they work and the size of the organizations for which they work. They are, to some degree, akin to the elite physicians who practice in the hospitals of important medical schools. They and their settings are few in number but powerful in setting the norms for the field.

The number of organizations that carry out national or otherwise large-scale evaluations with a high degree of technical competence actually is quite small. But in terms of both visibility and evaluation dollars expended, they occupy a strategic position in the field. For example, the funds awarded to six large evaluation research contractors funded by the

Department of Education in the late seventies (Raizen and Rossi, 1980) constituted more than two-thirds of all that department's evaluation funds. Similar degrees of concentration can be seen in the evaluation activities of the U.S. Departments of Health and Human Resources, Labor, and Agriculture. Most of these large contracts were awarded to for-profit social research firms (such as Abt Associates, Mathematica, and SRI International, to name a few) as well as to not-for-profit research organizations and universities (examples are Battelle Memorial Institute, the Rand Corporation, and the Manpower Development Research Corporation). A handful of research-oriented universities with affiliated research institutes (e.g., NORC at the University of Chicago and the Institute for Social Research at the University of Michigan) are also the recipients of grants and contracts for undertaking large-scale evaluations. In addition, the evaluation units of federal agencies that contract for and fund evaluation research and a few of the large national foundations, also include significant numbers of highly trained evaluators on their staffs. Within the federal government perhaps the highest concentration of skilled evaluators is found in the Evaluation Division of the General Accounting Office, where a large group of evaluation specialists have extended the activities of this key "watchdog" organization from auditing to the assessment of appropriate program implementation and the estimation of the impact of federal initiatives.

Most of the senior persons who work in "elite" organizations have doctorates in one of the social sciences or from professional schools that offer an evaluation concentration. For example, Abt Associates of Cambridge, Massachusetts, one of the largest for-profit social research firms, had more than 150 Ph.D.s on its payroll at the peak of its activities in 1979. (Incidentally, at the time, Abt Associates had a larger contingency of Ph.D. social scientists on its payroll than either of the two major universities in Cambridge, MIT and Harvard.)

Among the features of these for-profit and nonprofit elite organizations that are the contractees for most large-scale evaluations is a continual concern with the quality of their work. In part this has come about because of critiques of their earlier efforts, which were not as well conducted technically as those done by persons in academic institutions (Bernstein and Freeman, 1975). But as they came to dominate the field, at least in terms of large-scale evaluations, and as they found sponsors of evaluations increasingly using criteria of technical competence in selecting contractors, the technical quality of their efforts have improved markedly; so, too, have the competencies of their staffs, and they now compete for the best-trained persons in applied work. Also, they have found it to be in their self-interest to urge staff to publish in professional journals, participate actively in professional organizations, and engage in frontier efforts to improve the state of the art. To the extent that there is a general movement toward professionalism, these organizations are its leaders.

THE SOCIAL ECOLOGY OF
THE EVALUATION FIELD

While the field may be diverse, as we have documented in our discussion of the profession of evaluation, virtually all evaluators do see their work as purposeful; the rationale for doing applied work is to influence the actions and thinking of the broad category of persons who effect social change, and who in their policy and action roles use the findings and conclusions provided by evaluators.

The likelihood of evaluations being used is dependent upon a recognition that the interpersonal and political contexts in which they are undertaken are the key determinants of their utilization. Successful evaluations and successful evaluators continually need to assess the social ecology of the arena in which they work. The starting point for doing so is the recognition of the range of stakeholders who directly or indirectly facilitate or impede the usefulness of their efforts, both as evaluators go about doing their work and in stakeholders' responses to their products. We would argue that this is as true of the lonely evaluator situated in a single school, hospital, or social agency as it is of those who are associated with elite organizations.

The Range of Stakeholders

In an abstract sense, every citizen who should be concerned with the efficacy and efficiency of efforts to improve human and social conditions has a stake in an evaluation's outcome. In practice, however, the stakeholder group concerned with any given evaluation effort is narrower, consisting of those who have direct and visible interests in the program. Various stakeholders typically have different perspectives on the meaning and importance of an evaluation's findings, a source of potential conflict between these persons and the evaluator. No matter what an evaluation's results, there are some to whom the findings are good news and some to whom they are bad news.

To evaluate is to make judgments; to conduct an evaluation is to provide findings that can be used to make judgments. The distinction between making judgments and providing information upon which judgments can be based is useful and clear in the abstract, but it is often difficult to delineate in practice. Some stakeholders may perceive the results of an evaluation to be critical judgments and may react accordingly.

Who are the parties typically involved in the use of evaluation results? Listed below are some of the stakeholder groups that either directly participate or become interested in the evaluation process and its results:

- *Policymakers and Decision Makers:* Persons responsible for deciding whether a program is to be instituted, continued, discontinued, expanded, or curtailed.

- *Program Sponsors:* Organizations that initiate and fund the program to be evaluated.

- *Evaluation Sponsors:* Organizations that initiate and fund the evaluation. (Sometimes the evaluation sponsors and the program sponsors are identical.)

- *Target Participants:* Persons, households, or other units who participate in the program or receive the intervention services under evaluation.

- *Program Management:* Group responsible for overseeing and coordinating the intervention program.

- *Program Staff:* Personnel responsible for actual delivery of the intervention (e.g., teachers).

- *Evaluators:* Groups or individuals responsible for the design and/or conduct of the evaluation.

- *Program Competitors:* Organizations or groups who compete for available resources.

- *Contextual Stakeholders:* Organizations, groups, individuals, and other units in the immediate environment of a program (e.g., local government officials or influentials situated on or near the program site).

- *Evaluation Community:* Other evaluators, either organized or not, who read and evaluate evaluations for their technical quality.

Although these ten groups do not represent all parties conceivably interested and involved in the "politics of evaluation," they are the stakeholders who often may pay attention to the outcomes of an evaluation and who also may participate in one way or another in the conduct of an evaluation.

Note that the last paragraph emphasizes that these ten groups are *potential* audiences for an evaluation and *potential* participants in its conduct. This means that in any given case, all may be involved, or just one or two.

Very little is known about how evaluation audiences are formed and activated. It is not completely clear how the interests of each of the ten potential groups are engaged and acted upon in particular cases. Perhaps the only reliable prediction that can be made is that evaluation sponsors, program managers, and program staff are most likely to be attentive to an evaluation during its conduct and after a report has been issued. Of course, these reactions are quite understandable, since these groups usually have the most at stake in program continuation and it is their activities that are most clearly judged by the evaluation report.

Especially problematic are the reactions of beneficiaries (targets) of a program. Although in many programs beneficiaries would appear to have the strongest stake in an evaluation's outcome, they are often the least prepared to make their voices heard. Target beneficiaries are often unorganized, geographically scattered, often poorly educated and unskilled in political communication, and sometimes reluctant even to identify themselves. When target beneficiaries do make themselves heard in the course of an evaluation, it is often through organizations aspiring to represent them. For example, homeless persons rarely make themselves heard in the discussion of programs directed at relieving their distressful conditions. But members of the National Coalition for the Homeless, an organization composed mainly of persons who are not homeless, will often act as spokespersons in policy discussions dealing with the homeless problem.

There are two important consequences of the phenomenon of multiple stakeholders. First, evaluators must accept the fact that their efforts are but one input into the complex mosaic from which decisions and actions eventuate. Second, there are invariably strains that result from the conflicts in interests of these stakeholders. One can partially eliminate or minimize these strains by anticipating and planning for them, but they come with the turf and many simply have to be lived with or addressed on an ad hoc basis.

Evaluation as a Political Process

At every time point during a program's evolution and operations, evaluation results can be useful in the decision-making process. In the earliest phases of program design, evaluations can provide the basic data about social problems that make possible the design of sensitive and appropriate services. While prototype programs are being tested, prospective evaluations may provide definitive estimates of net effects. After programs have been in operation, evaluations can provide considerable information about accountability issues.

In some cases, project sponsors may contract for an evaluation with the strong anticipation that it will critically influence continuation, modification, or termination of a project. In those cases, the evaluator may be under pressure to produce information quickly, so that decisions can be made expeditiously. In short, evaluators may have a receptive audience.

In other situations, evaluators may complete their assessments of an intervention only to discover that decision makers react slowly to their findings (Cox, 1977). Even more disconcerting are the occasions when a program is continued, modified, or terminated without regard to an evaluation's valuable and often expensively obtained information.

Although in such circumstances evaluators may feel as though their labors have been in vain, the decision-making process is indeed complex. As we have noted, one can expect only that the results of an evaluation will be but one of the elements in decision-making. This is clearly revealed in the 1915 controversy over the evaluation of the Gary plan in New York City (see Exhibit 9-B).

There are many parties involved in a human service program, as we noted earlier. Program sponsors, managers, and operators, and sometimes the participants, often have very high stakes in the continuation of a program, and their unsupportable but enthusiastic claims may often be given more weight than the results of an evaluation. The outcomes of typical American political processes may be viewed as balancing a variety of interests; the outcome of an evaluation is simply a single argument on one side or another. To imagine otherwise would be to claim that evaluators occupy a place in the political decision-making process that commands the power of veto, a role that would strip decision makers of their prerogatives. Under such circumstances evaluators would become philosopher kings, whose pronouncements on particular programs would override those of all the other parties involved.

In any political system sensitive to weighing, assessing, and balancing the conflicting claims and interests of a number of constituencies, one can expect an evaluation to play the role of expert witness, testifying to the degree of a program's effectiveness. A jury of decision makers and other stakeholders may give such testimony more weight than uninformed opinion or shrewd guessing, but it is they, not the witness, who reach a verdict.

In short, we argue here that the proper role of evaluation is to contribute to the political process the best possible knowledge on evaluation issues. Evaluations and evaluators should not attempt to supplant the political process.

Consequences of Multiple Stakeholders

The multiplicity of stakeholders for evaluations generates strains for the evaluators in three basic ways: *First,* evaluators are often unsure whose

Exhibit 9-B: Politics and Evaluation

[This exhibit concerns the introduction of a new plan of school organization into the New York City schools in the period around World War I. The so-called Gary plan modeled schools after the new mass production factories; with children being placed on "shifts" and moved in "platoons" from subject mattter to subject matter. The Gary plan was introduced into the New York City schools by a new school board appointed by a reform mayor. The account below is a description of how evaluation results entered into the political struggle between the new school board and the existing school system administration.]

The Gary plan initially had been introduced into two New York schools on a pilot basis, and the Ettinger plan into a number of other schools. Superintendent Maxwell, resentful of interference in his professional domain and suspicious of the intent of Mitchel's administration, had already expressed his feelings about the Gary plan as it was operating in Angelo Patri's school: "Well, I visited that school [PS 45, Bronx] the other day, and the only thing I saw was a lot of children digging in a lot." Despite the superintendent's views, the Gary system had been extended to twelve schools in the Bronx, and there were plans to extend it further.

The cry for more research before extending the plan was raised by a school board member. In the summer of 1915, Superintendent Maxwell ordered an evaluative study of the Gary plan as it had been implemented in the New York schools. The job was given to B. R. Buckingham, an educational psychologist in the research department of the New York City schools and a pioneer in the development of academic achievement tests.

Buckingham used his newly developed academic achievement tests to compare two Gary-organized schools, six schools organized on the Ettinger plan, and eight traditionally organized schools. The traditionally organized schools came out best on the average, while the two Gary-organized schools averaged poorest. Buckingham's report was highly critical of the eager proponents of the Gary system, who made premature statements concerning its superiority to other forms of schooling.

No sooner had the Buckingham report appeared than a veritable storm of rebuttal followed, both in the press and in professional journals. Howard W. Nudd, executive director of the Public Education Association, wrote a detailed critique of the Buckingham report, published in the *New York Globe*, the *New York Times*, *School and Society*, and the *Journal of Education*.

Nudd counterattacked on technical grounds. First, he showed that at the time Buckingham conducted his tests, the Gary plan had been in operation in one school for only four months, and in the other for less than three weeks. He asserted that much of the equipment requested by Wirt had not been provided, and that the work of the Gary schools had been seriously disturbed by the constant stream of visitors who characteristically descend on a program that achieves visibility. In a detailed, school-by-school comparison, Nudd showed that in one of the Gary-organized schools 90 percent of the pupils came from immigrant homes where Italian was their first tongue, while some of the comparison schools were largely populated by middle-class, native American children. Moreover, pupils in one of the Gary schools had excellent test scores. When scores from that school alone were compared with those from other schools, the Gary school was seen to stand very well, indeed. When scores were averaged with the second Gary school, the overall result put the Gary plan well behind.

Buckingham had no answer to the contention of inadequate controls, but he argued that he was dealing not with two schools, six schools, and eight schools, but with measurements on over 11,000 children, and therefore his study represented a substantial test of the Gary scheme. He justified undertaking his study early on the grounds that the Gary plan, already in operation in twelve Bronx schools, was being pushed on the New York schools and superintendent precipitously. As noted above, there was pressure from the mayor's office to extend the plan throughout the New York schools, and to make any increase in the education budget contingent on wholesale adoption of the Gary system. Buckingham concluded that Superintendent Maxwell was obligated to undertake a study of the schools to determine their success in giving instruction in the "fundamental subjects," and not in terms of any other values or goals of the Gary plan.

The president of the Board of Education found it advantageous to cite Nudd's interpretation of the Buckingham report in debate at the Board of Education meeting. Superintendent Maxwell continued to

cite the Buckingham study as evidence against the effectiveness of
the Gary plan, even a year and a half later.

SOURCE: Adapted from A. Levine and M. Levine, "The Social Context of
Evaluative Research: A Case Study," *Evaluation Quarterly* 1 (November 1977):
520-523.

perspective they should take in designing an evaluation. Is the proper
perspective that of the society as a whole, the government agency involved, the program staff, the clients, or any of the other groups listed
above? For some evaluators, especially those who aspire to provide help
and advice on fine-tuning programs, the primary audience often appears to
be the program staff. For those evaluators whose evaluations have been
mandated by a legislative body, the primary audience may appear to be the
community, state, or nation as a whole.

In Chapter 8, the different accounting perspectives for conducting
efficiency analyses were discussed. We made the point that there is no
single proper perspective, but that all perspectives are equally legitimate.
The clients' or targets' perspective cannot claim any more legitimacy than
that of the program or the government agency funding the program. The
responsibility of the evaluator is not to take one of the many perspectives
as *the* legitimate one, but to be clear from which perspectives a particular
evaluation is being undertaken and to give recognition explicitly to the
existence of other perspectives. In other words, in reporting the results of
an evaluation, an evaluator should acknowledge, for example, that the
evaluation was conducted from the viewpoint of the program administrators and that there also exist the alternative perspectives of the society as a
whole and of the client targets.

Second, the evaluator must realize that sponsors of evaluations may
"turn" on evaluators when their results contradict the policies and programs they advocate. Evaluators often anticipate negative reactions from
other stakeholder groups but are dismayed and unprepared for the responses of the sponsors of evaluations to findings that are contrary to
those expected or desired. Evaluators are in a very difficult position when
this occurs. It may leave them open, for example, to attacks by other
stakeholders, which they expected would be fended off by the evaluation
sponsors. There are legitimate grounds for concern: Sponsor recommendations are a major source of referrals for additional work in the case of
outside evaluators, and the provider of the paycheck for inside ones. An
illustration is provided in Exhibit 9-C.

Exhibit 9-C: The Consequences of Contrary Results

In the late 1950s NORC was given the commission to conduct an evaluation of the impact of federal graduate fellowship programs on recruitment to various fields in the humanities and in the social, physical, and biological sciences. The funders of the evaluation were among the most prestigious bodies in their respective fields, including the National Academy of Sciences, the Social Science Research Council, and the American Council of Learned Societies. The study findings (Davis, 1962) were that graduate stipends did little to influence the distribution of graduate students among fields.

Indeed, the major impact of graduate fellowships was to shift the burden of support for graduate study away from the employment activities of graduate students' spouses to the federal government.

Of course, the prestigious sponsors of the evaluation had hoped that the evaluation they sponsored would show that federal graduate fellowship policies affected substantially the distribution of students among fields. Such findings would have bolstered their requests to Congress for more fellowship funds. In their reactions to the findings of the report, the sponsors acted like most disappointed sponsors, and hardly as peers and colleagues (as NORC staff naively expected). They hired technical experts to go over the report in great detail to uncover possible technical errors. Severe (and perhaps unwarranted) criticisms were leveled at the research design, writing style, vocabulary used, and even the format for statistical tables.

SOURCE: Adapted from Peter H. Rossi, "Boobytraps and Pitfalls in the Evaluation of Social Action Programs." *Proceedings of the Social Statistics Section, American Statistical Association* (1966).

Third, strain is introduced because of the difficulties in establishing proper modes for communicating with different stakeholders. The vocabulary of evaluation is no more complicated and esoteric than the vocabularies of the social science fields from which it is derived, but that does not make it understandable and accessible to lay audiences. To take a concrete illustration: The concept of "random" plays an important role in impact assessment. Technically, the concept has a precise and nonpejorative meaning, as given in Chapter 5. In lay language, however, "random" often has connotations of "haphazard," "careless," "aimless," "casual," and so on, all of which have pejorative connotations. To advocate the "random" allocation of targets to experimental and control groups means something quite precise and delimited to evaluation researchers, but may connote something quite different to lay audiences. Evaluators use the term "random" at their peril if they do not take care to qualify and specify its meaning at the same time.

It may be too much to expect of an evaluator that he or she should master the subtleties of communication with widely diverse audiences in discussing evaluations and outcomes. Yet, the problem of communication remains an important obstacle to the full acceptance of evaluation, and evaluators are well advised to make provision for careful assessment of the communicability of their findings, a topic we will discuss further below.

There are two additional strains in doing evaluations, compared with conventional social research, that are consequences of the multiple stakeholders and the fact that the evaluator is engaged in a political process. One is the difference between political time and evaluation time. The other is the contrast between policy significance and statistical significance.

Political Time and Evaluation Time

Evaluations, especially of impact, take time. As a rule, the tighter and more elegant the study design, the longer the evaluation takes. Large-scale social experiments that gauge the effects of major innovative programs may require four to eight years to complete and document. The political and program worlds move at a much faster pace. Policymakers and project sponsors often want to know in a matter of weeks or months whether or not a program is achieving its goals.

Evaluators often encounter pressure to complete their assessments more quickly than the best methods permit, as well as to release preliminary results before they are completely firm. At times, evaluators are asked for their "impressions" of effectiveness, even though they have stressed that such impressions are liable to be useless in the absence of firm results.

Also, the planning and procurement procedures within organizations that sponsor evaluations make it difficult to undertake timely studies. In most cases, procedures must be approved at several levels and by a number of key stakeholders. As outlined in Exhibit 9-D, the typical evaluation done under contract to the U.S. Department of Education requires three years from conception to completion. While both governmental and private-sector sponsors have tried to develop mechanisms to speed up the planning and procurement processes, the workings of their bureaucracies, legal requirements related to contracting, and the need to establish agreement on the evaluation questions and design hinder these efforts.

Exhibit 9-D: Typical Time Required for Undertaking a U.S. Department of Education Evaluation Contract

Total anticipated
working time: 12 months
Contract duration: 18 months
Total elapsed time: 3 years

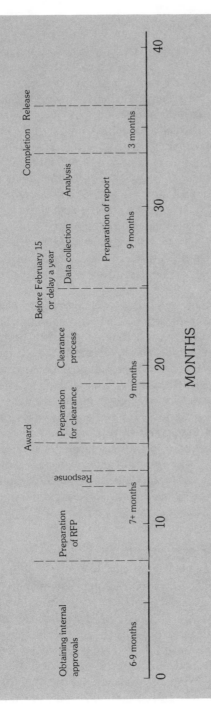

MONTHS

SOURCE: Reproduced from *Program Evaluation in Education*, by Senta A. Raizen and Peter H. Rossi, National Academy Press, Washington, DC, 1981.

It is not clear what can be done to reduce the pressures that arise from the different time schedules of evaluation and decision-making. It is self-evident that a long-term study should not be undertaken if the information is needed before the evaluation can be completed. It may be better in such circumstances to rely on expert opinion or another of the more judgmental evaluation methods discussed in Chapter 7. It would clearly be better to have some information—as sound in technical quality as possible, given time constraints—than to have no information at all.

A more strategic approach is to confine technically complex evaluations to pilot or prototype projects for interventions that are not likely to be implemented on a large scale in the near future. Thus, randomized controlled experiments may be most appropriate to evaluate the worth of new programs (initially implemented on a small scale) before such programs appear on the agendas of decision-making bodies. Extensive cross-sectional analyses may be applied to programs that have a history of steady support.

A final strategy for evaluators is to anticipate the direction of programs and policy activities, rather than be forced, within tight time constraints, to respond to the demands of other parties. One proposal that has attracted some attention is to establish independent evaluation institutes dedicated to examining, on a pilot or prototype basis, interventions that might one day be in demand. Such national evaluation centers could assess the worth of alternative social programs addressed to policy issues foreseen to be important a decade or more ahead. While this proposal has some attractive features, especially to professional evaluators, it is not at all clear that it is possible to forecast accurately what the next decade's social issues will be. As things stand now, we believe that the tension caused by the disparities between political and research time will continue to be a problem in the employment of evaluation as a useful tool for policymakers and project managers.

The Issue of
Policy Significance

Although an evaluation outcome may produce results that all would agree are statistically significant and generalizable, the net outcome may still not be of any policy significance (Sechrest and Yeaton, 1982). That is, there are situations in which the findings may pass most of the tests we discussed in Chapter 5 but are too small to be relevant to policy, planning, and managerial action. For example, the Sesame Street evaluation discussed in Chapter 6 found that children viewing the program were statistically different from nonviewers in their knowledge of the alphabet. Substantively, the difference amounted to only several letters, and hence may have had little policy significance (Cook et al., 1975).

The issue of what the magnitude of a difference must be to have policy significance varies from field to field. In education, an important gain is sometimes defined as one with a magnitude of at least one-half a standard deviation. One formal way of providing data for such judgments is to conduct cost-benefit and cost-effectiveness analyses, as discussed in Chapter 8. Doing so allows judgments to be made on the basis of whether resources are effectively expended compared with the costs and benefits of alternative projects.

Another, more diffuse, criterion is to make judgments of the social worth of the change in outcome. Small magnitudes of change have policy significance when social worth is high, but larger magnitudes are necessary when social worth is low. Thus, a program of nutritional education that reduces clinically observable cases of malnutrition in children by 2 percent may be policy significant; a consumer education project that reduces the purchase of unnecessary small household appliances by 10 percent may not be policy significant.

The availability of alternative interventions must also be taken into account. For example, in a country with high saturation of television sets and a formal educational system that requires extensive resources and a long period to modify, small gains from educational television may be policy significant; the same magnitude of change would not be viewed positively if rapid changes at low cost were possible in the formal educational system.

Policy significance emerges as an issue in another guise, also. Too often a prospective program may be tested without sufficient understanding of how the policy issues are seen by those decision makers who will have to approve the enactment of the program into statutes. Hence, while the evaluation of the program in question may be flawless, its findings may prove irrelevant. In the New Jersey-Pennsylvania Income Maintenance Experiment, the experiment designers posed as their central issue the following question: How large is the work disincentive effect of an income maintenance plan? But, by the time the experiment was completed and congressional committees were considering various income maintenance plans, the key issue was not the work disincentive effect. Rather, members of Congress were more concerned with how many different forms of welfare could be consolidated into one comprehensive package without ignoring important needs of the poor and without creating many inequities (Rossi and Lyall, 1974).

Since a major purpose of impact assessments, and of evaluative activities generally, is to help decision makers form and adopt public policies, the research must be sensitive to the various policy issues involved. The goals of a project must resemble those articulated by policymakers in deliberations on the issues of concern. A carefully designed randomized experiment showing that a reduction in certain regressive taxes would lead to an improvement in worker productivity may be irrelevant if decision makers are more concerned with motivating entrepreneurs and attracting potential investments.

Responsible impact assessment design necessarily involves, if at all possible, some contact with relevant decision makers to ascertain their interests in the project being tested. For an innovative project that is not currently being discussed by decision makers but is being tested because it may become the subject of future discussion, the evaluators and sponsors of the test of impact effectiveness must rely on informed guesses about what policy issues might arise. For other projects, the processes of obtaining decision maker opinions are quite straightforward. One may consult the proceedings of deliberative bodies (e.g., government committee hearings or legislative debates), interview decision makers' staffs, or consult decision makers directly. Indeed, it is just this issue that has led to the development of evaluability assessments, discussed in Chapter 2.

Although we have geared this discussion toward impact evaluations, the same issues pervade delivery system (process and accountability) evaluations. For example, in order to fine-tune a program's target eligibility requirements to increase coverage and reduce bias, one must examine statistical significance and magnitudes of difference, estimating what results are due to the changed criteria for target coverage, to bias, or to chance.

Interpreting evaluation results, then, requires considerations that go beyond methodology. The fact that evaluations are conducted according to the canons of social research may make them superior to other modes of judging social programs, but evaluations provide only superfluous information unless they are designed to draw on the values and preferences involved in policymaking, program planning, and management. Their weaknesses, in this regard, tend to center on how research questions are stated and how findings are interpreted (Datta, 1980). To maximize the utility of evaluation findings, evaluators must be sensitive to two levels of policy considerations.

First, programs that address problems perceived as critical require better (that is, more rigorous) assessments than interventions related to trivial concerns. Technical decisions, such as setting levels of statistical significance and magnitude, should be informed by the nature of policy and program considerations. Such decisions are always a matter of judgment and sensitivity. Even when formal efficiency analyses (see Chapter 8) are undertaken, the issue remains. For example, the decision to use an individual, program, or community accounting perspective is determined by policy and sponsorship considerations.

Second, evaluation findings must be assessed according to their generalizability, whether the findings are policy and program significant, and whether the program clearly fits need (as expressed by the many factors involved in the policymaking process).

The Missing Engineering Tradition

In the long term, evaluators—indeed, all applied researchers—and their stakeholders must develop an "engineering tradition," something currently missing from most of the social sciences. Engineers are distinguished from their "pure science" counterparts by their concern with working out the details of how scientific knowledge can be used in addressing "real-life" problems. It is one thing to know that gases expand when heated and that each gas has its own expansion coefficient; it is another to be able to use that principle in the mass production of economical, high-quality gas turbine engines.

Similar engineering problems exist with respect to social science findings. For example, one of the important social science principles upon which Fairweather's (1974) Lodge program for mental patients is built is that social supports in the form of peer groups can be very beneficial to individuals who are going through stressful periods of transition. This idea has been around in the social sciences for a long time. The engineering problem is how to construct such groups *de novo*. Fairweather and his colleagues spent years developing techniques for organizing mental hospital wards into supportive peer groups and then devising ways of training others to employ those techniques successfully.

Developing a good prototype model of a program, however, often is not sufficient to solve the engineering problem. This point was forcefully illustrated by what at first appeared to be a promising experiment supported by the U.S. Department of Education (Williams and Elmore, 1976). Since there were so many different—and sometimes contradictory—teaching styles and procedures being advocated in the educational community, the department thought it would be a fine idea to run a "competition" among them to find which would be most effective. Six models would be chosen by a panel of experts as the most promising of the contenders and would then be installed in a set of schools and operated by the model builders, with appropriate control schools and classes to provide the baseline measures of learning that would enable the evaluators to decide on the best models.

The advocates of different teaching models competed, six were chosen, and volunteer school systems came forward to try each of the models. The embarrassing finding was that none of the models was beyond the prototype stage. "Production" models, including necessary instructions, procedures for training the teachers, descriptions of the equipment needed, and so on, had simply never been developed.

The first year of the Planned Variation Experiment was spent in developing more or less workable models of each of the learning methods, but some of the contractees never managed to get their production models in good enough shape that the schools were willing to adopt them. The end result was simply several years of fruitless tinkering and no field test of the different methods.

Basic Science Models and Policy-Oriented Models

Social scientists often do not grasp the difference in emphasis required in developing a causal model to explain a phenomenon and formulating a model in order to affect the phenomenon purposefully. For example, much of the criminal behavior of young men is explainable by the extent of such behavior among males in their social network—fathers, brothers, other male relatives, friends, neighbors, schoolmates, and so on. This is a fascinating finding that affords many insights into the areal and ethnic distributions of crime rates. However, it is not a useful finding in terms of affecting the crime rate, because it is difficult to develop a public policy that would redistribute the social networks of young men. Short of yanking young males out of their settings and putting them into other environments, it is not at all clear than anything can be done to affect the social networks of young males. Removing them from their environments is not a viable policy, at least until this country changes drastically, and such a change would not necessarily be for the better.

In contrast, a weaker determinant of crime that can be the basis for a crime-control program has to do with potential criminals' subjective probabilities of being caught for committing a crime, being convicted if caught, and going to prison if convicted. The willingness to engage in crime is sluggishly and weakly related to these subjective probabilities: The more a person believes that he or she will be caught committing a crime, the more likely he or she thinks it is that conviction will follow arrest, and the more likely he or she thinks it is that imprisonment will follow conviction, the lower the probability of criminal behavior. Thus, to some extent the incidence of criminal acts is reduced if police are effective in arresting criminals, if prosecutors are diligent in obtaining convictions, and if the courts have a harsh sentencing policy. None of the relationships described above yields correlations much above .30, yet these findings are much more salient for controlling crime than the social network explanation mentioned above. Mayors and police chiefs can implement programs that increase the proportion of criminals apprehended, prosecutors can work harder at obtaining convictions, and judges can refuse to plea bargain. Moreover, dissemination of these policy changes in ways that reach the potential offenders would, in itself, have some modest impact on the crime rate.

Sensitivity to Policy Space

Roughly defined, policy space is that set of alternative policies under consideration at any given point in time. Of consequence is the fact that policy space keeps changing in response to influentials' efforts to garner support from other influentials and from ordinary community members. This decade's policy space with respect to crime control is dominated by programs of long sentences for selected types of criminals. In contrast, during the 1970s, it focused on developing community-based treatment centers as an alternative to imprisonment, on the grounds that prisons were breeding places for crime and that criminals would be better helped in close contact with the normal, civilian world.

The volatility of policy space is illustrated in the example given earlier of the TARP experiments conducted in the late 1970s on the effectiveness of short-term financial support for reducing recidivism in recently released felons. Whatever the merits of the Georgia and Texas TARP experiments, by the time the evaluation findings were available federal policy space had changed so drastically (with the election of Ronald Reagan) that there was simply no way the policies that emerged from those experiments would be considered.

It is hoped that these observations about the organization and dynamics of conducting evaluations in the context of the social policy and program world sensitizes evaluators to the importance of "scouting" the terrain when embarking on an evaluation and warns them to remain alert to ecological changes that may occur during the evaluation process. Such efforts may be at least as important to the successful conduct of evaluation activities as the appropriateness of the technical procedures employed.

UTILIZATION OF EVALUATION RESULTS

As a starting point, the conventional three-way classification of the ways evaluations are used is helpful (Rich, 1977; Leviton and Hughes, 1979, 1981). Evaluators prize the *direct* or *instrumental* use of their evaluations. "Direct" use refers to the documented and specific use of evaluation findings by decision makers and other stakeholders. For example, evaluation data showing that patients of community health centers are hospitalized fewer times than patients treated in the ambulatory clinics of hospitals have been used by Congress and health policymakers in developing medical care programs for the poor (Freeman et al., 1982).

The second type of utilization is referred to as "conceptual" use. As Rich (1977) defines it, conceptual utilization is the use of evaluations to influence thinking about issues in a general way. An example is the current effort to control the costs of delivering health and welfare services, stimulated at least in part by evaluations of their efficacy and ratio of costs to benefits. These evaluations did not lead to the adoption of specific programs or policies, but provided evidence that current ways of delivering health care were costly and inefficient.

The third type of utilization—*persuasive* use—refers to enlisting evaluation results in efforts either to defend or to attack political positions—in other words, to support or refute the status quo. For example, one of the frequent rationales used by the Reagan administration in defending the cutting of social programs is the lack of clear findings of positive impacts in the evaluations of major social programs. Persuasive use is similar to speechwriters inserting quotes into political speeches whether they are applicable or not. The persuasive use of evaluations is, for the most part, out of the hands of either program evaluators or sponsors and will not concern us further in this chapter.

Do Evaluations Have Direct Utility?

Disappointment about the limited utilization of evaluations is largely due to the seemingly abundant evidence that they have had very limited amounts of instrumental use. It is clear that many evaluations initiated for their direct utility fell short of that mark. However, it is only in the past several years that the extent of direct use has been studied systematically at all. These recent efforts challenge the previously held belief that evaluations do not have direct utility.

One careful study (Leviton and Boruch, 1983), for example, examined the direct use of evaluations sponsored by the U.S. Department of Education. The authors found numerous instances in which evaluation results brought about important program changes, and even more incidents in which they were influential in decisions made, although they were not the sole input in the decision-making process.

An interesting case study (Brown, 1982) documents the direct impact of a Congressional Budget Office evaluation on the House and Senate votes on legislation requiring special equipment on buses in order to facilitate the use of public transportation by the handicapped. Unfortunately, there are insufficient case studies such as Brown's report on requirements for bus transportation. In general, there are only fragmented findings on the direct use of evaluations. However, it would appear that there is a fair degree of instrumental utilization, contrary to the views expressed when the earlier editions of this book appeared. Unfortunately, a pessimistic view of the amount of direct utilization is still widely held among both evaluators and potential consumers of evaluations.

In instances where evaluations fail to be used instrumentally, evaluators may feel as though their labors have been in vain. In many cases, as we have discussed, one can expect only that the results of an evaluation will be but *one* of the elements in decision-making. This is clearly revealed in the 1915 controversy over the evaluation of the Gary plan in New York (see Exhibit 9-B).

Subsequently, we will suggest some means of increasing the utilization of evaluations. Most of these suggestions are particularly relevant to increasing the direct use of studies. However, it is also important to value the conceptual use of evaluations appropriately.

Conceptual Use of Evaluations

No doubt every evaluator has occasional megalomaniacal dreams in which a grateful world receives with adulation the findings of his or her evaluation and puts them immediately and directly to use. Most of our megalomaniacal dreams must remain just dreams. We would argue, however, that the conceptual use of evaluations often provides important inputs into policy and program development, and should not be compared with ending the race in second place. Conceptual utilization may not be as visible to peers or sponsors as direct utilization, but it may in the end have important impacts on the community as a whole or on critical segments of it.

Under the term "conceptual use" we refer to the variety of ways in which evaluations indirectly influence policies, programs, and procedures. These range from simply sensitizing persons and groups about current and emerging social problems to influencing future program and policy development by examining the results of a series of evaluations together (see the discussion of meta-evaluations in Chapter 6).

Evaluations perform a sensitizing role by documenting the incidence, prevalence, and distinguishing features of social problems. Diagnostic evaluation activities, described in Chapter 2, have provided clearer and more precise understanding of changes occurring in the family system, critical information on the location and distribution of unemployed persons, and provide more meaningful descriptions of the social world around us in many other ways.

Impact assessments also have conceptual utility. A specific example is the current concern in medical care policy development with "notch" groups. Evaluations of programs to provide medical care to the poor have found that the very poor, eligible for public programs such as Medicaid, often are adequately provided with health services. Those just above them—thus the term "notch" group—who are not eligible for public programs tend to fall between the cracks. Because they have low income and are not program eligible, they have decidedly more difficulty in obtaining medical services. When seriously ill, they constitute a major burden on community hospitals, which cannot turn them away but can receive reimbursement from neither the patients nor the government. Concern with the near poor or "notch" group is increasing because of their exclusion from a wide range of health, mental health, and social service programs.

An interesting example of a study that has had considerable long-term impact conceptually is Coleman's report (Coleman et al., 1966) on educational opportunity. It changed conventional wisdom about the characteristics of good and bad educational settings, turning policy and program interest away from problems of fiscal support to consideration of how to improve teaching methods. The initial impetus for the Coleman study was a 1964 congressional mandate to the Office of Education to provide information on the quality of educational opportunities provided to minority students in the United States.

Conceptual use of evaluation results creeps into the policy and program worlds via many different routes, usually circuitous, that are difficult to trace. For example, Coleman's report to the Office of Education did not become a Government Printing Office best-seller. It is unlikely that more than a few hundred people actually read it cover to cover, but journalists wrote about it, essayists summarized its arguments, and major editorial writers mentioned it. Through these communication brokers, the findings became known to policymakers in the education field and to politicians at all levels of government.

In 1967, a year after his report was published by the Government Printing Office, Coleman was convinced that it had been buried in the National Archives and would never emerge again. Eventually, however, Coleman's findings—in one form or another—reached a wide and influential audience. Indeed, by the time Coleman and his associates (Caplan and Nelson, 1973) questioned Washington political figures about which social scientists had influenced them, Coleman's name was among the most prominently and consistently mentioned.

Some of the conceptual utilizations of evaluations may be described simply as consciousness raising. For example, the development of early childhood education programs was stimulated by the evaluation findings resulting from an impact assessment of *Sesame Street*. The evaluation found that while the program does have an impact on young children's educational skills, the magnitude of the effect was not as much as the program staff and sponsors had imagined it would be. Prior to the evaluation, some educators were convinced that *Sesame Street* represented the "final solution," and that they could turn their attention to other educational problems. The evaluation findings led to the conviction that early childhood education was in need of further research and development.

Another important conceptual use of evaluations is to document that some current practice or approach is definitely wrong. A striking illustration of this function of evaluation is the consistent negative findings concerning the impacts of various efforts to rehabilitate convicted felons. The net effect of these programs is effectively zero: Criminals who have participated in rehabilitation programs are as likely to return to a life of crime as those who have not (Lipton et al., 1975). Even worse, the outcomes of the evaluation researches support the so-called Iron Law of Evaluation Studies, namely, the better an evaluation study is technically, the less likely it is to show positive program effects. These negative findings have facilitated the shift in policymaker attention away from rehabilitation efforts to crime prevention.

As in the case of direct utilization, evaluators have an obligation to do their work in ways that maximize conceptual utilization. In a sense, it is more difficult to design efforts to maximize conceptual utilization than it is to design them to optimize direct use. To the extent that evaluators are hired guns and turn to new ventures after completing an evaluation, they may not be around or have the resources to follow through on promoting conceptual utilization. Sponsors of evaluations and other stakeholders who maintain a more consistent commitment to particular social policy and social problem areas have to assume some—if not the major portion— of the responsibility for maximizing the conceptual use of evaluations, and often are in a position to perform the broker function discussed above.

Variables Affecting Utilization

In studies of the use of social research in general and evaluations in particular, five conditions appear to affect utilization consistently (Leviton and Hughes, 1981):

1. relevance

2. communication between evaluators and users

3. information processing by users

4. plausibility of evaluation results

5. user involvement or advocacy

The importance of these conditions and their relative contributions to utilization have been studied carefully by Weiss and Bucuvalas (1980). They questioned 155 decision makers in the mental health field on their reactions to 50 actual research reports. Weiss and Bucuvalas found that decision makers apply both a truth test and a utility test in screening social research reports. Truth is judged on two bases: research quality and conformity to prior knowledge and expectations. "Utility" refers to feasibility potential and degree of challenge to current policy. Weiss and Bucuvalas's study provides convincing evidence of the complexity of the utilization process (see Exhibit 9-E).

Guidelines for Maximizing Utilization

Out of the research on utilization and the real-world experiences of evaluators have emerged a number of guidelines for increasing utilization. These have been summarized by Solomon and Shortell (1981) and are briefly noted here for reference:

1. Evaluators must understand the cognitive styles of decision makers. For instance, there is no point in presenting a complex piece of analysis to a politician who cannot or will not make use of such material. Thus, reports and oral presentations tailored to the specific audience may be more appropriate than, say, academic journal articles directed toward a narrow "scholarly" group.

2. Evaluation results must be timely and available when needed. Evaluation findings must therefore balance timing and accessibility of findings with thoroughness and completeness of analysis. Evaluators may have to risk criticism from some of their academic colleagues, whose standards of scholarship cannot always be met because of the need for rapid results and crisp reporting.

3. Evaluations must respect stakeholders' program commitments. Evaluations are conducted for specific sets of individuals and organizations, and their usefulness demands wide participation in the evaluation design process to ensure sensitivity to stakeholders' interests. Differences in values and outlooks between clients and evaluators should be explicated at the outset of a study and should be a determinant of whether or not a particular evaluation is undertaken by a particular evaluation team.

4. Utilization and dissemination plans should be part of the evaluation design. Evaluation findings are most likely to be used if the evaluation effort includes "educating" potential users about the strengths and limitations of

Exhibit 9-E: Truth Tests and Utility Tests

In coping with incoming floods of information, decision makers invoke three basic frames of reference. One is the relevance of the content of the study to their sphere of responsibility, another is the trustworthiness of the study, and the third is the direction that it provides. The latter two frames, which we have called truth and utility tests, are each composed of two interdependent components:

Truth test: Is the research trustworthy? Can I rely on it? Will it hold up under attack? The two specific components are:

1. Research Quality: Was the research conducted by proper scientific methods?

2. Conformity to User Expectations: Are the results compatible with my experience, knowledge, and values?

Utility test: Does the research provide direction? Does it yield guidance—either for immediate action or for considering alternative approaches to problems? The two specific components are:

1. Action Orientation: Does the research show how to make feasible changes in things that can feasibly be changed?

2. Challenge to the Status Quo: Does the research challenge current philosophy, program, or practice? Does it offer new perspectives?

Together with Relevance (that is, the match between the topic of the research and the person's job responsibilities), these four components constitute the frames of reference by which decision makers assess social science research. Research Quality and Conformity to User Expectations form a single truth test in that their effects are contingent on each other: Research Quality is less important for the usefulness of a study when results are congruent with officials' prior knowledge than when results are unexpected or counterintuitive. Action Orientation and Challenge to the Status Quo represent alternative functions that a study can serve. They constitute a utility test, since the kind of explicit and practical direction captured by the Action Orientation frame is more important for a study's usefulness when the study provides little criticism or reorientation (Challenge to the Status Quo) than it is when Challenge is high. Conversely, the criticisms of programs and the new perspectives embedded in Challenge to the Status Quo add more to usefulness when a study lacks prescriptions for implementation.

SOURCE: Adapted, with permission, from Carol H. Weiss and Michael J. Bucuvalas, "Truth Tests and Utility Tests: Decision-Makers' Frames of Reference for Social Science Research," *American Sociological Review*, Vol. 45 (April), 1980: 302-313.

the effort, the degree to which they may expect definitive results, how the information from the evaluation can be communicated effectively by decision makers to their constituencies, and what criticisms and other reactions may be anticipated.

5. Evaluations should include an assessment of utilization. Evaluators and decision makers must not only share an understanding of the purposes for which a study is undertaken, but also agree on the criteria by which its successful utilization may be judged.

It should be evident that while these guidelines are relevant to the utilization of all program evaluations, the roles of evaluation consumers differ and affect the uses to which information is put and consequently mechanisms to maximize utility. In particular, if evaluations are to influence legislation and far-reaching policies, they must be conducted and "packaged" in ways that meet the needs of potential users. From a study of congressional staff with major responsibilities for the development of educational legislation, Florio et al. (1979) compiled a useful summary of requirements, which we present in Exhibit 9-F.

Disseminating Evaluation Results

Utilization, of course, requires dissemination. "Dissemination," for our purposes, refers to the set of activities by which knowledge about evaluation findings is made available to relevant audiences. Dissemination is a definite responsibility of evaluation researchers.

Our discussion of dissemination brings us back to the need to identify relevant stakeholders. Obviously, the results must be communicated in ways that make them intelligible to the various stakeholder groups. Particularly, external evaluation groups generally provide sponsors with "technical reports" that include detailed and complete (not to mention honest) descriptions of the evaluation's design, data collection methods, analysis procedures, results, suggestions for further research, and rec-ommendations regarding the program (if a monitoring or impact evalua-

Exhibit 9-F: Educational Inquiry: The Unmet Potential

The interviewees mentioned over 90 steps that could be taken to improve the use of educational studies in the formation of legislative policy. The most common themes, which reflect the current barriers to such use, are the ways in which research and assessment reports are presented and the failure to meet the needs demanded by the policy cycles in Congress.

The table summarizes the responses to the question of how to improve the use of available information.

Staffers struck a common theme of work and information overload problems associated with the job. They rarely have time to "evaluate the evaluations," let alone read through the "voluminous reports" that come across their desks. This was at the root of the repeated call for executive summaries in the front matter of reports, which would allow them to judge the relevance of the contents and determine if further reading for substance was necessary. Although 16 (61%) of the staffers complained of an information overload problem, 19 (73%) also indicated that they were often forced to generate their own data relevant to political and policy questions. As one staffer put it, "We have no overload of useful and understandable information."

The timing of the study reports and their relevance to questions and problems before the Congress were major barriers repeatedly mentioned by congressional staff. Mary Moore, senior policy analyst for the Assistant Secretary of Education (HEW) and one of the sources of policy-relevant information, compares the policy process to a "moving train." She suggests that information providers have the obligation to know the policy cycle and meet it on its own terms.

The credibility problem is also one that plagues social inquiry. Bertram Carp, Deputy Director of the White House Domestic Policy staff and former aide to Vice-President Mondale when he was a senator, said that "all social science suffers from the perception that it is unreliable and not policy-relevant." His comments were reflected by several of the staffers interviewed—for example, "research rarely provides definitive conclusions," or "for every finding, others negate it," or "educational research can rarely be replicated and there are few standards that can be applied to assess the research products."

One went so far as to call project evaluations "lies," then reconsidered and called them "embellishments."

Again, it must be pointed out that the distinctions among different types of inquiry—research, evaluation, data collection, and so on—are rarely made by the recipients of knowledge and information. If project evaluations are viewed as fabrications, it reflects negatively on the entire educational inquiry community.

Even when policy-relevant research is presented in time to meet the "moving train," staffers complain of having "too much unassimilable information," or that "studies are poorly packaged," contain too much technical jargon, and are too "self-serving." Several said that researchers write for other researchers and rarely, except in congressionally mandated studies, tailor their language to the decision-making audiences in the legislative process. A theme underlying many of these observations is that the research and evaluation community does have the needed knowledge and information available. This indicates that there is less than a clear understanding of the limitations on the contributions which can be made by the educational inquiry community.

Improving the Use of Educational Studies

Format & Presentation (45)
Relevance to Congressional Needs (25)

Use executive summary (13)

Clarify language/eliminate jargon (7)

Use charts and visual displays (6)

Synthesize available findings (4)

Present data in concise fashion (4)

Use examples of results (4)

Make concrete recommendations (3)

Provide references to more information (3)

Index data (1)

Meet timing of legislative cycle and process (9)

Have policy-relevant information (9)

Demonstrate a greater understanding of the political arena in Congress (4)

Make appropriate information available throughout the legislative process (3)

Credibility

Develop direct relationships with staff early and throughout the conduct of a study (13)

Have sources with a strong reputation (5)

Have more accurate and unbiased information (3)

Do not have results that are overly cautious (1)

Note: Times mentioned are in parentheses.

SOURCE: Adapted, with permission, from David H. Florio, Michael M. Behrmann, and Diane L. Goltz, "What Do Policy Makers Think of Evaluational Research & Evaluation? Or Do They?" *Educational Evaluation and Policy Analysis*, Vol. 1, January 1979, pp. 61-87. Copyright 1979, American Educational Research Association, Washington, DC.

tion), as well as a discussion of the data and analysis limitations. Most technical reports are read only by peers, and rarely by the stakeholders who count. Many of these stakeholders simply are not accustomed to reading voluminous documents, do not have the time to do so, and may not be able to understand them in any case.

Therefore, every evaluator must learn to be a secondary disseminator, catering to the particular stakeholders relevant to his or her evaluation activities. "Secondary dissemination" refers to the communication of research results and any recommendations they yield in ways that meet the needs of stakeholders (as opposed to "primary" dissemination, which in most cases is the technical report). Secondary dissemination takes many forms: abbreviated versions of technical reports (often called "executive summaries"), slick "special reports" that are issued regularly by evaluation groups of the evaluation responses, memos, oral presentations complete with slides and graphic displays, and sometimes even movies or videotapes. The objective of secondary dissemination is simple—to provide results in ways that can be comprehended by the legendary "intelligent layperson," a figure as elusive as the equally legendary Bigfoot (but for whose existence better evidence abounds).

Proper preparation of secondary dissemination documents is an art form unknown to most in the evaluation field, for few opportunities for learning are available during academic training. The "trick" in secondary communication is to find the appropriate style for the presentation of research findings using language and form understandable to the "intelligent layperson." The *language* should be on a reasonable vocabulary level that is as free as possible from technical terms of the esoteric sort and the *form* of secondary dissemination documents should be succinct—that is, short enough that they are not formidable.

Probably the best advice that can be given is that if the evaluator does not have the talents to disseminate his or her findings in ways that maximize utilization—and few of us do—an investment in experts is justified. After all, as we have stressed, evaluations are undertaken as purposeful activities; they are useless unless used.

EPILOGUE

There are many reasons to expect continued support of evaluation activities. First, decision makers, planners, project staffs, and target participants are increasingly skeptical of common sense and conventional wisdom as sufficient bases upon which to design social programs that will achieve their intended goals. Decades of attempts to solve the problems represented by explosive population growth, the maldistribution of resources within and between societies, popular discontent, crime, educational deficiencies among adults and children, drug and alcohol abuse, and weaknesses in traditional institutions such as the family have led to a realization that these are obstinate and difficult issues to face. This skepticism has led policymakers and decision makers to seek ways of learning more quickly and efficiently from their mistakes and of capitalizing more rapidly on effective measures.

A second major reason for the growth of evaluation research has been the development of knowledge and technical procedures in the social sciences. The refinement of sample survey procedures has provided an important information-gathering method. When coupled with more traditional experimental methods in the form of field experiments, these procedures become a powerful means of testing social programs. Advances in measurement, statistical theory, and substantive knowledge in the social sciences have added to the ability of social scientists to take on the special tasks of evaluation research.

Finally, regardless of the shifts that occur in the political climate, significant numbers of persons almost everywhere have come to insist that communal and personal problems are not fixed features of the human condition, but subject to change and amelioration through the reconstruction of social institutions. We believe more than our ancestors did that community life can be improved, and that the lot of all persons can be enhanced by the betterment of the disadvantaged and deprived.

At the same time, almost worldwide, we are confronted with severely limited resources for welfare, health, and other social programs. It is tempting to hope that we can simply wish away unemployment, crime, homelessness—all the social ills with which we are familiar—and to believe that "moral reconstruction" will diminish the need for effective and efficient social programs. But it is catastrophically naive to think that doing so will solve our problems.

The prognosis is troublesome, in the short term at least, when we contemplate the variety and number of concerns that require urgent action in contrast to the resources being committed to their amelioration and control. It is clear that sensible, orderly procedures are required if we are to choose which problems to confront first, and to decide which programs to implement in order to deal with them. Our position is clear: Systematic evaluations are invaluable to current and future efforts to improve the lot of humankind.

REFERENCES

Abt Associates
    1977   An Overview of the Experimental Housing Allowance Program Demand Experiments. Cambridge, MA: Abt Associates.

Abt, C. C.
    1978   "The Public Good, the Private Good, and the Government Good in the Evaluation of Social Programs: How Inept Government Requirements Increase Costs and Reduce Effectiveness." Evaluation Quarterly 2 (November): 620-630.

Adams, B. and B. Sherman
    1978   "Sunset Implementation: A Positive Partnership to Make Government Work." Public Administration Review 36 (January/February): 78-81.

Aday, L. A., R. Andersen, et al.
    1984   "Hospital-Sponsored Primary Care, II: Impact on Patient Access." American Journal of Public Health 74 (August): 792-798.

Aiken, L. H., R. J. Blendon, D. E. Rogers, and H. E. Freeman
    1980   "Evaluating a Private Foundation's Health Program." Evaluation and Program Planning 3 (April): 119-129.

Augustin, M. S., E. Stevens, and D. Hicks
    1973   "An Evaluation of the Effectiveness of a Children and Youth Project." Health Services Report 88 (December): 942-946.

Barnouw, B. S. and G. G. Cain
    1977   "A Reanalysis of the Effect of Head Start on Cognitive Development: Methodology and Empirical Findings." Journal of Human Resources 12 (Spring): 177-197.

Barnouw, B. S., G. G. Cain, and A. Goldberger
    1980   "Issues in the Analysis of Selectivity Bias," in E. W. Stromsdorfer and G. Farkas (eds.) Evaluation Studies Review Annual, Volume 5. Beverly Hills, CA: Sage Publications.

Basilevsky, A. and D. Hum
    1984   Experimental Social Programs and Analytic Methods: An Evaluation of the U.S. Income Maintenance Projects. New York: Academic.

Bell, R., S. P. Klein, H. M. Bohannan, et al.
    1984   Treatment Effects in the National Preventive Dentistry Demonstration Program. Santa Monica, CA: Rand Corporation.

Bennett, C. A. and A. A. Lumsdaine
    1975   Evaluation and Experiment. New York: Academic.

Berk, R. A.
    1983   "An Introduction to Sample Selection Bias in Sociological Data." American Sociological Review 48: 386-398.

Berk, R. A., T. Cooley, C. J. LaCivita, and K. Sredl
    1981   Saving Water: Lessons in Conservation from the Great California Drought, 1976-1977. Cambridge, MA: Abt Books.

Berk, R. A. and D. Rauma
    1983   "Capitalizing on Non-Random Assignment to Treatment: A Regression Continuity Analysis of a Crime Control Program." Journal of the American Statistical Association 78 (March): 21-28.

Berk, R. A. and S. C. Ray
    1982   "Selection Biases in Sociological Data." Social Science Research 11: 3-40.

Berk, R. A. and P. H. Rossi
    1976   "Doing Good or Worse: Evaluation Research Politically Re-Examined." Social Problems 23 (February): 337-349.

Bernstein, I. N. and H. E. Freeman
    1975   Academic and Entrepreneurial Research. New York: Russell Sage.

Blalock, H. M., Jr.
    1979   Social Statistics (2nd ed., rev.). New York: McGraw-Hill.

Blalock, H. M., Jr., and A. Blalock (eds.)
    1968   Methodology in Social Research. New York: McGraw-Hill.

Bogart, L. (ed.)
  1969 Social Research and the Desegregation of the United States Army. Chicago: Markham.
Bohrnstedt, G. W.
  1970 "Reliability and Validity Assessment in Attitude Measurement," pp. 80-99 in G. F. Summers (ed.) Attitude Measurement. Skokie, IL: Rand McNally.
  1982 "Measurement," in P. H. Rossi et al. (eds.) Handbook of Survey Research. New York: Academic.
Boruch, R. F.
  1975 "On Common Contentions About Randomized Field Experiments," pp. 107-142 in R. F. Boruch and H. W. Riecken (eds.) Experimental Testing of Public Policy: The Proceedings of the 1974 Social Science Research Council Conference on Social Experiments. Boulder, CO: Westview.
Boruch, R. F., A. J. McSweeney, and E. J. Soderstrom
  1978 "Randomized Field Experiments for Program Planning, Development, and Evaluation: An Illustrative Bibliography." Evaluation Quarterly 2 (November): 655-695.
Bozzo, R. M., E. L. Kane, and S. Mittenthal
  1977 Evaluation of the State of Delaware's Human Service Delivery System. Washington, DC: National Institute for Advanced Studies.
Bradburn, N. and S. Sudman
  1982 Asking Questions: A Practical Guide to Questionnaire Design. San Francisco: Jossey-Bass.
Bremner, R.
  1956 From the Depths: The Discovery of Poverty in America. New York: New York University Press.
Brewster, M. A., I. Crespi, R. Kaluzny, J. Ohls, and C. Thomas
  1980 "Homeowner Warranties: A Study of the Need and Demand for Protection Against Unanticipated Repair Expenses." Journal of the American Real Estate and Urban Economics Association 8 (2): 207-215.
Bridges, W. and J. Oppenheim
  1977 "Racial Discrimination in Chicago's Storefront Banks." Evaluation Quarterly 1 (February): 159-171.
Bryant, E. and K. Rupp
  1984 Summary of Net Impact Results. Rockville, MD: Westat.
Bulmer, M.
  1982 The Uses of Social Research. London: George Allen & Unwin.
Burstein, L., H. Freeman, and P. H. Rossi (eds.)
  1985 Collecting Evaluation Data: Problems and Solutions. Beverly Hills, CA: Sage Publications.
Cadman, D., L. W. Chambers, et al.
  1984 "The Usefulness of the Denver Developmental Screening Test to Predict Kindergarten Problems in a General Community Population." American Journal of Public Health 75 (October): 1093-1097.
Cain, G. G.
  1975 "Regression and Selection Models to Improve Nonexperimental Comparisons," pp. 297-317 in C. A. Bennett and A. A. Lumsdaine (eds.) Evaluation and Experiment. New York: Academic.
Campbell, D. T.
  1969 "Reforms as Experiments." American Psychologist 24 (April): 409-429.
Campbell, D. T. and R. F. Boruch
  1975 "Making the Case for Randomized Assignment to Treatments by Considering the Alternatives: Six Ways in Which Quasi-Experimental Evaluations in Compensatory Education Tend to Underestimate Effects," pp. 195-296 in C. A. Bennett and A. A. Lumsdaine (eds.) Evaluation and Experiment. New York: Academic.

Campbell, D. T. and A. Erlebacher
  1970 "How Regression Artifacts in Quasi-Experimental Evaluations Can Mistakenly Make Compensatory Education Look Harmful," pp. 185-210 in J. Helmuth (ed.) The Disadvantaged Child, Volume 3: Education: A National Debate. New York: Brunner/Mazel.
Campbell, D. T. and J. C. Stanley
  1966 Experimental and Quasi-Experimental Designs for Research. Skokie, IL: Rand McNally.
Caplan, N. and S. D. Nelson
  1973 "On Being Useful: The Nature and Consequences of Psychological Research on Social Problems." American Psychologist 28 (March): 199-211.
Carlson, D. B. and J. D. Heinberg
  1977 How Housing Allowances Work. Washington, DC: Urban Institute.
Carnoy, M.
  1975 "The Economic Costs and Returns to Educational Television." Economic Development and Cultural Change 23 (January): 207-248.
Caro, F. G. (ed.)
  1971 Readings in Evaluation Research. New York: Russell Sage.
Carter, R.
  1983 The Accountable Agency. Beverly Hills, CA: Sage Publications.
Cernea, M. and B. J. Tepping
  1977 A System for Monitoring and Evaluating Agricultural Extension Projects. Washington, DC: World Bank.
Chelimsky, E.
  1978 "Differing Perspectives of Evaluation," pp. 19-38 in C. C. Rentz and R. R. Rentz (eds.) Evaluating Federally Sponsored Programs: New Directions for Program Evaluation 2 (Summer). San Francisco: Jossey-Bass.
  1983 "Program Evaluation and Appropriate Governmental Change." Annals of the American Academy of Political and Social Science 466 (March): 103-118.
  1985 "Program Evaluation and the Use of Extant Data," in L. Burstein et al. (eds.) Collecting Evaluation Data: Problems and Solutions. Beverly Hills, CA: Sage Publications.
Chen, H-t. and P. H. Rossi
  1980 "The Multi-Goal, Theory-Driven Approach to Evaluation: A Model Linking Basic and Applied Social Science." Social Forces 59 (September): 106-122.
Cicirelli, V. G. et al.
  1969 The Impact of Head Start. Athens, OH: Westinghouse Learning Corporation and Ohio University.
Cohen, J.
  1977 Statistical Power Analysis for the Behavioral Sciences (rev. ed.). New York: Academic.
Coleman, J. S., T. Hoffer, and S. Kilgore
  1981 Public and Private Schools: High School and Beyond. Chicago: National Opinion Research Center.
Coleman, J. S. et al.
  1966 Equality of Educational Opportunity. Washington, DC: Government Printing Office.
Conlisk, J.
  1977 "A Further Look at the Hansen-Weisbrod-Pechman Debate." Journal of Human Resources 12 (Spring): 147-163.
Conner, R. F.
  1977 "Selecting a Control Group: An Analysis of the Randomization Process in Twelve Social Reform Programs." Evaluation Quarterly 1 (May): 195-244.
Cook, T. D., H. Appleton, R. F. Conner, A. Shaffer, G. Tamkin, and S. J. Weber
  1975 "Sesame Street" Revisited. New York: Russell Sage.

Cook, T. D. and D. T. Campbell
  1976 "The Design and Conduct of Quasi-Experiments and True Experiments in Field Settings," pp. 223-326 in M. D. Dunnette (ed.) Handbook of Industrial and Organizational Research. Skokie, IL: Rand McNally.
  1979 Quasi-Experimentation Design and Analysis Issues for Field Settings. Skokie, IL: Rand McNally.
Cook, T. D., J. Levinson-Rose, and W. E. Pollard
  1980 "The Misutilization of Evaluation Research: Some Pitfalls of Definition." Knowledge: Creation, Diffusion, Utilization 1 (June): 477-498.
Cook, T. D. and C. S. Reichardt
  1976 "Guidelines—Statistical Analysis of Nonequivalent Control Group Designs: A Guide to Some Current Literature." Evaluation 3 (May): 136-138.
Cook, T. D. and C. S. Reichardt (eds.)
  1979 Qualitative and Quantitative Methods in Evaluation Research. Beverly Hills, CA: Sage Publications.
Cooley, W. W. and G. Leinhardt
  1980 "The Instructional Dimensions Study." Educational Evaluation and Policy Analysis 2 (January): 7-25.
Cooper, A. M. and M. B. Sobell
  1979 "Does Alcohol Education Prevent Alcohol Problems? Need for Evaluation." Journal of Alcohol and Drug Education 25 (January): 54-63.
Cox, G. B.
  1977 "Managerial Style: Implications for the Utilization of Program Evaluation Information." Evaluation Quarterly 1 (August): 499-508.
  1980 "Involuntary Patient Flow: A Computer Simulation of a Psychiatric Ward." Evaluation Review 4 (October): 571-584.
Cronbach, L. J.
  1982 Designing Evaluations of Educational and Social Programs. San Francisco: Jossey-Bass.
Cronbach, L. J. and Associates
  1980 Toward Reform of Program Evaluation. San Francisco: Jossey-Bass.
Crone, C. D.
  1977 "Evaluation: Autopsy or Checkup?" World Education Reports 15 (October): 3-13.
Cutright, P. and F. S. Jaffe
  1977 Impact of Family Planning Programs on Fertility: The U.S. Experience. New York: Praeger.
Datta, L.
  1977 "Does It Work When It Has Been Tried? And Half Full or Half Empty?" pp. 301-319 in M. Guttentag and S. Saar (eds.) Evaluation Studies Review Annual, Volume 2. Beverly Hills, CA: Sage Publications.
  1980 "Interpreting Data: A Case Study from the Career Intern Program Evaluation." Evaluation Review 4 (August): 481-506.
Davis, J. A.
  1962 Stipends and Spouses: The Finances of American Arts and Sciences Graduate Students. Chicago: University of Chicago Press.
Davis, M. W.
  1984 "Anatomy of Decision Support." Datamation 30 (June 15): 201-208.
Deaux, E. and J. W. Callaghan
  1984 "Estimating Statewide Health-Risk Behavior: A Comparison of Telephone and Key Informant Survey Approaches." Evaluation Review 8 (August): 467-492.
Deutsch, S. J.
  1979 "Lies, Damn Lies and Statistics: A Rejoinder to the Comment by Hay and McCleary." Evaluation Quarterly 3 (May): 315-328.
Deutsch, S. J. and F. B. Alt
  1977 "The Effect of Massachusetts' Gun Control Law on Gun-Related Crimes in the City of Boston." Evaluation Quarterly 1 (November): 543-567.

Diaz-Guerrero, R., I. Reyes-Lagunes, D. B. Witzke, and W. H. Holtzman
 1976 "Plaza Sesamo in Mexico: An Evaluation." Journal of Communication 26 (Spring): 145-154.
Edwards, W., M. Guttentag, and K. Snapper
 1975 "A Decision-Theoretic Approach to Evaluation Research," pp. 139-182 in E. L. Struening and M. Guttentag (eds.) Handbook of Evaluation Research, Volume 1. Beverly Hills, CA: Sage Publications.
Elliott, D. C. et al.
 1976 Research Handbook for Community Planning and Feedback Instruments, Volume 1 (rev.). Boulder, CO: Behavioral Research Institute.
Fairweather, G. W. and L. G. Tornatzky
 1977 Experimental Methods for Social Policy Research. Elmsford, NY: Pergamon.
Feaster, J. G. and G. B. Perkins
 1973 Families in the Expanded Food and Nutrition Education Program: Comparison of Food Stamp and Food Distribution Program Participants and Nonparticipants. Washington, DC: U.S. Department of Agriculture.
Federal Statistical System
 1976 Social Indicators 1976. Washington, DC: U.S. Department of Commerce.
Festinger, L.
 1964 "Behavioral Support for Opinion Changes." Public Opinion Quarterly 28 (Fall): 404-417.
Fink, A., J. Kosecoff, et al.
 1984 "Consensus Methods: Characteristics and Guidelines for Use." American Journal of Public Health 74 (September): 979-983.
Fisher, R. A.
 1935 The Design of Experiments (1st ed.). London: Oliver & Boyd.
Florio, D. H., M. M. Behrmann, and D. L. Goltz
 1979 "What Do Policy Makers Think of Evaluational Research and Evaluation? Or Do They?" Educational Evaluation and Policy Analysis 1 (January): 61-87.
Fraker, T. and R. Maynard
 1984 The Use of Comparison Group Designs in Evaluations of Employment Related Programs. Princeton, NJ: Mathematica Policy Research.
Franke, R. H. and J. D. Kaul
 1978 "The Hawthorne Experiments: First Statistical Interpretation." American Sociological Review 43 (October): 623-642.
Franklin, J. L. and J. H. Thrasher
 1976 An Introduction to Program Evaluation. New York: John Wiley.
Freeman, H. E.
 1977 "The Present Status of Evaluation Research," pp. 17-51 in M. Guttentag and S. Saar (eds.) Evaluation Studies Review Annual, Volume 2. Beverly Hills, CA: Sage Publications.
 1983 "A Federal Evaluation Agenda for the 1980s: Some Speculations and Suggestions." Educational Evaluation and Policy Analysis 5 (Summer): 185-194.
Freeman, H. E., K. J. Kiecolt, and H. M. Allen III
 1982 "Community Health Centers: An Initiative of Enduring Utility." Milbank Memorial Fund Quarterly 60 (Spring): 245-267.
Freeman, H. E., R. E. Klein, J. Kagan, and C. Yarbrough
 1977 "Relations Between Nutrition and Cognition in Rural Guatemala." American Journal of Public Health 67 (March): 223-239.
Freeman, H. and P. H. Rossi
 1984 "Furthering the Applied Side of Sociology." American Sociological Review 49 (August): 571-580.
Freeman, H. E., P. H. Rossi, and S. R. Wright
 1980 Doing Evaluations. Paris: Organisation for Economic Cooperation and Development.
Freeman, H. E. and C. C. Sherwood
 1970 Social Research and Social Policy. Englewood Cliffs, NJ: Prentice-Hall.

Freeman, H. E. and M. A. Solomon
  1979 "The Next Decade in Evaluation Research." Evaluation and Program Planning 2 (March): 255-262.
Gall, J. E., Jr., and D. D. Norwood
  1977 Demonstration and Evaluation of a Total Hospital Information System. Hyattsville, MD: National Center for Health Services Research.
Garms, W. I.
  1971 "A Benefit-Cost Analysis of the Upward Bound Program." Journal of Human Resources 6 (Spring): 206-220.
Geisel, M. S., R. Roll, and R. S. Wettick, Jr.
  1969 "The Effectiveness of State and Local Regulation of Handguns: A Statistical Analysis." Duke Law Journal (August): 647-676.
General Accounting Office
  1984 An Evaluation of the 1981 AFDC Changes: Initial Analysis. Washington, DC: Author.
Glass, G. V, B. McGaw, and M. L. Smith
  1981 Meta-Analysis in Social Research. Beverly Hills, CA: Sage Publications.
Gleser, G. C., B. L. Green, and C. Winget
  1981 Prolonged Psychosocial Effects of Disaster. New York: Academic.
Goldman, J.
  1977 "A Randomization Procedure for 'Trickle-Process' Evaluations." Evaluation Quarterly 1 (August): 493-498.
Gramlich, E. M. and P. P. Koshel
  1975 Educational Performance Contracting: An Evaluation of an Experiment. Washington, DC: Brookings.
Gray, C. M., C. J. Conover, and T. M. Hennessey
  1978 "Cost Effectiveness of Residential Community Corrections: An Analytical Prototype." Evaluation Quarterly 2 (August): 375-400.
Greeley, A. M., W. C. McCready, and K. McCourt
  1976 Catholic Schools in a Declining Church. Kansas City: Sheed & Ward.
Greeley, A. M. and P. H. Rossi
  1966 The Education of Catholic Americans. Chicago: Aldine.
Green, L. W., H. C. Gustafson, W. Griffiths, and D. Yaukey
  1972 The Dacca Family Planning Experiment. Berkeley: University of California Press.
Guba, E. G. and Y. S. Lincoln
  1981 Effective Evaluation: Improving the Usefulness of Evaluation Results Through Responsive and Naturalistic Approaches. San Francisco: Jossey-Bass.
Guttentag, M. and E. L. Struening (eds.)
  1975 Handbook of Evaluation Research, Volume 2. Beverly Hills, CA: Sage Publications.
Hannan, T.
  1976 "The Benefits and Costs of Methadone Maintenance." Public Policy 24 (Spring): 197-226
Hansen, W. L. and F. H. Nelson
  1976 "The Distributional Efficiency of Benefits for a Student Financing Program with Payment Obligations Contingent upon Future Income." Proceedings of the Inaugural Convention of the Eastern Economic Association 2(3, Supplement, July): 83-98.
Hanushek, E. A. and J. E. Jackson
  1977 Statistical Methods for Social Scientists. New York: Academic.
Hay, R., Jr., and R. McCleary
  1979 "Box-Tiao Time Series Models for Impact Assessment: A Comment on the Recent Work of Deutsch and Alt." Evaluation Quarterly 3 (May): 277-314.
Hayes, S. P., Jr.
  1959 Evaluating Development Projects. Paris: UNESCO.

Heckman, J.
   1980   "Sample Selection Bias as a Specification Error," in E. W. Stromsdorfer and G. Farkas (eds.) Evaluation Studies Review Annual, Volume 5. Beverly Hills, CA: Sage Publications.

Heumann, L. F.
   1979   "Racial Integration in Residential Neighborhoods: Toward More Precise Measures and Analysis." Evaluation Quarterly 3 (February): 59-80.

Hibbs, D. A., Jr.
   1977   "On Analyzing the Effects of Policy Interventions: Box-Jenkins and Box-Tiao Versus Structural Equation Models," pp. 137-139 in D. R. Heise (ed.) Sociological Methodology 1977. San Francisco: Jossey-Bass.

Hornik, J., H. Gates, and C. Costanzo
   1981   Technical Manual for Management Information System. Northampton, MA: Mental Patients Advocacy Project, Western Massachusetts Legal Services.

Hovland, C. I., A. A. Lumsdaine, and F. D. Sheffield
   1949   Experiments in Mass Communication, Volume III: The American Soldier. Princeton, NJ: Princeton University Press.

Hunter, J. E., F. L. Schmidt, and G. B. Jackson
   1982   Meta-Analysis: Cumulating Research Findings Across Studies. Beverly Hills, CA: Sage Publications.

Ingle, H.
   1976   "Reconsidering the Use of Television for Educational Reform: The Case of El Salvador," pp. 114-139 in R. F. Arnove (ed.) Educational Television: Policy Critique and Guide for Developing Countries. New York: Praeger.

Irwin, J.
   1970   The Felon. Englewood Cliffs, NJ: Prentice-Hall.

Kagan, J., R. B. Kearsley, and P. R. Zelazo
   1977   "The Effects of Infant Day Care on Psychological Development." Evaluation Quarterly 1 (February): 109-142.

Kassebaum, G., D. Ward, and D. Wilner
   1971   Prison Treatment and Parole Survival. New York: John Wiley.

Kazdin, A. E.
   1982   Single-Case Research Designs. New York: Oxford.

Kelling, G., T. Pate, D. Dieckman, and C. E. Brown
   1974   The Kansas City Preventive Patrol Experiment: A Technical Report. Washington, DC: Police Foundation.

Kennedy, S. D.
   1980   Final Report of the Housing Allowance Demand Experiment. Cambridge, MA: Abt Associates.

Kershaw, D. and J. Fair
   1976   The New Jersey Income-Maintenance Experiment, Volume 1. New York: Academic.

Kiresuk, T.
   1973   "Goal Attainment Scaling at a County Mental Health Service." Evaluation 1(1): 12-18.

Kirschner Associates, Inc.
   1975   Programs for Older Americans: Setting and Monitoring; A Reference Manual. Washington, DC: Department of Health, Education and Welfare, Office of Human Development.

Kish, L.
   1965   Survey Sampling. New York: John Wiley.

Klarman, H. E.
   1974   "Application of Cost-Benefit Analysis to the Health Services and the Special Case of Technologic Innovation." Journal of Health Services 4 (Spring): 325-352.

Kmenta, J.
   1971   Elements of Econometrics. New York: Macmillan.

Krasner, L. and A. C. Houts
  1984 "A Study of the 'Value' Systems of Behavioral Scientists." American Sociologist 39 (August): 840-850.
Krug, A. S.
  1967 "The Relationship Between Firearms Licensing Laws and Crime Rates." Congressional Record 113, Part 15 (July 25): 200060-200064.
Lambert, C., Jr., and H. E. Freeman
  1967 The Clinic Habit. New Haven, CT: College and University Press.
Landsberg, G.
  1983 "Program Utilization and Service Utilization Studies: A Key Tool for Evaluation." New Directions in Program Evaluation 20 (December): 93-103.
Lash, T. W. and H. Sigal
  1976 State of the Child: New York City. New York: Foundation for Child Development.
Levin, H. M.
  1975 "Cost-Effective Analysis in Evaluation Research," pp. 89-124 in M. Guttentag and E. L. Struening (eds.) Handbook of Evaluation Research, Volume 2. Beverly Hills, CA: Sage Publications.
  1983 Cost Effectiveness: A Primer. Beverly Hills, CA: Sage Publications.
Levine, A. and M. Levine
  1977 "The Social Context of Evaluation Research: A Case Study." Evaluation Quarterly 1 (November): 515-542.
Levine, R. A., M. A. Solomon, G. Hellstern, and H. Wohlman (eds.)
  1981 Evaluation Research and Practice: Comparative and International Perspectives. Beverly Hills, CA: Sage Publications.
Leviton, L. C. and R. F. Boruch
  1983 "Contributions of Evaluations to Educational Programs." Evaluation Review 7 (October): 563-599.
Leviton, L. C. and E.F.X. Hughes
  1979 Utilization of Evaluations. Evanston, IL: Northwestern University Center for Health Services and Policy Research.
  1981 "Research on the Utilization of Evaluations: A Review and Synthesis." Evaluation Review 5 (August): 525-548.
Lieberman, H. M.
  1974 "Evaluating the Quality of Ambulatory Pediatric Care at a Neighborhood Health Center: Creative Use of a Chart Review." Clinical Pediatrics 3 (January): 52-55.
Light, R. J. and D. B. Pillemer
  1984 Summing Up: The Science of Reviewing Research. Cambridge, MA: Harvard University Press.
Lipton, D., R. Martinson, and L. Wilkins
  1975 The Effectiveness of Correctional Treatment: A Survey of Evaluation Studies. New York: Praeger.
Little, I.M.D. and J. A. Mirrlees
  1974 Project Appraisal and Planning for Developing Countries. New York: Basic Books.
Lynn, L. E., Jr.
  1980 Designing Public Policy. Santa Monica, CA: Scott, Foresman.
Main, E. D.
  1968 "A Nationwide Evaluation of the MDTA Institutional Job Training." Journal of Human Resources 3 (Spring): 159-170.
Maki, J. E., D. M. Hoffman, and R. A. Berk
  1978 "A Time Series Analysis of the Impact of a Water Conservation Campaign." Evaluation Quarterly 2 (February): 107-118.
Marks, S. D., M. R. Greenlick, A. V. Hurtodo, J. D. Johnson, and I. Henderson
  1980 "Ambulatory Surgery in an HMO." Medical Care 18 (February): 127-146.

Mathematica Policy Research
   1983   Final Report of the Seattle-Denver Income Maintenance Experiment, Volume 2. Princeton: Mathematica Policy Research.
Mayo, J. K., R. C. Hornik, and E. G. McAnany
   1976   Educational Reform with Television: The El Salvador Experience. Palo Alto, CA: Stanford University Press.
McCleary, R. and R. Hay, Jr.
   1980   Applied Time Series Analysis for the Social Sciences. Beverly Hills, CA: Sage Publications.
McLaughlin, M. W.
   1975   Evaluation and Reform: The Elementary and Secondary Education Act of 1965/Title I. Cambridge, MA: Ballinger.
Mielke, K. W. and J. W. Swinehart
   1976   Evaluation of the Feeling Good Television Series. New York: Children's Television Workshop.
Milavsky, J. R., R. C. Kessler, H. W. Stipp, and W. S. Rubens
   1982   Television and Aggression: A Panel Study. New York: Academic.
Miles, M. B. and A. M. Huberman
   1984   Qualitative Data Analysis: A Sourcebook of New Methods. Beverly Hills, CA: Sage Publications.
Miley, A. D., B. L. Lively, and R. D. McDonald
   1978   "An Index of Mental Health System Performance." Evaluation Quarterly 2 (February): 119-126.
Morris, L. L. and C. T. Fitz-Gibbon
   1978   How to Measure Program Implementation. Volume 4 in L.L. Morris (ed.) Program Evaluation Kit (8 volumes). Beverly Hills, CA: Sage Publications.
Mosteller, F. and D. P. Moynihan (eds.)
   1972   On Equality of Educational Opportunity. New York: Vintage Books.
Murray, C.
   1984   Losing Ground: American Social Policy 1950-1980. New York: Basic Books.
Murray, D. R.
   1975   "Handguns, Gun Control Laws, and Firearm Violence." Social Problems 23 (October): 81-93.
Murray, S.
   1980   The National Evaluation of the PUSH for Excellence Project. Washington, DC: American Institutes for Research.
Myers, D. E. and R. C. Rockwell
   1984   "Large-Scale Data Bases: Who Produces Them, How to Obtain Them, What They Contain." New Directions for Program Evaluation 22 (June): 5-25.
Namboodiri, N. K., L. F. Carter, and H. M. Blalock, Jr.
   1975   Applied Multivariate Analysis and Experimental Designs. New York: McGraw-Hill.
National Center for Health Services Research
   1977   Emergency Medical Services Systems Research Projects, 1977. Washington, DC: Author.
National Institute of Mental Health
   1976   A Working Manual of Simple Program Evaluation Techniques for Community Mental Health Centers. Washington, DC: Government Printing Office.
Nay, J. N., J. W. Scanlon, R. E. Schmidt, and J. S. Wholey
   1976   "If You Don't Care Where You Get To, Then It Doesn't Matter Which Way You Go," pp. 97-120 in C. C. Abt (ed.) The Evaluation of Social Programs. Beverly Hills, CA: Sage Publications.
Nicholson, W. and S. R. Wright
   1977   "Participants' Understanding of the Treatment in Policy Experimentation." Evaluation Quarterly 1 (May): 245-268.

Noble, J. H., Jr.
　1977　"The Limits of Cost-Benefit Analysis as a Guide to Priority Setting in Rehabilitation." Evaluation Quarterly 1 (August): 347-380.
Nunnally, J. C. and R. L. Durham
　1975　"Validity, Reliability, and Special Problems of Measurement in Evaluation Research," pp. 289-352 in E. L. Struening and M. Guttentag (eds.) Handbook of Evaluation Research, Volume 1. Beverly Hills, CA: Sage Publications.
Office of Income Security Policy
　1983　Overview of the Seattle-Denver Income Maintenance Final Report. Washington, DC: U.S. Department of Health and Human Services.
Oman, R. C. and S. R. Chitwood
　1984　"Management Evaluation Studies: Factors Affecting the Acceptance of Recommendations." Evaluation Review 8 (June): 283-305.
Orshansky, M.
　1969　"Perspectives on Poverty: How Poverty is Measured." Monthly Labor Review 92 (February): 37-41.
Patton, M. Q.
　1980　Qualitative Evaluation Methods. Beverly Hills, CA: Sage Publications.
Pierce, G. L. and W. J. Bowers
　1979　The Impact of the Bartley Fox Gun Law on Crime in Massachusetts. Boston: Center for Applied Social Research, Northeastern University.
Polivka, L. and E. Steg
　1978　"Program Evaluation and Policy Development: Bridging the Gap." Evaluation Quarterly 3 (November): 696-707.
Pressman, J. L. and D. L. Rubinfeld
　1973　Implementation. Berkeley: University of California Press.
Pyndyck, R. S. and D. L. Rubinfeld
　1976　Econometric Models and Economic Forecasts. New York: McGraw-Hill.
Quigley, P. A., L. Morris, and G. Hammett
　1976　The Choctaw Home-Centered Family Education Demonstration Project. Tucson, AZ: Behavior Associates.
Raizen, S. A. and P. H. Rossi (eds.)
　1981　Program Evaluation in Education: When? How? To What Ends? Washington, DC: National Academy Press.
Reeves, B. F.
　1970　The First Year of Sesame Street: The Formative Research. New York: Children's Television Workshop.
Reiss, A. J., Jr.
　1971　The Police and the Public. New Haven, CT: Yale University Press.
　1985　"Some Failures in Designing Data Collection that Distorts Results," in L. Burstein et al. (eds.) Collecting Evaluation Data: Problems and Solutions. Beverly Hills, CA: Sage Publications.
Ribich, T. I. and J. L. Murphy
　1975　"The Economic Returns to Increased Educational Spending." Journal of Human Resources 10 (Winter): 56-77.
Rich, R. F.
　1977　"Uses of Social Science Information by Federal Bureaucrats," in C.H. Weiss (ed.) Using Social Research for Public Policy Making. Lexington, MA: D.C. Heath.
Riecken, H. W. and R. F. Boruch (eds.)
　1974　Social Experimentation: A Method of Planning and Evaluating Social Intervention. New York: Academic.
Robert Wood Johnson Foundation
　1980　Annual Report. Princeton, NJ: Author.
Robertson, D. B.
　1984　"Program Implementation Versus Program Design." Policy Studies Review 3 (May): 391-405.

Robins, P. K., R. G. Spiegelman, S. Weiner, and J. G. Bell (eds.)
  1980   A Guaranteed Annual Income: Evidence from a Social Experiment. New York: Academic.
Roethlisberger, F. J. and W. Dickson
  1939   Management and the Worker. Cambridge, MA: Harvard University Press.
Roos, L. L., Jr., N. P. Roos, and B. McKinley
  1977   "Implementing Randomization." Policy Analysis 3 (Fall): 547-560.
Ross, H. L., D. T. Campbell, and G. V Glass
  1970   "Determining the Social Effects of a Legal Reform: The British Breathalyzer Crackdown of 1967." American Behavioral Scientist 3 (March/April): 494-509.
Rossi, A. S.
  1966   "Abortion Laws and Their Victims." Trans-Action (September/October).
Rossi, P. H.
  1978   "Issues in the Evaluation of Human Services Delivery." Evaluation Quarterly 2 (November): 573-599.
  1979   "Critical Decisions in Evaluation Studies." New Directions for Testing and Measurement 1: 79-88.
  1983   "Pussycats, Weasels or Percherons? Current Prospects for the Social Sciences Under the Reagan Administration." Evaluation News 4 (February): 12-27.
Rossi, P. H. (ed.)
  1982   "Standards for Evaluation Practice." New Directions for Program Evaluation 15 (September).
Rossi, P. H., R. A. Berk, and B. K. Eidson
  1974   Roots of Urban Discontent. New York: John Wiley.
Rossi, P. H., R. A. Berk, and K. J. Lenihan
  1980   Money, Work and Crime: Some Experimental Evidence. New York: Academic.
Rossi, P. H. and R. A. Dentler
  1961   The Politics of Urban Renewal. New York: Free Press.
Rossi, P. H. and H. E. Freeman
  1982   Evaluation: A Systematic Approach (2nd ed.). Beverly Hills, CA: Sage Publications.
Rossi, P. H. and K. Lyall
  1976   Reforming Public Welfare. New York: Russell Sage.
Rossi, P. H. and W. Williams (eds.)
  1972   Evaluating Social Programs. New York: Seminar.
Rossi, P. H., J. D. Wright, and A. Anderson (eds.)
  1983   Handbook of Survey Research. New York: Academic.
Rossi, P. H. and S. R. Wright
  1977   "Evaluation Research: An Assessment of Theory, Practice, and Politics." Evaluation Quarterly 1 (February): 5-52.
Rutman, L.
  1980   Planning Useful Evaluations: Evaluability Assessment. Beverly Hills, CA: Sage Publications.
St. Pierre, R. G.
  1983a "Congressional Input to Program Evaluation." Evaluation Review 7 (August): 411-436.
St. Pierre, R. G. (ed.)
  1983b "Management and Organization of Program Evaluation." New Directions for Program Evaluation 18 (June).
Salamon, L. M.
  1974   The Time Dimension in Policy Evaluation: The Case of the New Deal Land-Reform Experiments. Durham, NC: Center for Urban and Regional Development Policy, Duke University. (Reprinted in Public Policy 27[2], 1979.)
Schatzman, L. and A. L. Strauss
  1973   Field Research: Strategies for a Natural Sociology. Englewood Cliffs, NJ: Prentice-Hall.

Schmidt, R. E., J. W. Scanlon, and J. B. Bell
  1978 Evaluability Assessment: Making Public Programs Work Better. Washington, DC:
        Urban Institute.
Schneider, A. L.
  1982 "Studying Policy Implementation." Evaluation Review 6 (December): 715-730.
Sechrest, L. and W. H. Yeaton
  1982 "Magnitudes of Experimental Effects in Social Science Research." Evaluation
        Review 6 (October): 579-600.
Seitz, S. T.
  1972 "Firearms, Homicide and Gun Control Effectiveness." Law and Society Review 6
        (May): 595-613.
Sewell, W. H. and R. M. Hauser
  1975 Education, Occupation and Earnings: Achievement in the Early Career. New
        York: Academic.
Sherman, L.
  1980 Experimental Interventions in the Treatment of Spouse Abuse. Washington, DC:
        Police Foundation.
Sherwood, C. C., J. N. Morris, and S. Sherwood
  1975 "A Multivariate, Nonrandomized Matching Technique for Studying the Impact of
        Social Interventions," pp. 183-224 in E. L. Struening and M. Guttentag (eds.)
        Handbook of Evaluation Research, Volume 1. Beverly Hills, CA: Sage
        Publications.
Shlay, A. and P. H. Rossi
  1981 "Putting Politics into Urban Ecology: Estimating the Net Effects of Zoning."
        American Sociological Review 46 (October).
Shortell, S. M. and W. C. Richardson
  1978 Health Program Evaluation. St. Louis: C. V. Mosby.
Shortell, S. M., T. M. Wickizer, and J.R.C. Wheeler
  1984 "Hospital-Sponsored Primary Care, I: Organizational and Financial Effects."
        American Journal of Public Health 74 (August): 784-791.
Skipper, J. K., Jr., and R. C. Leonard
  1968 "Children, Stress and Hospitalization." Journal of Health and Social Behavior 9
        (December): 275-287.
Smith, M. L., G. V Glass, and T. I. Miller
  1980 The Benefits of Psychotherapy: An Evaluation. Baltimore: Johns Hopkins
        University Press.
Solomon, M. A. and S. M. Shortell
  1981 "Designing Health Policy Research for Utilization." Health Policy Quarterly 1
        (May): 216-237.
Squire, L. and H. G. van de Tak
  1975 Economic Analysis of Projects. Baltimore: Johns Hopkins University Press.
SRI International
  1983 Final Report of the Seattle-Denver Income Maintenance Experiment, Volume I.
        Palo Alto, CA: SRI International.
Stephan, A. S.
  1935 "Prospects and Possibilities: The New Deal and the New Social Research." Social
        Forces 13 (May).
Stokey, E. and R. Zeckhauser
  1978 A Primer for Policy Analyses. New York: Norton.
Stouffer, S. A. et al.
  1949 The American Soldier: Combat and Its Aftermath. Manhattan, KS: Military
        Affairs/Aerospace Historian.
Struening, E. L. and M. Guttentag (eds.)
  1975 Handbook of Evaluation Research, Volume 1. Beverly Hills, CA: Sage
        Publications.

Struyk, R. J. and M. Bendick (eds.)
    1981 Housing Vouchers for the Poor: Lessons from a National Experiment. Washington, DC: Urban Institute.
Stuart, H. D. and A. M. Cruze
    1976 "Estimates of the Target Population for Upward Bound and Talent Search Programs." Durham, NC: Research Triangle Institute.
Suchman, E.
    1967 Evaluative Research. New York: Russell Sage.
Sudman, S.
    1976 Applied Sampling. New York: Academic.
Tessler, R. and D. Mechanic
    1975 "Consumer Satisfaction with Prepaid Group Practice: A Comparative Study." Journal of Health and Social Behavior 16 (March): 95-113.
Thompson, M.
    1980 Benefit-Cost Analysis for Program Evaluation. Beverly Hills, CA: Sage Publications.
Torgerson, W. S.
    1958 Theory and Method of Scaling. New York: John Wiley.
Trochim, W.M.K.
    1984 Research Design for Program Evaluation: The Regression Discontinuity Approach. Beverly Hills, CA: Sage Publications.
UNCO, Inc.
    1975 National Childcare Consumer Study. Washington, DC: Author.
U.S. Department of Justice
    1977 Criminal Victimization Surveys in Boston: A National Crime Survey Report. Washington, DC: Government Printing Office.
van de Vall, M. and C. A. Bolas
    1981 "External vs. Internal Social Policy Researchers." Knowledge: Creation, Diffusion, Utilization 2 (June): 461-481.
Vanecko, J. J. and B. Jacobs
    1970 Reports from the 100-City CAP Evaluation: The Impact of the Community Action Program on Institutional Change. Chicago: National Opinion Research Center.
Watts, H. W., J. K. Peck, and M. Taussig
    1977 "Site Selection, Representativeness of the Sample, and Possible Attrition Bias," pp. 441-446 in H. W. Watts and A. Rees (eds.) The New Jersey Income-Maintenance Experiment, Volume 3. New York: Academic.
Weick, K. E.
    1984 "Small Wins: Redefining the Scale of Social Problems." American Psychologist 39 (January): 40-49.
Weiss, A. T.
    1975 "The Consumer Model of Assessing Community Mental Health Needs." Evaluation 2: 71.
Weiss, C. H.
    1972 Evaluating Action Programs: Readings in Social Action and Education. Boston: Allyn & Bacon.
Weiss, C. H. and M. J. Bucuvalas
    1980a "Truth Tests and Utility Tests: Decision-Makers' Frames of Reference for Social Science Research." American Sociological Review 45 (April): 302-313.
    1980b Social Science Research and Decision-Making. New York: Columbia University Press.
Weissert, W., T. Wan, B. Livieratos, and S. Katz
    1980 "Effects and Costs of Day-Care Services for the Chronically Ill: A Randomized Experiment." Medical Care 18(6): 567-584.
Westat, Inc.
    1976- Continuous Longitudinal Manpower Survey, Reports 1-10. Rockville, MD:
    1980 Author.

Wholey, J. S.
 1977 "Evaluability Assessment," pp. 41-56 in L. Rutman (ed.) Evaluation Research Methods: A Basic Guide. Beverly Hills, CA: Sage Publications.
 1979 Evaluation: Promise and Performance. Washington, DC: Urban Institute.
 1981 "Using Evaluation to Improve Program Performance," pp. 92-106 in R. A. Levine et al. (eds.) Evaluation Research and Practice: Comparative and International Perspectives. Beverly Hills, CA: Sage Publications.
Wholey, J. S., J. W. Scanlon, H. Duffy, J. S. Fukumoto, and L. M. Vogt
 1970 Federal Evaluation Policy. Washington, DC: Urban Institute.
Williams, W.
 1980 The Implementation Perspective. Berkeley: University of California Press.
Williams, W. and R. F. Elmore (eds.)
 1976 Social Program Implementation. New York: Academic.
Wilner, D. M., R. P. Walkely, T. C. Pinkerton, and M. Tayback
 1962 The Housing Environment and Family Life. Baltimore: Johns Hopkins University Press.
Wilson, J. Q. (ed.)
 1966 Urban Renewal: The Record and the Controversy. Cambridge: MIT Press.
Wolfe, B.
 1977 "A Cost-Effectiveness Analysis of Reductions in School Expenditures: An Application of an Educational Production Function." Journal of Education Finance 2 (Spring): 407-418.
Wortman, P. M., C. S. Reichardt, and R. G. St. Pierre
 1978 "The First Year of the Education Voucher Demonstration: A Secondary Analysis of Student Achievement Test Scores." Evaluation Quarterly 2 (May): 193-214.
Wright, J. D., P. H. Rossi, K. Daly, and E. Weber-Burdin
 1981 Weapons, Crime and Violence in America. Amherst, MA: Social and Demographic Research Institute.
Wright, J. D., P. H. Rossi, S. R. Wright, and E. Weber-Burdin
 1979 After the Clean-Up: Long-Range Effects of Natural Disasters. Beverly Hills, CA: Sage Publications.
Zaidan, G. C.
 1971 The Costs and Benefits of Family Planning Programs. Washington, DC: World Bank.
Zeckhauser, R.
 1975 "Procedures for Valuing Lives." Public Policy 23 (Fall): 419-464.

PETER H. ROSSI is currently Stuart A. Rice Professor of Sociology and Director of the Social and Demographic Research Institute at the University of Massachusetts at Amherst, and coeditor of *Social Science Research*. He has been on the faculties of Harvard University, Johns Hopkins University, and the University of Chicago, where he also served as Director of the National Opinion Research Center. He has been a consultant on research methods and evaluation to (among others) the National Science Foundation, the National Institute of Mental Health, the Federal Trade Commission, and the Russell Sage Foundation. His research has largely been concerned with the application of social research methods to social issues, and he is currently engaged in research on natural disasters and criminal justice. His works include *Prison Reform and State Elites* (with R. A. Berk, 1977), *Money, Work and Crime* (with R. A. Berk and K. J. Lenihan, 1980), and *Handbook of Survey Research* (with J. D. Wright and A. Anderson, 1983). In 1979-80 Professor Rossi was president of the American Sociological Association, and in 1981 he received the Evaluation Research Society's Myrdal Award for contributions to evaluation research methods. He was the 1985 recipient of the Common Wealth Award for Career Contributions to Sociology. He was also awarded the 1985 Donald Campbell Award for outstanding methodological innovation in public policy studies.

HOWARD E. FREEMAN is Professor of Sociology at the University of California, Los Angeles, and was the founding director of its Institute for Social Science Research. From 1963 to 1972 he was Morse Professor of Urban Studies at Brandeis University, and has been associated with Harvard University, the Ford Foundation, and the Russell Sage Foundation. Currently, Professor Freeman is a research adviser to the Robert Wood Johnson Foundation and the coeditor of *Evaluation Review: A Journal of Applied Social Research*. He is former editor of the *Journal of Health and Social Behavior* and associate editor of *American Sociological Review* and *Social Problems*. His books include *Social Problems: A Policy Perspective* and *The Mental Patient Comes Home*. He is coeditor of the *Handbook of Medical Sociology* and *Collecting Evaluation Data*, as well as the 1978 edition of the *Policy Studies Review Annual* and the 1980 edition of the *Evaluation Studies Review Annual*. Dr. Freeman is a member of the Institute of Medicine, National Academy of Sciences. He undertakes evaluations in the health and mental health fields.